P9-CRZ-964

BEVERLY ANN MATTHEWS
1106 E. WASHINGTON ST.
BLOOMINGTON, IL 61701

FUNDAMENTALS OF PARALEGALISM

Thomas E. Eimermann

Illinois State University

FUNDAMENTALS OF PARALEGALISM

Little, Brown and Company
Boston   Toronto

Library of Congress Catalog Card No. 79-92801

10 9 8 7 6 5 4 3   ISBN 0-316-23120-7

MV
Published simultaneously in Canada
by Little, Brown & Company (Canada) Limited

Printed in the United States of America

The author wishes to acknowledge the use of the following material, reprinted with permission of the publisher.

Text excerpts
   Pages 37–38: From ABA Special Committee on Legal Assistants, *Liberating the Lawyer.* Reprinted by permission of the American Bar Association. *Pages 46, 47–48:* From ABA Special Committee on Legal Assistants, *Certification of Legal Assistants.* Reprinted by permission of the American Bar Association. *Pages 78–79:* From the National Association of Legal Assistants Code of Ethics and Professional Responsibility. Reprinted by permission of the National Association of Legal Assistants, Inc. *Pages 79–80:* From the American Bar Association Code of Professional Responsibility. Reprinted by permission of the American Bar Association. *Pages 91–92, 95, 97, 99–100:* From Albert Benjamin, *The Helping Interview,* 2d ed. Copyright © 1974 by Houghton Mifflin Company. Reprinted by permission.

Figures
   FIG. 7.1, *American Jurisprudence 2d,* Vol. 49, p. 708. FIG. 7.2, *American Jurisprudence 2d,* Vol. 49, June 1979 Pocket Supplement, p. 53. FIG. 7.3, *American Jurisprudence 2d,* Vol. 49, p. 1. FIG. 7.4, *American Jurisprudence 2d,* Vol. 49, p. 28. FIG. 7.5, *American Jurisprudence 2d,* Vol. 50, p. 1159. Copyright © 1970 by Lawyers Co-operative Publishing Company, Rochester, New York. FIG. 7.6, *Corpus Juris Secundum,* Vol. 51C, pp. 776–777. FIG. 7.7, *Corpus Juris Secundum,* Vol. 51C, p. 1. FIG. 7.8, *Corpus Juris Secundum,* Vol. 51C, 1979 Pocket Supplement, p. 48. FIG. 7.9, *Corpus Juris Secundum,* Vol. 51C, p. 12. FIG. 7.10, *Corpus Juris Secundum,* Vol. 52A, p. 929. Copyright © 1969 by West Publishing Company, St. Paul, Minn. FIG. 7.11, *Corpus Juris Secundum,* General Index vol. A–Complex, p. 1. Copyright © 1959 by West Publishing Company, St. Paul, Minn. FIG. 7.12, *Illinois Law and Practice,* Landlord and Tenant volume, p. 431. Copyright © 1956 by West Publishing Company. FIG. 7.13, *Illinois Law and Practice,* Pocket Supplement to Landlord and Tenant volume, p. 85. Copyright © 1978 by West Publishing Company. FIG. 7.14, *Index to Legal Periodicals,* Sept. 1976–Aug. 1977, p. 279. Copyright 1976, 1977, 1978, by The H.W. Wilson Company. FIG. 7.15, *American Law Reports 3d,* Vol. 40, pp. 646–648. FIG. 7.16, *American Law Reports 3d,* Vol. 40, p. 653. Copyright © 1971 by the Lawyers Co-operative Publishing Company. FIG. 7.17, *American Law Reports 2d–3d,* Quick Index, p. 398. Copyright © 1973 by Lawyers Co-operative Publish-

To the memory of
Eggert W. Giere
an outstanding teacher
and influential mentor

Preface

This book is designed to serve as a text for introductory paralegal and legal assistant courses. It presents basic information about the functions of a legal assistant in the American legal system and attempts to develop fundamental paralegal skills. Rather than emulating the style of most law school materials, it presents a simplified descriptive analysis of the facts and concepts a paralegal needs to know in order to function effectively in the legal environment. The presentation does not assume any previous legal knowledge and carefully defines the legal terms introduced.

Part I describes the organization of the American legal system and the role of the paralegal within the system. The text opens with these topics because I believe the reader should have an overview of how the legal system operates and the function of the paralegal before attempting to learn specific skills.

Legal controversies can involve disputes over what in fact occurred or the interpretation and application of the law, or both. Part II covers the manner in which a paralegal gathers the facts, and Part III considers how to find and interpret the law. Part IV discusses how the facts and the law are integrated in preparation for a trial, an administrative hearing, or an appeal.

The chapters in these sections supply basic factual information on rules of evidence, content of hospital records, content of legal reference books, elements of various pleadings, procedures in an administrative hearing, and the organization of an appellate brief. Equally important, these chapters contain instructions on how the paralegal should approach practical problems. At the end of each of these chapters there are questions and projects that will assist the reader in applying new skills to concrete problems.

The final chapter attempts to assist readers in evaluating their prospects in this emerging profession. It takes a realistic look at the rewards and the frustrations that usually accompany positions in the field, and should lead to a knowledgeable career choice.

The instructor's manual that accompanies this text contains learning objectives, projects, use of classroom time, and exam questions for each chapter, to help in coordinating reading assignments with class work and homework projects.

In any undertaking of this magnitude the author owes a great deal to the contributions of many individuals, and I am no exception. A special note of gratitude is due to Jim Knecht, Suzanne Little, Fred Moore, Harry Poling, Barb Schmidt, Tom Smith, and the other paralegals and attorneys who provided practical insights and examples to complement the academic and theoretical aspects of this book. Alberta Carr did an outstanding job of editing, typing, and proofreading the manuscript. Her experience and dedication to the project were influential and greatly appreciated. Editors Greg Franklin and Will Ethridge and book editor Cynthia Chapin of Little, Brown were always there with the answers I needed and the encouragement to continue. Finally, a special note of thanks is due to my wife and children for their special patience and understanding.

Contents

PART II
FINDING THE FACTS

PART III
FINDING THE LAW

PART IV
PREPARING THE CASE

List of Figures

FUNDAMENTALS OF PARALEGALISM

PART I

LAW AND THE PARALEGAL

The decade of the 1970s saw the acceptance of paralegals and rapid growth in their numbers. Today there can be little doubt as to the viability of paralegalism and the increasingly important part it will play in the legal delivery systems in the United States.

This text is designed to introduce the reader to the various roles the paralegal can play as well as to provide an understanding of the legal and ethical limitations placed on those roles. Equally important, it is designed to provide the type of background knowledge required of someone seeking a career in this promising field.

The book is introductory in nature and concentrates on building a foundation of basic knowledge and skill development. The reader should acquire a general understanding of the way the legal system operates, how to locate relevant statutes and court cases, how to interpret what is found, and how to relay that information according to the accepted forms of legal communication. The text does not attempt to develop substantive legal knowledge in any particular field or to analyze the rules of procedure for any specific jurisdiction. However, the material provided should make it easier for the reader to acquire such knowledge through additional reading, course work, or on-the-job experience.

Chapter 1 provides an overview of the American legal system. Before paralegals can begin to learn about their role, they must have some understanding of the general organization and operation of the legal system. Chapter 2 then explores the historical development of paralegals and the various roles they can play. Chapter 3, in turn, analyzes the limitations placed on paralegals by unauthorized practice of law statutes and professional codes of ethics.

CHAPTER 1

The American Legal System

The American legal system is a complex set of institutions that vary in structure and procedure. Each of the fifty states, along with the federal government, runs its own set of courts under its own set of rules. And while the laws of one state are often similar to the laws of another state, each can ultimately determine for itself what those laws will be.* Thus where one state may choose to legalize gambling, another may not. Where one state may choose to allow no-fault divorces, another may not.

Some look upon this diversity as one of the great strengths of our political system. They argue that it encourages experimentation and innovation in allowing the residents of Georgia, for example, to establish rules of conduct that differ from those established by the residents of Nevada. Critics, on the other hand,

---

*This is because the United States operates under a system of government known as federalism. The United States Constitution divides the power to make various types of laws between the national government and the states. Subject to the restraints imposed by the Constitution itself, the states are in many areas free to determine what their own laws will be.

point to the problems it creates for interstate business and travel. Among other effects, it forces large corporations and other out-of-state parties to utilize the services of local attorneys and makes it more difficult for an attorney (or a paralegal) to move a practice from one state to another.

THE FUNCTIONS OF LAW

Despite the fact that the laws themselves sometimes differ, the development and enforcement of those laws are essential functions of all fifty states as well as the federal government. Indeed, the development and enforcement of the law are essential governmental functions in all developed societies.

While the form of the law may vary (constitutional, statutory, administrative, etc.), the law itself defines the type of conduct that is either prohibited or required. The criminal code usually prohibits the unauthorized taking of property that belongs to someone else. Tax laws require that certain types of individuals or corporations give part of their income to the government. The laws can apply to the behavior of individuals, businesses, and even governments themselves. Thus municipalities may be prohibited from dumping raw sewage into lakes and rivers, and the police prohibited from conducting unreasonable searches and seizures.

In order to be considered laws, these rules of conduct must be promulgated and enforced by the appropriate governmental agencies. Only the United States Congress can make federal statutory law. Administrative agencies can promulgate regulations only when they are acting under a proper delegation of legislative authority. The principles of the common law must be applied through a judge sitting in a court of competent jurisdiction.*

---

*All courts have some restrictions on the types of cases they can entertain. Constitutions and legislatures assign certain types of cases to particular courts. If a case is within a particular court's jurisdiction, it means that the court has the legal authority to hear that case. Jursisdiction can be based on the nature of the parties involved, the subject matter, or the location of the incident being litigated.

These rules of conduct also carry with them certain sanctions that can be imposed upon those who fail to follow the rules. When individuals violate a section of the criminal law they may be fined, sent to prison, or in some cases even suffer loss of life. Persons who violate sections of the civil law may be forced to pay various penalties or damage awards. Similarly, they may be forced to carry out the terms of a contract or even to return to work after having been out on a strike. Police who conduct illegal searches and seizures may be denied the right to use that evidence in court and may even be forced to pay damages to the injured party. Even presidents can be cited for contempt if they fail to turn over subpoenaed materials.

While there may be a great deal of debate over the wisdom and appropriateness of a particular law (as there is, for example, over the issue of legalizing marijuana), there is general agreement that laws themselves are necessary. As the Task Force on Law and Law Enforcement reported to the National Commission on the Causes and Prevention of Violence:

> Human welfare demands, at a minimum, sufficient order to insure that such basic needs as food production, shelter and child rearing be satisfied, not in a state of constant chaos and conflict, but on a peaceful, orderly basis with a reasonable level of day–to–day security. . . .
> When a society becomes highly complex, mobile, and pluralistic; the beneficiary, yet also the victim, of extremely rapid technological change; and when at the same time, and partly as a result of these factors, the influence of traditional stabilizing institutions such as family, church, and community wanes, then that society of necessity becomes increasingly dependent on highly structured, formalistic systems of law and government to maintain social order. . . . For better or worse, we are by necessity increasingly committed to our formal legal institutions as the paramount agency of social control.[1]

It has thus been increasingly left to the legal system to define and enforce the rules of the society. Some of these rules are heavily influenced by the religious and moral beliefs of various elements in the society (e.g., restrictions on abortions, pornography, and gambling), while others (e.g., traffic regulations) have no moral content at all. Nevertheless, they help to provide the type of order and predictability that are essential elements of our modern society.

SOURCES OF LAW

Laws can come from several different sources. They can come from federal, state, and local governments, and they can come from legislatures, administrators, and judges. Generally speaking, though, when people think of law they think first of the legislative enactments of their state legislatures. This is because we are usually more aware of the state's criminal code than we are of other forms of law. Even though we have probably never read it, we picture a ponderous statute book filled with "thou shalt nots."

Statutory law consists of the enactments of legislative bodies. These legislative bodies can be the United States Congress, a state legislature, or a village board. These enactments are then published in the form of statutes or ordinances. Since the wording of these statutes is occasionally ambiguous, the judges who are called upon to apply them serve as the ultimate arbitrators of their meaning.

Administrative law is similar to statutory law in that it usually consists of fairly specific regulations that are written in a form similar to statutes. Whereas statutory law is made by the legislative branch, administrative law is made by the executive branch or by independent regulatory agencies. These agencies can promulgate regulations in limited areas under the appropriate grants of authority from the legislative branch. As in the case of statutes, the judge who is called upon to apply the regulation becomes the ultimate arbitrator of its meaning.

A third type of law is that which is referred to as the common law. Common law consists of various legal principles that have evolved through the years from analysis of specific court decisions. Ultimately, these principles can be traced back to fifteenth-century England, though they have been modified through the years by various state courts. When a legal dispute involves a subject that is not adequately covered by the other types of law, the judge will apply the principles of the common law. In other words, in the absence of pronouncements from the constitution or a legislative or administrative body, the judge looks to the decisions of other judges in similar circumstances.

Closely related to the concept of common law is the term equity. The English Chancery Court allowed judges a freer hand in reaching a just result in situations where the common law had become too rigid and technical. Judges today are allowed to use their equity powers to "do justice" where specific laws do not cover the situation. Equity powers are primarily utilized in cases involving property rights and include the powers of a judge to issue an injunction or to order specific performance.* They allow the judge to take preventive or remedial action, when otherwise the law would limit their decision to monetary award after the damage has been done.

The final source of law is the constitution itself. The prescriptions laid out in the constitution (as they are interpreted by the judges) constitute the highest form of man-made law. In order to be valid, statutes and administrative regulations must not conflict with the principles laid down in the Constitution of the United States or the state involved.

CRIMINAL LAW AND CIVIL LAW

Just as law can be classified on the basis of its source, so too it can be divided into the general categories of criminal law and civil law. Both types consist of rules of conduct that have been laid down by the appropriate legal authorities, but they differ with regard to the manner in which they are enforced (Table 1.1).

When an individual violates a part of the criminal law, society considers itself to be the offended party, and it takes a much more active role in the sanctioning process. Thus when Peter Jones burglarizes Sam Smith's home, the criminal law looks upon that act as an offense against society itself rather than as simply a matter between Smith and Jones. When the case goes to court, it is listed as *People v. Jones* or *State v. Jones*. Government attorneys prosecute the accused party, and the victim is merely a witness. The criminal law seeks not to redress the losses of the victim but to maintain the vitality of the rule of conduct involved. If a court of law determines that a provision of the criminal law has been violated, it may impose two broad types of sanctions — loss of liberty and financial penalty. Most commonly, the loss of liberty involves spending a few days in the county jail to several years in a state penitentiary. It can, however, range all the way from unsupervised probation to the inflicting of the death penalty. While a

---

*Specific performance requires that a party carry through on a proper contract that has not been fulfilled.

TABLE 1.1
Comparison of Criminal and Civil Cases

Characteristic	Criminal	Civil
Source of the law	Government	Government
Offended party	Society	Individual
Investigation and "prosecution" of violations	Government	Individual
Burden of proof	Beyond a reasonable doubt	Preponderance of the evidence
Sanctions used	Fines, imprisonment, death	Monetary damages, injunctions, specific performance, etc.
Beneficiary of sanctions	Society	Individual

negotiated settlement will occasionally contain some provisions for restitution, the fines that are assessed as part of the criminal process become the property of the state rather than the victim.

In civil cases, on the other hand, the government takes a much more passive role. It develops the basic rules of conduct and provides a judicial system for the application of those rules, but it is left to the aggrieved party to prosecute a case. Thus when one party defaults on the terms of a contract, the other party must hire a lawyer and initiate the legal process on an individual basis.

Consistent with this more active role for the individual is the fact that when plaintiffs triumph they benefit directly from the outcome. Under the civil law the party who is found to be at fault can be required to directly compensate the victim for various types of injuries sustained. Even when the damages are punitive (designed to punish the wrongdoer) rather than compensatory, the plaintiff becomes the beneficiary rather than the government.* In addition to awarding damages, civil court judges can issue injunctions and dissolve marriages.

Due to the more serious consequences of violating criminal laws, different standards of proof are applied. On the criminal side, the prosecution is required to prove its case "beyond a reasonable doubt," while in civil actions the plaintiff need only meet the "preponderance of the evidence" standard. The "beyond a reasonable doubt" standard is usually explained to jurors as being the degree of doubt that causes a reasonable person to refrain from acting. "Preponderance of the evidence," on the other hand, is usually understood to mean that the facts asserted are more likely to be true than not true. A study conducted by Rita James Simon and Linda Mahan showed that judges tend to equate "beyond a reasonable doubt" with a median probability of approximately 8.8 out of 10, while jurors averaged approximately 8.6 out of 10. "Preponderance of the evidence" was interpreted by the judges as a median probability of 5.4 out of 10, with 7.1 out of 10 being the median for jurors.[2] Clearly the criminal law requires a greater degree of proof before its sanctions can be applied.

Readers should bear in mind that a single act could become the basis for actions in both the criminal and civil courts. For example, the victim of a battery could sue the attacker for civil damages at the same time the state is prosecuting the attacker on a criminal charge. The driver of an automobile involved in a traffic accident may receive a traffic ticket from the police and at the same time be sued by someone else involved in the accident. In certain types of antitrust cases the government can choose between seeking criminal charges and civil damages.

Felonies, Misdemeanors, and Other Crimes

Serious crimes like murder, rape, armed robbery, and aggravated assault are classified as felonies. Felonies generally involve a punishment that can include a year or more in a state prison. Misdemeanors include charges such as disorderly conduct and

---

*It should be noted that the government can become a plaintiff in a civil suit. Under these circumstances the governmental plaintiff benefits in the same way a private plaintiff does.

criminal damage to property. When incarceration is called for in such cases, it is usually less than one year and is served in a county jail. Today the criminal law in most jurisdictions is entirely statutory in nature, and the legislature determines whether a given act is to be considered a felony or a misdemeanor.

The criminal codes of most states typically include: crimes against persons (homicide, kidnapping, sex offenses, assault, and battery), crimes against property (theft, robbery, burglary, arson, and trespass), crimes against the public health or decency (drug laws, abortion, bribery, and disorderly conduct), and crimes against the government itself (treason and official misconduct). The federal criminal law tends to focus on interstate activities.

Many times criminal charges overlap and represent gradations on a spectrum. For example, murder, voluntary manslaughter, involuntary manslaughter, and reckless homicide all involve the taking of a human life. They differ primarily in terms of the intent of the person responsible for the killing. Compare the way in which these offenses are defined in the Illinois criminal code:

A person who kills an individual without lawful justification commits murder if, in performing the acts which cause the death;
   (1) He either intends to kill or do great bodily harm to that individual or another, or knows that such acts will cause death to that individual or another; or
   (2) He knows that such acts create a strong probability of death or great bodily harm to that individual or another; or
   (3) He is attempting or committing a forcible felony other than voluntary manslaughter.[3]

. . .

A person who kills an individual without lawful justification commits voluntary manslaughter if at the time of the killing he is acting under a sudden and intense passion resulting from serious provocation by:
   (1) The individual killed, or
   (2) Another whom the offender endeavors to kill, but he negligently or accidentally causes the death of the individual killed.[4]

. . .

A person who kills an individual without lawful justification commits involuntary manslaughter if his acts whether lawful or unlawful which cause the death are such as are likely to cause death or great bodily harm to some individual, and he performs them recklessly. If the acts which cause the death consist of the driving of a motor vehicle, the person may be prosecuted for reckless homicide or if he is prosecuted for involuntary manslaughter, he may be found guilty of the included offense of reckless homicide.[5]

In a similar fashion the misdemeanor of assault becomes the felony of aggravated assault when either the assailant uses a deadly weapon or the victim of the assault is a teacher or policeman.[6] This type of overlapping of charges often provides a basis for reaching compromise agreements through the plea bargaining process.*

While the state criminal code itself can usually be broken down neatly into felonies and misdemeanors, there are some other types of quasi-criminal law situations of which the reader should be aware. Traffic laws are usually codified in a different part of the state's statutes and do not carry the same stigma as do violations of the criminal law. Nevertheless the judicial proceedings used to enforce these traffic laws are criminal in nature. The state takes it upon itself to prosecute offenders who in turn must be found guilty "beyond a reasonable doubt." Some juvenile proceedings are also criminal in nature. Local ordinances for matters like garbage disposal and barking dogs are additional examples of quasi-criminal proceedings.

Commercial Law

The offenses of fraud and deceptive practices are examples of applications of the criminal law to business transactions. Most of the law relating to commercial transactions falls on the civil side of the ledger. The sections of the law usually referred to as contracts, sales, negotiable instruments, and insurance are all closely related. They lay the ground rules upon which our modern system of commercial enterprise is built.

*It is commonly estimated that between 75 and 90 percent of all criminal cases are disposed of through the plea bargaining process rather than by going to trial. In a typical plea bargain the defendant agrees to plead guilty to a lesser charge. The prosecutor is assured of getting a conviction without having to go through the time and expense of a trial or to risk losing the case. The defendant usually comes away with a lighter sentence than he or she would expect to receive if the case had gone to trial.

A contract is a promise that is enforceable in a court of law. Contract law specifies the conditions that must be met in order to have a valid contract. It lays down some rules for interpreting contracts and for what should be done when one is violated. Another part of the law spells out the conditions under which bills and notes will be accepted. Still another area carefully defines the conditions under which various types of sales can take place and what a buyer's and seller's remedies will be.

The law on business organizations spells out the conditions required to form a partnership or a corporation. Detailed rules have been developed involving such concerns as issuing stocks, maintaining corporate records, powers of the directors, and obligations toward stockholders. Antitrust laws prohibit certain kinds of mergers and marketing activities. Labor law specifies certain relationships between employers and employees.

Property

Property is another area of the law that is closely related to commercial transactions. The law defines the rights and obligations of owners of real and personal property. Real property consists of fixed and immovable possessions like land and buildings. Personal property refers to possessions like automobiles, stocks and bonds, jewelry, and other common objects people own.

Liens and mortgages delineate the conditions under which property can be used to secure debts. Bailments relate to the responsibilities of the various parties involved in repairing or storing someone else's property.

The area of estate planning involves the development of a plan for disposing of an individual's property after death. A will is a legal document in which the owner of the property specifies the manner in which it should be distributed, and in some cases names an individual (the executor) who is to be responsible for carrying out those wishes. Estate plans often include various types of life insurance and occasionally the establishment of trusts. A trust is a legal relationship in which one party holds property for the benefit of another.

Probate refers to the process of proving that a will is genuine and then distributing the deceased's property according to the will and the various tax laws.

Torts

The term torts covers a variety of noncriminal, noncontractual wrongs. A tort exists where a person (or a person's property) is harmed as a direct result of another person's failure to carry out a legal duty.

The most common type of tort action involves negligence. Negligence is the failure to use proper care when carrying out a legal duty. In order to bring a tort action for negligence, the injured party must establish that an injury was suffered because the party being sued failed to do what a reasonable and prudent person would ordinarily have done under the same circumstances. A prudent person is supposed to foresee when an injury might reasonably result from some action. When motorists drive, for example, they have a legal duty to keep their vehicles under control to the extent that injury to others is avoided. If the road is snow covered it must be reasonably anticipated that it will be harder to stop an automobile and thus it must be driven at a slower speed. While the motorist is not required to anticipate the negligent acts of others, reasonable steps to avoid an accident must be taken once a negligent act has been observed. Thus if driver A observes driver B attempting to back out onto a busy highway, driver A must attempt to slow down and anticipate the danger.

Tort law is a highly complex area of the law involving a multitude of concepts like contributory negligence, assumed risk, imputed negligence, and strict liability. This brief survey of various types of law does not allow for the explanation of all these concepts. At this point it is sufficient to have a general idea of the types of factors involved in tort actions.

In addition to motor vehicle accidents, negligence can involve the manufacture and distribution of faulty products, maintenance of unsafe premises, and malpractice actions. Nor do all torts involve negligence. Tort actions can also involve assault and battery, false imprisonment, malicious prosecution, libel and slander, and various unfair business practices.

Interpersonal Relationships

Still another area of the civil law involves the legal relationships between husband and wife and between parent and child. It involves the law relating to marriage — annulment, separation, and divorce; adoption; guardianship; and the legal status of infants and incompetent persons. When conflicts arise, the law provides principles which become the basis of the courts' settlement in these areas.

TYPES OF COURTS

At first glance, the judicial systems of this country present a very confusing mixture of titles and functions. This is due in large part to the fact that there are actually fifty-one different court systems (the federal system plus one for each state). Not only are their jurisdictions divided in different ways, but the same types of courts often have different names. The basic trial court, for example, is called the Court of Common Pleas in Pennsylvania, the District Court in Minnesota, the Circuit Court in Illinois, the Superior Court in California, and the Supreme Court in New York. Some systems have justices of the peace and/or magistrates, while others do not. Rather than attempt to provide a description of each of these fifty-one court systems, we will simply review some general patterns found in them and leave it to the reader to search out the details of specific states.*

The courts involved can generally be divided into two main types: trial courts and appellate courts (Table 1.2). The trial court is the one which is charged with the basic handling of a case. In its more glorious moments it receives the evidence and the arguments presented by the opposing attorneys and then determines if the plaintiff has proven the case or whether the defendant is guilty of a criminal offense. Most of the time, however, is spent in far less dramatic proceedings in which the court receives plea agreements and ratifies out-of-court settlements. The appellate court, on the other hand, selectively reviews those decisions.

In order to truly understand the difference between the two, it is necessary to distinguish between questions of law and questions of fact. In most cases the meaning of the law is relatively clear, but the facts themselves are very much in dispute. It is

*Relatively simple explanations of most state court systems can be found in books and pamphlets published by the state. These organization manuals are usually available in the reference section of most libraries.

TABLE 1.2
Comparison of Trial and Appellate Courts

Characteristic	Trial Courts	Appellate Courts
Decision makers	One judge and sometimes a jury[a]	Majority vote of three or more judges
Presentation of arguments by attorneys	Yes	Yes
Testimony of witnesses and introduction of physical evidence	Yes	No
Determination of questions of fact	Yes	No
Interpretation of the law	Judge — yes Jury — no	Yes

[a]In most jurisdictions the juries' decisions must be unanimous. While most juries consist of twelve people, some courts use six-person juries for some types of cases.

quite clear that under the criminal codes of most states, it is a crime for someone other than a physician, pharmacist, or other authorized medical person to sell or distribute narcotic drugs. When someone is on trial for selling narcotics, the focus is usually on whether the accused did in fact sell narcotics — a question of fact rather than of interpretation of the law. The evidence usually consists of an undercover police agent testifying that the accused did indeed sell the agent a substance that lab reports identify as a narcotic.

While the primary focus of most trials is on factual issues, there are times when legal issues are involved as well. In the example cited above the defendant might admit to selling the drug but claim an entrapment defense. The entrapment doctrine prohibits law enforcement officers from instigating criminal acts by otherwise innocent persons in order to lure them into committing a crime. Even with the entrapment defense, the primary emphasis is still on determining the facts. The most important fact is the defendant's predisposition to commit the crime.* However, there are occasions where interpretation of the entrapment doctrine itself is unclear — then there is a legal question. When Charles Hampton was arrested by Federal Drug Enforcement Administration agents in 1974, he claimed an entrapment defense on the basis that government agents had supplied him with a drug, then later arrested him for selling the very same drug to another government agent. This contention presented a legal question as well as a factual one.†

During the course of a trial there may be numerous legal issues raised involving the conduct of the trial itself. Should a particular piece of evidence be excluded because it was the product of an illegal search and seizure? Should plaintiff's attorney be able to pursue a certain line of questioning? Should the judge present a particular set of instructions to the jury? Has the defendant's trial been tainted by prejudicial publicity? Then too, there is always the possibility of challenging the constitutionality of the statute itself. Thus a doctor charged with performing an illegal abortion could argue that the law he is charged with violating is itself unconstitutional.

When legal issues are raised in the trial courts they are ruled upon by the presiding judge. The trial then goes ahead on the basis of the judge's ruling. If it is ruled that the testimony is not admissible, then the trial goes on without it. If the judge rules that the search was not illegal, then the objects discovered in that search are admitted as evidence. On the basis of the evidence that has been allowed, the jury then resolves the factual questions. Was the defendant at the scene of the crime as two impar-

---

*Had the defendant ever committed such a criminal act or thought of committing such an act before? If the government merely provided the opportunity to commit the crime, it is not guilty of entrapment; but if it actually placed the idea of committing the crime in an otherwise innocent person's mind, then it is entrapment.

†In *Hampton v. United States*, 425 U.S. 484, 96 S.Ct. 1646 (1976), the U.S. Supreme Court resolved the issue against Hampton. The court ruled that as long as the defendant was predisposed to commit the crime anyway, it was not entrapment.

tial witnesses have testified, or was he, as three of his friends testified, across town playing poker? Was the fact that the defendant was driving 55 miles per hour on a snow-packed road the proximate cause of the plaintiff's injuries? What is appropriate compensation for never being able to walk again? If it is a bench trial rather than a jury trial, the judge will decide the factual questions as well as the legal ones.

Once these issues have been settled by the trial court, the losing party can usually have an appellate court review his case. (Most states and the federal government provide for one appeal as a matter of right in most types of cases. Additional appeals are usually at the discretion of the higher court.) That appeals court will ordinarily limit itself to reviewing the legal issues. Once it has been determined at the trial court level that the defendant did fire the shot that killed the murder victim — or that the defendant's conduct was not the proximate cause of the plaintiff's injuries — those factual issues are settled and are not open to review on appeal.

If the appellate court determines that a significant legal error* was made in the way the trial was conducted, it will usually cancel the original outcome and direct that the trial be conducted over again. Thus the reversal of a criminal conviction does not necessarily mean that the defendant will go free. The government can retry the person without being in violation of the double jeopardy clause.† On the other hand, if a key piece of evidence has been ruled to be inadmissible, the government may choose not to retry the defendant because it may feel that its case is too weak without the excluded evidence.

Whereas a single judge presides over a trial court, groups of judges act together in appellate courts. The decisions at the appellate level are based on a majority vote of the judges who are participating. Lower level appellate judges usually work in rotating panels of three while in the upper level appellate courts all of the judges jointly decide each case. There are no witnesses giving

---

*If the error is deemed to be very minor and not to have affected the result, the court labels it as "harmless error" and allows the decision to stand.

†Double jeopardy is a situation in which a person is tried more than once for the same offense. The Fifth and Fourteenth Amendments to the Constitution prohibit various forms of double jeopardy.

testimony in the appellate courts and, of course, no juries. The judges merely review the trial transcript and the written briefs from the lawyers. Sometimes they have oral arguments in which they listen to the verbal arguments of opposing attorneys and then have an opportunity to question them.

The Federal Courts

The federal courts and their relationships are shown in Figure 1.1.

The basic trial court in the federal judiciary is the district court. The entire country is divided into ninety-four distinct districts. Each state has its own district with the larger states having several districts within their borders. There are over 500 district judges spread among these ninety-four districts. These courts also have magistrates who supervise court calendars, hear procedural motions, and issue subpoenas and some writs. These

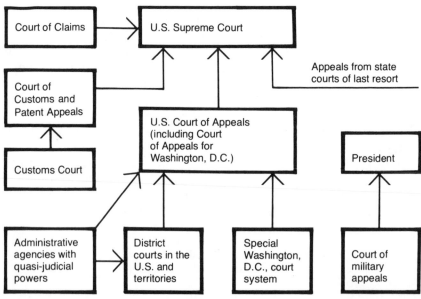

FIGURE 1.1
Organization of the Federal Courts

courts deal with federal criminal violations; civil cases of over $10,000 that arise under the Constitution, laws, or treaties of the United States; admiralty and maritime matters; civil cases of over $10,000 where the parties are citizens of different states; and certain actions of administrative agencies.

The basic appellate court in the federal system is the United States Court of Appeals, sometimes called the circuit court. The nation has been divided into eleven appellate circuits covering all ninety-four district courts as well as the District of Columbia court system. The judges usually decide cases in rotating groups of three. These appellate courts have jurisdiction over appeals from the district courts, independent regulatory agencies, the U.S. Tax Court, and territorial courts.

The United States Supreme Court is at the top of the federal judicial system. Here all nine justices hear and decide every case as a group. The Constitution gives them original jurisdiction* in cases between the United States and a state; between two or more states; by a state against a citizen of another state, an alien, or a foreign country;† and any case involving foreign ambassadors, ministers, or consuls. The Supreme Court, however, prefers to have the district courts handle these types of cases whenever it is possible to do so. It considers its primary function to be that of serving as the court of last resort (the final appellate body) for the entire federal judicial system as well as for the state courts when certain cases involve important questions of federal law.

In addition to the courts discussed above, there are some highly specialized courts such as the Customs Court, the Court of Claims, the Court of Customs and Patent Appeals, and the Court of Military Appeals. They have very little relevance to the average person and do not need to be elaborated on in this type of general overview.

Judges in the major federal courts are appointed by the president with the consent of the Senate and serve until they either retire, die, or are removed by impeachment.

---

*Original jurisdiction means that the court has the authority to act as the trial court rather than to review as an appellate court.

†The Constitution originally gave citizens of one state the right to sue the government of another state in the federal courts, but the Eleventh Amendment cancelled that right.

State Court Systems

State court systems are often much more complex than the federal system (Figure 1.2). Rather than having one basic trial court, states often have a variety of specialized courts such as traffic courts, family courts, juvenile courts, and probate courts. Judges selected for these courts hear only cases falling within the jurisdiction of that court.

Some states maintain a system of justices of the peace or magistrate courts for minor civil and criminal matters. These courts are not considered to be "courts of record." That means that no record is kept from which a party could appeal the case. A losing party must therefore initiate a complete new trial in a higher level trial court.

The states maintain either one or two levels of appellate courts

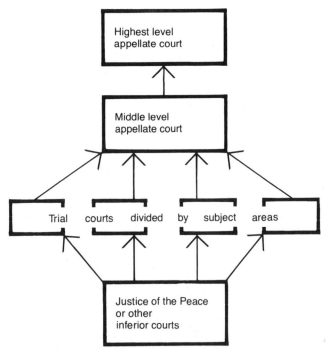

FIGURE 1.2
Organization of a Typical State Court System

to review the proceedings of these lower courts. The larger states have generally gone to a two-tiered system like that in operation at the federal level. The intermediate level appellate courts usually sit in panels while their courts of last resort sit as a whole. Appeals to the highest court are generally discretionary.

State courts have exclusive jurisdiction (only these state courts have authority to hear that kind of case) over matters which do not fall within the purview or scope of the federal courts. In some areas, both the federal and state courts have authority to hear the same types of cases (concurrent jurisdiction). Whenever a federal law or a provision of the U.S. Constitution is involved, the federal courts have the right to the final say.

Judges for the state courts are selected in a variety of ways. Some are appointed by the state's chief executive and/or the state legislature. Others are selected in either partisan or nonpartisan elections. Still others use a modification on what has come to be known as the Missouri plan. These systems generally involve a special panel of lawyers and lay persons nominating a few candidates for the vacancy. The governor then appoints from among this select group. A year or two later the appointee goes before the electorate in a special retention election. In such an election the voters are asked simply whether Judge X should be retained.

CRIMINAL PROCEDURE

Just as the structure and organization of the court systems vary from one state to another, so too do the details of criminal and civil procedure (Figure 1.3). Nevertheless, the procedures that these courts have adopted also have much in common, and while the details may vary, the major stages are much the same.

Theoretically the criminal process is supposed to start with a judge issuing a warrant for the defendant's arrest after the judge has been presented with probable cause* through a formal criminal complaint. The police then presumably arrest the defendant. In fact, most arrests are made before any warrant is ever issued. Usually the police arrest a suspect without a warrant and then

---

*Probable cause is usually interpreted as meaning that the available knowledge about the facts and circumstances would lead a reasonable man to conclude that the suspect probably had committed the crime.

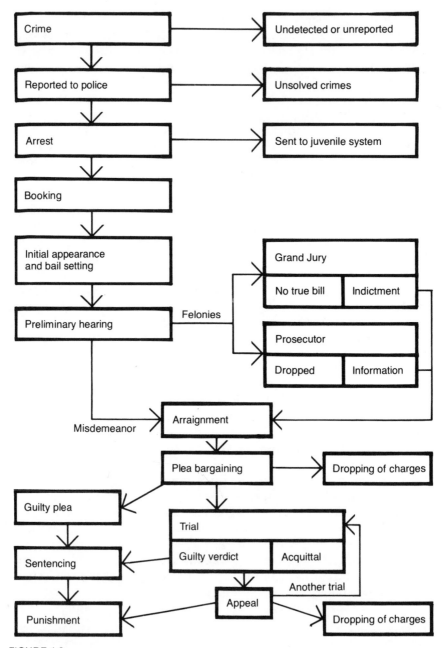

FIGURE 1.3
Criminal Procedure

draw up the criminal complaint. Such a procedure is proper under most state laws as long as at the time of the arrest the law enforcement officer had reasonable grounds to believe the suspect was committing or had committed a crime.

As soon as the defendant is brought back to the police station, a clerical process known as the booking takes place. The arrest is recorded in the department's records and the defendant may be fingerprinted and photographed. Within a reasonable amount of time (a few hours or the next morning if brought in overnight) the defendant must be brought before a judge (or magistrate) to be formally told of the charges and to have bail set.* (In some cases the defendant may be released on personal recognizance and therefore not have to post a cash bond.)

If the defendant is charged with a felony, a preliminary hearing will be held to determine whether there is probable cause to hold the defendant for the grand jury (if the state utilizes a grand jury) or for a trial. While the preliminary hearing is often waived, it can be used as a discovery tool and can be a useful way of getting a witness on the record.

The federal government and some states use grand juries at this point. The grand jury is made up of representative lay persons who are charged with reviewing the government's case to determine if there is enough evidence to justify holding the defendant for trial. The grand jury can also act as an investigative body and ultimately determine that a person whom the police have not charged with a crime should be. The Watergate grand jury is probably the most famous example of this latter function. If the grand jury decides that a defendant should be prosecuted, it returns an indictment or true bill. If the defendant has already been arrested he or she is then brought to court for the arraignment, formally told about the indictment, and renders an official plea. It is also at this point that the defendant notifies the court of the desire to exercise the right to a jury trial. If the person named in the indictment has not been previously arrested, an arrest warrant is issued at this time.

In states that do not use the grand jury the prosecutor draws up a formal list of charges called an information. This document then serves as the basis for the arraignment.

---

*In some states the amount of bail is preset for minor offenses and the accused can bail out at the police station prior to the initial court appearance.

Prior to the trial there will probably be various motions argued before the judge relating to the amount of discovery* to be allowed and the exclusion of certain evidence. It is also likely that at this time the prosecution and the defense will engage in the practice of plea bargaining.

If no plea agreement is reached, the trial itself constitutes the next stage of the criminal process. If it is a jury trial, it will begin with selection of the jurors. Through a process known as *voir dire*, either the judge alone or the judge plus the attorneys involved question the potential jurors in an attempt to discover their qualifications. Potential jurors can be dismissed by the judge on the basis of either a challenge for cause or a peremptory challenge. The judge dismisses a juror for cause when convinced that the person cannot adequately serve as an impartial attentive juror. The number of such challenges for cause is unlimited, but it is the judge, not the attorney, who makes the judgment. On the other hand, each side receives a set number of peremptory challenges, and these challenges are automatically enforced. They are strictly limited, and both sides usually must use them very carefully.

The trial begins with an opening statement by the prosecution in which the government explains what it thinks it will prove during the trial. The defense attorney can then either make an opening statement giving the defendant's side of the story or can wait until ready to present witnesses for the defense. The opening statement is followed by the prosecution's presentation of the evidence. This consists of the testimonies of various witnesses and, possibly, the presentation of documentary or physical evidence. Following the initial testimony from each prosecution witness the defense counsel is allowed to cross-examine the witness. This is followed by the prosecutor's redirect and possibly the defendant's re-cross-examination.

When the prosecution is ready to rest its case the defense will ordinarily move for a directed verdict on the basis that the prosecution failed to carry its required burden of proof with respect to all of the elements of the crime. If the judge grants the motion

---

*Discovery is the process by which one side can obtain relevant information about the case from the other side. It is designed to give both sides adequate opportunities to prepare their cases and to avoid major surprises at the time of the trial itself.

(which rarely happens), the case is dismissed. If not, the defense goes on to present its side of the case. The same format of direct examination and cross-examination, then re-direct and re-cross is followed. Each side has an opportunity to present rebuttal evidence in the same format. The trial is ended with the presentation of the closing arguments and (if it is a jury trial) the instructions to the jury.

If the judge or the jury returns a verdict of not guilty, the matter is ended at that point. If one or more guilty verdicts are returned, the judge will usually set a date for a sentencing hearing. This hearing offers the opportunity to examine the recommendations of corrections personnel as well as special circumstances presented by the defense. The amount of discretion a judge has in sentencing varies greatly from one state to another and from one crime to another. Many times the judge has the option of placing the defendant on probation or even suspending the sentence.

The appeals procedure begins with a post-trial motion for a new trial. While these motions are seldom successful, they are in most states a necessary part of the appeals process. Only after the trial judge has turned down such a motion is the door to the appellate court opened. Motions of intent to appeal are then filed and the court reporter is directed to prepare an official record of the case. This record along with the appellate briefs from both sides forms the basic materials upon which the appeal is examined by the appellate court. If oral arguments are involved the attorneys will have an opportunity to make a verbal presentation, and the judge will have the opportunity to question the attorneys about the implications of their positions.

In criminal cases it is also possible to seek review of a conviction through a writ of habeas corpus. The conditions under which this takes place are fairly complex and a discussion of them also goes beyond the scope of this chapter.

CIVIL PROCEDURE

Civil suits are initiated with the filing of a complaint (Figure 1.4). This complaint must state who are the parties to the suit, what legal rights have been violated, and the specific events that constitute the violation of those rights. A tenant plaintiff might name

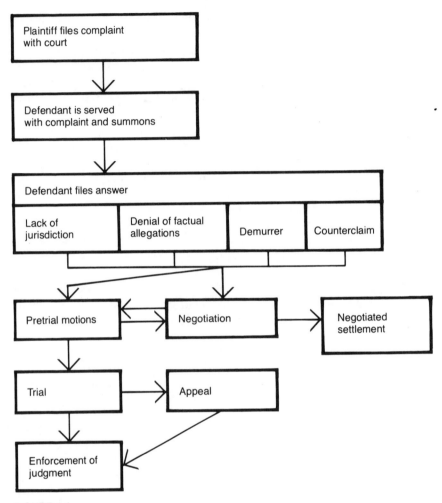

FIGURE 1.4
Civil Procedure

his landlord as the defendant and allege that the landlord had violated the plaintiff's rights to peaceably enjoy the premises and endangered health and safety by cutting off the utilities in the middle of winter. In addition to the above three elements, the complaint must also indicate the basis for the court's jurisdiction and venue as well as the relief being sought. Jurisdiction refers to the statutory or constitutional authority for a particular type of court to hear a particular type of case. Venue relates to the physical location of the court in relation to the location of the parties or the location of the incident that sparked the dispute (e.g., the cause of action). The relief requested depends on the nature of the case. In the example cited above, the plaintiff would probably ask for monetary damages and an injunction to prohibit the landlord from taking similar action in the future.

The next stage in the civil process consists of serving the defendant with a summons and a copy of the complaint. The summons is simply a legal notice informing the recipient that a lawsuit has been filed against him or her and that if an appearance in court is not made at a certain time and place the recipient runs the risk of having the suit decided against him or her without even being present (e.g., a default judgment).

Once served the defendant usually rushes out to a lawyer's office with the complaint. The attorney, having been hired by the defendant, then files an answer with the court. The answer can include one or more of the following elements: a challenge to the court's authority to hear the case; a denial of the facts stated in the complaint; a demurrer; or a counterclaim. A demurrer is a position which asserts that even if the facts alleged in the complaint were true (though the defendant does not necessarily concede that they are), no cause of action would exist. In other words, even if it happened the way the plaintiff claims it did, the law does not provide a remedy for such a situation. A counterclaim simply turns the tables and alleges a cause of action on the part of the original defendant against the original plaintiff. The challenge to the court's jurisdiction and the demurrer are both legal questions that usually are disposed of through pretrial motions. Where there is a denial of some of the facts the case must proceed to the trial stage.

Between the time that the defendant's answer has been filed and the date of the trial itself, motions are heard, pretrial conferences and negotiations take place, and both sides utilize various discovery mechanisms to find out more about the other side's case. Much of the time these negotiations result in all parties reaching a compromise agreement.

When the parties are unable to reach a negotiated settlement and go to trial the actual trial procedures closely parallel those used in criminal trials. The role of the plaintiff's attorney in a civil case corresponds to that of the prosecutor in a criminal trial. The role of the defense attorney is essentially the same in both. Bear in mind, though, that whereas the prosecutor has to present proof beyond a reasonable doubt, the plaintiff must only prove the case by the preponderance of the evidence standard.

When the verdict is rendered (either by a judge or jury) the judge enters the results into the court record. In addition to indicating which party triumphed and what if any relief was granted, the judge also assigns the court costs involved. Under some statutes it is possible to award attorneys' fees, also. If the judgment has not been satisfied voluntarily within a reasonable amount of time, the winner can return to the court to obtain a writ of execution. This is an order to the sheriff to seize and sell enough of the loser's property to satisfy the judgment with the proceeds of the sale.

The appellate process is also similar to that used in criminal cases, except for the fact that there is no writ of habeas corpus available.

ADMINISTRATIVE PROCEDURE

As discussed earlier in this chapter, administrative agencies have the authority to make legally binding rules and regulations in their specialized areas. At the federal level one finds agencies like the Internal Revenue Service, the Federal Trade Commission, the Interstate Commerce Commission, the Equal Employment Opportunity Commission, and the Occupational Safety and Health Agency. At the state levels there are similar agencies with similar functions.

When these agency rules and regulations are violated, there is a quasi-criminal administrative procedure invoked in which the investigative section of the agency brings charges of wrongdoing before administrative law judges. The adjudicative staffs are usually structured in such a way as to insure their neutrality and the hearing examiners soon develop an expertise in the technical areas for which the agency is responsible.

The procedures utilized in these administrative hearings generally resemble those involved in courtrooms, except that the rules of evidence are not as strict and due process guarantees are not as extensive. Both the regulations developed by the agency and specific adjudicatory decisions can usually be taken to the courts for review.*

SUMMARY

The development and enforcement of law is an essential governmental function in all developed societies. These laws regulate human conduct by imposing duties to do certain things and prohibiting other types of behavior. Under the federalist system of government in the United States, the states and the national government share the responsibility for formulating these laws.

The United States Constitution lays down fundamental legal principles and assigns powers to the various branches of government and the subunits (local governments). All law must be consistent with the dictates of the Constitution. Statutory law consists of the enactments of legislative bodies in the federal, state, and local governments. Administrative law is formulated by the executive branches and independent regulatory agencies. In situations where none of these laws resolve the conflict, the judge turns to the common law. In so doing the judge follows principles that are derived from previous decisions in related cases.

Whereas the civil law is designed to redress private wrongs, the criminal law is designed to punish those whose conduct offends the society as a whole. In criminal law the state assumes the burden of prosecuting a case, while in the civil area the offended individual must pursue the matter personally. In both situations the state does provide judicial apparatus for arbitrating the dispute. There are also major differences between civil and criminal cases with respect to the burden of proof required and the sanctions that are imposed.

Criminal law is divided into felonies and misdemeanors. Felonies are those that the legislature considers to be the more serious offenses and that carry penalties ranging from a year in prison to the death penalty. There are also quasi-criminal proceedings involving juveniles, traffic offenses, and ordinance enforcement actions. In this chapter we have divided civil law into

*Both the procedures used and the basis for review are discussed in greater detail in Chapter 9.

the four general categories of commercial transactions, property rights, torts, and interpersonal relations. Contracts, negligence, agency, and corporations are examples of the ways in which these general categories can be further subdivided.

It is important that the reader understand the basic difference between trial courts and appellate courts. It is the trial court that not only makes the initial decision in a dispute but also develops the record that appellate courts review. The appellate courts do not take additional testimony about the facts of the dispute and will rarely substitute their own factual conclusions for those of the trial judge or jury. The appellate courts focus on reviewing the legal issues involved in a case. They examine the interpretation given to the law by the trial judge and procedures that were employed during the trial.

Compared to most state judiciaries the federal judicial system is relatively simple. The district court serves as a trial court of general jurisdiction (e.g., it can hear cases involving a wide variety of criminal and civil matters). The court of appeals provides the first level of review and then the Supreme Court sits as the court of last resort (the final appellate body). State court systems often have a variety of specialized courts at the trial level. Some have only one level of review, while others have a two-tiered system like the federal model.

While specific rules of criminal and civil procedure are quite complex and vary from one jurisdiction to the next, basic stages in the process are alike. Criminal cases begin with arrest and then proceed through various stages: the defendant is informed of the charges that are pending, given a chance to be released on bail, given a preliminary determination of probable guilt by a judge or grand jury, and then brought to trial. In most cases the defendant negotiates a plea bargain rather than going through with the trial. Guilty verdicts (and guilty pleas) are followed by sentencing and punishment. Civil cases, on the other hand, are begun when the plaintiff files a complaint and serves the defendant with a summons. The defendant's response can involve a variety of pre-trial motions and counterclaims. If negotiations fail, the case ends up in a courtroom trial that closely parallels the procedures used in a criminal case. If the judgment is not satisfied voluntarily, the winner can return to obtain a writ of execution.

Administrative proceedings are quasi-judicial in nature. They borrow many of the procedures used in the courts but are generally conducted in a more informal manner and without the strict rules of evidence. Both administrative and judicial procedures will be discussed in greater detail in Part IV.

While there is a great deal of variation among the federal judicial system and the states systems, they also have a great deal in common. This chapter has attempted to present the basic principles and procedures of these systems. The mastery of the materials is a prerequisite to the reader's future exploration of specific court systems and substantive areas of the law.

KEY TERMS

administrative law	injunction
appellate court	jurisdiction
bail	law
beyond a reasonable doubt	misdemeanor
civil law	ordinance
common law	preponderance of the evidence
complaint	plaintiff
constitutional law	preliminary hearing
criminal law	statutory law
defendant	summons
entrapment	tort
equity	trial court
felony	true bill
grand jury	venue
indictment	writ of execution
information	

REVIEW QUESTIONS

1. What is the basic function of law in our society?

2. Under what conditions does a judge apply the common law?

3. What are the primary differences between criminal law and civil law?

4. What are the primary differences between trial courts and appellate courts?

5. From what judicial bodies can you appeal directly to the United States Supreme Court?

6. What are the methods used for selecting judges in the federal and the state courts?

7. What are the primary differences between the stages in a criminal proceeding and a civil one?

DISCUSSION QUESTIONS

1. Do you agree with the assertion that laws are in fact necessary? Many believe we have too much law today. Do you agree? If you do feel that we have too many laws, which ones should be eliminated? Do we still need additional laws in some areas?

2. What is the proper relationship between the law and morality? When, if ever, should laws be based on moral codes or used to enforce moral values?

3. Should there be less variation in the law from one state to the next? Do the advantages of diversity really outweigh the disadvantages?

4. How important is the method by which judges are selected? Which method do you think is best and why?

PROJECTS

1. Read the United States Constitution and then make a list of the powers that are assigned to each of the following categories:
   a. Powers that are delegated to the federal government;
   b. Powers that neither the states nor the federal government can exercise; and

    c. Powers that states (but not the federal government) are specifically prohibited from exercising.

2. Diagram your own state's court system. Use Figures 1.1 and 1.2 as examples.

REFERENCES

1. James S. Campbell, Joseph R. Sahid, and David P. Stang, *Law and Order Reconsidered: Report of the Task Force on Law and Law Enforcement to the National Commission on the Causes and Prevention of Violence* (New York: Bantam Books, 1970), pp. 3 and 5.

2. Rita James Simon and Linda Mahan, "Quantifying Burdens of Proof," *Law and Society Review* 5, no. 3 (February 1971): 319–30.

3. 38 *Illinois Revised Statutes*, §9–1.

4. 38 *Illinois Revised Statutes*, §9–2.

5. 38 *Illinois Revised Statutes*, §9–3.

6. 38 *Illinois Revised Statutes*, §§12–1 and 12–2.

CHAPTER 2

Paralegalism: What's in a Name?

Paralegal, legal assistant, legal advocate, lay assistant, legal adjunct, and law clerk — these are all labels that have been used at one time or another to identify an individual who, while lacking membership in the bar, nevertheless takes on a variety of important legal tasks. The paralegal is an individual who is part of a group critical to the future delivery of legal services in this country — a group that represents, in the words of one legal scholar, "an idea whose time has come."[1]

The prefix *para* carries the meanings of "near" or "beside"; "similar to" or "subordinate to." Thus a paralegal is one who works near or beside a lawyer, one who is similar to a lawyer, or one who is subordinate to a lawyer. All three connotations are useful in helping us arrive at an understanding of what a paralegal really is. Paralegals do indeed perform tasks that lawyers have often performed in the past. They do work near lawyers, and they are considered to be subordinate to lawyers.

Paralegals are individuals with legal skills that give them competence to perform such functions as gathering and analyzing facts, researching legal questions, preparing various types of legal documents, making logistical preparations for legal proceedings, managing a law office, and even representing clients in certain administrative hearings. A well-trained paralegal working under the supervision of an attorney can do just about anything but give legal advice to clients and appear in formal judicial proceedings.

In 1971 the American Bar Association's Standing Committee on Ethics and Responsibility adopted the title *legal assistant* as the proper designation for a person performing paralegal functions.[2] This text, however, will utilize the term *paralegal* since in the author's opinion it conveys a more meaningful description of a more comprehensive role.

In this chapter we will review some of the historical events that have led to the current recognition of paralegals, we will note how one becomes a paralegal, and we will explore some of the specific tasks a paralegal is likely to perform.

HISTORICAL DEVELOPMENT AND RECOGNITION

At the time the United States was founded there was a general distrust of lawyers and an attempt to get along without them.[3] Many of the old justice of the peace systems did not even require that the judge have legal training. As the nation evolved it soon became apparent that lawyers did serve an essential function, and they rapidly came to dominate both the legal and the political systems.

Up to the twentieth century legal education was haphazard and access to the profession was widely obtainable. Lawyers learned the law by serving an apprenticeship or clerkship with a practicing attorney and then simply reading the law on their own. Permission to practice was obtained by presenting themselves to a local judge for examination. Without any set standards the admission criteria differed widely, and personal influence was an inevitable factor. Since judges usually abided by the decisions of their colleagues, the standards for admission were determined by the most lenient judge in the state.[4]

These attorneys operated almost totally on their own. Not only were most of them sole practitioners, they did not even use secretaries. The apprentice law clerks assisted in the longhand preparation of legal documents but most contributed little else to the attorney's practice.[5] Indeed, rather than being paid for their contributions, many had to pay the attorney for the privilege of occupying a desk in his office.[6]

Development of the Need for Paralegals

The introduction of the typewriter and the telephone, along with the movement toward partnership arrangements, led most attorneys to hire lay assistants for such clerical duties as answering the telephone, typing letters and documents, and keeping the books. After the development of law schools replaced the old apprenticeship or clerkship arrangement, some attorneys utilized law school students as research clerks. By and large, however, most attorneys resisted delegating any of their legal tasks.

In the meantime several major professional groups in this country had begun to make extensive use of paraprofessionals. This movement was led by medical doctors who, even prior to the Civil War, had begun utilizing nurses as paraprofessionals. The doctors learned that by delegating such tasks as taking temperatures and giving injections they had more time to devote to what they considered to be the more challenging and rewarding aspects of their profession. As the sophistication of the medical sciences grew, so too did the diversity of paraprofessionals. Today the field is populated by such positions as registered nurses, licensed practical nurses, and nurses' aides; by physical therapists, occupational therapists, and inhalation therapists; and by radiologic technologists, laboratory technicians, operating room technicians, and medical records technicians. According to one estimate there are now approximately eleven paramedical personnel for every doctor in this country.[7] Other professionals who have made extensive use of paraprofessionals include dentists, architects, teachers, and even law enforcement personnel.

The fact that the average medical doctor's income is more than twice that of the average lawyer is just one of the factors which eventually led attorneys to reevaluate their traditional reluctance to delegate their work.[8]

The American Bar Association's Special Committee of Legal Assistants commissioned Kline Strong of the University of Utah Law Research Institute to study the economics of utilizing paralegals. Strong studied 104 law firms of four partners or less.

He analyzed typical legal tasks in terms of tasks performed by a lawyer, tasks performed by a paralegal, and tasks performed by a secretary. He then calculated how much money would be saved by the use of a paralegal as opposed to the lawyer and secretary alone. Figuring an hourly rate at $3.00 per hour for secretaries, $5.00 per hour for paralegals, and $40.00 per hour for lawyers, Strong concluded that the firm utilizing a paralegal could form a corporation for a client for $127.50, while it would cost the non-paralegal firm $253.50 in billable time. If the firm charged a flat $300 fee for the act of forming a corporation, it could increase its profit from $46.50 to $172.50, while leaving the attorney with 3.5 extra hours to spend on other cases. The secret, says Strong, is to have each procedure completed by the least expensive persons competent to handle that procedure. Even if the attorney were to save just one hour a day through utilization of a paralegal, he would be freeing himself to earn another $9,600 per year at the billable rate of $40.00 per hour. Spread over a 25-year period, that one hour of paralegal assistance could increase an attorney's income by $240,000.[9]

American Bar Association Recognition and Encouragement

While both governmental agencies and private law firms had been having lay personnel perform some paralegal functions, the established bar did not really begin to give much attention to the paralegal situation until the late 1960s. In 1967 the American Bar Association (ABA) issued a significant formal ethics opinion that clarified the legitimacy of delegating legal work to non-lawyers.[10] When the association's revised Code of Professional Responsibility and Canons of Judicial Ethics was promulgated in 1969, Ethical Consideration 3-6 favorably supported the extensive use of paralegals. In August of 1968, the ABA's House of Delegates adopted Report Number 3 of the association's Special Committee on Availability of Legal Services. That report contained the following recommendation:

> Recognizing that freeing a lawyer from tedious and routine detail thus conserving his time and energy for truly legal problems will enable him to render his professional services to more people, thereby making

legal services more fully available to the public, this Committee rec-
ommends:

1. That the legal profession recognize that there are many tasks in
   serving a client's needs which can be performed by a trained, nonlawyer assistant working under the direction and supervision of a
   lawyer;
2. That the profession encourage the training and employment of
   such employees; and
3. That there be created a special committee of this Association to
   consider:
   (a) The kinds of tasks which may be competently performed by a
       nonlawyer working under the direction and supervision of a
       lawyer;
   (b) The nature of the training which may be required is provided
       to develop competence and proficiency in the performance of
       such tasks;
   (c) The role, if any, to be played by the legal profession and the bar
       in providing such training;
   (d) The desirability of recognizing competence and proficiency in
       such assistants as by academic recognition or other suitable
       means; and
   (e) All appropriate methods for developing, encouraging, and in-
       creasing the training and utilization of nonlawyer assistants to
       better enable lawyers to discharge their professional respon-
       sibilities.[11]

The association then formed the Special Committee on Lay Assistants for Lawyers to carry out recommendation number three.

In 1971 this special ABA committee (renamed the Special
Committee on Legal Assistants) released preliminary drafts of
reports reviewing the use of paraprofessionals in other professions, reporting the results of research done on paralegal usage,
and suggesting guidelines for the training of paralegals.[12] This
special committee was awarded the status of a standing committee in 1975.

In 1972 the National Paralegal Institute was founded under an
Office of Economic Opportunity (OEO) grant with the charge of
supporting and promoting the use of paralegals in public sectors
of the law (especially in legal services offices). It was designed to
assist in the development of training programs and materials as
well as acting as a watchdog to ensure that the certification process would not needlessly cripple paralegal use in the public sec-
tor.[13]

Growth in Use of Paralegals

It is clear that with the formal recognition accorded paralegals by the ABA there has been an increased use of paralegals within all aspects of the profession. When Prentice-Hall conducted a survey of 311 Missouri attorneys in 1963, 63 percent of the respondents replied that they did not feel they could make use of a lay technician.[14] Five years later a survey of St. Louis area lawyers found that only 29 percent failed to see a need for paralegals.[15]

While Strong's study demonstrated that the utilization of a paralegal is profitable for small firms as well as large, large firms have so far made a greater use of their services. This is due in part to the fact that such firms tend to be more specialized and do a higher volume of business. Their greater size also means that they probably have a more efficient management system and that delegation (to junior associates) is already a common practice.

Government agencies have also made wide use of paralegals. Since these agencies must operate within fixed budgets and cannot simply pass the cost of their services on to the client, they have utilized paralegals to stretch their resources.

This was particularly true of the legal services programs funded by the Office of Economic Opportunity. One survey conducted in the early 1970s showed that 45 percent of the agency's offices employed paralegals. While most used only one or two, a few had as many as twenty.[16] By 1977 the Legal Service Corporation (successor to the old OEO program) employed approximately 1,300 paralegals, and approximately 60 percent of their programs used paralegals in administrative hearings.[17]

While they were called legal research analysts rather than legal assistants, the Justice Department has been using paralegals since 1964. Today the department employs approximately 400 paralegals and 800 legal technicians.[18] (See Figure 2.1 for an explanation of the classification system currently used by the Office of Personnel Management.) The Federal Trade Commission, the Equal Employment Opportunity Commission, the National Labor Relations Board, and the Environmental Protection Agency all use paralegal investigators. The Department of Health and Education's Bureau of Hearings and Appeals has used lay employees to prepare and present disability cases.[19] The Interstate Commerce Commission recently revised its rules to delegate to paralegals the task of processing applications.[20]

FIGURE 2.1
Paralegal Classifications in the Federal Civil Service System

1. *Paralegal Specialist Series, GS-950*
   This new series has been developed to meet the needs of a number of agencies who have established paralegal positions and who plan establishment of many more such positions to provide better utilization of legal personnel. Generally, these positions have been classified in the Legal Clerical and Administrative Series, GS-986; the Legal Assistance Series, GS-954; or the Adjudicating Series, GS-960.

   A large number of these positions involve the application of substantial legal knowledge in performing responsible assignments in support of attorneys. For such positions a law degree is a desirable qualification though not a necessary one because the work does not require full professional legal competence; however, legal education is a consideration in ranking candidates.

   Because of the required level of discretion and independent judgment in the application of substantial legal knowledge and the relevance of college-level education, this occupation has been identified as a two-grade interval occupation for which the Professional and Administrative Career Examination (PACE) is appropriate. Test 500 may be used as a factor for inservice placement; it may not be used on a pass-fail basis.

   Positions classifiable to the new Paralegal Specialist Series include most positions previously classified in the Legal Assistance Series, GS-954, and the Adjudicating Series, GS-960; these series are hereby abolished. The Paralegal Specialist Series also includes some of the higher level administrative positions, requiring quasi-legal knowledge, previously classified in the Legal Clerical and Administrative Series, GS-986.

2. *Legal Clerk and Technician Series, GS-986*
   The title and series definition for this one-grade interval series has been revised, and a new qualification standard has been provided. The qualification standard for the Legal and Kindred Group, GS-900 (Legal Assistant, GS-5/6 and Clerk, GS-4) issued in June 1962 is rescinded.

   Inclusion of technician levels in this series provides a career bridge between legal clerical positions and positions in the Paralegal Specialist Series.

3. *Professional Legal Occupations*
   When the classification standard for the General Attorney Series, GS-905, was developed, in 1959, the Commission agreed with the Federal Bar Association that, by definition, professional legal work should be that which requires bar membership. At that time there were a number of series identified as professional legal occupations not requiring bar membership. Commission studies of these occupations have resulted in some cases in setting up new quasi-legal series, e.g., for claims examining and land law examining po-

FIGURE 2.1 — Continued

sitions formerly in the Adjudicating Series, GS-960, or in the case of Estate Tax Examining and Trade Mark Examining, determining that the positions characteristic of the occupation did generally require professional competence and should be classified in the General Attorney Series, GS-905. The Estate Tax Examining Series, GS-920, and the Trade Mark Examining Series, GS-1241, were redefined as quasi-legal series or nonprofessional series to provide an appropriate series for those few incumbents who were not members of the bar. Thus, the Legal Assistance Series, GS-954 and the Adjudicating Series, GS-960, both of which are defined as involving professional legal work not requiring bar membership, are anomalies not appropriate for continued use and have been abolished. The classification standard for the Legal Assistance Series, GS-954, issued in May 1951, and revised in March 1957 and October 1965, is rescinded.

For the same reason, the series definition for the Deportation and Exclusion Examining Series, GS-942, has been revised to delete reference to professional legal work not requiring admission to the bar. (Note: The qualification standard for the Hearings and Appeals Series, GS-930, may be used for positions in the Deportation and Exclusion Examining Series, GS-942, with appropriate selective factors.)

Source: *United States Civil Service Commission Bulletin No. 930-17*, Washington, D.C., August 11, 1975.

At the state level administrative agencies are also beginning to utilize paralegals in their operations. The nature of their positions roughly parallels those at the federal level. Even some state legislatures have begun to recognize the use of paralegals on their own committee staffs. In Illinois, for example, the Joint Committee on Administrative Rules created the position of a rules analyst for a nonlawyer to assist in research of proposed rule making and existing agency rules and regulations. The position called for a person with "knowledge of the use of legal source materials and state government organization and operations."[21]

In addition to law offices and government agencies, banks, insurance companies, and other private corporations also make use of paralegals. Banks are most likely to use them in their trust departments while insurance companies employ them in claims work as well as in their corporate law departments. The paralegals' expertise has also made them useful additions to the staffs of trade associations and lobbying groups.

The paralegal profession has been growing so rapidly that it is difficult to determine its true size. One prominent 1977 estimate put the figure at that time at approximately 70,000.[22] It seems clear that the number will continue to grow during the next decade as well.

Compensation

Salaries quite naturally vary from one part of the country to another and are influenced by the type of education the paralegal has had. One recent survey of 381 law firms throughout the United States and Canada reported that paralegals with both a bachelor's degree and formal paralegal training received a median annual compensation of $13,000.[23]

Generally speaking, those working in larger firms and in the East and Midwest are able to command higher salaries. In Chicago, starting salaries average around $10,000 and some experienced paralegals make as much as $25,000.[24] On the other hand, many legal services programs start paralegals in the $7,000 to $8,000 range. Federal civil service positions for paralegals can begin at anywhere from the GS-5 level to GS-11 (or approximately $10,000 to $18,000 under today's standards). Starting salaries in the state civil service systems generally fall within the $8,000 to $12,000 range.

EDUCATION AND CERTIFICATION

In the early years of this nation's history, those who could convince a judge that they knew enough law could be attorneys. Today those who can convice an employer that they know enough law can be paralegals. But just as the various bar associations gradually standardized and institutionalized the education and licensing of attorneys, so too the bar associations have recently turned their attention to the standards for admission into the ranks of legal paraprofessionals.

On-the-Job Training

Prior to 1970, one learned to be a paralegal exclusively through some sort of on-the-job training. Many lawyers simply delegated discretionary tasks to their secretaries after having explained how it was to be done.* Occasionally someone with a special skill, such as accounting, would be brought in for specific clients' problems.

In spite of the growth of formal educational programs, many employers still use some in-house training. While some use it only as a supplement to the formal training, others rely on it exclusively. The Legal Services Corporation, for one, does a great deal of in-house training of paralegals working in its legal aid offices. Many programs specifically designate an experienced paralegal as a training coordinator with the responsibility for orienting new paralegals and developing additional training for current employees.

Formal Educational Programs

Formal paralegal education can probably be traced most directly to a series of short courses for paralegals which began in 1968 at the University of Denver College of Law. In 1969 the Law School and the College of Human Services at Columbia University ran an experimental program to train paralegals for newly created jobs with legal services offices in New York city.[25] Antioch School of Law was the first law school to closely integrate a comprehensive paralegal curriculum with the regular juris doctor program. With few exceptions, though, law schools have not become directly involved in paralegal education.

Meramac Community College of St. Louis was the first of a large number of junior and community colleges to offer a paralegal education program with a series of night classes in September of 1969. Today, the junior colleges dominate (in terms of numbers) the delivery system for paralegal education.

Most of the junior college programs attempt to follow closely the recommendations and accreditation standards of the American Bar Association. Within the standard two-year period the student is expected to combine general education courses in areas such as English, history, and the social sciences with a legal education component. The legal education portion is generally di-

---

*It should be noted here that many experienced legal secretaries do perform some paralegal tasks even though they do not receive formal recognition for doing so.

vided into general courses that introduce the student to law and the operation of the legal system and specialized courses that teach specific paralegal skills. The ABA originally required a combination of 45 semester hours in general education and introductory law courses along with 15 semester hours of legal specialty courses. However, that has recently been reduced to 30 and 15 hours respectively.

Some bachelor degree-granting colleges and universities have also developed formal paralegal programs. Some of these have been incorporated into the regular four-year degree program. In these types of programs, a student merely substitutes a major in legal studies (or some similar title for the paralegal courses) for a traditional major in English, political science, or business.

At other universities paralegal programs have been assigned to extension or continuing education divisions and are segregated from the institution's regular degree programs. Sometimes they simply offer a series of short noncredit courses for working professionals, and at other times they offer special certificate programs at either the graduate or the undergraduate level. Such programs are usually three to four months in duration and concentrate on a specialized area of legal training.

Still another educational delivery system is represented by the private business school. In 1970 the Institute for Paralegal Training opened in Philadelphia. Formed by three practicing attorneys expressly for providing paralegal training, the institute developed three-month specialty courses at the post-bachelor level. Several other private institutions have since followed suit.

The growth in paralegal programs has been phenomenal. From these humble beginnings in 1968, 1969, and 1970 it grew until by the middle of 1973 there were thirty-one programs operating on a continuous basis.[26] By January 1980 over 250 programs were known to exist in the United States.[27]

ABA and State Accreditation

Given this explosion of programs, it is not surprising that in 1972 the American Bar Association's House of Delegates directed the Special Committee on Legal Assistants to concentrate its efforts on the development of standards for accreditation of formal education programs directed to the training of legal paraprofessionals. Pursuant to that directive the committee held a special conference of interested parties in May of 1973 on the campus of the University of Denver School of Law. In August of 1973 the House of Delegates formally adopted a set of standards for accrediting educational programs and gave the responsibility for administering those standards to the Standing Committee on Legal Assistants. Some state bar associations have also begun to accredit programs.[28]

As of January 1980, only fifty-one of the more than 250 programs had been granted either provisional or final ABA approval. The practical impact of having such accreditation is still most uncertain, for accreditation means only that some agency or organization (in this case the ABA) has recognized that the school's program meets certain predetermined standards. Whereas graduation from an ABA-accredited law school is a prerequisite to taking the bar examination in most states, graduation from an approved paralegal program is not a formal prerequisite for employment as a legal assistant. While graduation from such a program may influence a prospective employer, it is not tied to any type of certification or licensing standards.

The Certification Question

Certification refers to the formal recognition by a nongovernmental organization that an individual has met some predetermined set of qualifications. That set of qualifications may or may not include graduation from an accredited educational program and may or may not include passage of some examination. When the government engages in the licensing of occupations it is in effect formally limiting the practice of those occupations to individuals who have met certain predetermined qualifications. Those qualifications may also include graduation from an accredited educational program and/or the passage of some examination. The primary difference between certification and licensure is that licensing has the force of law behind it. Whereas an employer may be more inclined to hire an individual who has been certified, there is nothing that prohibits him from hiring someone who is not. On the other hand, where a state has chosen to license an occupation, it is illegal for anyone not so licensed to engage in that occupation.

At the conclusion of a 1971 report to the ABA House of Delegates, the Special Committee on Legal Assistants stated, "On the basis of the study of lay personnel in other professions, it appears essential that the organized bar take an active role in development and control of the licensing and certification standards of all lay employees for the legal profession."[29] In February 1972, the House of Delegates adopted a resolution instructing its Special Committee on Legal Assistants to develop "standards for ascertaining the proficiency of legal paraprofessionals."[30]

Since the ABA had been giving a great deal of attention to the role of paraprofessionals in the medical professions, the use of some type of certification or licensing arrangement seemed to be a logical next step. However, after the committee began to study the matter more thoroughly and after they held a series of public hearings on the issue during the winter of 1974–1975, its outlook on the matter began to change. The majority of the approximately fifty organizations which participated in the hearings were against the ABA's attempting to establish standards for certification at that time.

Advocates of certification have argued that it would provide the paralegals who were certified with increased status, greater salaries, and greater mobility. They also argue that certification would provide both potential employers and the public at large with an assurance of a certain level of competence.

Opponents have disputed the contention that certification is needed to protect the public. The idea has been expounded that since the consuming public lacks the expertise to be able to judge the person's qualifications, an organization that does have the expertise must do it for them. However, in this case, the consuming public is not faced with the decision of choosing among individuals claiming to be qualified paralegals. The consumer of legal services chooses his attorney (who is licensed) and it is up to the attorney to select the paralegals who will work on the client's case. The attorney does possess the expertise to judge the paralegals' qualifications.

Opponents of certification also have disputed the contention that certification will increase the paralegal's status, salary, or mobility. It has been argued that wages reflect both the value of that individual's contribution to the employer and the current conditions of the employment market and that certification is unlikely to change either of these. It has been further argued that unlike a field such as nursing, mobility is limited by one's degree of specialization and the fact that the law varies from one state to the next. Neither of these factors, it has been asserted, would be affected by certification.

Additional controversies arise when one begins to contemplate what the standards of certification might be. Should there be a requirement for some post-secondary education? Should graduation from an accredited program be required? If there is a requirement for formal education, will it tend to restrict access to white middle-class individuals and tend to screen out the poor and minorities? Is it really appropriate to eliminate the on-the-job training route of access? If on-the-job training is allowed, what kind of reasonable standards can be used to assess the validity of that training?

If a standardized test is going to be used, what will it test? At the present time lawyers are expected to be qualified as generalists and bar examinations are designed to test all major fields of legal knowledge. Does it make sense to require all paralegals to be generalists also? Many of the existing educational programs are geared to producing narrow-field specialists. Why should a paralegal whose work is in the area of real estate be expected to know about forming corporations? Are not certain skills as important as substantive legal knowledge? Can standardized tests be designed to adequately test paralegal skills?

Who is the appropriate certifying agency? The bar associations have tended to assume that it is their role to conduct this certification process. However, many paralegals are now asserting that it should be their prerogative rather than that of the bar. Is there a conflict of interest in giving this privilege to the bar association?

When the Special Committee on Legal Assistants released its report on the certification question, it concluded that:

1. The occupation of legal assistant is in a dynamic stage of development and will likely undergo further changes.
2. The numerous associations of legal assistants, which have been created throughout the country, further reflect the dynamic characteristics of this occupation. However, there is no organization as yet that can be identified as fully representative of and qualified to speak for legal assistants.
3. In addition to the investigations that have been and are being undertaken, there is need for a broadly based, national study to

analyze the roles and functions, and the means by which the competencies may be measured.

4. Whether or not certification may in the future be considered to be an appropriate means to identify qualified legal assistants, it is premature to initiate such a program at this stage of development and before the competencies required to perform the roles and functions of legal assistants have been adequately defined.

5. If certification of legal assistants should eventually be undertaken,
    (a) the goal of such a program should be primarily to provide the general public with legal services, more widely available, more efficiently offered, and at lower cost, and
    (b) the operation of such a program should be national in scope and under the supervision of a board that includes lawyers, legal assistants, educators, and members of the general public.

6. It is appropriate that the legal profession, through the American Bar Association, continue to exercise the initiative and some control in considering issues related to the possible future certification of legal assistants, and in exercising this initiative and control seek the joint cooperation of appropriate and representative national associations of legal assistants, state and local bar associations, educators, and the general public.[31]

While the ABA may have decided it was premature to begin to certify paralegals, the Oregon State Bar Association did not. The certification program there involves: (1) an educational requirement (associate degree and completion of approved paralegal training program); (2) a work experience requirement (equivalent of two years of practical experience as a paralegal); and (3) satisfactory completion of a comprehensive examination covering general skills (e.g., interviewing, investigation, and legal research) and substantive areas of Oregon Law. Between 1974 and 1979 approximately twenty paralegals received certification under this program.[32]

The state bar associations in California, Illinois, Michigan, Nevada, and Wyoming have also considered certification at one time or another, but as of this writing none have been adopted.

While the National Federation of Paralegals (which is made up of fifteen state and local paralegal associations) is opposed to certification at this time, the National Association of Legal Assistants (an outgrowth of the National Association of Legal Secretaries) has been operating its own certification program since 1976. In order to qualify for their certified legal assistant designation the individual must pass a two-day comprehensive examination and then participate in continuing legal education activities.

The exam appears to be heavily oriented to law office management, legal research, and a general overview of substantive areas of the law. In order to take the examination the paralegal must meet one of five education and experience requirements. At one end of the scale, a graduate of an ABA-approved training program needs one year of experience, while a person who is certified as a professional legal secretary or who has worked seven years as a paralegal can take the exam without evidence of any post-secondary education. By the end of 1979 the National Association of Legal Assistants had certified 224 persons in thirty-five states.[33]

To date, the certification question remains a hotly debated question within the legal community. The programs that have been instituted have affected relatively few individuals, and there are no legal or ethical obligations for lawyers either to refrain from hiring uncertified paralegals or to pay certified ones more. Likewise, certified paralegals are subject to the same legal restrictions on their activities as other paralegals.

PARALEGAL FUNCTIONS

We have reviewed the development of the paralegal movement and the ways in which one can become a paralegal. Now it is time to look a little closer at what a paralegal actually does. This overview of paralegal tasks will be directed at simply providing the reader with a general feeling for the type of work various kinds of paralegals actually do. It is not designed to be a complete description of how these tasks are actually performed, and it is definitely not designed to teach anyone how to perform these tasks.*

General Functions

Generally speaking, a client's initial contact is directly with the attorney. Only after the attorney has analyzed the nature of the

*Subsequent chapters are designed to teach generally applicable paralegal skills in interviewing, factual investigation, legal research, the drafting of legal memoranda, and briefs. The text is not designed to teach the specific steps involved in handling various types of law practice nor to familiarize students with documents related to any particular substantive area.

client's problem, explained his fee, and established a lawyer-client relationship will the paralegal be brought into the picture. However, in some legal aid offices and some group legal services offices the client may actually meet with the paralegal first.* In these instances the paralegal records the type of information the lawyer will need to analyze the case and may screen clients to determine their eligibility for the service. Once the attorney has analyzed the client's problem the tasks assigned to the paralegal will depend upon which area of the law is involved.

Corporate Law

A paralegal who works in the corporate law area engages in a great deal of document drafting and record keeping. Whether the paralegal is working for a private firm that handles the affairs of corporate clients or for the legal department of a corporation the duties will be similar.

Depending on their ability and experience, paralegals would participate in the drafting of articles of incorporation, corporate bylaws, resolutions, notices and waivers, stock options, and shareholder agreements. Paralegals are also given responsibility for keeping track of the many filing requirement dates and completing the various report forms that are required by statutes and administrative regulations.

Corporate law paralegals also do such tasks as researching the availability of a corporate name, keeping track of pending legislation or administrative regulations that would affect the operations of corporate clients, and keeping shareholder records.

Real Estate Law

In real estate transactions, the paralegal's duties consist primarily of assembling all of the appropriate documents that are part of a typical real estate transaction. The paralegal may be called upon to examine public records to determine the legal description

---

*The type of group legal services office referred to here is one in which the clients (or their employers) have already paid for a particular package of legal services.

of the property being sold, who the legal owners are, whether there are encumbrances* on the property, what its assessed valuation is, and when the taxes are due.

After consulting with the supervising attorney as to which clauses should be included, the paralegal will often be given responsibility for drafting real estate sales contracts, leasing agreements, and land trust arrangements. He or she may also be given responsibility for drawing up the settlement sheets and ordering title insurance and mortgage releases. The drawing up of the settlement sheets involves calculating taxes owed and various credits that are due to either the buyer or seller. The paralegal will probably also be called upon to take responsibility for coordinating the closing date with the parties to the sale, the attorneys, and the mortgage lender's representative.

Estate Planning and Probate

In planning an estate, paralegals can be used extensively in gathering routine factual data about the individual and his assets. To assist the attorney in deciding what course of action to follow, the paralegal may be asked to do legal research and calculate various tax consequences, utilizing different alternatives. Once the attorney has decided on which combination of options the client should use, the paralegal can do preliminary drafting of the wills and trust agreements being used.

Paralegals can also perform a number of important tasks in implementing the estate plan. For example, they can change the beneficiary designations of life insurance policies and pension plans, can prepare gift tax returns when needed, and can handle the reregistration of real estate, stocks, and bonds for living trusts.

In probating an estate, the paralegal can again be delegated the task of gathering all the relevant information and documents. It is usually the paralegal's duty to inventory all aspects of the

---

*An encumbrance is a charge or liability that has been placed on the property. For example, if a person has not paid a contractor for work done on that person's house, that contractor can place a lien on the property. The government can place a lien on the property if the taxes have not been paid. The property then cannot be sold until those encumbrances are removed.

estate, to handle correspondence with heirs, the attorney general's office, insurance companies, and other relevant parties.

Probate paralegals can also be responsible for keeping track of all court dates and other relevant deadlines. As these deadlines approach, they should make sure that the appropriate petitions, affidavits,* and tax forms have been prepared. Paralegals are often used to do many of the calculations involved in completing estate tax and inheritance tax forms.

Litigation

The types of activities which have been discussed in the areas of corporate law, real estate, and estate planning and probate have involved drawing up contracts and other forms of agreement as well as filing routine reports. When disputes arise about the meaning of those contracts, corporate bylaws, leases, and so on, the lawyers involved will attempt to negotiate a settlement. If they are unsuccessful, they will have to resort to litigation† to resolve the dispute. If a dispute arises over the question of somebody's negligence, it too will have to be litigated if the parties are unable to resolve it through negotiation. Still other matters, such as a divorce or a criminal charge, must be formally litigated even if the parties involved have mutually agreed upon settlement. In other words, litigation cuts across substantive divisions of the law, and could involve questions of corporate or real estate law as well as questions of negligence or criminal law.

When paralegals are involved in litigation activities, their duties tend to fall within one or more of the following general categories: (1) researching the facts, (2) researching the law, (3) drafting relevant documents, and (4) coordinating logistical concerns. Specifically, they might be assigned the task of undertaking extensive interviews with the client and friendly witnesses. One of their main tasks may simply be locating potential witnesses. When depositions and/or interrogatories are in order, the paralegal can be assigned the task of drafting the questions to be

---

*An affidavit is a written statement in which the person making the statement (the affiant) swears before a proper official (usually a notary public) that the content of the statement is correct.

†Litigation is a term which is used to identify a dispute which has been turned into a formal lawsuit. In other words, either a civil or criminal complaint has been officially filed in the courts.

used, drafting responses to the opposing side's questions, and summarizing that side's answers.* With respect to physical and documentary evidence, the paralegal can arrange to secure relevant photographs and medical records. Paralegals may even research the amount of money awarded by juries for similar cases in that jurisdiction.

If the case involves legal as well as factual questions, properly trained paralegals are capable of doing much of the time-consuming legal research. They can utilize the standard legal reference works to locate important statutes and cases and then produce an internal memorandum summarizing the situation for the attorney.

As the lawsuit progresses through the various procedural stages, paralegals are often assigned responsibility for administering the "tickler" system.† The paralegal is thus assigned the task of seeing that appropriate praecipes, pleadings, and motions are filed on time.‡ Part of that responsibility often includes the drafting of the appropriate document for the attorney's approval.

As the case proceeds to the trial stage, paralegals can assist the attorney by summarizing and indexing all of the information gained from the various interviews, interrogatories, and depositions. They can also develop appropriate exhibits for the attorney to introduce. Another important function consists of contacting all the relevant witnesses to make sure they understand when and where they are supposed to testify. During the trial the paralegals can take notes and help the attorney locate the key questions, exhibits, and other references they intend to use.

If an appeal is taken, the paralegal usually has responsibility for filing the notice of appeal and ordering copies of the record and a transcript of the trial. After these materials have been received, the paralegal is usually assigned the task of abstracting or digest-

---

*A deposition is the taking of a witness's sworn testimony out of court and prior to the actual trial. Interrogatories are formal written questions sent to the other side as a means of obtaining factual information.

†A "tickler" system is a procedure designed to give advance warning to all important dates (i.e., when a motion is due or a hearing is scheduled).

‡A praecipe is a formal request that the court clerk take some action in a situation where a judge's approval is not required. Pleadings are the formal complaints and answers submitted by the parties which define the nature of the lawsuit. A motion is a request that the judge make a ruling or that some other action be taken (i.e., a motion to not allow certain evidence to be introduced).

ing* them, and undertaking more legal research. These activities usually culminate in the preparation of a preliminary draft of the brief.

The Systems Approach

Paralegal usage has been spurred by the development of law office systems. Kline Strong, a law school professor who apparently holds the only Ph.D. in Law Office Management in existence, has been credited with being the major designer of these types of systems.[34] Utilizing the assistance of fellow law school professors and some 4,050 man hours of law student labor, Strong developed systems for divorce, probate, and corporate law in 1971. The following year he developed law office systems for bankruptcy, collections, real estate transactions, and the administration of intestate estates.† Those were followed in succeeding years by systems in estate planning and public securities issues.[35]

Strong's systems and others that have followed are based on the development of a master information listing. It is usually the paralegal's responsibility to see that all of the information called for on the master form is supplied. This master information form is then correlated to a set of standardized practice forms so that the blanks on the forms are numbered to correspond to specific items on the master information list.

A third element of the systems is a checklist that reminds the paralegal of the various tasks that have to be accomplished and when they should be done. If it is all done correctly, the attorney can thus be assured that all of the important information will be collected and that all of the proper forms will be prepared and that they will be completed by the appropriate date.

General Administration

In addition to the legal activities described above, some paralegals are given general administrative duties. These administrative

---

*Abstracting involves the preparation of a summary of the contents of documents being abstracted. Digesting involves not only summarizing, but also classifying and organizing the documents.

†An intestate estate is one in which the deceased did not leave a will.

duties can include hiring the clerical staff, seeing that the office machines are kept in proper repair, coordinating the keeping of time records and overseeing the billing process, keeping the library up to date, and answering clients' inquiries about the status of their cases.

SUMMARY

Paralegals or legal assistants are individuals who, although they lack membership in the bar, nevertheless do possess legal knowledge and skills, and do (under the supervision of a licensed attorney) perform a variety of legal tasks. They gather and analyze facts, research legal questions, assist in the preparation of legal documents, and perform administrative functions. They can even represent clients before some administrative tribunals. Indeed, about the only things they cannot do (provided they are working under the supervision of an attorney) are give legal advice and represent clients in formal judicial proceedings.

As the practice of law has grown in terms of sophistication and specialization and as lawyers have moved from solo practice into larger firms, the potential for utilizing paralegals has also grown. Taking a lesson from the medical profession, lawyers have begun to see the economic advantage of delegating some of their work to well-trained paraprofessionals.

In 1967 the American Bar Association issued a significant ethics opinion that clarified the legitimacy of delegating legal work to nonlawyers and in 1968 it created a special committee to encourage the training and employment of paralegals.

Since then the paralegal profession has grown rapidly. While the use of paralegals is clearly appropriate in all types of legal settings, the fact remains that so far they have been used most heavily in large firms and legal aid agencies. Salaries vary widely from one area to another and from one employer to another. Starting salaries are most likely to fall in the $8,000 to $12,000 range, while experienced paralegals may earn as much as $25,000.

During the 1970s a large number of educational institutions began to operate paralegal training programs. Today such programs exist at the junior college level, the bachelor degree level, and the post-bachelor degree level. These programs are offered by established public and private colleges and universities as well as by specialized business schools. In spite of the growth of these formal training programs, the Legal Services Corporation and other employers still engage in extensive on-the-job training programs of their own.

While the American Bar Association has become involved in the accreditation of paralegal training programs, it has determined that it would be premature to begin a certification program at this time. Nevertheless, several other organizations (both state bar associations and paralegal associations) have begun or are considering certification standards. Advocates of certification claim that it will increase the status, pay, and mobility of paralegals, as well as assuring attorneys and the public of a higher level of competence. Opponents dispute these assertions and question whether the profession has developed to the point where objectively measurable standards can be established.

The specific tasks paralegals perform depend a great deal on the type of employer and the area of the law that is involved. While the specific information that is being gathered, the specific documents that are being drafted, and the law that is being researched vary from one setting to the next, the basic skills are common to all areas. Parts II, III, and IV of this text will concentrate on building those general skills. Chapter 3 discusses the restrictions and obligations that accompany the paralegal's role.

KEY TERMS

abstracting	lay person
accreditation	legal assistant
affiant	licensure
affidavit	litigation
apprentice	motion
certification	paralegal
deposition	pleadings
digesting	praecipe
encumbrance	systems approach
interrogatory	tickler system

REVIEW QUESTIONS

1. What actions did the American Bar Association take to influence the use of paralegals?

2. What other factors have led to the increased use of paralegals?

3. Who, other than private law firms, is likely to employ paralegals?

4. In what ways do typical junior college paralegal programs differ from those at the post-bachelor degree level?

5. What is the ABA's current position on accreditation and licensing?

6. What are the primary duties of a paralegal working in the litigation area? In the corporate area? In the estate planning and probate area? In the real estate area?

7. In what ways does the systems approach encourage the use of paralegals?

DISCUSSION QUESTIONS

1. What are the relative strengths and weaknesses of the various types of paralegal training programs? If you were going to employ a paralegal, which type of program would you seek a graduate from? Why?

2. What, in your estimation, are the most compelling arguments in favor of certification of paralegals? What are the most compelling arguments against? If certification were to be mandated, what do you think the standards should be? If a test were to be used, what would be the nature of the material covered and the format of the test? Would there be an education requirement? What groups would participate in the establishment of these standards?

PROJECTS

1. Find out if there have been any formal discussions in the bar association in your state with regard to certification of paralegals. (One method of doing this involves searching through back issues of the state bar journal.) If there have been any proposals or actions, what positions were taken?

2. Find out if there is a paralegal association in your city or state. Has it taken a position on the certification issue?

3. How many professions are licensed in your state? What types of requirements have been established in those areas?

4. Find out if your state civil service system has established any job classifications that are specifically geared to paralegals. How many classifications can you identify that might be appropriate for a well-trained paralegal (even if the position may not formally require paralegal training or experience)?

REFERENCES

1. Lester Brickman, "Expansion of Lawyering Process Through a New Delivery System: The Emergence and the State of Legal Paraprofessionalism," *Columbia Law Review* 71 (1971): 1,176.

2. ABA Informal Opinion 1185 (1971). The American Bar Association Special Committee on Lay Assistants for Lawyers also formally changed its name to the Special Committee on Legal Assistants.

3. Anton-Hermann Chroust, *The Rise of the Legal Profession in America*, vol. 1 (Norman: University of Oklahoma Press, 1965), pp. 27–29. *See* also James Willard Hurst, *The Growth of American Law* (Boston: Little, Brown and Company, 1950), pp. 251–52.

4. Hurst, *The Growth of American Law*, pp. 276–85.

5. Paul Hamlin, *Legal Education in Colonial New York* (New York: New York University, 1939), chapter three, pp. 35–55.

6. Joseph Henry Beale, "The History of Legal Education," in *Law: A Century of Progress 1835–1935*, vol. 1 (New York: New York University Press, 1937), p. 105.

7. William Statsky, *Introduction to Paralegalism* (St. Paul, Minnesota: West Publishing Company, 1974), p. 19.

8. In an address to an Illinois Institute for Continuing Legal Education Workshop on October 20, 1973, Kline Strong (a prominent leader in the paralegal movement) made direct reference to this income differential as an incentive for making more extensive use of paralegals.

9. ABA Special Committee on Legal Assistants, *Liberating the Lawyer: The Utilization of Legal Assistants by Law Firms in the United States.* Preliminary draft, June 1971, pp. 43–49.

10. ABA Opinion 316.

11. ABA Special Committee on Legal Assistants, *Liberating the Lawyer,* pp. v–vii.

12. ABA Special Committee on Legal Assistants, *Training for Legal Assistants* (preliminary draft, 1971), *Proposed Curriculum for Training of Law Office Personnel* (preliminary draft, April 1971), *Liberating the Lawyer* (preliminary draft, June 1971), and *The Paraprofessional in Medicine, Dentistry, and Architecture* (preliminary draft, October 1971).

13. William Frey, "A Short Review of the Paralegal Movement," *Clearinghouse Review* 7 (December 1973): 466.

14. Missouri Bar Association, *A Motivational Study of Public Attitudes and Law Office Management,* 1963, p. 140.

15. Bar Association of Metropolitan St. Louis, *Sample Feasibility Survey Questionnaire Results of Survey,* 1968, p. 2. This survey was related to the proposed establishment of a legal assistant training program at Meramac Community College.

16. *Ibid.,* p. 463.

17. Catherine Day-Jermany, *Status Report on Paralegal Training and Career Development* (Washington, D.C.: Legal Services Corporation, February 1977), pp. 2 and 18.

18. As reported by Kathryn Braeman, Deputy Director of the Office of Information, Law and Policy, at ABA Conference for Legal Assistant Program Directors and Educators, October 26, 1979.

19. Frey, "A Short Review of the Paralegal Movement," pp. 464–65.

20. Interstate Commerce Commission, Revision of Application Procedures. Ex Parte No. 55 (Sub no. 25).

21. Quoted from official announcement of the Joint Committee on Administrative Rules of the Illinois General Assembly, dated October 1, 1978.

22. Carole A. Carmichael, "Employment Picture Bright for the Trained Paralegal," *Chicago Tribune,* 16 September 1977.

23. Manuel Galvan, "Law-grad Pay Meets Inflation Rate," *Chicago Daily Law Bulletin,* May 11, 1979, p. 3.

24. Jim Mlynarski, "Paralegals: They're Gaining Acceptance," *Chicago Daily Law Bulletin,* January 19, 1979, p. 3.

25. William Statsky, "Paraprofessionals: Expanding the Legal Service Delivery Team," *Journal of Legal Education* 24 (1972): 397.

26. William G. Haemmel, "Paralegals/Legal Assistants — A Report of the Advances of the New Professional," *American Business Law Journal* (1973): 112.

27. As reported by Terri Ford, Staff Director, American Bar Association, Standing Committee on Legal Assistants, in telephone conversation January 7, 1980.

28. Reported in *National Paralegal Reporter* (October 1976): 2.

29. American Bar Association Special Committee on Legal Assistants, *Certification of Legal Assistants,* 1975, p. 7.

30. *Ibid.,* p. 8.

31. *Ibid.,* pp. 28–29.

32. Juanita Fuller, "Oregon State Bar Certification Program," *Outlook* (Publication of Illinois Paralegal Association), May 1979, p. 3.

33. As reported by Dorthea Jorde, President of the National Association of Legal Assistants at ABA, National Conference for Legal Assistant Program Directors and Educators, October 26, 1979.

34. Stuart Gullickson, "Lawyering Systems," *University of Toledo Law Review* 4 (Spring 1973): 399.

35. *Ibid.*

CHAPTER 3

Legal and Ethical Responsibilities

Paralegals are not just involved in an occupation, they are part of a profession. They are quite properly considered to be professionals, not only because their work involves specialized expertise and training, but also because they are subject to highly developed ethical responsibilities that do not apply to other groups in the society. Paralegals hold positions of responsibility and trust. Their actions directly and indirectly affect the well-being of their clients. It is therefore essential that paralegals be aware of both their legal limitations and their ethical responsibilities.

This chapter examines what constitutes the unauthorized practice of law and the nature of a paralegal's ethical obligations. Since both topics help to define just what paralegals can and cannot do, it follows quite naturally the discussion of paralegal tasks contained in Chapter 2. The reader will find that the chapter contains frequent and sometimes lengthy quotations from the opinions of many different courts. They have been included not only to convey the substance of the court's decision but also to begin to familiarize the reader with the language and style of court opinions.

UNAUTHORIZED PRACTICE OF LAW

Historical Development of the Lawyers' Monopoly

Chapter 2 briefly mentioned the distrust early Americans had for lawyers. Nevertheless, American lawyers soon exerted their influence and rapidly developed an exclusive franchise for most legal business. While the standards for admission to the bar were quite haphazard, American courts quickly adopted the English model that prohibited a person from practicing law until the court had satisfied itself that the person's training and character made him fit for such an assignment.[1] Through the years, the state legislatures have developed statutes limiting the practice of law to individuals who have met qualifications spelled out by the legislature. The courts have uniformly upheld such statutes on the basis of their being reasonable attempts to protect the public's interests.[2]

In *West Virginia State Bar v. Earley,* the court offered the following typical justification for its restrictions on the practice of law.

> The justification for excluding from the practice of law persons who are not admitted to the bar and for limiting and restricting such practice to licensed members of the legal profession is not the protection of the members of the bar from competition or the creation of a monopoly for the members of the legal profession, but is instead the protection of the public from being advised and represented in legal matters by unqualified and undisciplined persons over whom the judicial department of the government could exercise slight or no control.[3]

Note especially that the court is not only concerned about the qualifications of the person giving the advice. There are clearly instances in which individual accountants, real estate brokers, and insurance brokers possess more accurate and up-to-date substantive legal knowledge than do some lawyers. In many cases, these lay persons are instructed on the meaning of the law by lawyers who are specialists in that field (e.g., where an insurance broker goes to a special seminar on the tax advantages of certain types of trust arrangements). Accountants and lawyers often read the same publications relating to the meaning of recent changes in the Internal Revenue Act.

In most unauthorized practice of law cases, there is no assertion that the nonlawyer gave bad advice or drew up an improper contract. In *State ex rel Johnson v. Childe,* for example, the court even concedes that Childe may be more knowledgeable about the establishing of transportation and service rates for common carriers than most lawyers would be.

> It is urged as a defense that to acquire and possess the knowledge necessary to have reasonable skill and efficiency in the handling of matters relating to the fixing and revision of transportation and service rates and charges of common carriers requires years of intensive and undivided study which few lawyers, if any, have undertaken. This is not a defense. We do not doubt that respondent possesses high qualifications in the transportation rate field. But the fact that he can qualify as an expert in a particular field will not permit his engaging lawfully in the profession of the law without a license to do so.[4]

The court's real concern in the unauthorized practice of law area seems to focus on the ability of the judicial branch to exercise control over those who practice law. As Lloyd Derby has noted, lawyers possess basic legal skills and ethical restraints which their lay competitors do not. Writing in the *California Law Review,* Derby supports this position with references to those portions of the Code of Professional Responsibility which protect against conflict of interest and impose a strict fiduciary* standard for attorney-client relations.[5]

Recognized Exceptions for Court Appearances

When it comes to appearing in court, there are only two widely recognized exceptions to the lawyers' monopoly. One is the statutory exception spelled out for a few minor courts of no record (often called justice of the peace courts). The other involves the right to represent oneself.

*A fiduciary relationship is one in which a person acts for another in a position of trust.

Surprisingly, there was even some doubt about the layman's right to represent himself until the United States Supreme Court clarified the issue in *Faretta v. California.* Speaking for the majority, Mr. Justice Stewart stated:

> The Sixth Amendment does not provide merely that a defense shall be made for the accused; it grants to the accused personally the right to make his defense. It is the accused, not counsel, who must be "informed of the nature and cause of the accusation," who must be "confronted with witnesses against him," and who must be accorded "compulsory process for obtaining witnesses in his favor." Although not stated in the Amendment in so many words, the right to self-representation — to make one's own defense personally — is thus necessarily implied by the structure of the Amendment. The right to defend is given directly to the accused; for it is he who suffers the consequences if the defense fails.
>
> The counsel provision supplements this design. It speaks of the "assistance" of counsel, and an assistant, however expert, is still an assistant. The language and spirit of the Sixth Amendment contemplate that counsel, like the other defense tools guaranteed by the Amendment, shall be an aid to a willing defendant — not an organ of the State interposed between an unwilling defendant and his right to defend himself personally. To thrust counsel upon the accused, against his considered wish, thus violates the logic of the Amendment. In such a case, counsel is not an assistant, but a master; and the right to make a defense is stripped of the personal character upon which the Amendment insists.
>
> . . .
>
> It is undeniable that in most criminal prosecutions defendants could better defend with counsel's guidance than by their own unskilled efforts. But where the defendant will not voluntarily accept representation by counsel, the potential advantage of a lawyer's training and experience can be realized, if at all, only imperfectly. To force a lawyer on a defendant can only lead him to believe that the law contrives against him. Moreover, it is not inconceivable that in some rare instances, the defendant might in fact present his case more effectively by conducting his own defense. Personal liberties are not rooted in the law of averages. The right to defend is personal. The defendant, and not his lawyer or the State, will bear the personal consequences of a conviction. It is the defendant, therefore, who must be free personally to decide whether in his particular case counsel is to his advantage. And although he may conduct his own defense ultimately to his own detriment, his

choice must be honored out of "that respect for the individual which is the lifeblood of the law. . . ."[6]

While there have been a few instances in which judges have allowed defendants to proceed with a lay assistant,[7] a federal district court recently rejected the contention that the Sixth Amendment provided a constitutional right for defendants to be represented by nonlawyers.[8]

Today's holdings that there is no right or privilege for a layman to practice law or to have unlicensed representation by a layman have as their corollary the recognition of a compelling state interest in the practice of law of sufficient magnitude to allow the state to circumscribe activity in the area.[9]

Preparing Documents and Giving Advice

The practice of law involves more than simply appearing in court. As one court noted:

Practice of law under modern conditions consists in no small part of work performed outside of any court and having no immediate relation to proceedings in court. It embraces conveyancing, the giving of legal advice on a large variety of subjects, and the preparation and execution of legal instruments covering an extensive field of business and trust relations and other affairs. Although these transactions may have no direct connection with court proceedings, they are always subject to become involved in litigation. They require in many aspects a high degree of legal skill, a wide experience with men and affairs, and great capacity for adaptation to difficult and complex situations. . . . No valid distinction, so far as concerns the questions set forth in the order, can be drawn between that part of the work of the lawyer which involves appearance in court and that part which involves advice and drafting of instruments in his office. . . . In this country the practice of law includes both forms of legal service; there is no separation, as in England, into barristers and solicitors. It is of importance to the welfare of the public that these manifold customary functions be performed by persons possessed of adequate learning and skill, of sound moral character, and acting at all times under the heavy trust obligation to clients which rests upon all attorneys. The underlying reasons which prevent corporations, associations, and individuals other than members of the bar from appearing before the courts apply with equal force to the performance of these customary functions of attorneys and counsellors at law outside of courts. . . .[10]

As that same court went on to state, however, the lines are not always clear.

The occasional drafting of simple deeds, and other legal instruments when not conducted as an occupation or yielding substantial income may fall outside the practice of the law. The gratuitous furnishing of legal aid to the poor and unfortunate without means in the pursuit of any civil remedy, as matter of charity, the search of records of real estate to ascertain what may there be disclosed without giving opinion or advice as to the legal effect of what is found, the work of an accountant dissociated from legal advice, do not constitute the practice of law. There may be other kindred pursuits of the same character. All these activities, however, lie close to the border line and may easily become or be accompanied by practice of the law. The giving of advice as to investments in stocks, bonds, and other securities, in real or personal property, and in making tax returns falls within the same category.[11]

These lines are most often challenged by the activities of real estate brokers, tax consultants, and estate planning specialists. In *Oregon State Bar v. John H. Miller & Co.*, for example, the Oregon Supreme Court wrestled with a situation in which a nonlawyer insurance salesman advised his clients on estate planning questions.

Much of the advice contained in the report to the client could not be given without an understanding of various aspects of the law, principally the law of taxation. Most of the advice is in terms of "suggestions." In each instance the client is urged to consult his own attorney. But whether the report takes the form of suggestions for further study or as a recommendation that the suggestions be subjected to further scrutiny by a lawyer, the fact remains that the client receives advice from defendants and the advice involves the application of legal principles. This constitutes the practice of law.[12]

. . .

An insurance salesman can explain to his prospective customer alternative methods of disposing of assets, including life insurance, which are available to taxpayers *generally*. He may inform his prospect in general terms that life insurance may be an effective means of minimizing his taxes. He cannot properly advise a prospective purchaser with respect to his *specific* need for life insurance as against some other form of disposition of his estate, unless the advice can be given without drawing upon the law to explain the basis for making the choice of alternatives.[13]

Another borderline area that has received a lot of attention lately is the sale of "Do-It-Yourself Divorce Kits." Generally speaking, the courts have found that the mere advertisement and sale of do-it-yourself legal forms do not constitute the unauthorized practice of law.[14] The following case, however, makes an important distinction between simply selling the forms and filling them out.

Florida Bar v. Brumbaugh

Supreme Court of Florida
355 So.2d 1186 (1978)

Respondent, Marilyn Brumbaugh, is not and has never been a member of the Florida Bar, and is, therefore, not licensed to practice law within this state. She has advertised in various local newspapers as "Marilyn's Secretarial Service" offering to perform typing services for "Do-It-Yourself" divorces, wills, resumes, and bankruptcies. The Florida Bar charges that she performed unauthorized legal services by preparing for her customers those legal documents necessary in an uncontested dissolution of marriage proceeding and by advising her customers as to the costs involved and the procedures which should be followed in order to obtain a dissolution of marriage. For this service, Ms. Brumbaugh charges a fee of $50.

. . .

With regard to the charges made against Marilyn Brumbaugh, this Court appointed a referee to receive evidence and to make findings of fact, conclusions of law, and recommendations as to the disposition of the case. The referee found that respondent, under the guise of a "secretarial" or "typing" service prepares, for a fee, all papers deemed by her to be needed for the pleading, filing, and securing of a dissolution of marriage, as well as detailed instructions as to how the suit should be filed, notice served, hearings set, trial conducted, and the final decree secured. The referee also found that in one instance, respondent prepared a quit claim deed in reference to the marital property of the parties. The referee determined that respondent's contention that she merely operates a typing service is rebutted by numerous facts in evidence. Ms. Brumbaugh has no blank forms either to sell or to fill out. Rather, she types up the documents for her customers after they have asked her to prepare a petition or an entire set of dissolution of marriage papers. Prior to typing up the papers, respondent asks her customers whether custody, child support, or alimony is involved. Respondent has four sets of dissolution of marriage papers, and she chooses which set is appropriate for the particular customer. She then types out those papers, filling in the blank spaces with the appropriate information. Respondent instructs her customers how the papers are to be signed, where they are to be filed, and how the customer should arrange for a final hearing.

. . .

This case does not arise out of a complaint by any of Ms. Brumbaugh's customers as to improper advice or unethical conduct. It has been initiated by members of The Florida Bar who believe her to be practicing law without a license. The evidence introduced at the hearing below shows that none of respondent's customers believed that she was an attorney, or that she was acting as an attorney in their behalf. Respondent's advertisements clearly addressed themselves to people who wish to do their own divorces. These customers knew that they had to have "some type of papers" to file in order to obtain their dissolution of marriage. Respondent never handled contested divorces. During the past two years respondent has assisted several hundred customers in obtaining their own divorces. The record shows that while some of her customers told respondent exactly what they wanted, generally respondent would ask her customers for the necessary information needed to fill out the divorce papers, such as the names and addresses of the parties, the place and duration of residency in this state, whether there was any property settlement to be resolved, or any determination as to custody and support of children. Finally, each petition contained the bare allegation that the marriage was irretrievably broken. Respondent would then inform the parties as to which documents needed to be signed, by whom, how many copies of each paper should be filed, where and when they should be filed, the costs involved, and what witness testimony is necessary at the court hearing. Apparently, Ms. Brumbaugh no longer informs the parties verbally as to the proper procedures for the filing of the papers, but offers to let them copy papers described as "suggested procedural education."

. . .

The legal forms necessary to obtain such an uncontested dissolution of marriage are susceptible of standardization. This Court has allowed the sale of legal forms on this and other subjects, provided that they do not carry with them what purports to be instructions on how to fill out such forms or how they are to be used.

. . .

Although there is a danger that some published material might give false or misleading information, that is not a sufficient reason to justify its total ban. We must assume that our citizens will generally use such publications for what they are worth in the preparation of their cases, and further assume that most persons will not rely on these materials in the same way they would rely on the advice of an attorney or other persons holding themselves out as having expertise in the area. The tendency of persons seeking legal assistance to place their trust in the individual purporting to have expertise in the area necessitates this Court's regulation of such attorney-client relationships, so as to require that persons giving such advice have at least a minimal amount of legal training and experience. Although Marilyn Brumbaugh never held herself out as an attorney, it is clear that her clients placed some reliance upon her to properly prepare the necessary legal forms for their dissolution proceedings. To this extent we believe that Ms. Brumbaugh overstepped proper bounds and engaged in the unauthorized practice of law. We hold that Ms. Brumbaugh, and others in similar situations, may sell printed material purporting to explain legal practice and procedure to the public in general and she may sell sample legal forms. . . . Further, we hold that it is not improper for Marilyn Brumbaugh to engage in a secretarial service, typing such forms for her clients, provided that she only copy the information given to her in writing by her clients. In addition, Ms. Brumbaugh may advertise her business activities of providing secretarial and notary services and selling legal forms and general printed information. However, Marilyn Brumbaugh must not, in conjunction with her business, engage in advising clients as to the various remedies available to them, or otherwise assist them in preparing those forms necessary for a dissolution proceeding. More specifically, Marilyn Brumbaugh may not make inquiries nor answer questions from her clients as to the particular forms which might be necessary, how best to fill out such forms, where to properly file such forms, and how to present necessary evidence at the court hearings. Our specific holding with regard to the dissolution of marriage also applies to other unauthorized legal assistance such as the preparation of wills or real estate transaction documents. While Marilyn Brumbaugh may legally sell forms in these areas, and type up instruments which have been completed by clients, she must not engage in personal legal assistance in conjunction with her business activities, including the correction of errors and omissions.

One interesting exception to the prohibition of a layman preparing legal documents is found in *Johnson v. Avery.*[15] Here the United States Supreme Court asserted that in the absence of adequate assistance from licensed attorneys, nonlawyer prisoners could assist their fellow inmates in drawing up writs of habeas corpus and related pleadings. A theory can be developed which would imply that laymen could assist people in other areas as well when there is an absence of adequate legal services (perhaps because legal aid is inadequate and they cannot afford to pay a private attorney's fee). However, aside from approving the use of third-year law students, the courts have shown little inclination to accept such an application of *Johnson* outside the prison walls.

It is important that paralegals remain cognizant of those activities which constitute the practice of law. When they are working with licensed attorneys, paralegals can engage in some activities which are ordinarily reserved for lawyers alone. However, if they are not working under an attorney's supervision they have no more right to practice law than the rest of the public does, and they can be equally guilty of unauthorized practice.

Administrative Tribunals

The question of unauthorized practice of law also arises in the context of administrative hearings. Many governmental agencies at both the federal and state level hold quasi-judicial proceedings. These proceedings are labeled quasi-judicial because they employ some aspects of court procedure and serve the basic function of adjudicating disputes. However, they are not considered to be courts of law, and their decisions do not carry the same legal effect as those of courts of law. Examples include workmen's compensation appeals boards, rate hearings before commerce commissions, and pre-termination welfare hearings.

At the federal level the Administrative Procedure Act states that:

A person compelled to appear in person before an agency or representative thereof is entitled to be accompanied, represented, and advised by counsel or, if permitted by the agency, *by other qualified representatives*. . . . [Emphasis added.][16]

Several agencies have made provisions for such lay representation.[17]

In *Sperry v. State of Florida*,[18] the United States Supreme Court upheld the right of the Patent Office to authorize non-lawyers to practice before it. The court ruled that the Patent Office regulations in question were a legitimate exercise of authority that had been properly delegated by Congress. It further ruled that this congressional authorization superseded conflicting provisions of the state of Florida's attorney licensing act. Thus, even though the preparation and prosecution of patent applications for others constituted the practice of law under Florida statutes, these statutes could not be applied to the practices of a federal agency.

While some states have also adopted rules which allow lay persons to represent clients in administrative hearings, some state judiciaries have struck them down on the basis that they violated the unauthorized practice of law statute and usurped the judiciary's inherent power to control the practice of law. The following case is typical of this approach.

West Virginia State Bar v. Earley

Supreme Court of Appeals, West Virginia
109 S.E. 2d. 420 (1959)

The bill of complaint charges that the defendant, an adult resident of Boomer, Fayette County, West Virginia, who has never been admitted or licensed to engage in the practice of law within the State of West Virginia or to represent that he is qualified or authorized to engage in such practice, has been for several years and is now engaged in the practice of law within the State of West Virginia and represents that he is qualified and authorized to engage in such practice, in violation of the provisions of Section 4, Article 2, Chapter 30, Code, 1931. . . . It specifically alleges that the defendant, during the period 1951 to 1955, did advise and represent eleven separate claimants in adversary proceedings before the State Compensation Commissioner of West Virginia in hearings and proceedings before the commissioner or his duly appointed trial examiners and in behalf of two such claimants prepared notices of appeal to the Workmen's Compensation Appeal Board from awards and rulings of the commissioner involving issues of fact and questions of law.

. . .

The answer of the defendant admits that he appeared before the State Compensation Commissioner in behalf of the claimants in the proceedings mentioned in the bill of complaint and filed notices of appeal to the Workmen's Compensation Appeal Board in the two instances mentioned in the bill of complaint but denies that he advised any of the claimants represented by him or other persons with respect to their legal rights and remedies. The answer also denies that the defendant has engaged in the practice of law or represented that he was qualified and authorized to practice law within the State of West Virginia and alleges that by virtue of a rule, which permits persons to appear before the commissioner by attorney or agent, promulgated by the State Compensation Commissioner under the statute which confers upon the commissioner the authority to promulgate reasonable rules and regulations, and because he was permitted by the commissioner to appear in such proceedings, he has the right as an agent to represent claimants in proceedings and hearings before the commissioner; that he received no compensation for services performed by him in behalf of claimants; and that such services were incidental to his employment by a local union, Local 89, United Chemical Workers, CIO, of which the claimants whom he represented were members.

. . .

This court has provided by its rule effective May 1, 1947, that: "The relation of attorney and client exists, and one is deemed to be practicing law, whenever . . . ; (3) one undertakes, with or without compensation, to represent the interest of another before any tribunal — judicial, administrative or executive — otherwise than in the presentation of facts, figures, or factual conclusions, as distinguished from legal conclusions in respect to such facts and figures, except that one may appear as agent before a justice of the peace, and a regular bona fide employee may perform legal services for his regular employer in matters relating solely to the internal affairs of such employer, as distinguished from such services rendered to others."

It is clear beyond question that the defendant, in appearing as agent in behalf of claimants for compensation at hearings before the State Compensation Commissioner, an administrative agency or tribunal, and his duly appointed trial examiners and in preparing notices of appeal from the rulings of the commissioner to the appeal board, as admitted in the agreed statement of facts stipulated by counsel, engaged in the practice of law and that such conduct on his part constituted the unauthorized practice of law which may be prevented by injunction.

By his appearance before the commissioner, although without compensation other than his salary as incidental to his employment, the defendant represented another person before a tribunal of the character mentioned in the rule and his activity was not within any of the exceptions mentioned in the third provision of the rule. The State Compensation Commissioner is not a judicial tribunal but an administrative agency which may properly be considered as an administrative tribunal of the government of this state. . . . The particular tribunal, however, is not important, for it is well settled that it is the character of the act, and not the place where it is performed, which is the decisive factor in determining whether the act constitutes the practice of law. . . . As to the character of the acts of the defendant numerous decisions of appellate courts in different jurisdictions hold that an appearance before a compensation commission, an industrial commission, or a public service commission, or any of its examiners, referees, or individual commissioners, in behalf of another person in a representative capacity in adversary proceedings constitutes the practice of law.

. . .

Section 13, Article 1, Chapter 23, Code, 1931, empowering the State Compensation Commissioner to adopt reasonable and proper rules of procedure and to regulate and provide for the method of taking proof and evidence, does not undertake to authorize him to promulgate a rule by which a layman may appear as an agent in behalf of a claimant or employer in hearings before the commissioner and by permission of the commissioner practice before him. But even if the statute attempted to authorize the commissioner to promulgate a rule of that character such provision of the statute would be void as a legislative encroachment upon the inherent power of the judicial department of the government. The State Compensation Commissioner, as an administrative agency or tribunal, is without power or authority by rule or otherwise to permit an agent who is not a duly licensed attorney to practice before him and any provision of Rule 21 which attempts to permit an agent who is not a duly licensed attorney to practice before the commissioner is void and of no force or effect.

Not all state courts have taken this type of restrictive position, however, and paralegals can participate in some administrative hearings on the state as well as the federal level.[19]

AUTHORITY THROUGH DELEGATION

The cases discussed in the preceding section all involved the activities of a nonlawyer who was working independently. When a nonlawyer works under the supervision of a licensed attorney, however, functions can legitimately be performed which would not otherwise have been allowed.

The American Bar Association's Format Ethics Opinion Number 316 provides a clear statement of the role that nonlawyers can play in the office of a licensed attorney. It states:

> A lawyer can employ lay secretaries, lay investigators, lay detectives, lay researchers, accountants, lay scriveners, nonlawyer draftsmen, or nonlawyer researchers. In fact, he may employ nonlawyers to do any task for him except counsel clients about law matters, engage directly in the practice of law, appear in court, or appear in formal proceedings as part of the judicial process, so long as it is he who takes the work and vouches for it to the client and becomes responsible to the client. In other words, we do not limit the kind of assistance the lawyer can acquire in any way to persons who are admitted to the Bar, so long as the nonlawyers do not do things that lawyers may not do or do things that lawyers only may do.[20]

When the canons of ethics were revised, the new code of professional responsibility included the following authorization to use paralegals:

> A lawyer often delegates tasks to clerks, secretaries, and other lay persons. Such delegation is proper if the lawyer maintains a direct relationship with his client, supervises the delegated work, and has complete professional responsibility for the work product. This delegation enables a lawyer to render legal service more economically and efficiently.[21]

It thus seems apparent that in addition to granting formal recognition to paralegals, the American Bar Association included a broad grant of authority for paralegals to undertake various legal activities — provided of course that they do so under the supervision of a licensed attorney.

It is quite clear that paralegals can interview clients for the purposes of attaining information that is relevant to the handling of their cases. This principle was confirmed in *Procunier v. Martinez* when the United States Supreme Court ruled that a prison could not prohibit law students or legal paraprofessionals from talking with the prisoners on the same conditions as attorneys.[22]

When paralegals are involved in interviewing clients or in handling a client's confidential files, they are covered by the protections of the attorney-client privilege. While they are covered to the same extent that a lawyer is, those protections are not absolute. Rather, the application of the privilege depends upon the situation.

[The privilege applies]

"(1) Where legal advice of any kind is sought (2) from a professional legal adviser in his capacity as such, (3) the communications relating to that purpose, (4) made in confidence (5) by the client, (6) are at his instance permanently protected (7) from disclosure by himself or by the legal adviser, (8) except the protection be waived."[23]

"The privilege applies only if (1) the asserted holder of the privilege is or sought to become a client; (2) the person to whom the communication was made (a) is a member of the bar of a court, or his subordinate and (b) in connection with this communication is acting as a lawyer; (3) the communication relates to a fact of which the attorney was informed (a) by his client (b) without the presence of strangers (c) for the purpose of securing primarily either (i) an opinion on law or (ii) legal services or (iii) assistance in some legal proceeding, and not (d) for the purpose of committing a crime or tort; and (4) the privilege has been (a) claimed and (b) not waived by the client."[24]

Nothing in the policy of the privilege suggests that attorneys, simply by placing accountants, scientists, or investigators on their payrolls and maintaining them in their offices, should be able to invest all communications by clients to such persons with a privilege the law has not seen fit to extend when the latter are operating under their own steam. On the other hand, in contrast to the Tudor times when the privilege was first recognized, . . . the complexities of modern existence prevent attorneys from effectively handling clients' affairs without the help of others; few lawyers could practice without the assistance of secretaries, file clerks, telephone operators, messengers, clerks not yet admitted to the bar, and aides of other sorts. "The assistance of these agents being indispensable to his work and the communications of the client being often necessarily committed to them by the attorney or by the client himself, the privilege must include all the persons who act as the attorney's agents."[25]

While paralegals can thus act on behalf of the attorney and with the full attorney-client privilege in collecting information from the client, their role in giving information to the client is more limited. Paralegals cannot give legal advice to the client. Note, however, that paralegals can do the legal research which serves as the basis for the attorney's advice, and can relay that advice on to the client on behalf of the attorney.*

It is also clear that paralegals can prepare legal documents as long as they are reviewed by a licensed attorney before they are implemented.

While paralegals can sit at the counsel table with the attorneys and confer with them during the course of the trial, they cannot participate directly in the trial process. Some jurisdictions, however, do allow paralegals to present nonsubstantive motions in the absence of their employer. Note that distinction in the following case:

People v. Alexander

Appellate Court of Illinois
53 Ill. App. 2d. 299, 202 N.E. 2d. 841 (1964)

This is an appeal from a judgment order adjudging defendant guilty of contempt of court for the unauthorized practice of law. The Supreme Court transferred this case to our court and it is to be considered here as a direct contempt.

Defendant is a clerk employed by a firm of attorneys and is not licensed as a lawyer, although he is studying to be an attorney. On October 19, 1962, defendant was present in court when the case of *Ryan v. Monson* was called. Thereafter, he prepared an order spreading of record the fact that after a trial of the case *Ryan v. Monson* the jury had disagreed and continuing the case until October 22. The trial judge added to that order "a mistrial declared."

. . .

In his testimony defendant stated that after the case was called on October 19, he and plaintiff's attorney in the *Ryan v. Monson* case stepped up; that the judge inquired whether they knew of the dis-

---

*The attorney must have established a personal relationship with the client and the paralegal must be merely the carrier of the advice rather than the source.

agreement by the jury; that the court requested that an order be prepared spreading the mistrial of record; that both defendant and plaintiff's lawyer sat down at a counsel's table and defendant wrote the order which they then presented to the judge in chambers.

An order of court reciting the verdict of a jury or setting out its failure to agree on a verdict is the responsibility of the court and the court clerk is usually ordered by the court to enter an order showing the result of a jury's deliberations. This is reflected in *Freeport Motor Casualty Co. v. Tharp,* 406 Ill. 295, at 299, 94 N.E. 2d 139, at 141, where the court stated:

"It is equally clear that a *judgment* exists in this State from the time the court acts even though it may not have been formally written on the record by the clerk. *People ex rel. Holbrook v. Petit,* 266 Ill. 628, 107 N.E. 830; *People ex rel Waite v. Bristow,* 391 Ill. 101, 62 N.E. 2d 545. And there is a well-recognized distinction between *rendering* a judgment and entering a judgment. The former is the judicial act of the court in pronouncing its ruling or finding in the controversy; the latter is the ministerial act of the clerk in preserving the record of that decision. The terms are used antithetically, each in its distinctive correct legal sense. *Blatchford v. Newberry,* 100 Ill. 484."

. . .

The preparation of an order, in the instant case, with the collaboration of opposing counsel was a ministerial act for the benefit of the court and a mere recordation of what had transpired. We cannot hold that this conduct of defendant constituted the unauthorized practice of law.

We agree with the trial judge that clerks should not be permitted to make motions or participate in other proceedings which can be considered as "managing" the litigation. However, if apprising the court of an employer's engagement or inability to be present constitutes the making of a motion, we must hold that clerks may make such motions for continuances without being guilty of the unauthorized practice of law. Certainly with the large volume of cases appearing on the trial calls these days, it is imperative that this practice be followed.

. . .

We cannot add to the heavy burden of lawyers who in addition to responding to trial calls must answer pre-trial calls and motion calls — all held in the morning — by insisting that a lawyer must personally appear to present to a court a motion for a continuance on grounds of engagement or inability to appear because of illness or other unexpected circumstances. To reduce the backlog, trial lawyers should be kept busy actually trying lawsuits and not answering court calls.

In all aspects of a paralegal's work the employing attorney will ultimately be held responsible for the work product. Supervision encompasses both direction and inspection. The lawyer has a responsibility to carefully describe the manner in which he wants the paralegal to approach the task; to be available for feedback; and to review the final product. The amount of time spent and the depth of the review will naturally depend on the difficulty of the task and the paralegal's experience in completing similar assignments. If the attorney fails to catch a paralegal's error, it will in most cases have the same legal effect as if the attorney himself had made the error.[26]

Besides the possibility of disciplinary action for failing to properly supervise a paralegal's work, the attorney could be sued in a tort action for negligence. The employing attorney could be found negligent for the failure to supervise as well as under the doctrine of *respondeat superior.**

There is some question as to what standard of care a court would impose in such a case. If the suit were based on improper supervision, the standard would likely be that of comparable work done by other attorneys who possess ordinary legal knowledge and skills. If the suit were based on the *respondeat superior* doctrine alone, it might be argued that the standard of care would be that of comparable work done by other paralegals who possess a minimum degree of skill and knowledge.[27] In either case, though, the attorney and the paralegal would appear to be covered by the principle that a professional is not liable for an error in judgment.[28]

ETHICAL RESPONSIBILITIES

Codes of Paralegal Responsibility

Since paralegals hold positions of trust and may by their actions have significant consequences on the lives of their firms' clients, it is essential that they adhere to a strict code of professional

---

*A Latin term, it means "Let the master answer." It is a legal principle that the employer is held responsible for the actions of an employee which are done in the course of employment.

ethics. The National Association of Legal Assistants has developed the following:

Canon 1: A legal assistant shall not perform any of the duties that lawyers only may perform nor do things that lawyers themselves may not do.

Canon 2: A legal assistant may perform any task delegated and supervised by a lawyer so long as the lawyer is responsible to the client, maintains a direct relationship with the client, and assumes full professional responsibility for the work product.

Canon 3: A legal assistant shall not engage in the practice of law by giving legal advice, appearing in court, setting fees, or accepting cases.

Canon 4: A legal assistant shall not act in matters involving professional legal judgment as the services of a lawyer are essential in the public interest whenever the exercise of such judgment is required.

Canon 5: A legal assistant must act prudently in determining the extent to which a client may be assisted without the presence of a lawyer.

Canon 6: A legal assistant shall not engage in the unauthorized practice of law and shall assist in preventing the unauthorized practice of law.

Canon 7: A legal assistant must protect the confidences of a client, and it shall be unethical for a legal assistant to violate any statute now in effect or hereafter to be enacted controlling privileged communications.

Canon 8: It is the obligation of the legal assistant to avoid conduct which would cause the lawyer to be unethical or even appear to be unethical, and loyalty to the employer is incumbent upon the legal assistant.

Canon 9: A legal assistant shall work continually to maintain integrity and a high degree of competency throughout the legal profession.

Canon 10: A legal assistant shall strive for perfection through education in order to better assist the legal profession in fulfilling its duty of making legal services available to clients and the public.

Canon 11: A legal assistant shall do all other things incidental, necessary, or expedient for the attainment of the ethics and responsibilities imposed by statute or rule of court.

Canon 12: A legal assistant is governed by the American Bar Association Code of Professional Responsibility.[29]

Note that Canon 12 makes reference to the American Bar Association's Code of Professional Responsibility. Given the fact that the employing attorney will ultimately be held accountable for the paralegal's acts, it is imperative that the paralegal be familiar with this document as well.

The ABA's Code of Professional Responsibility consists of nine canons. These canons are broad statements of general norms, e.g., "A lawyer should assist in maintaining the integrity and competence of the legal profession."[30] Each of the nine canons is supplemented by various "Ethical Considerations" and "Disciplinary Rules." The Ethical Considerations (EC) are aspirational statements concerning the objectives toward which members of the profession are supposed to strive, e.g., "A lawyer should maintain high standards of professional conduct and should encourage fellow lawyers to do likewise."[31] Disciplinary Rules (DR), on the other hand, are mandatory in character. They establish a minimum level of behavior below which no lawyer can fall without being subject to a disciplinary action, e.g., "A lawyer shall not form a partnership with a nonlawyer if any of the activities of the partnership consist of the practice of law."[32]

The nine canons of the American Bar Association Code of Professional Responsibility are listed below, verbatim, along with the author's summary of the nature of their coverage.

Canon 1: A lawyer should assist in maintaining the integrity and competence of the legal profession.

This canon and its accompanying ethical considerations and disciplinary rules state in essence that lawyers should make sure that high requirements are established for entrance into the profession; that those who are in it should follow the rules; and that they should report colleagues who do not.

Canon 2: A lawyer should assist the legal profession in fulfilling its duty to make legal counsel available.

Through its ethical considerations and disciplinary rules, this canon is primarily concerned with the topics of solicitation and advertising, specialization, and the amount and division of fees.

Canon 3:   A lawyer should assist in preventing the unauthorized practice of law.

The material associated with this canon deals with a lawyer's relationships with lay personnel. In addition to discussing delegation to paralegals (EC 306), it also discusses relationships to banks, collection agencies, insurance companies, and so forth.

Canon 4:   A lawyer should preserve the confidences and secrets of a client.

This section discusses the circumstances under which the confidences of a client can be revealed. EC 4-2 states in part that "It is a matter of common knowledge that the normal operation of a law office exposes confidential professional information to non-lawyer employees of the office, particularly secretaries and those having access to the files; and this obligates a lawyer to exercise care in selecting and training his employees so that the sanctity of all confidences and secrets of his clients may be preserved."

Canon 5:   A lawyer should exercise independent professional judgment on behalf of a client.

This material deals with the proper handling of potential conflicts of interest.

Canon 6:   A lawyer should represent a client completely.

Once the attorney takes on a client, he should devote the necessary time and energy to do the job correctly.

Canon 7:   A lawyer should represent a client zealously within the bounds of the law.

This section discusses topics such as the proper and improper ways of communicating with adverse parties, witnesses, judges, and juries. It also covers aspects of trial conduct.

Canon 8:   A lawyer should assist in improving the legal system.

Topics discussed in this section include seeking and holding political office and criticism of judges and other public officials.

Canon 9:   A lawyer should avoid even the appearance of professional impropriety.

These EC's and DR's are primarily concerned with conditions of employment and the use of clients' funds.

Paralegals should also be aware of the existence of formal and informal opinions issued by the ABA's Committee on Ethics and Professional Responsibility. An opinion is designated by the committee as formal if it is believed to be of broad general interest. It is designated as informal when it is of comparatively narrow scope, involving a problem thought to arise less frequently. Formal Opinions numbered 323 and above and Informal Opinions numbered 1120 and above have been issued since the revision of the old canons of ethics into the new code of professional responsibility.*

Opinions of special interest to paralegals include F85, F316, I315, I329, I344, I523, I909, I998, I1193, and I1274, concerning the duties and functions of lay personnel; I123, I124, I619, I660, I845, I909, I1000, I1185, I1278, and I1367, concerning the listing of lay personnel on business cards, stationery, and the like; and I325, I326, and I792, concerning fees and fringe benefits.

State and local bar associations tend to use these ABA materials as models and adopt similar versions of the code of professional responsibility. They also issue opinions concerning the proper standard of behavior in specific situations.† The reader is urged to become familiar with these local materials as well.

Enforcement of Ethical Responsibilities

An attorney found to have seriously breached the ethical requirements of the profession can be reprimanded, suspended, or even disbarred.‡ While the specific mechanisms for doing this

---

*The practice of issuing advisory opinions in unauthorized practice of law cases has recently come under attack as being an anti-competitive device which violates the Sherman Antitrust Act. See *Surety Title Insurance Agency, Inc. v. Virginia State Bar*, 431 F. Supp. 298 (1977).

†Some state bar associations have recently adopted specific guidelines covering the use of paralegals.

‡A reprimand is a public censure or simply an announcement that the attorney's conduct has been found to be in violation of the code of ethics. A suspension means that the attorney is prohibited from practicing law during some fixed time period, but can expect to return to practice later. A disbarment implies a permanent removal of one's license to practice law.

vary from one state to another, it is ultimately up to the state's judiciary to impose a suspension or a disbarment. In so doing, the courts will rely primarily upon the standards of conduct that are spelled out in the state bar association's ethics code (which, of course, is generally modeled after the ABA).

However, since there is no licensing procedure for paralegals, there is no formal enforcement mechanism for disciplining those who violate their ethical responsibilities. A paralegal who participates in the unauthorized practice of law can be prosecuted under that state's statute on unauthorized practice of law. Beyond that, it is left to the paralegal's employer to enforce the required standards of ethical conduct. Remember that the supervising attorney is held responsible for the actions of one's lay employees.

SUMMARY

The practice of law has been limited to individuals who have been admitted to the bar (i.e., licensed to practice) in their respective states. This monopoly has been justified as a legitimate means of protecting the public from those who do not have either the necessary legal knowledge or the ethical responsibilities which admission to the bar is supposed to guarantee. While persons have a constitutional right to act as their own attorneys, there is no right to be represented by someone else who is not an attorney.

The practice of law is not limited to those activities which take place in a courtroom. It also extends to the giving of legal advice and the preparation of legal documents. It is often difficult, however, to identify when the legitimate business activities of real estate brokers, tax accountants, and others cross over into the forbidden practice of law.

Lay appearances before administrative tribunals are sometimes allowed and at other times prohibited. It depends on whether the legislative branch and the administrative agency have authorized such practices, and whether the courts have approved. State courts cannot restrict the rights of a federal agency to allow lay representation in its own tribunals even if the hearings take place in that state.

When paralegals work under the proper supervision of an attorney, they can legitimately perform functions which would otherwise have been considered unauthorized practice. While they cannot give legal advice or present substantive matters in court, they can communicate with clients under the protection of the attorney–client privilege, and they can draft legal documents.

As professionals, paralegals have ethical responsibilities to their profession, their employers, and their clients. The paralegal has a responsibility to maintain the confidentiality of the attorney–client relationship. The paralegal must give the best effort one is capable of giving to the client's case, but must also avoid participating in fraud or trickery. The paralegal must not take any action which would be unethical for an attorney to take. The paralegal must bear in mind that the supervising attorney can ultimately be held responsible for the paralegal's actions.

KEY TERMS

admitted to the bar	informal opinion
Code of Professional Responsibility	lay person
	license
disbarment	practice of law
Disciplinary Rule	professional reprimand
Ethical Consideration	*respondeat superior*
fiduciary	suspension
formal opinion	

REVIEW QUESTIONS

1. What is the judiciary's justification for granting a monopoly to lawyers?

2. Under what circumstances does a person have a legal right to be represented by a nonlawyer?

3. When does the selling of insurance cross over into the practice of law?

4. Under what conditions is it legitimate for a nonlawyer to market do-it-yourself divorce kits?

5. What activities are paralegals prohibited from undertaking even when they are operating under the supervision of a licensed attorney?

6. What are the means of enforcing a paralegal's ethical responsibilities?

DISCUSSION QUESTIONS

1. In *Faretta v. California* the court emphasizes that the government does not have a right to protect the defendant from his own incompetence as an attorney. Do you agree? Should the court have the power to protect persons from knowingly selecting a nonlawyer to represent them?

2. If real estate brokers as part of the licensing requirement are both tested for their knowledge in the area and held accountable for a code of ethics, is the public's interest adequately protected to the point where they should be able to compete with lawyers in that limited area? Should the state require a person to have a complete knowledge of all areas of the law (as they do lawyers) before they can advise people about the law in a single specialized area (as might a tax accountant)?

3. With reference to *Oregon State Bar v. John H. Miller & Co.* and *Florida Bar v. Brumbaugh*, where do you think the lines should be drawn?

4. What are the advantages and disadvantages to the public of allowing lay representation at administrative hearings?

PROJECTS

1. Compare and contrast the ABA Code of Professional Responsibility with the ethics code adopted by the bar association in your state. Also contrast official opinions related to the use of paralegals.

2. Investigate and report on the procedures that are used for disciplining attorneys in your state.

REFERENCES

1. *See* discussion in *Turner v. American Bar Association*, 407 F. Supp. 451, 474 (1975).
2. *Ex parte Garland*, 4 Wall. 333 (1867); *Schware v. Board of Examiners*, 353 U.S. 232 (1957); *Konigsberg v. State Bar*, 353 U.S. 252 (1956); and numerous state cases including *Chicago Bar Association v. United Taxpayers of America*, 312 Ill. App. 243, 38 N.E. 2d 349; *People v. Alfani*, 227 N.Y. 334, 125 N.E. 671; and *West Virginia State Bar v. Earley*, 109 S.E. 2d 420.
3. *West Virginia State Bar v. Earley*, 109 S.E. 2d 420, 435 (1959).
4. *State ex rel Johnson v. Childe*, 295 N.W. 381, 382 (Neb. 1941).
5. *See* Lloyd Derby, "The Unauthorized Practice of Law by Laymen and Lay Associates," *California Law Review* 54 (1966): 1,331; 1,363.
6. *Faretta v. California*, 421 U.S. 806 (1975).
7. *See*, for example, *U.S. v. Stockheimer*, 385 F. Supp. 979 (W.D. Wisc., 1974). Judge Doyle held that in the absence of any constitutional or federal statutory provision compelling him to forbid or not forbid the defendant's use of a lay assistant, he would use his discretion to allow it.
8. *Turner v. American Bar Association*, 407 F. Supp. 451 (N.D. Texas, 1975), affirmed 539 F.2d 715 and 542 F.2d 56.
9. *Ibid.*, 481.
10. *In re Opinion of the Justices*, 194 N.E. 313, 317 (1935).
11. *Ibid.*, 317 and 318.
12. *Oregon State Bar v. John H. Miller & Co.*, 385 P.2d 181, 182 (Ore., 1963).
13. *Ibid.*, 183.
14. *See*, for example, *New York County Lawyers Assn. v. Dacey*, 21 N.Y.2d 694, 287 N.Y.S.2d 422, 234 N.E.2d 459 (1967); *Oregon State Bar v. Gilchrist*, 272 Or. 552, 538 P.2d 913 (1975); *State v. Winder*, 348 N.Y.S.2d 270 (1973); *Colorado Bar Association v. Miles*, 557 P.2d 1202 (Colo. 1976); and *In re Thompson*, 574 S.W.2d 365 (Mo.1978). But see also Florida Bar v. Brumbaugh, 355 So.2d 1186 (Fla. 1978); and *Palmer v. Unauthorized Practice Committee of the State Bar of Texas*, 438 S.W.2d 374 (Tex. Civ. App. 1969).
15. *Johnson v. Avery*, 393 U.S. 483 (1969).
16. 5 USCA §555(b) (1967).
17. These agencies include the Patent Office, the Social Security Administration, and the Department of Immigration and Naturalization.
18. *Sperry v. State of Florida*, 373 U.S. 379 (1963).
19. *Toplis & Harding v. Murphy*, 384 Ill. 463, 52 N.E.2d 505 (1943), for example, stresses that in Illinois unemployment compensation hearings are not considered "judicial proceedings" and that they involve questions of fact rather than questions of law.
20. ABA Formal Opinion No. 316 (January 1967).
21. ABA "Code of Professional Responsibility," EC 3-6 (1969).
22. 416 U.S. 396, 94 S. Ct. 1800, 40 L.Ed.2d 224 (1974).
23. John Henry Wigmore, *Evidence* (Boston: Little, Brown & Company, McNaughton rev. 1961), Vol. 8, p. 554.
24. *U.S. v. United Shoe Machinery Corporation*, 89 F. Supp. 357, 358–59 (D. Mass., 1950).
25. *U.S. v. Kovel*, 296 F.2d 918, 921 (1961).
26. *State v. Barrett*, 207 Kan. 178, 483 P.2d 1111 (1971); and *Vaughn v. California*, 100 Cal. Rptr. 713, 494 P.2d 1257 (1972).
27. *See* B. Davis, "On the Question of Negligence: The Paraprofessional," *Toledo Law Review* 4 (1973): 553, 556. It has been held that laymen practicing be-

fore Workmen's Compensation Board are not held to the same degree of care as an attorney. *Bland v. Reed*, 261 Cal. App. 2d 445, 67 Cal. Rptr. 859 (1968).

28. *Ibid.*, 557.

29. National Association of Legal Assistants, *Code of Ethics and Professional Responsibility* (Tulsa, Okla.: NALA, 1975).

30. Canon 1.

31. EC 1–5.

32. DR 3–103.

PART II

FINDING THE FACTS

The resolution of a legal conflict involves the application of general principles of law to a specific set of facts. Before attorneys can advise a course of action for the client to take, they need to know the factual details of the client's situation. When attorneys file a lawsuit, they need to specify a great deal about the facts in the initial complaint. Good trial attorneys will never proceed to trial without a firm expectation of what the various witnesses are likely to say. Getting the facts straight is thus central to the practice of law. It is an area in which paralegals can make major contributions.

Chapter 4 will discuss the ways in which these facts are gathered. It begins with the initial client interview in the law office and covers such topics as the gathering of testimony from witnesses, the taking of photographs, and the collection of documentary and physical evidence.

Since the ultimate line of inquiry must be not only "What happened?" but "What can I use in court?" the chapter will also provide a brief overview of some of the most important aspects of the rules of evidence.

CHAPTER 4

Interviewing and Investigation

For the attorney, some important knowledge of the factual details of a client's situation can be obtained from documentary evidence (such as police reports, medical reports, contracts, and photographs) and personal observation (e.g., visiting the scene of an accident or examining the condition of an apartment). However, knowledge of many of the most important facts is usually gained by interviewing clients and witnesses. It is therefore essential that attorneys and their paralegals develop considerable skills in using the interviewing process.*

THE CLIENT INTERVIEW

Depending on the procedures established in the office in which they work, paralegals may be involved in several types of inter-

*One common criticism of law schools is that their curriculums usually contain little or nothing in the way of course work in this vital area. Hopefully, paralegal programs will not be guilty of similar omissions.

view situations. These situations can include the initial client interview, follow-up interviews with the client (either in the office or in the field), and field interviews with both friendly and hostile witnesses.

In many legal aid and some group legal services programs, the client will be interviewed by a paralegal prior to meeting with an attorney. In most legal aid programs the first order of business is the determination of whether the client meets the program's financial eligibility standards. This amounts to obtaining information about the client's income, assets, and debts, as well as the number of dependents. (In soliciting such personal financial information it is very important that the interviewer explain why such information is necessary.) This information may then need to be verified in some fashion and examined in light of the agency's eligibility standards.

Once it has been determined that the client is financially eligible for the program's services, paralegals then proceed to gather information about the nature of the client's problems. Here the paralegal must gather enough factual information to separate the legal problems from the nonlegal ones, and to be able to provide the agency's attorneys with the type of information they need to begin solving the legal problems. The paralegal should also be able to help these clients obtain assistance from appropriate social service agencies for their nonlegal concerns.

While in some law offices the attorneys prefer to have paralegals collect a considerable amount of information about their clients' problems before they meet with them personally, in others the attorneys prefer to handle the initial interview on their own and then utilize paralegals for obtaining follow-up information. In most private law firms the attorneys conduct the initial interviews themselves. This is usually related to their desire to impress the client, to reserve the right to make an immediate decision as to whether to accept the case, and to negotiate the fee arrangement.* Once the attorney-client relationship has been established the attorney may then choose to either bring the paralegal into the interview or completely turn the client over to the paralegal for the gathering of further information about the client's case.

---

*In legal aid, group legal services, and legal clinics the types of cases accepted are usually spelled out by established policies and the fees are either nonexistent, prepaid, or standardized.

No matter how productive the initial interview, it is often necessary to go back to the client at a later date to gather additional facts. This can be done by having the client come back into the office, by going to the client's home or office, or perhaps by simply using the telephone. The paralegal may have to interview other persons who have knowledge of the facts of the dispute and these interviews may also take place in a variety of settings.

Principles of Good Communication

The authors of a recent book on communication problems reported having seen the following sign in a lawyer's office:

> I know you believe you understand what you think I said, but I am not sure you realize that what you heard is not what I meant.[1]

It would probably be worthwhile if every law office prominently displayed such a sign because it points out a common communication problem — the listener is not getting the message the speaker has intended to convey.

The communications process begins with the speaker's desire to send a message to another party. Before a message can be sent, however, he or she must decide what combination of words, gestures, and facial expressions should be used. Then the speaker must actually transmit the message using these symbols. The listener, on the other hand, must first be alert enough to accurately perceive which symbols the speaker is using. Then the listener must in turn decide what meaning should be attached to these symbols. It is quite possible for two different people to receive different messages from the same set of words and gestures. We are constantly faced with the possibility that our listeners do not comprehend the meaning we intend to convey and that in turn we do not accurately perceive the messages they send to us.

The development of good listening skills is essential to the understanding of what the person being interviewed is really saying. As Alfred Benjamin has written in an excellent book on interviewing skills:

> Listening requires, first of all, that we not be preoccupied, for if we are we cannot fully attend. Secondly, listening involves hearing the way

things are being said, the tone used, the expressions and gestures employed. In addition, listening includes the effort to hear what is not being said, what is only hinted at, what is perhaps being held back, what lies beneath or beyond the surface. We hear with our ears, but we listen with our eyes and mind and heart and skin and guts as well.[2]

Good listening involves not only a recognition of what the interviewee perceives to be the facts, but how he or she feels about those facts as well. As Thomas Shaffer stresses in his discussion on legal interviewing, "Feelings are facts." Even though statements which begin with "I think" or "I feel" are not ordinarily admissible in a court of law, it is important that the attorney knows a person thinks or feels that way.[3]

The interviewer learns about these feelings not only from statements in which the interviewee says that he feels angry or that she resents the action of someone else but from a variety of gestures and expressions. As Makay and Gaw explain:

While we are engaged in conversations with another, we are being continuously bombarded with messages from the other's face or hands or posture, the sound of his or her voice, the distance that separates us, the amount of time we spend together and spend looking at each other, and so on. We can't escape from nonverbal communication.[4]

These nonverbal messages can be either conscious or unconscious and either intentional or unintentional. A smile is both intentional and conscious. A quivering voice is usually conscious yet unintentional.[5]

The interviewer must work at being a good listener. It is especially important that one avoid the trap of allowing previous experiences to color perception of the case at hand. After a paralegal has interviewed dozens of clients with landlord-tenant disputes there is a danger that the interviewer will begin to think in terms of stereotyped categories. One can then begin to assume that simply because something happened one way in a similar case, it happened the same way in the case at hand. The danger is that having once categorized the current case, the interviewer will fail to hear what the interviewee is really saying. The danger is even greater when the interviewer has undergone a similar experience.

Communication is a two-way street and the interviewer also

has an obligation to make sure the person being interviewed really understands what the interviewer is saying. While the interviewer cannot very well give the client a lesson on good listening, one should be very conscious of the words, expressions, and gestures used as well as the reactions they evoke. To as great a degree as possible, the interviewer's vocabulary should be modified to fit the interviewee's educational and cultural background.* Great efforts should be made to keep legal jargon out of the conversation. Above all, the interviewer needs to be alert for signals that the other person does not really understand what is being said. In those cases, the interviewer must go back and try to restate the message in different terms.

Putting the Subject at Ease

Communication between the interviewer and the interviewee can also be improved by having the interview take place in a comfortable and quiet location in which there will be privacy and a lack of interruptions. The provision of such facilities helps to establish good rapport. The avoidance of interruptions from phone calls and secretaries shows respect for the interviewee and helps to build trust.

Communication can be facilitated or impeded by a circumstance as simple as where the parties are seated during the interview. The traditional arrangement is to have either the lawyer or the paralegal seated behind a large imposing desk that reinforces the authority image. The client is then seated across the desk — usually in a chair that is lower than that of the interviewer. Such a seating arrangement intimidates clients and does not serve to put them at ease.

Figure 4.1 shows the basic seating arrangements available in most offices. Arrangements A, B, and C all utilize a desk and side chairs while arrangement D gets away from the desk and involves chairs placed around an end table or lamp table of some sort. The behavioral science literature suggests quite strongly that D is the arrangement most conducive to good communica-

---

*This does not mean that a middle-aged, middle-class white should attempt to talk like a young ghetto black. It does mean that the interviewer should seek to use key words the interviewee will understand.

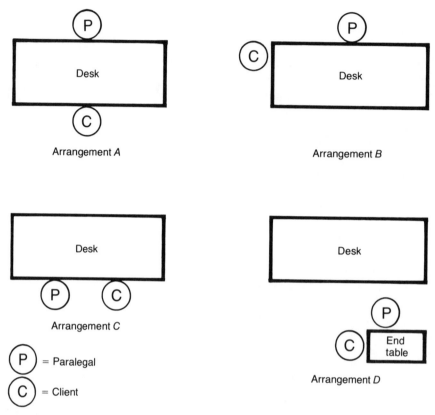

FIGURE 4.1
Alternative Seating Arrangements for Interviews

tion. It places the interviewer and the interviewee on an equal level at a distance that facilitates personal communication.* It also has the advantage of providing comfortable eye contact. It allows the two parties either to look directly at each other or to easily glance away at a 90° angle. About the only disadvantage is that it is more difficult for the interviewer to take notes. In effect, the interviewer now has to balance a legal pad on a knee.

*While the parties should be close, they should not be so close as to invade their private sphere. The social sphere, which is considered the optimal space for this type of communication, is found to be approximately two to four feet from the other person.

In order to avoid this disadvantage (and in smaller offices where such end table arrangements may not be available), it would be wise for the paralegal to utilize arrangement B. This positioning of client and paralegal offers the same advantages of distance and eye contact. It also provides the interviewer with a good place to take notes.

While the taking of notes can be distractive, it is really essential in most legal interviewing situations. The paralegal has to get the facts correctly and cannot afford to rely on memory until the interview can be written up. Indeed, as Benjamin suggests:

> In our culture, when note taking is discriminately handled, it is not resented. On the contrary, its absence may be looked upon as negligence or lack of interest.[6]

The ability to see the types of notes which are being taken (which is possible from positions B and D) is thought to strengthen the trusting aspect of the relationship.

In addition to the factors discussed above, the general conduct of the interviewer has a lot to do with putting the client at ease. Allen Ivey identifies three aspects of what he calls "attending behavior."[7]

To begin with, the interviewer needs to be *comfortable and relaxed*. Ivey advises interviewers to:

> Relax physically; feel the presence of the chair as you are sitting on it. Let your posture be comfortable and your movements natural; for example, if you usually move and gesture a good deal, feel free to do so at this time.[8]

The interviewer's sense of relaxation can go a long way toward placing the interviewee at ease.

Secondly, Ivey stresses the importance of initiating and maintaining *eye contact*. He warns, however, that such eye contact can be overdone.

> A varied use of eye contact is most effective, as staring fixedly or with undue intensity usually makes the client uneasy. If you are going to listen to someone, look at them.[9]

The final element in attending behavior is *verbal following*:

. . . the interviewer's use of comments which follow directly from what the interviewee is saying. By directing one's comments and questions to the topics provided by the client, one not only helps him develop an area of discussion, but reinforces the client's free expression, resulting in more spontaneity and animation in the client's talking.[10]

Starting the Interview

The handling of the initial contact between client and paralegal can have a lot to do with establishing a meaningful rapport. If the attorney either begins the interview while the paralegal is present or calls in the paralegal at some point during the course of the client's visit, it is the attorney's responsibility to introduce and explain the paralegal's presence. On the other hand, if the paralegal is meeting the interviewee without a previous introduction, the paralegal should enter the reception room, greet with an introduction, and personally accompany the client to the office. The traditional handshake is still an effective gesture to show interest in and respect for the person to whom one is being introduced. Women paralegals may find it a particularly effective way of establishing a professional relationship with male clients or witnesses.

As part of the introduction process, the paralegal should give a brief explanation of this role. The person being interviewed has a right to know who the interviewer is and that the interviewer is not a lawyer. On the other hand, there is no need to launch into a five minute description of everything a paralegal can or cannot do. The paralegal's role should be described in relatively simple positive terms. For example: "I am a paralegal — not an attorney. My job involves gathering the basic facts for (attorney's name). I will be working with him/her on your case." If the paralegal handles administrative hearings, one can explain the type of representation given and the amount of experience.

If the interview situation involves a client's initial visit to the law office, the paralegal should allow the client to introduce the problem in the manner and at the pace most comfortable for the client. The interviewer should be willing to engage in some small talk about the weather or about the parking situation until the client feels relaxed enough to move on to the nature of the problem. If after some awkward periods of silence, the client seems to have trouble discussing the specific situation, the paralegal can initiate the conversation with an inquiry such as: "Well, Mr./ Mrs. . . . what is it that brings you in to see us?"

It is very important that the paralegal have the clients describe the nature of the problem on their own initiative rather than in response to specific questions from the interviewer. As Benjamin warns:

> If we begin the helping interview by asking questions and getting answers, asking more questions and getting more answers, we are setting up a pattern from which neither we nor surely the interviewee will be able to extricate himself. By offering him no alternative we shall be teaching him that in this situation it is up to us to ask the questions and up to him to answer them. What is worse, having already become accustomed to this pattern from previous experience, he may readily adapt himself to it. Here again, he will perceive himself as an object, an object who answers when asked and otherwise keeps his mouth closed — and undoubtedly his mind and heart as well.[11]

The net result is that communication will be reduced and valuable information may not be volunteered. A further danger is that the interviewer will have to concentrate so much on framing the next question that he will fail to listen to what his client is really saying.

Keeping the Interview Going

While the interviewer needs to avoid a straight question-and-answer format, carefully selected questions are an important part of most interview situations. When properly used, questions can clarify areas of ambiguity and assist the interviewee in telling the story. The secret to successful interviewing lies in asking the questions in the proper form and at the proper time.

To begin, one needs to be familiar with the forms a question can take. Consider, for instance, the difference between open and closed questions. Open questions such as "How did the accident take place?" provide some focus to the interview without greatly limiting the freedom of the respondent. On the other hand, closed questions are by their nature very specific and usually demand very short answers: "What color was the car that hit you?" "How far in advance did you see it coming?" "Was the sun shining in your face at the time?" Note that if the interviewee, in responding to the general open question, fails to discuss the point at which the other car was first seen, the interviewer can always follow it up with a more specific closed question. However, if the interviewer, in answering a closed question, fails to ask about the condition of the roadway, it is unlikely to be volunteered by the interviewee.

Earlier in this chapter, we emphasized that "feelings are facts." The emotional state of the client in relating the incident, as well as the emotional state of the various parties at the time of the incident, are important. Responses to open questions are much more likely to reveal these emotional factors. Compare the information given by the client in response to the different forms of questions from the paralegal.

INTERVIEW NO. 1

Paralegal: Did you receive a written eviction notice?

Client: Yes.

INTERVIEW NO. 2

Paralegal: How did you find out that you were going to be evicted?

Client: The landlord came up to me around 7 o'clock in the evening while I was sitting on the front porch with some other residents. He yelled something about my being a no good troublemaker because I was always complaining to the city inspections department. Then he stuck this eviction notice in my hand, stomped off.

Thus it can be seen that one usually obtains better information from open questions. The closed variety should be reserved for pulling together potentially important details the interviewee may have overlooked.

Once the client has begun to expound on one of these open questions, the interviewer should attempt to keep the conversation going through the use of minimal encourages to talk, paraphrasing, and reflection of feelings. The minimal encourages to talk, as Ivey labels it, involves one or two words or very short phrases that are designed simply to communicate that the interviewer is hearing what is being said, and that the interviewee should continue with his or her narrative. These minimal encourages include:

"Then?" "And?" "So?"
Repetition of a key word or two.
"Could you tell me more?"
"How do you feel about that?"
"Could you give me an example?"
"What does that mean to you?"
"Um-hm." [12]

Minimal encourages also include head nods and various other gestures. [13]

Paraphrasing is simply the process of repeating, in a shortened form, what the interviewee has just finished saying. It serves three basic functions:

1. To convey to the client that you are with him, that you are trying to understand what he is saying;
2. To crystallize a client's comments by repeating what he has said in a more concise manner; and
3. To check the interviewer's own perceptions to make sure he really does understand what the client is describing. [14]

For example, if a client relates a rather involved conversation with a bill collector, the interviewer might respond: "So the bill collector threatened to get you fired if you didn't pay by Tuesday. Is that right?"

Whereas the paraphrasing reflects the interviewee's perception of the facts, reflection of feeling centers on his or her emotions. It demonstrates that the interviewer has been listening closely and understands the feelings which have been expressed. [15] In responding to these feelings, the goal is to communicate an understanding of the way the client feels — a sense of empathy. It is not necessary to show acceptance for the person's feelings — just that those feelings are respected. As Benjamin puts it:

. . . acceptance means treating the interviewee as an equal and regarding his thoughts and feelings with sincere respect. It does not mean agreeing; it does not mean thinking or feeling the way he does; it does not mean valuing what he values. It is, rather, the attitude that the interviewee has as much right to his ideas, feelings, and values as I have to mine and that I want to do my utmost to understand his life space in terms of his ideas, feelings, and values rather than in terms of my own.[16]

After listening to a client describe an incident in which her husband made derogatory remarks about her at a party, the interviewer might comment: "You must have felt pretty angry about being embarrassed in front of your friends."

When using either the paraphrasing or the reflection of feeling technique, the interviewer should deliver the feedback in a tentative tone of voice. This offers the interviewee a chance to respond by either (1) affirming that the stated understanding is correct, (2) correcting what was a false understanding on the interviewer's part, (3) elaborating further on the topic, or (4) some combination of the first three. These techniques will show the interviewee that the interviewer is listening and will force clarification of the presentation.

Nonverbal behavior also plays an important role in the feedback process. Earlier in this chapter we discussed the importance of the interviewer being sensitive to various forms of nonverbal communication. Remember that just as the client sends nonverbal cues to the interviewer, so too the interviewer sends nonverbal cues to the client. The paralegal must therefore remain conscious of nonverbal behavior and the effect it is having on the client.

A good interviewer will also try to avoid using "why" questions because they have come to connote disapproval and displeasure.[17] They put the interviewee on the defensive and erode the relationship of trust the interviewer is supposed to be building. While there are occasions when these why questions can legitimately be used (i.e., "Why did you move out of your apartment?"), they should be especially avoided where matters of values and judgment are involved.[18]

Bear in mind that the paralegal has an obligation to seek out all relevant information — including that which may be damaging to the client's case. It is necessary to explain to the client that the attorney needs to know about any damaging evidence to be prepared to deal with it. The client needs to be reminded that there may be cross-examination during the trial and the opposing side is likely to bring up any damaging evidence at that time. The client can also be told that what may appear to be damaging may in fact turn out to be beneficial. Whenever possible the paralegal should try to avoid situations in which the client is found to be lying to either the lawyer or the paralegal. Before you ask a client if he or she was speeding at the time of the accident, the client should be gently forewarned that the police report will probably show a speed that has been estimated on the basis of skid marks.[19]

Ending the Interview

As mentioned previously, the interviewer should let the client begin the interview on his or her own terms. General open questions are used along with minimal encourages, paraphrasing, and reflections of feeling. Closed questions are used for following up and clarifying details in the later stages of the interview. Near the end the paralegal should summarize his or her understanding of the client's problem in order to ensure accuracy and to give the client a chance to add any additional information which may have been overlooked.

Once these steps have been completed, the paralegal should collect, or make arrangements to collect, copies of all relevant legal documents. These documents should be photocopied and returned to the client as soon as possible. If the client is going to have to sign any authorization forms, it is usually wise to get those taken care of at the same time.

The client should also be told what to expect next from the office — whether to expect to see the attorney soon and just what the nature of the next contact with the attorney's office might be. In the case of legal aid work it may be appropriate to refer the client to various social service agencies that can assist in some other ways.

It is also important at this stage that paralegals remember the ethical prohibitions that apply to their role. Clients will often attempt to elicit advice and opinions about their cases from the paralegal. The paralegal needs to remember that paralegals cannot give legal advice and that the clients should not be given false expectations about the outcomes of their cases. Likewise, the paralegal must remember to respect the clients' rights to confidentiality.

As soon as possible after the interview the paralegal should review and polish the notes on the case while the matter is still fresh. These notes, along with the copies that were made of relevant documents, should then be placed in the appropriate office file.

THE INVESTIGATION

After having completed the initial client interview, the attorney and the paralegal will have a fair idea of the general nature of the case. The client, however, seldom knows all of the relevant facts: "Why wasn't the traffic signal operating?" "Why did the brakes fail?" "Why did the welfare worker deny your client's requested benefits?" and "Does the condition of the apartment violate any provisions of the housing codes?" are examples of relevant factual questions that the client might not be able to answer.

Even when the client can provide an answer it will be necessary to confirm the client's perceptions of those facts. The client's perception is sometimes biased and inaccurate. It therefore needs to be verified through the examination of other witnesses as well as through physical and documentary evidence.

Attorneys may do much of this investigative work on their own, they may hire an outside investigator, or they may utilize a paralegal on their own staff.* If the attorney does attempt to do the actual investigative work, an awkward position could develop when it comes to laying the proper foundation for photographs or impeaching the testimony of a witness. It is much better if the attorney is able to call somebody else to the witness stand to give this type of testimony.

Above all else the investigator must conduct an unbiased search for the truth. In order to protect the client's interests the attorney must be aware of the unfavorable as well as favorable factors in the case. If there is a witness or a document that contradicts the client's story, the attorney needs to know about it. Good attorneys seek to avoid surprises and they rely on sound investigation to accomplish that end.

The nature of the investigation will, of course, vary considera-

---

*The author considers investigation to be a paralegal function. It is a law-related activity performed by a lay person for an attorney.

bly with the area of law involved, as well as with the particular facts of the case at hand. Negligence cases require a great deal of investigative work. Damaged cars, broken machines, and injured persons all have to be examined. Witnesses have to be interviewed at length in order to determine the existence of negligence on the part of one or more parties to the accident. In workmen's compensation cases negligence is not an issue but the extent of damage is. Likewise the extent to which an injury was work related becomes an important aspect of the investigation. In probate an investigation could involve either locating missing heirs or attempting to determine what the mental state of the deceased was at the time the will was written.

The underlying skills in all areas are basically the same. Whether a witness is being sought to testify about an automobile accident or an armed robbery, the problems of locating that witness or of gaining cooperation are often the same. Investigators must be resourceful and persistent without being obnoxious. Persons are not usually located on the first try and investigators must be able to cope with the prospect of frequently ending up on dead-end roads. Investigators must also be patient for they often will spend many hours just sitting around waiting for people. The hours will be irregular and they will often have to work while others play. Yet the area of investigation is indeed one of the most challenging and rewarding activities in which a paralegal can participate.

The Rules of Evidence

When an investigator goes out on a case, he or she needs to think not only in terms of finding the truth, but in terms of how the situation can be presented in a court of law. For as even the most casual television viewer knows, the courts in this land operate under some very specific rules about when something can be introduced as evidence in a trial and when it cannot. Thus the proficient investigator needs to have a working knowledge of the basic principles of evidence.

Evidence, in the general sense, is information. It can be in the form of testimony, documents, or physical objects. When a judge rules that something is admissible evidence, he or she is permitting that piece of evidence to be presented as proof of some fact involved in the lawsuit. The judge's decision to admit or not admit evidence involves the application of various established legal principles. The conditions which must be met in order to introduce something into evidence depend to some extent on the particular type of evidence involved but all types of evidence must be relevant and material.

Relevancy refers to the probative value of the evidence: Does the presentation of this evidence lead one to logically conclude that an asserted fact is either more probable or less probable? Materiality is usually thought of as either a subcategory of relevancy or simply an equivalent. It relates to whether the evidence is part of the specific issues being tried in the case at hand. For example, the fact that a plaintiff suffered an injury in a previous automobile accident would be relevant and material only if the injury had been to the same part of the body injured in the case at hand.[20] Relevancy alone does not insure admissibility. Thus a gruesome photograph of the condition of the victim of a mutilation murder may be relevant yet excluded because of the probability that it would inflame the jury.[21]

In addition to being relevant the evidence must be competent. With respect to oral testimony from witnesses, it must be established that the witness is:

1. *Capable of expressing himself* so as to be understood by the jury (either directly or through an interpreter); and
2. *Capable of understanding the duty to tell the truth;* and
3. *Has personal knowledge and recollection* regarding the particular matter upon which he is called to testify (except where opinion testimony is permissible).[22]

The first two factors usually involve the age or mental condition of the witness. The third involves the meaning of hearsay evidence.

In nontechnical terms, hearsay is in effect rumor or secondhand information. It is "information that has been told to a witness by someone else."[23] For example, imagine a situation in which Doris tells Sue that she saw Bill, the defendant in a divorce suit, check into a motel with his secretary. Sue would not be allowed to testify about what her friend Doris has told her. Sue has no personal knowledge about Bill's roommates. She did not see Bill and his secretary herself.

There are some circumstances in which hearsay evidence is admitted. These exceptions to the hearsay rule include dying declarations, spontaneous utterances, former testimony, depositions, confessions and admissions, and business records.[24] In all cases, there are three conditions which must be met:

1. Generally, the original declarant must be unavailable to testify;
2. The declaration must be one which sheds some light upon the establishment of the true facts of the case and the information cannot be presented through any other source.
3. There must be some test of the trustworthiness of the statement in lieu of the oath and the right of cross-examination.[25]

A more detailed discussion of each of these exceptions would go far beyond the scope of this book and would be a major part of one of the most difficult of law school courses. Generally speaking, it is sufficient for the paralegal to be able to recognize when there are potential problems with the hearsay rule. Paralegals should then consult with their supervising attorney concerning the correct approach to be taken.

It is also essential to always be aware of the differences between facts and opinions. When a witness testifies that he saw the defendant's automobile strike the plaintiff's car broadside, he is testifying about a fact he observed. But when that same witness states that the defendant was driving too fast for the icy condition of the road, he is stating an opinion. Sometimes opinion evidence is admissible, while other times it is not. So-called expert witnesses can give opinion evidence in situations where lay witnesses cannot.

Lay witnesses (regular witnesses who have not been shown to have any special expertise) can give opinions on such subjects as the speed of moving vehicles; the similarity of a person's voice or handwriting to that of someone's voice or handwriting with which they are familiar; and whether or not a person is angry or intoxicated. In order to be allowed to venture such opinions, the trial judge must be satisfied that:

1. The witness personally observed or perceived that upon which he renders an opinion;

2. The matter must be one about which normal persons regularly form opinions (speed, size, sound, color, etc.); and
3. Giving an opinion is the best way of getting the matter to the jury . . . i.e., the facts upon which the opinion rests are not as meaningful as the opinion itself.[26]

An expert witness is "a person who possesses skill and knowledge in some art, trade, science, or profession that is beyond and above that of the *average* man."[27] While jurors are usually impressed by the amount of formal education a witness has and are especially impressed when the witness has authored books or articles on the subject, formal education itself is not a requirement for being an expert witness.[28] There has been at least one occasion when a burglar was taken from the penitentiary to act in court as an expert witness on techniques for breaking and entering. The expert witness can only testify as to his or her opinion, however, when it falls within the area of the witness's established expertise and goes beyond the knowledge of the common man or woman. If the expert witness has personal knowledge of the facts upon which the opinion is based (as in the case of a physician who has treated an injury personally) he or she can testify about that opinion directly. If the expert has no such personal knowledge (as in the case of a physician who did not treat an inury personally but is called upon to give an expert opinion on this injury's ramifications), the attorneys must present the witness with a series of hypothetical questions. These hypotheticals ask the witness to express an opinion on the basis of the information provided by the attorney during the questioning.

With testimonial evidence the judge or jury must rely on the descriptions and reports given by other people. In the case of real evidence (also referred to as physical or demonstrative evidence) the judge or jury is presented with tangible objects which speak for themselves. These tangible objects include not only such items as clothes and weapons but things like photographs, tape recordings, and maps as well. In a personal injury suit brought because the plaintiff has been paralyzed, for example, the plaintiff's lawyer may show a "one day in the life of . . ." type of movie in order to make the jury more aware of the full implications of the plaintiff's injuries.

Before such real evidence can be admitted it must be shown to be relevant and to be properly authenticated. For example, it is necessary to establish that the victim bled before the bloodstained clothes found in the defendant's apartment can be introduced into evidence. It is also necessary to establish that the blood-stained clothes being presented were in fact the same ones that were found in the defendant's apartment and that they are in the same condition as when they were found.*

In order to properly authenticate such physical evidence the investigator should (1) keep the object in his or her exclusive personal control from the time it is found until the time it is presented in court, (2) maintain a complete record of everyone involved in the chain-of-possession (i.e., everyone who handled it from the time it was found to the time it was presented in court), or (3) mark the object in a way that will make it easily distinguishable at a later time.[29]

The rules governing the authentication of photographs differ from one jurisdiction to the next. Most courts simply require that a witness who is familiar with an object or scene in the photograph testify that it is an accurate representation of that object or scene as it appeared at the time of the incident. On the other hand, a few courts require that the person who actually took the photograph testify about the type of camera and the settings used. Some require testimony relating to the developing process and the chain-of-possession.[30]

Written documents must also be relevant and authentic. Generally this means that the original document itself must be produced at the trial. This is due to the operation of the concept known as the best evidence rule. Proper testimony would of course have to establish that the document presented was in fact what it was purported to be. There are some circumstances, however, in which a copy may be considered admissible. Public records (official governmental documents as well as private deeds and mortgages which are officially recorded with the government) can be presented through the use of certified copies. In addition to presenting a copy showing an official seal and signature, an affidavit from the record's custodian is usually presented explaining what the record shows and attesting that it is an accu-

---

*There are some circumstances in which the evidence can be admitted even when its condition has changed. For example, if some of the blood had been removed for purposes of laboratory analysis, the bloodstained clothes could still be introduced if there was evidence as to what changed and why.

rate copy of the one on file.[31] Copies of private papers may be allowed when the original has been lost or destroyed, is in the hands of an adverse party who has refused to produce it, or in the hands of a third party who is outside the jurisdiction of the court's subpoena power.[32] In cases where the original is so voluminous that it is impractical to produce it in its entirety, the litigant is allowed to produce a summary.[33]

It is hoped that this brief discussion of some of the most basic principles of evidence will serve to make the reader sensitive to the complexities and potential problems of presenting factual information in a judicial proceeding. The investigator should provide the attorney with all of the facts possible, irrespective of whether or not they are admissible in court. Inadmissible evidence can often be used as the basis for obtaining evidence which is admissible. It can also be important in negotiating settlements. The resourceful attorney may be able to utilize one of the numerous exceptions in the rules to admit something which the paralegal thought to be inadmissible. It is very important that the investigator make every effort to gather information in an admissible form whenever it is possible to do so. Taking time to mark a piece of evidence or excluding a remark from a statement can mean the difference between being able to use the item in court or not being able to use it.

Getting Started

Generally speaking, the legal system is a rather slow-moving process in which delays and continuances are common. It is not uncommon for a period of four to five years to pass between the time of an accident and the eventual courtroom resolution of the negligence and damages issues which arose from that accident. For the investigator time is of the essence. Accident scenes change. Witnesses' memories fade. Witnesses move. Broken parts are repaired or discarded. Injuries heal. It is therefore essential that the investigator take certain actions as soon as humanly possible.

Before the investigator rushes off into the field, thought must be given to identifying just what it is that is being sought. It is a good idea to make a list of each of the facts the client has presented. Then thought must be given as to the types of physical, documentary, or testimonial evidence that will be needed to substantiate those facts. What important questions couldn't the client answer? How best can one go about answering those questions? The paralegal should find out if the attorney has some particular theory of negligence or some particular defense strategy in mind but should not let the investigation be limited by such an initial theory of the case.

After gaining some general idea of what is being sought and who will have to be interviewed, the investigation should be organized in the most productive and efficient way possible.

Physical and Photographic Evidence

The investigator usually begins by personally visiting the scene at which the events in question took place. In a situation involving an automobile accident, for example, the investigator should take a variety of photographs of both the damage to the vehicles involved and the condition of the roadway. Pictures should include any tire marks present and the condition of tires on the vehicles involved in the accident. If there is any suspicion that a faulty part may have been responsible, a series of close-up photographs should be taken of that part. Pictures of the scene should show the existence of all road signs and traffic control signals as well as any obstructions to the driver's vision. Wherever appropriate, the photographer should take pictures which show the nature of the injuries suffered.

Since dirt and debris usually fall off a car at the moment of impact, the investigator should look very carefully for this type of physical evidence. Spilled oil or antifreeze will often mark the point on the road at which the impact took place. The nature of damage to the headlights can indicate whether or not the lights were on at the time of the accident.*

When taking photographs of this type, the investigator should strive to reproduce as faithfully as possible that which the ordinary human being sees. Artistic urges and fancy camera angles must be subordinated to straightforward shots that show the proper depth perception. While some courts still prefer black and

---

*If the ends of the bulb broke cleanly and there are no signs of oxidation present, the lights were not on at the time of the impact.

white pictures over colored ones, most find both types equally acceptable.[34] Identification can be aided by placing a marker (such as a small chalk board or, for close-ups, a business card) in the area to be photographed.[35] This not only helps to establish the authenticity of the photo, it also helps viewers place the objects pictured in their proper perspective.*

In addition to taking photographs, the investigator should prepare detailed diagrams wherever they are appropriate. Such diagrams must, in order to be admissible, be drawn to scale. At the accident scene, for example, the investigator should carefully measure everything from the width of the street to the location of various traffic signs. This information should then be converted into one or more detailed diagrams. The diagrams can in turn be useful aids in interviewing witnesses as well as being used at the trial itself.

Locating Witnesses

Just as the investigator should take photographs as soon after the incident as possible, so too should the investigator locate and interview witnesses as soon as possible. The longer the delay, the more difficult it will be to find them and the less they will accurately remember.

During the initial interview the client should be asked to supply as much information as possible about both the identity and possible location of relevant witnesses. Depending on the type of event involved, police reports or newspaper articles should be checked for information about possible witnesses. (Figure 4.2 provides an example of a typical police report.) Whenever there is a chance that someone who lives or works nearby may have seen or heard something related to the event in question, the investigator should check with the occupants of all nearby buildings. If the event took place at a particular intersection at a particular time, one should observe and record the license numbers of automobiles which go through that intersection at approximately the same time every day. There is a good chance that the drivers

---

*On rare occasions a trial court will object to the marker on the basis that it has changed the scene. The investigator should therefore routinely take two photographs; one with the marker and one without. The second photo can then be introduced if there should happen to be an objection to the marker.

of some of those vehicles may have seen at least something relevant to the event in question. Sometimes the search for witnesses may also involve posting a notice in the area or even taking out a display advertisement in a local newspaper.

Occasionally an investigator will have a witness's name but will be unable to locate that witness either because of a missing address or the address is incorrect. When this occurs, there are a number of steps a resourceful investigator can take. While they are often out of date, the telephone book and the city directory are good starting points. If the person has moved, landlords, utility companies, neighbors, and relatives often know where they have moved. If the investigator knows where the person is employed, the witness can either be contacted there or the address can be obtained through the employer. If the individual being sought has school-age children, it may be possible to find out where their transcripts were forwarded through the school system. If the person is a member of a trade union or professional association, the national headquarters may be able to provide a current address. For a nominal fee the post office will provide address correction information. Still another method of search involves sending a certified letter marked for the addressee only and with a return receipt requested. If the witness has an unlisted telephone number, the local telephone company office may be willing to relay a message that an attorney is trying to reach someone in that household.[36]

In addition to locating lay witnesses, the investigator may also need to contact expert witnesses for a court appearance. The expert witnesses should be contacted early so that they can advise the investigator on the types of factual material that should be gathered (see Figure 4.3).

While most expert witnesses may be used in almost any type of case, they are most likely to be found in various types of negligence cases. In product liability and professional malpractice cases, an expert is usually needed to testify about the generally accepted practices and standards of that industry or profession. For example, in product liability cases the plaintiff must show that there was a defect in the design or manufacture of the product. As Anthony Golec states:

> To qualify as an expert in a products liability case, the engineer must demonstrate sufficient technical familiarity with the general type or class of product or equipment under consideration. He must also be

FIGURE 4.2
Sample Traffic Accident Report

POLICE

TRAFFIC ACCIDENT REPORT

POLICE ACCIDENT NO. A78-944 | INCIDENT NUMBER | Sheet 1 of 1 Sheets

I.D.O.T. USE ONLY

ON Number or Name of Highway or Street: 1. Linden Street | COUNTY: McLean | TOWNSHIP OR CITY: Normal

1 At Intersection With: Virginia Avenue (Number or Name of Intersecting Highway or Street)

2 If not at Intersection ____ Feet or ____ Miles (Circle 1) N E S W of ____ (Nearest Highway, Street, Bridge, or other Landmark)

DATE OF ACCIDENT (MO DAY YR): 2 02/02/78
TIME OF ACCIDENT: 6:54 A.M. (P.M.)
TOTAL UNITS INVOLVED
DAY OF THE WEEK: M T (W) T F S S

TYPE OF REPORT
CIRCLE ONE OR MORE: (1. Conventional) 2. Desk 3. Animal 4. Private Property 5. Hit & Run 6. Supplementary
CIRCLE ONE OR MORE: 1. Fatal (2. Injury) (3. Property Damage) (4. Arrest) 5. Interstate/Expressway

UNIT 1

DRIVER'S NAME Last First M.I.: 3. Hart, Thomas L. | DATE OF BIRTH Mo./Day/Yr.: 10/24/56 | 1. MALE 2. FEMALE | TAKEN TO: not | TAKEN BY: not | INJ. CODE: 0
DRIVER'S ADDRESS: 1700 North School, Apt. 27 | CITY/STATE/ZIP/PHONE: Normal, Ill. 61761 438-8638
DRIVER'S LICENSE NO: H620-8295-8308 | STATE: Il | CLASSIFICATION: A & M | RESTRICTIONS: None
COLOR: 4. Whi | YEAR: 66 | MODEL: Tempest 4 dr | MAKE: Pontiac | VEHICLE TYPE: Passenger | Total Occ. Unit 1 Including Driver: 1
VEHICLE OWNER: same as driver | VEHICLE REGIST. NO: TKL 177 | STATE: Il | YEAR: 78 | VEHICLE IDENTIFICATION NO.: 23369P268458
OWNER'S ADDRESS: same | CITY: same | STATE: Il
VEHICLE REMOVED BY: driver | VEHICLE REMOVED TO: driven | (1. DRIVEN AWAY) 2. TOWED AWAY

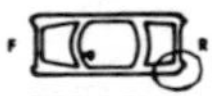
CIRCLE POINT OF CONTACT
$ 250.00 APPROX. COST TO REPAIR OR REPLACE

UNIT 2 OR PEDESTRIAN

[X] DRIVER'S NAME Last First M.I.: 5. Hooper, James B. | [ ] PEDESTRIAN | DATE OF BIRTH Mo./Day/Yr.: 02/25/07 | 1. MALE 2. FEMALE | TAKEN TO: not | TAKEN BY: not | INJ. CODE: 0
DRIVER'S ADDRESS: 1306 South Linden | CITY/STATE/ZIP/PHONE: Normal, Ill. 61761 436-6709
DRIVER'S LICENSE NO: H260-2199-7058 | STATE: Il | CLASSIFICATION: B | RESTRICTIONS: 1-0-0
COLOR: 6. Grn | YEAR: 73 | MODEL: Polara 4 dr | MAKE: Dodge | VEHICLE TYPE: Passenger | Total Occ. Unit 2 Including Driver: 3
VEHICLE OWNER: same as driver | VEHICLE REGIST. NO: CJ1316 | STATE: Il | YEAR: 78 | VEHICLE IDENTIFICATION NO: DM41K3F271053
OWNER'S ADDRESS: same | CITY: same | STATE: Il
VEHICLE REMOVED BY: driver | VEHICLE REMOVED TO: driver | 1. DRIVEN AWAY 2. TOWED AWAY

SEATING IN VEHICLE
1 2 3
4 5 6
STATION WAGON
7 8 9

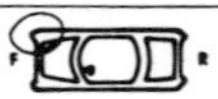
CIRCLE POINT OF CONTACT
$ Under 250.00 APPROX. COST TO REPAIR OR REPLACE

DAMAGE TO PROPERTY OTHER THAN VEHICLES

NAME OF OWNER OF PROPERTY: None | ADDRESS OF OWNER
NATURE OF DAMAGE | APPROX. COST OF REPAIR OR REPLACE $

TIME NOTIFIED OF ACCIDENT: 6:54 A.M. (P.M.) | DATE NOTIFIED OF ACCIDENT (MONTH DAY YEAR): 02/02/79 | DATE REPORT COMPLETED (MONTH DAY YEAR): 02/02/79 | 5235937
ARREST (NAME) Last First M.I.: Hart, Thomas L. | SECTION NUMBER: 11-904 | TICKET NUMBER: 12884
ARREST (NAME) Last First M.I.: one issued | SECTION NUMBER | TICKET NUMBER
SIGNATURE OF INVESTIGATING OFFICER: X D. Churchill | I.D. NUMBER: 602 | DISTRICT OF ASSIGNMENT: NPO #3 | COURT DATE: 03/05/79 | REVIEWING OFF.

(SR1733 - 300M - Rev. 3-78)

CODE FOR INJURY
Use only most serious one in each space for injury.
K-Dead Before Report Made
O-No Indication of Injury
A-Bleeding Wound, Distorted Member, or Had to be Carried From Scene
B-Other Visible Injury, as Bruises, Abrasions, Swelling, Limping, etc.
C-No Visible Injury But Momentary Unconsciousness or Complaint of Pain.

If witness place W in unit no. box

List Additional Passenger or Witness Information On a Separate Attached Sheet

PASSENGERS AND/OR WITNESSES

NAME Last First M.I.: 7. Hooper, Mrs. James
ADDRESS: 1306 S. Linden
CITY: Normal, | STATE: Il.
1-M 2-F: 2 | AGE: 69 | TAKEN TO: not
UNIT NO.: 2 | SEAT POS.: 2 | TAKEN BY: not | INJ. CODE: 0

NAME Last First M.I.: Williams, Ann
ADDRESS: 1306 South Linden
CITY: Normal, | STATE: Il.
1-M 2-F: 2 | AGE: 91 | TAKEN TO: St. Joseph's Hospital
UNIT NO.: 2 | SEAT POS.: 3 | TAKEN BY: AAA Ambulance | INJ. CODE: B

NAME Last First M.I.: DNA
ADDRESS
CITY | STATE
1-M 2-F | AGE | TAKEN TO:
UNIT NO. | SEAT POS. | TAKEN BY: | INJ. CODE

NAME Last First M.I.: DNA
ADDRESS
CITY | STATE
1-M 2-F | AGE | TAKEN TO:
UNIT NO. | SEAT POS. | TAKEN BY: | INJ. CODE

NAME Last First M.I.: DNA
ADDRESS
CITY | STATE
1-M 2-F | AGE | TAKEN TO:
UNIT NO. | SEAT POS. | TAKEN BY: | INJ. CODE

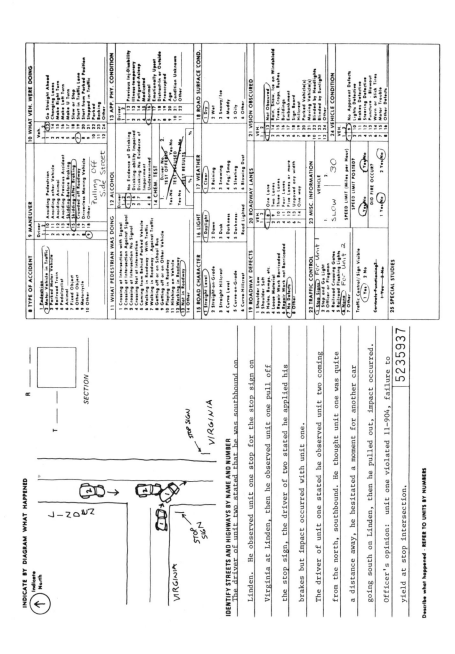

INDICATE BY DIAGRAM WHAT HAPPENED

IDENTIFY STREETS AND HIGHWAYS BY NAME AND NUMBER

The driver of unit two stated that he was southbound on Linden. He observed unit one stop for the stop sign on Virginia at Linden, then he observed unit one pull off the stop sign, the driver of two stated he applied his brakes but impact occurred with unit one.

The driver of unit one stated he observed unit two coming from the north, southbound. He thought unit one was quite a distance away, he hesitated a moment for another car going south on Linden, then he pulled out, impact occurred.

Officer's opinion: unit one violated 11-904, failure to yield at stop intersection.

Describe what happened · REFER TO UNITS BY NUMBERS

5235937

FIGURE 4.3
Letter to a Prospective Expert Witness

| **MINT & WALLER** | **Robert Mint** |
| **Trial Lawyers** | **Bruce Waller** |

500 First National Bank Bldg.
Bloomington, Illinois 61761   September 12, 1978

Prof. George Grain
Department of Agriculture
Rock State University
Rock, Iowa

Dear Prof. Grain:

This office represents a client who was injured while painting the roof of a metal grain bin. I am trying to locate an expert witness for consultation regarding design safety and possibly some court testimony, and thought you may be able to give me some help.

The grain bin was a cylindrical structure about twenty feet high with a cone-shaped metal roof on top of the cylinder at approximately 45 degrees pitch. The client slipped, lost his footing, and slid off the roof onto the ground.

A product liability suit has been filed in McLean County, Illinois. The complaint alleges that at the time the bin left the control of the defendant, it was not reasonably safe in that:

1. There was no railing, bar, or other device at the edge of the roof to prevent a person on the roof from sliding off;

2. There was no warning to persons who were climbing to the roof or on the roof of the danger of standing on the roof.

I would greatly appreciate it if you could send me any suggestions on possible expert witnesses. If you are interested in serving in this capacity, please send me your resumé and fee schedule. I would appreciate hearing from you even if you do not have any suggestions.

Sincerely yours,

Suzanne Little

Suzanne Little
Legal Assistant

able to describe a state-of-the-art knowledge at or before the date of manufacture of the product and often must have conducted appropriate tests with the product in question.[37]

An invaluable aid in locating such experts is Philo, Robb, and Goodman's *Lawyers' Desk Reference: Technical Sources for Conducting a Personal Injury Action*.[38] This reference work contains lists of experienced expert witnesses in many specialized areas.

It is usually a little harder to find expert witnesses in the medical area — especially when an allegation of malpractice is involved. Golec writes that:

> One of the formidable obstacles is the difficulty in obtaining the technical help of experts, namely other doctors, in a medical malpractice investigation and subsequent trial. The medical profession has historically been extremely reluctant to testify against its own, yet has also been extremely lax in policing itself and weeding out bad practitioners.[39]

Medical school faculty or doctors on the staffs of veterans' hospitals are often one of the best sources for locating doctors who are willing to testify in court.[40] In an area such as workmen's compensation, where the focus is on the nature of the employee's injury rather than the negligence of another professional, doctors are usually more willing to serve as expert witnesses.

Interviewing Witnesses

When conducting interviews the investigator should generally make advance arrangements to ensure that there will be adequate time available and that it will be at a time which is convenient for the witness.* The investigator must rely on the cooperation of the witness and should therefore make every effort to be accommodating. The interview can take place in the law

---

*There are occasions when it is better to simply appear at the witness's doorstep without advance notice. This is particularly true where there is reason to believe that the person might seek to get together with someone else to rehearse a story. See pages 116–117 for a more complete discussion of the problems of adverse witnesses.

office, in the witness's home, or even at the witness's place of work. The most important consideration is that it take place in a relatively peaceful setting where interruptions can be minimized. If at all possible, the interview should take place out of the presence of friends, family, or co-workers.*

As in the case of the client interview, it should begin on a rather open-ended basis. The witness should not be confronted with a series of yes or no questions. The witness may be approached as if the investigator had only a general knowledge of the situation and the witness is needed to fill in the details. The same types of feedback mechanisms discussed earlier in this chapter should be utilized (i.e., minimal encourages, paraphrasing, and reflection of feelings). As the interview progresses, the investigator can utilize more closed questions in order to pin down the essential details.

When a witness gives an evaluation of some person or event, the interviewer should probe to find the specific observations upon which that evaluation is based. Exactly what the witness said or heard personally must always be clarified as opposed to what was simply heard secondhand.

As the investigator conducts the interview, he should be carefully evaluating the person's strength as a witness in the courtroom: How convincing will the witness be on the witness stand? Will the witness be able to follow the questions easily or will the witness become confused easily? If the interviewee was an eyewitness to something or overheard something, the investigator should subtly test the witness's eyesight and/or hearing. If a person wears eyeglasses, it is wise to determine the type of prescription and whether the eyeglasses were worn at the time of the incident about which the testimony is to be given.

Generally speaking, the investigator should attempt to interview adverse witnesses first. Time is of the essence and it is important to get these witnesses on record before they have time to establish various defenses. If they have consulted with a lawyer, they have probably been told not to say anything to an inves-

---

*One exception to this rule may occur when a young child is being interviewed. Here it may be better to have a parent present in order to help put the child at ease. On the other hand, it is always possible that the child may be willing to tell the interviewer something about which he or she does not want the parents to know. Another exception is the situation in which an interpreter is needed because the witness cannot speak English.

tigator. (If it is determined that a witness has retained an attorney, that witness should only be approached through that attorney.) If the investigator contacts the adverse party soon enough, that person may not yet have talked to an attorney or have carefully developed all aspects of the story. Statements from such adverse witnesses can also readily identify the problem areas the paralegal's attorney may have and can provide clues for the type of information needed to impeach that testimony.

In approaching a hostile witness it is sometimes better to interview without making an appointment in advance. Such a strategy reduces the chances of the witness carefully rehearsing a story before the investigator's arrival.[41] It is important to be prepared for any eventuality, for it will probably be the only opportunity to talk to the hostile witness.

When witnesses appear to be reluctant to cooperate, the investigator should attempt to determine the cause for this reluctance: Are they friends of the other party or the victim? Do they fear some sort of retaliation? Are they simply afraid of being called to testify at the trial stage? The investigator can always point out that a statement given now may avoid the necessity of the person being subpoenaed to testify at a trial.

When interviewing friendly witnesses, the investigator must be especially careful not to use leading questions and to guard against the witness who is embellishing the truth in order to win approval or help a friend.

Taking Formal Statements

After having engaged the witness in conversation long enough to have established rapport and developed some idea about the types of things the person witnessed, most investigators attempt to take some type of formal statement.* While this statement cannot be

---

*It should be pointed out that there is some difference of opinion on the taking of formal statements. Because such statements are discoverable by the opposing side, some attorneys prefer not to take them. They simply rely on the investigative notes. If the witness changes the story, the attorney has the investigator testify about what the witness had told the investigator earlier. Such testimony is not likely to carry quite as much weight as a formal statement would. Where the attorney is really concerned about pinning a witness down for the record, a deposition can be taken. (See the last paragraph in this section for an explanation of depositions.)

used as direct evidence at the trial, it can be used as a vehicle through which the witness can refresh the memory or through which a hostile witness's testimony can be impeached. If a witness's testimony is detrimental to the investigator's side of the case, an attempt can possibly be made to show the judge or jury that the witness is not very credible. This might be accomplished by demonstrating that the testimony given in court is inconsistent with statements the witness made in an earlier statement out of court.

There are three main types of statements taken by investigators. The most common and the most widely recognized is the narrative type, in which the investigator records in his or her own handwriting what the witness is saying. (See Figure 4.4.) The investigator should simply take out a pad of legal paper and start writing. If the witness asks about the procedure, simply explain that pertinent facts are being recorded before they fade from memory. While the witness's words are not taken down verbatim, an attempt should be made to use his or her own phrases and descriptions as much as possible.

Figure 4.5 presents the manner in which a typical narrative statement is organized. The first section should supply as much information as possible about the witness. In addition to such items as name, address, and phone number, it should include information about employer, relatives, professional group memberships, social clubs, and even hobbies. Most of this information is simply for the purpose of making it possible to locate the witness in case of a move prior to the trial. This first section also should include information as to the date and location at which the statement is being given. If witnesses are present, that too should be mentioned.

The heart of the statement is the description of whatever it is that the witness observed. Usually it is presented in chronological order. In addition to describing the events themselves, it is important to have the witness carefully describe the environment in which those events took place. Thus in an automobile accident case, the witness would be asked to describe such matters as the weather and the existence of any temporary obstructions to a driver's view.

When witnesses use slang or improper English it should be included just as it was given. If, however, it is not clear what was intended by the phrase, the witness should be asked to clarify it. If

FIGURE 4.4
Sample Narrative Statement

I am Carl Jones. I am 27 years old and am married to Lois Jones. We have two children, Bobby and Lois. We live at 908 South Oak St., Atlanta, Illinois. My phone number is 663-1708. I am employed by Cutler-Hyde Co. on Rte #130 in Lincoln, Illinois. I am a drill press operator and earn $7.83 per hour. I am a representative with I work 40 to 48 hours. I am a member of the Drill Press Operators Union, the Elks and the V.F.W. My parents are Herman and Eleanor Jones. They live at Lodge #39, Marilena Blvd., Arkansas. Both of my parents are retired.

On March 17, 1979, at 10:30 p.m. while driving my 1974 Olds 88 Cutlass Royale, I was involved in an accident with Oscar Fee who was driving a 1977 Mercury Marquis. My car is roadster red and the Mercury is frost green. It is my understanding Calvin Houston is the owner of the 1977 Mercury. My car license number is CJ 309 and the license to the Mercury was CH 9231. The accident occurred at the intersection of Oakland Avenue and Regency Drive in Bloomington, Illinois. The occupants in my car were my wife Lois who was sitting in the right front seat, my son Bobby who was sleeping in the left rear seat, and my daughter Lois who was sitting up in the right

CJ

rear seat. There was just the driver in the Mercury. My wife and children and I were on the Oak House for an evening meal. We had been shopping at the Eastland Mall until about 8:30 and I let Lois directly to the Oak House from the Mall. I would just go in a few minutes drive from the Mall to the Oak House. We intended to eat at the Oak House and then go home to Atlanta. We left the restaurant at about 10:15.

The weather conditions were clear and the roads were dry. Oakland Avenue is a black top street running generally east and west. It is four lanes wide and is usually quite the lane to be 18 ft wide. Regency Drive is four lanes wide and generally runs north and south. It dead-ends at Oakland Avenue. Both streets are relatively level at this point. I'm not sure what the speed limits are in this area. I am not exactly sure what my speed was as I was not carrying on an argument. I would guess it was about 25 mph. This is a semi-commercial area. On the south side of Oakland is a big insurance company office and some small real estate office. There is a building on the northwest corner of the intersection that I think they call the NRE building. On the northeast corner is a Sunoco Service Station. This is a crossroads for traffic

CJ

FIGURE 4.4 — Continued

located on Legacy located on the north-west corner. The lighting conditions were average in my opinion, as I could see cars coming toward me and traveling in front of me.

I did not see the Opel Sedan when the accident happened. There are two ways to leave. One way is to get onto Legacy and head south. The other way is to drive past the east side of the Sunoco station and turn right onto Oakland. I would guess the drive on the east side of the Sunoco station ca 110 feet from the curb line of Legacy. I backpedaled up to Oakland and I could see a car on Oakland headed west. It was about 125 feet east of the drive I was using to exit. I made a rolling right turn into the low lane to the curb lined west on Oakland. I did what you might call a running start in that I didn't stop before entering Oakland. There was no sign at the drive no cars of I could see the car approaching my my left headed west. I would have it made. I was kind of irate because I waited a while was merging and the left thing I knew I saw the 1977 Mercury pulling out of Oakland from Legacy. The Mercury was headed south and was just crossing the white curb lane of Oakland when we collided. I don't think the Mercury driver even saw me as I'm sure he did not stop. I would judge his speed at 30 to 35 MPH

when I saw him I was only 10 feet away from him when I first saw him. I put on my brake and had all but stopped when he hit me. He left rear quarter panel of the Mercury hit the entire front end of my car. After the impact I ended up about 10 feet past Legacy still in the west curb lane of Oakland Avenue. The Mercury was angled toward the northeast and was sitting in the inside westbound lane on Oakland. At the eastbound curb lane I noticed about 15 feet of skid marks which had to be made by my car. I told Officer that he would notice where on the hill he was going. I pointed out the stop sign to him. He said "I never saw you at all." I told him that I had my lights on. I took him slow off from the impact and when I stopped. About that time the police came and crews anyone down. The officers name I think was Hegerty and Hagardy.

When we hit, my arm hit the steering of the right arm. The injury was to the upper part of my arm and chest. In addition, for the next day now that is all of my injuries. While I did a cut on her left by behind I think it hit the artery in my car. She had to have 34 stitches suturing from her left

door. Injured his ankle. He did
not have any further injuries. Our children
were not injured in the accident. They did
not miss any time from school, and staying
well, and are playing with the neighbor kids
every day. My wife Shirla is not employed
now nor has she been since our marriage
in 1967. We were taken to Catholic Hospital
by AAA Ambulance Service. The emergency room
doctor was Dr. Elmer Wills. Our family
doctor is a Bloomington doctor and he is Dr.
Frank Smith. He treated us while in the
hospital and continues to treat us at this
time. It is his opinion at this time that
I will be out of work for 6 to 8 weeks. I
can't run a drill press but am able to do a
lot of things around the house. I am left-
handed, and while I am getting well I have
been working on painting project in my den.

My car appears to be a total loss. The
estimate of damage is $838.73. The damage
is pretty much confined to the front and there
is some damage to the left rear quarter panel
and the new body paint.

I can think of nothing further to add.

CJ

concerning this accident.
I have read these 3 pages and
they are true.

Carl Jones   May 12, 1979

FIGURE 4.5
Standard Elements in a Narrative Statement for an Auto Accident

1. *Identity of the witness*

   Name

   Age, sex, and marital status

   Occupation and employer

   Residence and business address, phone numbers

   Organizational affiliations and other items that will help locate the person in the future

2. *Identification of the accident*

   Date, day of the week, time

   Location of the accident

   Type of accident

   Identification of parties involved (drivers, passengers, etc.)

   Were parties traveling as part of their job?

   Description of vehicles involved (owner, make, model, color, year, license number, serial number)

   Identification of potential witnesses

3. *Detailed description of scene of accident*

   Description of streets and highways

   a. Direction
   b. Width
   c. Number of lanes
   d. Grade
   e. Speed limit
   f. Traffic controls
   g. Type and condition of surface

   Weather conditions

   Buildings and other objects which could obstruct one's view.

4. *Detailed description of accident*

   Direction and speed of vehicles, pedestrians

   Status of traffic signals

Evasive action

Point of impact (on roadway and on each vehicle)

Final resting place of vehicles

Skid marks and debris

Statements made

Location of witnesses

5. *Bodily injuries (for each person injured)*

Part of body injured

Extent of injury

Nature of treatment (ambulance, hospital, doctor)

Nature of disability

Occupation and salary

Pre-existing medical problems

6. *Property damage*

To vehicles

To buildings, etc.

7. *Attestation clause*

Pages numbered

Corrections initialed

Signed by witness

the witness makes a value judgment, a request should be made for the basis for that judgment.[42] However, if a friendly witness makes some sort of racial slur or makes reference to hearsay evidence, it should not be included. The inclusion of such material could either make the statement inadmissible or allow the statement to later damage the witness's position. On the other hand, if such items occur in the statement of a hostile witness, they should be left in.[43]

The final stage of the statement is the verification phase. At the end of the statement the investigator should have the witness write: "I have read these ____ pages and they are true." Golec suggests adding the phrase, "This is all I know about this matter and all I can say about it," in order to protect against additional adverse material being brought forth at a later date.[44]

In writing up the statement the investigator should keep the margins even on all four sides and carefully number each page. It is best to use lined paper and to use every available line. These guidelines are designed to protect against possible charges that the statement was altered at some later date. The bottom line of each page should be skipped to leave room for the witness's initials.

When the statement has been completed, the investigator should hand it to the witness and ask that it be read to make sure the investigator recorded everything correctly. If any errors are pointed out, the investigator should make the changes and then ask the witness to initial the change. Finally, the witness should be asked to both sign the statement's verification clause at the end and to initial it at the bottom of each page.

If the witness cannot read, the investigator should have a neighbor or some neutral third party read the statement to the witness. If there are corrections, both the neighbor and the witness should initial them. The neighbor should then write something like: "I have read the above statement of ___ pages to _____ and he has said they are correct to the best of his knowledge." The neighbor then also signs. The witness also signs (or makes his mark) and initials in the regular manner. Since some people are too embarrassed to admit that they cannot read, the investigator should watch the person's eyes when he or she is asked to read over the statement. If the eyes stay fixed on one spot, it is probable that the witness is not really reading it.[45] The investigator must then probe the witness to determine illiteracy. A signed statement in and of itself is not worth much in court if it is later determined the witness could not read.

A second type of statement is one which is mechanically recorded. Usually, a plastic belt (dictaphone type) is used rather than magnetic tape because the belt is more difficult to alter.[46] At the beginning of the recorded statement the investigator should identify himself or herself; state the date, time, and location of the interview; and describe the make and model of the recording equipment being used.[47] The statement will then consist of the investigator's questions and the witness's answers. The same general format should be followed as when one is developing a written statement. At the end of each belt of tape the investigator should state that it is the end of the belt, naming the number, and ask the witness if the statements have been true and complete up to that point. Then at the end the entire interview should be played back for the witness. The recorder should then be turned on again and the witness asked if the tape has been played back and if it is true and complete. If there are any corrections, the witness should make those corrections at that time.[48]

A third type of statement is similar to the question and answer format discussed above, but a verbatim record is made by some- one taking shorthand. The person who has taken the shorthand then prepares a written transcript and attests to the accuracy of its contents.

There are both pros and cons with each method. The verbatim records are often best used with witnesses who are very old, very young, or hostile. In these cases it is preferable because it can help protect the investigator against charges that he or she ma- nipulated the witnesses or otherwise took unfair advantage of them. The recorded statement may also be helpful when the witness is unwilling to sign any written documents. As F. Lee Bailey and Henry Rothblatt remark:

> Many witnesses are sensitive about signing anything that looks like a document, but will permit the recording of their voices, perhaps not fully realizing that a properly recorded statement is as effective and legally binding as a written statement.[49]

When utilized with simple telephone interviews, the mechani- cally recorded statements can be big time-savers. However, as the statement becomes more complex or involved, it becomes in- creasingly more difficult to have people carry through with the elaborate authentication process suggested above. Another prob- lem with both the mechanically recorded and the shorthand methods is that the interviews often tend to ramble and thus the answers appear to be very disorganized.

Whatever the method used, the investigator should try to get some type of statement from each known witness. Even when a witness claims to know nothing about the event, it is wise to obtain a formal statement to that effect in order to protect oneself from a situation in which the witness has a change of mind and later becomes a star witness for the opposition. If the witness will not even make a negative statement, the investigator should carefully record the dates and circumstances under which those refusals came.[50]

Before leaving the topic of statements, it may be useful to distinguish the type of statements we have been discussing from depositions and interrogatories. A deposition is a question and answer session which takes place outside of the courtroom, but a session in which the witness is under oath and the entire event is recorded by a court reporter. Interrogatories are a set of written questions that are sent from one party in a lawsuit to another. These discovery devices will be discussed in greater detail in Chapter 8.

Obtaining Documentary Evidence

Depending on the nature of the case at hand, there may be a need for various kinds of documentary evidence. In any type of case involving a personal injury, for example, the injured party's medical records become an important factor. In a product liability suit, information about safety records and industry standards are usually vital to its outcome. Likewise, information about a company's financial position can be a key element in many types of cases.

If the patient has been hospitalized, the hospital itself will usually be the best source for information about the medical condition. In order to be accredited by the Joint Commission on Accreditation of Hospitals,* the institution must maintain a complete set of patient records that conform to the commission's specific standards. Private physicians, on the other hand, often keep little more than a record of a patient's charges and payments. When records are requested for a lawsuit, many physicians simply dictate a letter based on their rough notes. Figure 4.6 shows a typical response.

Hospital records usually begin with an admissions form which gives personal data which usually includes birth date and place of birth, marital status, occupation, religion, former names, relatives, insurance carrier, and a medical history. The admissions

---

*The Joint Commission on Accreditation of Hospitals is the major accrediting group in the United States and is jointly sponsored by the American Medical Association, the American College of Surgeons, the American College of Physicians, and the American Hospital Association.

FIGURE 4.6
Physician's Response to Request for Medical Records

(Date)

To: (Law Firm)

Re: (Patient's Name)

Dear Sir:
I have received your request and authorization for release of medical information.

This will confirm that Mr. _____ was hospitalized on (date), at _____ Hospital, for repair of a right recurrent inguinal hernia. His recovery from the surgery was satisfactory.

I did confirm severe arthritis, involving the back, neck, arms, and shoulders. In addition, he has had discogenic disease of the cervical spine treated surgically in the past.

It was my impression that he is totally disabled from employment and that this does appear to be permanent and progressive in character.

Very truly yours,

(Physician's name), M.D.

---

order will show the doctor's analysis of the reason for admission. The examination which is conducted at the time of admission* and the daily observations of temperature, blood pressure, pulse rate, skin condition, and so on will all be recorded as part of the hospital record. The order sheets will show the various laboratory tests and medications administered. Lab reports and consultation reports of other doctors should also be present in the record. Figure 4.7 provides an example of what the history and physical sections look like.

If an operation was performed, there should be a physician's report that includes such material as the type of surgical procedure used and what was observed about the patient's condition during the operation. The discharge summary will review the patient's condition upon admission, progress while in the hospi-

*While hospital policies vary, it must usually be done between five days before admission and the first day after admission.

FIGURE 4.7
History and Physical Section of Hospital Record

(Name of Hospital)	(Physician's Name)

(Patient's Name)

Admitted: (Date)

Room: _____

History and Physical

This fifty-four-year-old white male was brought to the emergency room after being injured in an automobile accident. The patient states that he was turning the corner and after turning the corner he became somewhat lightheaded and then everything went black and he hit a parked car. He was brought to the emergency room. He was complaining of some numbness of the lips. He was hyperventilating at the time and complaining of some low backache and pain over various parts of the body. X rays were taken of the skull, cervical spine, lumbosacral spine, pelvis, and left shoulder and all the X rays failed to reveal any evidence of fracture. There was considerable degenerative disc disease of the cervical and lumbar spine. He had a slight spondylolisthesis of L4 and L5. There was narrowing of the disc space of L4, L5, and marked degenerative changes of C5 and C6. The patient in the past has had a gallbladder removed. He has had a tonsillectomy. He has had a double hernia repaired and he has had a ruptured disc removed from his back. The patient has been under a lot of nervous tension recently. Recently he had been complaining of various arthritic pains. He has been taking Valium and Motrin at home. He has been complaining of some vague headaches with lightheadedness. The patient was first seen in his hospital bed the evening of admission at which time he was complaining of pain in the back and some pain in his hip. BP 130/90. Pulse 84. Respiration 16.

Head:	Negative.
Eyes:	Pupils are equal size and shape. React to light and accommodation.
Chest:	Symmetrical.
Lungs:	Clear to percussion and auscultation.
Heart:	Borders within normal limits. Regular rate and rhythm. No murmurs. No extrasystoles.
Abdomen:	Scaphoid. Liver, kidney, and spleen are not palpated. There are no masses or tenderness.
External genitalia:	Normal.
Admission diagnosis:	Syncope, multiple contusions, degenerative arthritis, anxiety reaction.

D: _____ T: _____ _____, M.D.

tal, the results of diagnostic procedures utilized, the condition of the patient on release, and a listing of any medication that was prescribed for the patient to be taken at home. See Figure 4.8.

Some states provide a statutory right for the patient (or the authorized agent) to review and copy these hospital records. Some states also provide access by the defendant to a plaintiff's hospital records when that plaintiff is alleging to have sustained injuries as a result of defendant's actions. In still other states no such rights to access exist and it is entirely up to each hospital to establish its own policies.

FIGURE 4.8
Discharge Summary Section of Hospital Records

(Name of hospital)

Hospital no. _____

Room no. _____

Date of admission: _____

Date of discharge: _____

Discharge Summary

Patient was admitted to the hospital after an automobile accident. He was seen then by the physician on call. During this hospitalization, he complains of multiple aches and pains over the entire body. His urinalysis reveals some hematuria, he was seen by (Physician's Name) who cystoscoped the patient. He had a normal brain scan, a normal EEG. He was discharged from the hospital, condition improved. Will be followed as an outpatient.

Final Diagnosis:
1. Syncope, etiology unknown
2. Osteoarthritis
3. Degenerative disc disease of the cervical and lumbar spine
4. Spondylodesis of L4 and L5, narrowing of the interval tubal disc space of L4, L5
5. Microscopic hematuria
6. Chronic prostatitis
7. Urethritis
8. Benign prostatic hypertrophy with secondary early lower urinary tract obstruction
9. Multiple contusions

Where access to hospital records is allowed (either by law or by decision of the hospital) the patient is usually required to sign a specific authorization form. In all states, however, the hospital must turn over patient records when a proper *subpoena duces tecum* has been issued by the courts.

Depending on the nature of the case, the investigator can often make great use of various types of governmental documents. City building departments have information on building construction plans and safety inspections. Coroners' offices have autopsy and inquest reports.* County recorders' offices have information on mortgages, bankruptcies, trusts, and judgments. License bureaus have all sorts of background information on license holders. The secretary of state's office and the federal Security and Exchange Commission have extensive data about the structure and financial position of corporations.

While the law differs from one state to the next, the general rule is that the public has a right to inspect public records during reasonable business hours. The right to inspect such documents carries with it the right to make copies. In order to both facilitate the process and protect the documents, most offices will provide a member of the public with photocopies of the document for a nominal service fee. At the federal level, the Freedom of Information Act requires each agency to make various records available to the public.[51] Exemptions are allowed, however, for such matters as defense and foreign policy secrets, trade secrets, confidential commercial or financial information, personnel and medical files, and investigatory files compiled for law enforcement purposes.

In product liability cases, the investigator will need to obtain copies of relevant industry standards established by both governmental agencies and voluntary associations. While the courts of different states vary with regard to their treatment of the admissibility of such codes, the modern trend seems to favor their use. The National Safety Council, the American Standards Institute, and the American Society of Safety Engineers are some of the most common sources of such standards. The *Lawyers' Desk*

---

*While the inquest results are generally not admissible as to the cause of death, the reports can still be used as an investigative tool. Testimony at an inquest could be used to inpeach a witness's testimony at the trial if it were inconsistent with that given at the inquest.

Reference: Technical Sources for Conducting a Personal Injury Action is a handy source for locating relevant organizations.[52] The American National Standards Institute and the Underwriters Laboratories publish catalogs which list the availability of published standards.

There will be times when important documentary evidence cannot be obtained from the sources mentioned above. Occasionally an investigator can obtain information from businesses, private individuals, and even governmental agencies despite the fact that there is no legal right to receive it. Approaching the correct people in a suitable manner can often gain voluntary cooperation. Where such cooperation is not forthcoming, the investigator will have to confer with the attorney about utilizing the subpoena power of the court.*

THE INVESTIGATIVE REPORT

The investigator's hard work will be of little use if it is not communicated effectively to the attorney. The format through which this information will be relayed will depend upon the needs of the parties involved. Usually the investigator prepares a formal report to describe what was done and to provide an analysis of the results. Statements, diagrams, or photographs which have been taken are then usually attached as appendices to the report. There may be only one comprehensive report or, in longer, more complex matters, a series of interim reports.

In the report's analysis section the investigator should isolate each factual question about which there is some dispute. For each one the investigator should then compare and contrast all aspects of the evidence (testimonial, physical, and documentary) which relate to that specific issue. It is at this point also that the investigator should draw attention to various factors that may affect a witness's credibility. For instance, if a given witness is hard of hearing or has a surly manner, that information should also be included.

While the investigator should work hard to present this information in a concise manner, it is most important that it be com-

---

*A *subpoena duces tecum* is a court order commanding a person to bring certain documents to court.

plete. Although an item might appear to be rather insignificant at the time the report is being prepared, it may become extremely important at some later date.

SUMMARY

In both civil and criminal suits, there is usually more of a dispute over what actually took place (the facts) than there is about the meaning of the law. While there are occasions in which both sides are willing to stipulate* to a particular description of the facts, it is much more likely that the major part of the attorney's energy will go toward convincing the court to adopt the client's view of the facts rather than the opponent's contrary view. A good paralegal should therefore be a skilled fact-finder.

The attorney's initial view of the facts ordinarily comes directly from the client at the time of the initial interview. In many legal aid programs, a paralegal conducts these initial fact-finding interviews. In other situations, the paralegal may be assigned to conduct an in-depth fact-gathering session with the client after the attorney has talked with the client on more general terms.

Whenever possible these interviews should take place in a comfortable and quiet location in which there will be privacy and a lack of interruptions. The seating arrangement should be one which facilitates personal communication rather than one that intimidates the person being interviewed. The interviewer should put the client at ease and should be conscious of the nonverbal as well as the verbal aspects of communication.

The paralegal should begin the interview by explaining the paralegal's role in terms the client will understand. The client should then be given the opportunity to describe the problem in the client's own terms, rather than falling into a situation in which the client merely responds to the interviewer's questions. The interviewer should follow up with direct questions in order to clarify areas of ambiguity and to assist the interviewee who becomes bogged down or forgets the train of thought. Minimal encourages to talk, paraphrasing, and reflections of feelings are

---

*A stipulation in this context involves an agreement by the attorneys for both sides that a particular description of the facts should be placed on the record.

useful techniques for keeping the interview moving ahead constructively.

In bringing the interview to an end it is wise to summarize one's understanding of what the client has said in order to ensure accuracy and to give the client a chance to add information which might have been overlooked. The paralegal should collect copies of all relevant documents and have the client sign appropriate authorization forms. Immediately afterward, notes from the interview should be reviewed and polished while the matter is still fresh in the interviewer's mind.

Since one cannot rely solely on the client's perception of the facts, the paralegal must be prepared to interview other witnesses as well as examine the physical and documentary evidence that is available. The attorney must be made aware of the unfavorable as well as the supportive evidence.

To as great an extent as possible, the paralegal should strive to collect information in a form that will be admissible in a court of law. One should therefore develop a basic understanding of the rules of evidence and what constitutes relevant and competent evidence. The investigator must be prepared to properly authenticate real evidence. Nevertheless, even inadmissible evidence can be useful and it should be collected even if it cannot be admitted in court.

Since physical surroundings change, witnesses' memories fade, and injuries heal, it is important that the paralegal begin the investigation as soon after the incident as possible. Time is particularly important when one is investigating an automobile accident or some similar event in which the physical evidence is likely to change or disappear. A good investigator attempts to preserve the scene in photographs and prepares scale diagrams which will help others to see what happened.

In cases which lend themselves to the use of expert witnesses, the paralegal should identify appropriate individuals and enlist their support. The experts can then be used as a resource for the investigation as well as witnesses at the trial.

The strategy utilized in approaching a witness will depend on whether the witness is perceived as being friendly or adverse. Whenever possible the investigator should take a formal statement from both types of witnesses. The most common type of statement involves having the interviewer transpose the witness's answers into a simple narrative account and then obtain the witness's signature to indicate that the account is accurate. Mechanically recorded statements make up a second type of statement, while typing a verbatim transcript constitutes the third. There are advantages and disadvantages to each strategy and the paralegal should use the one which best fits the particular situation at hand.

Medical records as well as various government documents are often very useful. The paralegal should therefore become familiar with both the content of such documents and the procedures for obtaining copies of them.

Finally, the paralegal should communicate all this information to the attorney through reports that effectively summarize and integrate the results of the investigation.

KEY TERMS

admissible evidence

attending behavior

attestation clause

closed questions

competent evidence

demonstrative evidence

documentary evidence

evidence

expert witness

hearsay evidence

lay witness

material evidence

minimal encourages to talk

narrative statement

open questions

paraphrasing

physical evidence

real evidence

recorded statement

reflection of feelings

relevant evidence

subpoena duces tecum

testimonial evidence

transcribed statement

verbal following

REVIEW QUESTIONS

1. What factors often contribute to poor communication?

2. What are the advantages and disadvantages of closed versus open questions?

3. Why should the interviewer avoid the use of why questions?

4. Under what circumstances is hearsay evidence admissible?

5. What must be done to properly authenticate real evidence?

6. What are the most common means of locating both lay and expert witnesses?

7. What are the primary elements that should be included in a standard narrative statement?

8. What type of information usually appears in hospital records?

DISCUSSION QUESTIONS

1. What are the advantages and disadvantages of having a paralegal (as opposed to the attorney) conduct the initial interview with a client? What are the advantages and disadvantages of having a paralegal rather than the attorney interview other witnesses?

2. Do you agree with the manner in which the author suggests paralegals explain their roles to the client? How might you improve upon this description?

3. Which type of evidence (testimonial, documentary, and physical) is most reliable? Which is least reliable? What are the potential advantages and disadvantages of each?

4. In attempting to locate witnesses, where does one draw the line between ethical and unethical behavior? What techniques would not be ethical?

PROJECTS

1. In reading medical reports, it is likely that you will come upon some unfamiliar terminology. Go to your library and familiarize yourself with medical reference works. You should find some that are specifically directed at lawyers. Now use several of these references to assist you in writing out a short explanation of each of the following medical terms: (1) pneumothorax, (2) hypertrophic changes, (3) spondylolisthesis, and (4) sciatica. Which references did you find most useful and why?

2. Locate a recent copy of *National Safety News* (try the library again). Carefully examine this publication of the National Safety Council and then write up a brief (one page) summary of the nature of its contents. In what ways could this publication be useful to some paralegals?

3. Pair off with a classmate or friend and practice conducting an interview with a new client. After the interview has been completed, analyze how it could have been improved.

4. Pair off with someone else as in number three above. This time have the other person play the role of a witness to an automobile accident. Develop a proper narrative statement on the basis of this interview.

REFERENCES

1. Gerald Nierenberg and Henry Calero, *Meta-Talk* (New York: Pocket Books, 1975), p. 16.
2. Alfred Benjamin, *The Helping Interview*, 2d ed. (Boston: Houghton Mifflin Company, 1974), p. 44.
3. Thomas Shaffer, *Legal Interviewing and Counseling* (St. Paul: West, 1976), p. 65.
4. John Makay and Beverly Gaw, *Personal and Interpersonal Communication: Dialogue with the Self and with Others* (Columbus: Charles E. Merrill, 1975), p. 58.
5. *Ibid.*, p. 67.
6. Benjamin, *The Helping Interview*, p. 58.
7. Allen E. Ivey, *Microcounseling: Innovations in Interviewing Training* (Springfield: Charles C. Thomas, 1971), pp. 35–50, 149–50.
8. *Ibid.*, p. 150.
9. *Ibid.*, p. 149.
10. *Ibid.*
11. Benjamin, *The Helping Interview*, p. 66.
12. Ivey, *Microcounseling: Innovations in Interviewing Training*, pp. 152 and 153.
13. *Ibid.*, p. 56.
14. *Ibid.*, p. 156.
15. *Ibid.*, p. 154.
16. Benjamin, *The Helping Interview*, p. 39.
17. *Ibid.*, p. 80.
18. *Ibid.*, p. 85.
19. Raymond Gordon, *Interviewing: Strategy, Techniques, and Tactics* (Homewood, Ill.: Dorsey Press, 1975), pp. 16 and 17.
20. William A. Rutter, *Evidence*, 8th ed. (Gardena, Calif.: Gilbert Law Summaries, 1973), p. 12.
21. *Ibid.*, p. 25.
22. *Ibid.*, p. 68.
23. Gilbert B. Stuckey, *Evidence for the Law Enforcement Officer*, 2d ed. (New York: McGraw-Hill, 1974), p. 128.

24. *See* Stuckey, *Evidence for the Law Enforcement Officer*, pp. 130–49, for a brief description of each category.

25. *Ibid.*, pp. 129–30.

26. Rutter, *Evidence*, p. 72.

27. Anthony M. Golec, *Techniques of Legal Investigation* (Springfield, Ill.: Charles C Thomas, 1976), pp. 53–54.

28. F. Lee Bailey and Henry B. Rothblatt, *Fundamentals of Criminal Advocacy* (Rochester: Lawyers Co-operative Publishing Company, 1974), p. 123.

29. Stuckey, *Evidence for the Law Enforcement Officer*, p. 210.

30. Rutter, *Evidence*, p. 25.

31. Golec, *Techniques of Legal Investigation*, pp. 260–61.

32. Rutter, *Evidence*, pp. 115–16.

33. *Ibid.*, p. 116; and Stuckey, *Evidence for the Law Enforcement Officer*, p. 259.

34. Golec, *Techniques of Legal Investigation*, p. 92; and Stuckey, *Evidence for the Law Enforcement Officer*, p. 296.

35. Stuckey, *Evidence for the Law Enforcement Officer*, p. 288.

36. Bailey and Rothblatt, *Fundamentals of Criminal Advocacy*, p. 56.

37. Golec, *Techniques of Legal Investigation*, p. 191.

38. Harry M. Philo, Dean A. Robb, and Richard M. Goodman, *Lawyers' Desk Reference: Technical Sources for Conducting a Personal Injury Action*, 5th ed. (Rochester: Lawyers Co-operative Publishing Company, 1975), supplemented annually. This handy reference also has information about relevant industry standards and various other background sources.

39. Golec, *Techniques of Legal Investigation*, p. 211.

40. *Ibid.*, p. 216.

41. *Ibid.*, p. 58.

42. *Ibid.*, p. 81.

43. Bailey and Rothblatt, *Fundamentals of Criminal Advocacy*, p. 105.

44. Golec, *Techniques of Legal Investigation*, p. 71.

45. *Ibid.*, p. 84.

46. *Ibid.*, p. 76.

47. Bailey and Rothblatt, *Fundamentals of Criminal Advocacy*, p. 99.

48. *Ibid.*, p. 100.

49. *Ibid.*, p. 99.

50. Golec, *Techniques of Legal Investigation*, pp. 61 and 62.

51. 5 USCA §552.

52. Philo, Robb, and Goodman, *Lawyers' Desk Reference: Technical Sources for Conducting a Personal Injury Action*.

PART III

FINDING
THE
LAW

As stated in the introduction to Part II, the resolution of a legal conflict involves the application of general principles of law to a specific set of facts. Whereas Part II discussed how paralegals gather the facts, this part will focus on the process of finding and analyzing the law.

The presentation of such materials usually begins with an overview of the resources located in a law library followed by an analysis of the contents of each specific set of reference books. This text, however, is organized to give the researcher a thorough understanding of the legal reasoning process before beginning to discuss the maze of encyclopedias, digests, and citators that make up only a small portion of a law library.

Chapter 5 focuses on case law. It examines the doctrine of *stare decisis* and the reasoning used to apply it. The chapter also explains where law cases are located and how they should be analyzed.

Chapter 6 looks at statutory, administrative, and constitutional law. In contrasting the legal reasoning processes involved it helps the reader to find and analyze constitutions, statutes, and administrative regulations. Special attention is paid to the various rules of construction that courts tend to use when interpreting these documents.

Chapter 7 introduces the various secondary sourcebooks found in most law libraries. These resources are discussed in the order of possible use in solving a legal research problem. The chapter presents the types of materials contained in these diverse volumes and offers methods for developing an effective legal research strategy. Since the final stage of the research process involves reporting the results, the last section of the chapter contains a legal memorandum format for analyzing and reporting research.

CHAPTER 5

Case
Law

In chapter 1 we discussed the fact that legislators, administrators, and judges had lawmaking authority and that the law therefore can be divided into constitutional law, statutory law, administrative law, and common law. These different types of law appear in different forms and in various resource books but are ultimately given their practical meaning by judges deciding specific court cases. If there is any question on the meaning of a particular statute or constitutional provision, the courts decide the binding interpretation. For this reason we will begin our analysis of how to find the law with an examination of published court opinions, and through these opinions we will begin to study the legal reasoning process.

FINDING THE CASE

Case Reporters

Generally the decisions of trial courts are summarily recorded in the official case file and then stored at the local courthouse. While the decision is of great consequence to the parties involved, it usually has little significance for others.* The decisions of appellate courts, on the other hand, usually involve legal issues rather than factual issues and are ordinarily accompanied by a detailed justification for the court's decision. Since these decisions have precedent value,† it is important that they be made more readily available to the general legal community. In order to accomplish this, they are published in "case reporters."

Case reporters, consisting of hundreds of volumes, are books that contain copies of the court's opinions. They are usually arranged in chronological order and divided into volumes according to the court that rendered the opinion. Thus, opinions of the United States District Courts are found in the *Federal Supplement* while opinions from the United States Court of Appeals are in the *Federal Reporter*.

West Publishing Company is the major publisher of case reporters, and the West National Reporter System covers all appellate court decisions in the fifty states. The complete West system is briefly described in Table 5.1.

In addition to being reported by West, the decisions of selected courts are also recorded by the federal government, many states, and other private publishing houses. The federal government publishes United States Supreme Court cases in the *United States Supreme Court Reports*, while the Lawyers' Co-operative Publishing Company prints the *United States Supreme Court Reports, Lawyers' Edition*. Both, like West's *Supreme Court Reporter*, publish the complete opinions of the United States Supreme Court.‡ Several of the more commonly used case reporters are listed in Table 5.2.

Reporters are divided into official and unofficial categories. They are official when published at the direction of state or federal statutes. All others are unofficial. Since the opinions published in the unofficial reporters are the same as those in the

---

*There are occasions where trial courts (especially United States District Courts) will produce opinions involving significant legal issues. When these opinions are produced they are published in the same manner as are the appellate court decisions.

†The term precedent will be explained in more detail shortly. For now it means the court's decision may be considered a factor in determining the interpretation of the law in another case.

‡United States Supreme Court opinions can also be found in a looseleaf service entitled *United States Law Week*.

FIGURE 5.1
Analysis of Case Citations

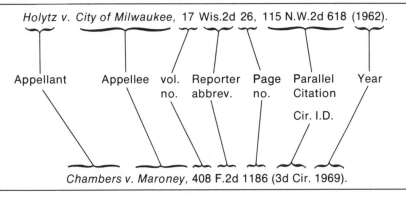

official ones, either can be used. However, when citing the case in briefs or other legal documents, the official citation should be stated first. While states differ as to the precedent value of decisions that are only published in unofficial reporters, most lawyers routinely include such citations when presenting their cases.

Case Citations

The legal citation is a way of referencing a case so that others will be able to find it, so care should be taken to always include the appropriate citation when making reference to a court case. The basic rules of case citation are discussed below. When difficult questions arise, one should consult the most recent edition of the *Harvard Citator* for a complete explanation of how to handle problems.[1]

Carefully examine Figure 5.1. Note that the citation begins with an abbreviated version of the names of the parties to the litigation. In the first case Janet Holytz, a minor, brought an appeal from a lower court decision that favored the City of Milwaukee. The party bringing the appeal (the appellant or petitioner) is usually listed first while the opposing side (the appellee or respondent) is listed second.* In the second example,

---

*Some states follow the practice of listing the name of the original plaintiff first no matter which party is bringing the appeal.

TABLE 5.1
West Case Reporters

Name of Case Reporter	Abbreviation	Courts Covered
Supreme Court Reporter	S. Ct.	U.S. Supreme Court
Federal Reporter	F.	U.S. Circuit Courts,
Federal Reporter, Second Series	F.2d	District Courts prior to 1932, and some specialized federal courts such as Court of Claims and Customs and Patent Appeals
Federal Supplement	F. Supp.	U.S. District Courts since 1932 and some decisions of Customs Court and Court of Claims
Federal Rules Decisions	F.R.D.	U.S. District Court Opinions involving Federal Rules of Civil Procedure and Federal Rules of Criminal Procedure
Atlantic Reporter	A.	State courts in Conn.,
Atlantic Reporter, Second Series	A.2d	Dela., Maine, Maryland, N.H., N.J., Penn., R.I., Vermont, and District of Columbia Municipal Court of Appeals
North Eastern Reporter	N.E.	State courts in Ill.,
North Eastern Reporter, Second Series	N.E.2d	Ind., Mass., N.Y., and Ohio
North Western Reporter	N.W.	State court cases in
North Western Reporter, Second Series	N.W.2d	Iowa, Mich., Minn., Nebr., N.D., S.D., and Wis.
Pacific Reporter	P.	State court cases in

Name of Case Reporter	Abbreviation	Courts Covered
Pacific Reporter, Second Series	P.2d	Alaska, Arizona, Calif., Colorado, Hawaii, Idaho, Kansas, Mont., Nevada, N.M., Okla., Oregon, Utah, Wash., and Wyo.
South Eastern Reporter	S.E.	State court cases in
South Eastern Reporter, Second Series	S.E.2d	Georgia, No. Car., So. Car., Va., and W.Va.
South Western Reporter	S.W.	State court cases in
South Western Reporter, Second Series	S.W.2d	Ark., Ky., Mo., Tenn., and Texas; also has cases from Indian territories
Southern Reporter	So.	State court cases in
Southern Reporter, Second Series	So.2d	Alabama, Georgia, La., and Miss.
New York Supplement	N.Y.S.	State court cases from
New York Supplement, Second Series	N.Y.S.2d	the state of New York
California Reporter	Cal.Rptr.	State court decisions from California

Frank Chambers is appealing a conviction for robbery by asking for a writ of habeas corpus against James F. Maroney, Superintendent of the State Correctional Institution.* (The party responsible for bringing the case to the court in question is usually listed first. This may or may not be the party who originated the litigation at the trial level.)

*The seeking of a writ of habeas corpus is a procedure in which the prisoner attempts to show the court that he is being held illegally by agents of the state. In instances such as this one it is a means of obtaining a federal court examination of the validity of a state criminal conviction.

TABLE 5.2

Commonly Used Case Reports Not Published by West

Name of Case Reporter	Abbreviation	Courts Covered
United States Supreme Court Reports	U.S.	U.S. Supreme Court
Lawyers' Edition, United States Supreme Court Reports	L.Ed.	U.S. Supreme Court
Lawyers' Edition, United States Supreme Court Reports, Second Series	L.Ed.2d.	U.S. Supreme Court
Court of Claims	Ct.Cl.	U.S. Court of Claims
Court of Customs and Patent Appeals Reports	C.C.P.A.	Court of Customs and Patent Appeals Customs Court
Customs Court Reports	Cust.Ct.	Customs Court
Federal Communications Commission Reports[a]	F.C.C.	Federal Communications Commission Decisions
Illinois Reports[b]	Ill.	Illinois Supreme
Illinois Reports, Second Series	Ill.2d	Court

This information is usually printed in prominent letters at the very beginning of the case. In determining the format for the first part of the citation, the major problem usually centers around which parts of the title should be omitted from the citation. As you can see above, the first names and initials of individuals are omitted. Frank Chambers v. James F. Maroney becomes simply *Chambers v. Maroney.* Maroney's title as superintendent of the State Correctional Institution is also omitted. On the other hand, first names or initials that are part of corporate names are included (e.g., *Williams v. D. L. Lewis & Co.*). The case name is always italic and common abbreviations such as Co., Bd., Inc., and Nat'l. can be used to shorten the title.

When there is more than one party on any side or when several

Name of Case Reporter	Abbreviation	Courts Covered
Illinois Appellate Court Reports	Ill.App.	Illinois Appellate Courts
Illinois Appellate Court Reports, Second Series	Ill.App.2d	Illinois Appellate Courts
Pennsylvania District and County Reports[b]	Pa.D.&C.	Pennsylvania District and County
Pennsylvania District and County Reports, Second Series	Pa.D.&C.2d	Courts
Pennsylvania State Reports	Pa.	Pennsylvania Courts not covered in other Case Reporters
Pennsylvania Superior Court Reports	Pa.Super.	Pennsylvania Superior Court

[a]This is simply one of several similar reports related to different regulatory agencies. The abbreviation corresponds to the agency.

[b]These are used to illustrate the pattern found in states that publish their own court opinions. Other states have similar names for their reporters.

cases have been consolidated, the citation only uses the names of the first parties listed on each side or the first case listed. When the state is a party to a case in its own courts, it is usually listed as *People v.* or *State v.* On the other hand, if a state is a party to a suit in federal court, the listing would be *Illinois v.*

Questions about what names to use in the title can often be resolved by consulting the table of cases at the front of the case reporter or by referring to the top of subsequent pages to see how the editors of the reporter abbreviated the cases.

Look back to the two examples given near the beginning of this section and note the use of abbreviations for case reporters. Table 5.1 shows that F.2d stands for the *Federal Reporter, Second Series,* and that N.W.2d stands for *North Western Reporter, Second Series.* The Wis.2d is similar to the Ill.2d used in Table 5.2. The use of these abbreviations tells the reader that *Holytz v. City of Milwaukee* can be found in both the *Wisconsin Reports, Second Series,* and the *North Western Reporter, Second Series.* *Chambers v. Maroney* can be found in the *Federal Reporter, Second Series.*

The numbers immediately in front of the reporter abbreviation stand for the number of the volume in which the case is found. The numbers immediately after the reporter abbreviation stand for the page number on which the case begins. Thus it can be seen that *Holytz v. City of Milwaukee* can be found both on page 26 of volume 17 of *Wisconsin Reports, Second Series,* and on page 618 of volume 115 of the *North Western Reporter, Second Series.* When two such citations are given for the same case they are referred to as parallel citations. Additional examples of parallel citations are:

> *Chambers v. Maroney,* 399 U.S. 42, 90 S. Ct. 1975, 26 L.Ed.2d 419 (1970).

> *McPherson v. Buick Motor Co.,* 217 N.Y. 282, 111 N.E. 1050 (Ct. App. 1916).

Following the identification of the volume and page of the reporters, the year in which the decision was rendered will appear in parentheses. *Holytz* was decided in 1962 and *Chambers* in 1969. In those cases where the identification of the court is not obvious from the type of reporter involved, there will be additional information about the court in parentheses. In the *Holytz* case a discerning reader can tell that the Wisconsin Supreme Court made the decision because only Supreme Court decisions from that state are published in *Wisconsin Reports.* In the *Chambers* case one can tell it is a decision from a United States Court of Appeals because it appears in the *Federal Reporter.* Note that information on which circuit was involved is included in the parentheses with the year. Table 5.3 explains some of the common abbreviations used to indicate the appropriate courts.

Up to this point the citations given have been for the case itself so the key page number given is the page on which the case begins. Sometimes a writer will make reference to a specific part of the court decision where a particular quote appears or where an issue is discussed. In these instances a second page number will appear after the page number on which the case begins; for

TABLE 5.3
Abbreviations for Courts

Abbreviation	Interpretation
(6th Cir. 1978)	Case was decided in the 6th Circuit in 1978
(D.C. Cir. 1972)	Case was decided in the Washington, D.C. Circuit in 1972
(D.C.R.I. 1969)	Case was decided in District Court of Rhode Island in 1969
(N.D.Ill. 1971)	Case was decided in District Court for the Northern District of Illinois in 1971
(Cal. 1952)	Case was decided in the California Supreme Court in 1952
(Ill. App. 1946)	Case was decided in the Illinois Appellate Courts in 1946

example, a quotation taken from page 1,189 of the *Chambers v. Maroney* decision would be cited as follows:

Chambers v. Maroney, 408 F.2d 1186, 1189 (3d Cir. 1969).

Sometimes citations will include information about prior or subsequent history of the case. For example:

Telex Corp. v. International Business Machines Corp., 367 F. Supp. 258 (N.D. Okl. 1973), 510 F.2d 894 (10th Cir. 1975), *cert. denied* 423 U.S. 802 (1975).

This citation indicates that the case was first decided by the Federal District Court for the Northern District of Oklahoma and can be found in volume 367 of the *Federal Supplement* beginning on page 258. The case was then appealed to the 10th Circuit where the decision is reported in volume 510 of the *Federal Reporter, Second Series*. The United States Supreme Court's decision not to grant *certiorari* is reported on page 802 of volume 423 of the *United States Supreme Court Reports*.

INTERPRETING COURT DECISIONS

Now we will turn our attention to the interpretation of court decisions, illustrated by United States Supreme Court's opinion in *Chambers v. Maroney*. This opinion was selected because it illustrates the elements of a typical decision and, in conjunction with *Texas v. White,* shows the amount of flexibility that courts can exercise in determining the precedent value of a specific case.* The identification of the basic elements, of course, applies to all written opinions.

The Case

Chambers v. Maroney

399 U.S. 42, 90 S. Ct. 1975 (1970)

Mr. Justice White delivered the opinion of the Court.

Issue The principal question in this case concerns the admissibility of evidence seized from an automobile, in which petitioner was riding at the time of his arrest, after the automobile was taken to a police station and was there *Judicial* thoroughly searched without a warrant. The Court of Appeals *History* for the Third Circuit found no violation of petitioner's Fourth *Disposition* Amendment rights. We affirm.

I

Facts During the night of May 20, 1963, a Gulf service station in North Braddock, Pennsylvania, was robbed by two men, each of whom carried and displayed a gun. The robbers took the currency from the cash register; the service station attendant, one Stephen Kovacich, was directed to place the coins in his right-hand glove, which was then taken by the robbers. Two teen-agers, who had earlier noticed a blue compact station wagon circling the block in the vicinity of the Gulf station, then saw the station wagon speed away from a parking lot close to the Gulf station. About the same time, they learned that the Gulf station had been robbed. They reported to police, who arrived immediately, that four men were in the station wagon and one was wearing a green sweater. Kovacich told the police that one of the men who robbed him

*See pages 160–170.

Facts

was wearing a green sweater and the other was wearing a trench coat. A description of the car and the two robbers was broadcast over the police radio. Within an hour, a light blue compact station wagon answering the description and carrying four men was stopped by the police about two miles from the Gulf station. Petitioner was one of the men in the station wagon. He was wearing a green sweater and there was a trench coat in the car. The occupants were arrested and the car was driven to the police station. In the course of a thorough search of the car at the station, the police found concealed in a compartment under the dashboard two .38–caliber revolvers (one loaded with dumdum bullets), a right-hand glove containing small change, and certain cards bearing the name of Raymond Havicon, the attendant at a Boron service station in McKeesport, Pennsylvania, who had been robbed at gunpoint on May 13, 1963. In the course of a warrant–authorized search of petitioner's home the day after petitioner's arrest, police found and seized certain .38–caliber ammunition, including some dumdum bullets similar to those found in one of the guns taken from the station wagon.

Judicial History

Petitioner was indicted for both robberies. His first trial ended in a mistrial but he was convicted of both robberies at the second trial. Both Kovacich and Havicon identified petitioner as one of the robbers. The materials taken from the station wagon were introduced into evidence, Kovacich identifying his glove and Havicon the cards taken in the May 13 robbery. The bullets seized at petitioner's house were also introduced over objections of petitioner's counsel. Petitioner was sentenced to a term of four to eight years' imprisonment for the May 13 robbery and to a term of two to seven years' imprisonment for the May 20 robbery, the sentences to run consecutively. Petitioner did not take a direct appeal from these convictions. In 1965, petitioner sought a writ of habeas corpus in the state court, which denied the writ after a brief evidentiary hearing; the denial of the writ was affirmed on appeal in the Pennsylvania appellate courts. Habeas corpus proceedings were then commenced in the United States District Court for the Western District of Pennsylvania. An order to show cause was issued. Based on the State's reponse and the state court record, the petition for habeas corpus was denied without a hearing. The Court of Appeals for the Third Circuit affirmed, 408 F.2d 1186 and we granted *certiorari,* 396 U.S. 900, 90 S. Ct. 225, 24 L.Ed.2d 177 (1969).

II

Decision

We pass quickly the claim that the search of the automobile was the fruit of an unlawful arrest. Both the courts below thought the arresting officers had probable cause to make the arrest. We agree. Having talked to the teen-age observers and to the victim Kovacich, the police had ample cause to stop a light blue compact station wagon carrying four men and to arrest the occupants, one of whom was wearing a green sweater and one of whom had a trench coat with him in the car.

Even so, the search that produced the incriminating evidence was made at the police station some time after the arrest and cannot be justified as a search incident to an arrest: "Once an accused is under arrest and in custody, then a search made at another place, without a warrant, is simply not incident to the arrest." *Preston v. United States,* 376 U.S. 364, 367, 84 S. Ct. 881, 883, 11 L.Ed.2d 777 (1964). *Dyke v. Taylor Implement Mfg. Co.,* 391 U.S. 216, 88 S. Ct. 1472, 20 L.Ed.2d 538 (1968), is to the same effect; the reasons that have been thought sufficient to justify warrantless searches carried out in connection with an arrest no longer obtain when the accused is safely in custody at the station house.

Reasoning

There are, however, alternative grounds arguably justifying the search of the car in this case. In *Preston, supra,* the arrest was for vagrancy; it was apparent that the officers had no cause to believe that evidence of crime was concealed in the auto. In *Dyke, supra,* the Court expressly rejected the suggestion that there was probable cause to search the car, 391 U.S., at 221–222, 88 S. Ct. 1475–1476. Here the situation is different, for the police had probable cause to believe that the robbers, carrying guns and the fruits of the crime, had fled the scene in a light blue compact station wagon which would be carrying four men, one wearing a green sweater and another wearing a trench coat. As the state courts correctly held, there was probable cause to arrest the occupants of the station wagon that the officers stopped; just as obviously was there probable cause to search the car for guns and stolen money.

In terms of the circumstances justifying a warrantless search, the Court has long distinguished between an automobile and a home or office. In *Carroll v. United States,* 267 U.S. 132, 45 S. Ct. 280, 69 L.Ed. 453 (1925), the issue was the admissibility in evidence of contraband liquor seized in a warrantless search of a car on the highway. After surveying the law from the time of the adoption of the Fourth Amendment onward, the Court held that automobiles and other conveyances may be searched without a warrant in circumstances that would not justify the search without a warrant of a house or an office, provided that there is probable cause to believe that the car contains articles that the officers are entitled to seize . . . .

Neither *Carroll, supra,* nor other cases in this Court require or suggest that in every conceivable circumstance the search of an auto even with probable cause may be made without the extra protection for privacy that a warrant affords. But the circumstances that furnish probable cause to search a particular auto for particular articles are most often unforeseeable; moreover, the opportunity to search is fleeting since a car is readily movable. Where this is true, as in *Carroll* and the case before us now, if an effective search is to be made at any time, either the search must be made immediately without a warrant or the car itself must be seized and held without a warrant for whatever period is necessary to obtain a warrant for the search.

Reasoning

In enforcing the Fourth Amendment's prohibition against unreasonable searches and seizures, the Court has insisted upon probable cause as a minimum requirement for a reasonable search permitted by the Constitution. As a general rule, it has also required the judgment of a magistrate on the probable-cause issue and the issuance of a warrant before a search is made. Only in exigent circumstances will the judgment of the police as to probable cause serve as a sufficient authorization for a search. *Carroll, supra,* holds a search warrant unnecessary where there is probable cause to search an automobile stopped on the highway; the car is movable, the occupants are alerted, and the car's contents may never be found again if a warrant must be obtained. Hence an immediate search is constitutionally permissible.

Arguably, because of the preference for a magistrate's judgment, only the immobilization of the car should be permitted until a search warrant is obtained; arguably, only the "lesser" intrusion is permissible until the magistrate authorizes the "greater." But which is the "greater" and which the "lesser" intrusion is itself a debatable question and the answer may depend on a variety of circumstances. For constitutional purposes, we see no difference between on the

Reasoning

one hand seizing and holding a car before presenting the probable cause issue to a magistrate and on the other hand carrying out an immediate search without a warrant. Given probable cause to search, either course is reasonable under the Fourth Amendment.

On the facts before us, the blue station wagon could have been searched on the spot when it was stopped since there was probable cause to search and it was a fleeting target for a search. The probable-cause factor still obtained at the station house and so did the mobility of the car unless the Fourth Amendment permits a warrantless seizure of the car and the denial of its use to anyone until a warrant is secured. In that event there is little to choose in terms of practical consequences between an immediate search without a warrant and the car's immobilization until a warrant is obtained. [It was not unreasonable in this case to take the car to the station house. All occupants in the car were arrested in a dark parking lot in the middle of the night. A careful search at that point was impractical and perhaps not safe for the officers, and it would serve the owner's convenience and the safety of his car to have the vehicle and the keys together at the station house.] The same consequences may not follow where there is unforeseeable cause to search a house. Compare *Vale v. Louisiana, ante,* 399 U.S. 30, 90 S. Ct. 1969, 26 L.Ed. 409. But as *Carroll, supra,* held, for the purposes of the Fourth Amendment there is a constitutional difference between houses and cars.

III

Decision

Neither of petitioner's remaining contentions warrants reversal of the judgment of the Court of Appeals. One of them

Issue

challenges the admissibility at trial of the .38-caliber ammunition seized in the course of a search of petitioner's house.

Reasoning

The circumstances relevant to this issue are somewhat confused, involving as they do questions of probable cause, a lost search warrant, and the Pennsylvania procedure for challenging the admissibility of evidence seized. Both the District Court and the Court of Appeals, however, after careful examination of the record, found that if there was error in admitting the ammunition, the error was harmless beyond a reasonable doubt. Having ourselves studied this record, we are not prepared to differ with the two courts below. See *Harrington v. California,* 395 U.S. 250, 89 S. Ct. 1726, 23 L.Ed.2d 284 (1969).

Issue

The final claim is that petitioner was not afforded the effective assistance of counsel. The facts pertinent to this claim

Facts

are these: The Legal Aid Society of Allegheny County was appointed to represent petitioner prior to his first trial. A representative of the society conferred with petitioner, and a member of its staff, Mr. Middleman, appeared for petitioner at the first trial. There is no claim that petitioner was not then adequately represented by fully prepared counsel. The difficulty arises out of the second trial. Apparently no one from the Legal Aid Society again conferred with petitioner until a few minutes before the second trial began. The attorney who then appeared to represent petitioner was not Mr. Middleman but Mr. Tamburo, another Legal Aid Society attorney. No charge is made that Mr. Tamburo was incompetent or inexperienced; rather the claim is that his appearance for petitioner was so belated that he could not have furnished effective legal assistance at the second trial. Without granting

Judicial History

an evidentiary hearing, the District Court rejected petitioner's claim. The Court of Appeals dealt with the matter in an extensive opinion. After carefully examining the state court record, which it had before it, the court found ample grounds for holding that the appearance of a different attorney at the second trial had not resulted in prejudice to petitioner. The

Reasoning

claim that Mr. Tamburo was unprepared centered around his allegedly inadequate efforts to have the guns and ammunition excluded from evidence. But the Court of Appeals found harmless any error in the admission of the bullets and ruled that the guns and other materials seized from the car were admissible evidence. Hence the claim of prejudice from the substitution of counsel was without substantial basis. In this posture of the case we are not inclined to disturb the judgment of the Court of Appeals as to what the state record shows with respect to the adequacy of counsel. Unquestionably, the courts should make every effort to effect early appointments of counsel in all cases. But we are not disposed to

Decision

fashion a *per se* ruling requiring reversal of every conviction following tardy appointment of counsel or to hold that, whenever a habeas corpus petition alleges a belated appointment, an evidentiary hearing must be held to determine whether the defendant has been denied his constitutional right to counsel. The Court of Appeals reached the right result in denying a hearing in this case.

Disposition

Affirmed.

The Facts

Under the principle of standing, courts are not supposed to decide abstract issues or render advisory opinions. Rather, they are supposed to decide cases that involve litigants who are personally affected by their decision. As discussed later in this chapter, the development of legal rules is tied to the court's decisions in specific cases. It is therefore essential that a case analysis begin with a thorough understanding of the facts.

In approaching a civil case the paralegal should ask the following types of questions: Who was the original plaintiff (the person who first brought the matter to court)? Who was the original defendant? If the plaintiff claims to have been injured by the defendant's actions, in what manner is this alleged injury to have taken place? What is the nature of the injury? What is the plaintiff asking the court to do about it? In criminal cases, questions should include: Who is the defendant? What is the nature of the alleged criminal activity? What governmental unit is undertaking the prosecution? What methods were employed by the police in obtaining the evidence used against the defendant? Was the trial conducted in accordance with the requirements of the due process clause?*

In *Chambers v. Maroney*, the state prosecuted Chambers for robbery because two witnesses identified him and the police found incriminating evidence in searches of the car in which he was riding and in his home. The police stopped the automobile because it matched the description of one seen at the robbery and because two of its occupants matched descriptions of the robbers. After arresting Chambers and three other suspects in a dark parking lot in the middle of the night, the police drove the auto to the station. They searched it at the police station, without a search warrant, and found two revolvers and property belonging to a robbery victim in a concealed compartment under the dashboard. They also discovered and seized ammunition that fitted the confiscated revolvers when they conducted a warrant-authorized search of Chambers's home the next day.

---

*This listing of questions is intended to be illustrative rather than exhaustive. Additional questions may need to be raised in the context of a specific case.

The incriminating evidence from both searches was used against Chambers at his trial. At both of his trials Chambers was represented by lawyers from the Legal Aid Society but by different individuals each time and he did not have the opportunity to confer with his attorney in the second trial until minutes before the trial began.

In analyzing the facts of a case, the paralegal must be sure to identify all the *relevant* facts; that is, the facts that are so essential to the court's decision that if they were to be changed the court's decision might also change. For example, the fact that Chambers was wearing a green sweater rather than a blue one would not ordinarily be important. In this case, however, it is important because his clothing matched that given in the description of the robber. The matching of the descriptions of the car and passengers establishes the probable cause used to justify the arrests and searches. On the other hand, there is nothing relevant about the description of the police who stopped them. Sometimes it is not clear whether or not a particular fact is essential to the decision. In this case, it is not altogether clear if it is important that the suspects were arrested in a dark parking lot at night.

The Judicial History

In addition to analyzing the facts that brought on the litigation in a specific case, the paralegal should analyze the manner in which other courts or administrative bodies have handled the same type of case. Since published opinions are usually the product of appellate courts, information is normally available about action taken by the trial court. If such a case was handled by a higher level appellate court, there will also be information about how lower level appellate courts disposed of the case.

In *Chambers v. Maroney*, the defendant's first trial ended in a mistrial while his second ended with his conviction for two robberies because the trial judge allowed the state to introduce the evidence found in the automobile and in the house. In 1965 Chambers sought but was denied a writ of habeas corpus in the state court. The Pennsylvania appellate courts affirmed the lower court's decision. Then Chambers began habeas corpus proceedings in the United States District Court, but the district court denied the petition and the court of appeals affirmed. The U.S. Supreme Court then granted *certiorari.**

The Issues

When a party takes a dispute to the courts, that party may be asking the court to resolve differences of opinion about the facts of the case and the meaning of the law.

These two types of disputes are called the issues of the case. The dispute that involves an event which is supposed to have taken place is an issue of fact. The dispute that involves the meaning or application of the law is a legal issue. While the appellate courts usually accept the trial court's interpretation of the facts there are occasions when appellate courts do make their own judgment concerning factual disputes.

Chambers raised several issues in his appeal: Did the police have probable cause to stop the auto and arrest the occupants? At the police station, did the police have a legal right to search the car Chambers was riding in without obtaining a search warrant first? If the trial court had improperly allowed the evidence seized in his home to be admitted, would it have had a harmful effect on the outcome of the trial? Did the defendant receive adequate counsel?

The Decision

Court opinions are useful because they indicate how the court decided the issues raised in a given case. The process of resolving the issues of fact in a case is usually not important to anyone beyond the parties of that case, but resolution of the legal issues can be quite significant for many others faced with similar situations. Under the precedent system used in United States courts, the legal interpretations of some courts can be binding on the decisions of other courts, and where the interpretations are not binding they may nevertheless be quite persuasive. Because

*The granting of a *writ of certiorari* means the Supreme Court agrees to review a case.

lawyers who wish to advise a client on the legality of a particular action need to determine the manner in which a previous decision might be applied, the court decision should be analyzed at two different levels: How was the issue settled in this particular case? What general principle of law has been enunciated by the way in which the court resolved this issue?

In the *Chambers* case we see the court ruled that the police did have probable cause to stop the automobile and arrest the occupants. The court also ruled that the police had a legal right to search the car at the station without first obtaining a search warrant. With respect to the admission of the ammunition found in the search of Chambers's home, the court concluded that even if there had been an error in admitting it, the error was harmless.* Finally, the court ruled that Chambers was not denied adequate assistance of counsel merely because he did not have an opportunity to confer with his legal aid lawyer until a few minutes before his second trial.

But what is the significance of the court's decision for future defendants? What general principles of law emerge that are likely to be applied to future cases? The answers to these questions are usually presented in the form of a holding. The holding is a statement that the law is to be interpreted in a certain way when a given set of facts exists. In order to better understand the scope of the holding it is necessary to explain the *ratio decidendi* and the *obiter dictum*. The *ratio decidendi* is a decision on the legal issues of a specific case that the judge has proper authority to decide. *Dictum* refers to comments the judge makes that are not necessary to the resolution of the issues of the case and are in effect a discussion of a hypothetical situation.

In the *Chambers* case one finds that the holding derived from the first issue is a very narrow one: When police observe an automobile matching the description of one seen circling and then speeding away from the scene of a robbery, and when police observe that the automobile contains two men who are wearing clothing that fits the description of clothing being worn by the robbers, then there is probable cause for the police to stop the automobile and arrest the occupants. Note that in stating the hold-

---

*Note the placement of the word "if." The court is not in fact deciding that the evidence was improperly admitted but it is saying that it would not make any difference. If it had been improperly admitted, the nature of the error was not great enough to affect the trial's outcome.

ing, the right to stop and arrest is clearly tied to the fact that the automobile and its occupants fit the descriptions of the auto at the scene of the robbery and of the robbers themselves.

It is difficult to formulate a holding for the second issue. The court says that the police in the *Chambers* case did have the right to search the auto without a warrant at the police station. The question is whether the court means to give the police the right to search an auto back at the station any time they have probable cause to search it at the scene of the arrest, or if the power to search it (without a warrant) back at the station only applies in situations (like this one) in which the auto is stopped in a dark parking lot at night. Five years after this case, in *Texas v. White*,[2] the justices of the Supreme Court argued among themselves as to the holding in *Chambers v. Maroney*. In a *per curiam* opinion* the court declared: "In *Chambers v. Maroney* we held that police officers with probable cause to search an automobile on the scene where it was stopped could constitutionally do so later at the station house without first obtaining a warrant."[3] However, Justices Marshall and Brennan argued in dissent that the majority misstated the true holding of the *Chambers* case.

> Only by misstating the holding of *Chambers v. Maroney,* 399 U.S. 42, 90 S. Ct. 1,975, 26 L.Ed.2d 419 (1970), can the Court make that case appear dispositive of this one. The Court in its brief *per curiam* opinion today extends *Chambers* to a clearly distinguishable factual setting, without having afforded the opportunity for full briefing and oral argument. . . .
>
> *Chambers* did not hold, as the Court suggests, "that police officers with probable cause to search an automobile on the scene where it was stopped could constitutionally do so later at the station house without first obtaining a warrant." . . . *Chambers* simply held that to be the rule when it is reasonable to take the car to the station house in the first place. . . . The Court in *Chambers* went on to hold that once the car was legitimately at the station house a prompt search could be conducted. But in recognition of the need to justify the seizure and removal of the car to the station house, the Court added:
>
>> "It was not unreasonable in this case to take the car to the station house. All occupants in the car were arrested in a dark

*This is a decision of the court in which the author is not identified. The form is usually used in short summary decisions.

parking lot in the middle of the night. A careful search at that point was impractical and perhaps not safe for the officers, and it would serve the owner's convenience and the safety of his car to have the vehicle and the keys together at the station house." *Id.*, at 52 n. 10, 90 S. Ct., at 1981.

In this case, the arrest took place at 1:30 in the afternoon, and there is no indication that an immediate search would have been either impractical or unsafe for the arresting officers. It may be, of course, that respondent preferred to have his car brought to the station house, but if his convenience was the concern of the police they should have consulted with him. Surely a seizure cannot be justified on the sole ground that a citizen might have consented to it as a matter of convenience. Since, then, there was no apparent justification for the warrantless removal of respondent's car, it is clear that this is a different case from *Chambers.*[4]

It is wise for the paralegal to utilize the more narrow of two competing holdings when analyzing a case but to remember that courts may adopt a broader interpretation at a later date.

The court's response to the third issue presented in the *Chambers* case is a narrow factual judgment concerning the lack of effect a possible error may have had. It does not lend itself to any significant holding.

With regard to the fourth issue, the court holds that the mere fact that an attorney is appointed minutes before a trial starts does not by itself require an evidentiary hearing on the right to counsel issue.

The Reasoning

Most written court opinions devote considerable space to justifying the court's decisions. In the reasoning sections the court usually follows established patterns of legal reasoning and reviews the relevant provisions of the constitution, statutes, and case law, and then relates the thought processes used to arrive at the court's judgment.

In the *Chambers* case the reasoning involves application of several previous cases which interpreted the meaning of the Fourth Amendment search and seizure clause. These patterns of reasoning will be presented in greater detail later in this chapter as well as in chapter 6.

The Disposition

After the court has explicated the relevant facts, stated and decided the issues, and justified its positions, it announces the actual disposition of the case, the next steps in the legal process. These steps usually consist of affirming (approving) or reversing (disapproving) the judgment of the lower court. If the case is affirmed the matter is considered settled, unless either the court that just decided the case changes its mind and grants a motion to reconsider it or a higher level appellate court decides to review it. If the lower court decision is reversed, the appellate court either sends the case back to the lower court to be done over again or substitutes its own judgment for that of the lower court. If it is sent back to the lower court, it is with the understanding that the lower court must act in a way which is not inconsistent with the principles of law the higher court laid down in its decision. If the decision of an intermediate appellate level court is then appealed to a still higher level appellate court, the case is not sent back to the lower level court until the higher court has reached its decision on the appeal.

In the *Chambers* case, the federal district court had denied Chambers's request for a writ of habeas corpus and the appeals court had affirmed that denial. In the decision reprinted here the Supreme Court affirmed the decision of the court of appeals. In the final result, Chambers did not obtain his writ of habeas corpus and must remain in his Pennsylvania prison until the Pennsylvania authorities choose to release him.

If the Supreme Court had supported Chambers's position on the right to counsel issue, it probably would have ordered the district court to hold an evidentiary hearing on the quality of legal assistance Chambers received. If the court had agreed with Chambers's assertion that the search of the automobile had been in violation of the Fourth Amendment, it would have required the Pennsylvania authorities either to grant him a new trial (at which the evidence seized in the search of the auto would not be admitted) or to release him from prison.

Figure 5.2 presents a case brief of *Chambers v. Maroney*. This case brief, which should not be confused with an appellate brief (which is discussed in chapter 10), seeks to isolate and summarize the various elements we have just been discussing.

FIGURE 5.2
A Model Case Brief

Heading:	*Chambers v. Maroney,* 399 U.S. 42, 90 S. Ct. 1975, 26 L.Ed.2d 419 (1970).

Facts: Police stopped an automobile in which Chambers and three others were riding because the auto matched the description of one seen at a recent robbery and because two of the occupants matched descriptions of the robbers. Rather than searching the auto at night in a dark parking lot in a dangerous section of town, the police removed it to the police station where they then searched it without a warrant. This search revealed two revolvers and property belonging to the robbery victim. Police also found and seized ammunition that fit the revolvers when they conducted a warrant-authorized search of Chambers's home the next day. The incriminating evidence seized in both searches was used against Chambers at his trial. At both of his trials, Chambers was represented by lawyers from the Legal Aid Society, but by different individuals each time. He did not have an opportunity to confer with his attorney at the second trial until minutes before the trial began.

Judicial History: Chambers was prosecuted for robbery. After his initial trial ended in a mistrial, he was convicted for two robberies. The trial judge allowed the state to introduce the evidence found in the automobile and in the house. After a Pennsylvania appellate court affirmed a lower state court's denial of a writ of habeas corpus, Chambers commenced this habeas corpus proceeding in the United States District Court. The writ was denied and the Court of Appeals affirmed. The United States Supreme Court then granted *certiorari.*

Specific Issues:

1. Did the police have probable cause to stop defendant's automobile and arrest the occupants? Yes

2. Did the police have a legal right to search defendant's automobile back at the station without having first obtained a search warrant? Yes

3. If the admission of the ammunition found in the search of defendant's house was improper, was it a harmless error? Yes

4. Was the defendant denied adequate assistance by counsel simply because he did not have an opportunity to confer with his second attorney until a few minutes before his second trial? No

(Continued)

FIGURE 5.2 — Continued

Holdings: 1. When police observe an automobile matching the description
of one that was seen circling and then speeding away from
the scene of a robbery, and when police observe that the automobile contains two men who are wearing clothing that fits
the description of clothing being worn by the robbers, then
there is probable cause for the police to stop the automobile
and arrest the occupants.

2. (Narrow interpretation) Police can remove an automobile to
the police station and search it there without a warrant if they
have probable cause to search it at the scene of the stop but
cannot reasonably do so (at night in a dangerous section of
town).

3. (Alternative broader interpretation) Police can search an automobile at the station house without a warrant any time they
have probable cause to search it at the scene of the arrest.

4. The mere fact that an attorney was appointed minutes before
the trial started does not by itself require an evidentiary hearing on the right to counsel issue.

Reasoning: I. Based on information supplied by eyewitnesses, police had
ample cause to stop the automobile.

II. It was not unreasonable to search the auto at the police station because the officers had sufficient probable cause to
have searched it at the scene.

A. *Preston v. United States* and *Dyke v. Taylor Implement
Mfg. Co.* are not applicable here because in those cases
the police lacked probable cause to believe that evidence
of a crime was concealed in the auto.

B. This situation is consistent with *Carroll v. U.S.* in which
police with probable cause could search the auto at the
scene without a warrant.

C. It was not practical for the police to search the vehicle at
the scene of the arrest.

D. The warrantless search at the police station was a lesser
intrusion on the defendant than it would have been if they
had immobilized the car until they could have gotten a
warrant.

III. The record indicates beyond a reasonable doubt that admitting the ammunition found in Chambers's house was harmless error.

IV. While a late appointment of counsel might result in a poor defense in some cases, there is no reason to believe that it did in this particular case or that it would necessarily do so in all cases.

Briefing a case like this often helps in understanding complex cases.

APPLYING COURT DECISIONS

In the American legal system individual case holdings form a basic unit of analysis. This is true not only when the common law is being interpreted but in situations involving statutory and constitutional law as well. Once a court interprets a section of a statute or constitutional provision, that court's interpretation becomes a case precedent which has to be considered in any future interpretations of that same section or provision.

Stare Decisis

Stare decisis is Latin for "Let the decision stand." It means that once a court has established a legal principle, other courts should adhere to that interpretation. *Stare decisis* provides stability and continuity and it allows people to act on the basis of a reasonable assurance that a legal obligation entered into one day will still be enforceable the next. It also ensures that one's legal rights are based on more than the idiosyncrasies of an individual judge.

The principle of *stare decisis* is applied through the use of a legal syllogism, for example:

Major Premise: A landlord cannot withhold a tenant's security deposit for maintenance and repair expenses that result from ordinary wear and tear.

Minor Premise: The dirt on the tenant's carpet was the result of ordinary wear and tear.

Conclusion: The landlord cannot withhold the tenant's security deposit to cover the cost of having the carpet cleaned.

The major premise is supposed to be selected on the basis of *stare decisis*. In other words, once a judge has ruled that a landlord cannot withhold a tenant's security deposit for maintenance and repair expenses that result from ordinary wear and tear, other judges should not substitute a premise which would say that they could.

The key stages in the decision process are the selections of the major and minor premises. The choice of the major premise (the proper *stare decisis* rule) often involves the exercise of a great deal of judicial discretion. The minor premise represents a factual judgment. Once the major and minor premises have been explicated, application of the accepted rules of deductive logic produce the conclusion.

Mandatory and Persuasive Authority

The concept of legal authority is an integral part of the *stare decisis* system. As discussed in chapter 1, there are fifty different state court systems plus a federal court system. Within each of these systems there are higher courts and lower courts, so not all court decisions carry equal weight.

Relevant precedent case decisions are either mandatory authority or persuasive authority. A decision is mandatory authority when it comes from a higher court in the state's own court system (or within the federal court system when it is a federal court deciding the case).* Figure 5.3 indicates the hierarchical nature of mandatory authority. Persuasive authority consists of the decisions of courts which do not constitute mandatory authority as well as the writings of legal scholars. Thus persuasive authority may include decisions of other states, legal encyclopedias, or law review articles. The state statutes and constitution are of course mandatory authority for the courts of that state and they are occasionally used as persuasive authority in other states.

Overturning Precedent

While legal scholars have long extolled the values of *stare decisis*, they have also seen a need for the law to grow with society's

---

*When a federal court is deciding a case involving an interpretation of state law, it must follow the interpretations given by that state's own courts.

changing needs so that courts do not repeat the mistakes of previous courts just because the other decision was rendered first.

In recognition of this need, the precedent system not only gives higher courts the right to reverse the decisions of lower courts, but it also gives courts the right to overrule their own previous decisions. Note how the Wisconsin Supreme Court overruled the common law doctrine of governmental immunity in the case of *Holytz v. City of Milwaukee.* The court emphasizes the extent to

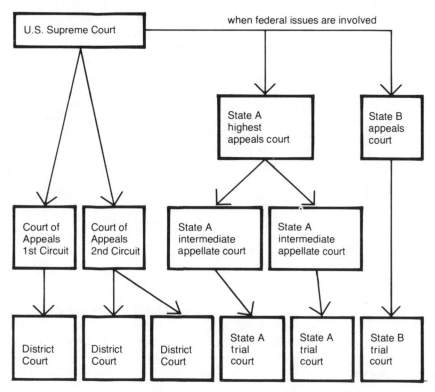

The decisions handed down by the various courts indicated are mandatory authority for the courts below them connected by an arrow. Thus a district court in the first circuit is required to follow the decisions of the court of appeals for the first circuit, but can consider the decisions of the second circuit court of appeals as only advisory. Likewise the decisions of State A's highest appellate court are mandatory authority for State A, but only persuasive authority for State B.

FIGURE 5.3
The Hierarchy of Precedents

which the doctrine of sovereign immunity was developed in a different era and is no longer appropriate.

Holytz v. City of Milwaukee

17 Wis.2d 26, 115 N.W.2d 618 (1962)

Gordon, Justice

The order of the trial court sustaining the respondent's demurrer to the complaint presents an issue with respect to the tort liability of a municipal corporation. The trial court found that on the facts alleged in the complaint the city was entitled to invoke the defense of municipal tort immunity. The appellants urge that the city may not invoke such defense because (a) the drinking fountain and the water meter pit trap door were created and maintained by the city in its proprietary capacity, or (b) the meter contraption constituted a nuisance and at the time the injury occurred the relationship of governor to governed did not exist between Janet Holytz and the city of Milwaukee, or (c) the trap door was an "attractive nuisance" that was not created or maintained by the city in a governmental capacity.

Upon the facts of this case, we consider that the trial judge was correct in his conclusion that, based upon the past decisions of this court, no cause of action was asserted in the complaint. However, we are now prepared to disavow those rulings of this court which have created and preserved the doctrine of governmental immunity from tort claims. This makes it unnecessary that we rest this case on the elusive issues mentioned in the foregoing paragraph; the case turns exclusively on our abrogation of the principle of governmental immunity from tort claims.

. . .

The rule of sovereign immunity developed in this country from an English doctrine and has been applied in the United States far beyond its original conception. The doctrine expanded to the point where the historical sovereignty of kings was relied upon to support a protective prerogative for municipalities. . . .

. . .

There are probably few tenets of American jurisprudence which have been so unanimously berated as the governmental immunity doctrine. This court and the highest courts of numerous other states have been unusually articulate in castigating the existing rule; text writers and law reviews have joined the chorus of denunciators. . . .

. . .

The immunization of municipalities from tort liability has been chipped away by a number of statutes in this state. Some examples are secs. 101.01 and 101.06, Wis. Stats. (safe place statute); sec. 345.05(1) (c) (2) (a), Wis. Stats. (motor vehicle accidents); sec. 270.58, Wis. Stats. (judgments against public officers); and sec. 81.15, Wis. Stats. (highway defects).

. . .

The defendant argues that any change in the municipal immunity doctrine should be addressed to the legislature. We recognize that earlier decisions of this court contemplated precisely that. See *Flamingo v. Waukesha,* 262 Wis. 219, 228, 55 N.W.2d 24 (1952) (concurring opinion); *Britten v. Eau Claire,* 260 Wis. 382, 386, 51 N.W.2d 30 (1951).

Not only have we previously expressed the view that any proposed change should be directed toward the legislature, but we also have expressed the view that the legislature's failure to enact a bill which had been introduced constituted ". . . an expression by the legislature that no change should be made. . . ." *Schwenkhoff v. Farmers Mut. Automobile Ins. Co.,* 6 Wis.2d 44, 47, 93 N.W.2d 867, 869 (1959).

We are satisfied that the governmental immunity doctrine has judicial origins. Upon careful consideration, we are now of the opinion that it is appropriate for this court to abolish this immunity notwithstanding the legislature's failure to adopt corrective enactments. . . .

On the other hand, courts sometimes choose not to overrule their prior decisions even when they admit that they are inconsistent in not doing so. Study the following sections from both the opinion of the court and a dissenting opinion in the most recent of several United States Supreme Court cases on the antitrust status of baseball.

Flood v. Kuhn

407 U.S. 258, 92 S. Ct. 2099, 32 L.Ed.2d 728 (1972)

Mr. Justice Blackmun delivered the opinion of the Court.

. . . Accordingly, we adhere once again to *Federal Baseball* and *Toolson* and to their application to professional baseball. We adhere also to *International Boxing* and *Radovich* and to their respective applications to professional boxing and professional football. If there is any inconsistency or illogic in all this, it is an inconsistency and illogic of long standing that is to be remedied by the Congress and not by this Court. If we were to act otherwise, we would be withdrawing from the conclusion as to congressional intent made in *Toolson* and from the concerns as to retrospectivity therein expressed. Under these circumstances, there is merit in consistency even though some might claim that beneath that consistency is a layer of inconsistency.[5]

. . .

Mr. Justice Marshall, with whom Mr. Justice Brennan joins, dissenting.

We do not lightly overrule our prior constructions of federal statutes, but when our errors deny substantial federal rights, like the right to compete freely and effectively to the best of one's ability as guaranteed by the antitrust laws, we must admit our error and correct it. We have done so before and we should do so again here. See, e.g., *Blonder-Tongue Laboratories, Inc. v. University of Illinois Foundation,* 402 U.S. 313, 91 S. Ct. 1434, 28 L.Ed.2d 788 (1971); *Boys Markets, Inc. v. Retail Clerks Union,* 398 U.S. 235, 241, 90 S. Ct. 1583, 1587, 26 L.Ed.2d 199 (1970).

To the extent that there is concern over any reliance interests that club owners may assert, they can be satisfied by making our decision prospective only. Baseball should be covered by the antitrust laws beginning with this case and henceforth, unless Congress decides otherwise.

Accordingly I would overrule *Federal Baseball Club* and *Toolson* and reverse the decision of the Court of Appeals.[6]

Sidestepping Precedent

Changes in the law are most likely to occur through a process of sidestepping existing precedents and selecting from among several alternate lines of precedents. Since the holding of any given case involves a particular set of facts, a judge can find that since the facts of the case at hand differ from those of the precedent, the rule of law laid down in the precedent case does not apply.

When lawyers are presenting their cases, they attempt to stress how the facts of their cases are similar to those of favorable precedents and different from those of unfavorable precedents. In *Texas v. White,*[7] the state of Texas argued that *Chambers v. Maroney** stood for the principle that whenever the police had the right to conduct a warrantless search of a suspect's automobile at the scene of the arrest, they also had the right to conduct such a warrantless search at the police station. White's lawyers, on the other hand, argued that *Chambers v. Maroney* stood for the principle that police could conduct a warrantless search of an au-

*See pages 163–165.

tomobile back at the station when conditions relating to the safety of the officers and the amount of available light made it impractical to conduct such a search on the scene. White's lawyers argued that since police could have safely searched White's car in the light, the *Chambers* case did not apply to White's situation.

Judge Cardozo's famous decision in *MacPherson v. Buick Motor Co.* demonstrates how the courts can utilize differing precedents. Note especially the way different factual situations are compared and how unfavorable precedents are dismissed.

MacPherson v. Buick Motor Co.

217 N.Y. 282, 111 N.E. 1,050 (Ct. App. 1916)

Cardozo, J. The defendant is a manufacturer of automobiles. It sold an automobile to a retail dealer. The retail dealer resold to the plaintiff. While the plaintiff was in the car it suddenly collapsed. He was thrown out and injured. One of the wheels was made of defective wood, and its spokes crumbled into fragments. The wheel was not made by the defendant; it was bought from another manufacturer. There is evidence, however, that its defects could have been discovered by reasonable inspection, and that inspection was omitted. There is no claim that the defendant knew of the defect and willfully concealed it. The case, in other words, is not brought within the rule of *Kuelling v. Lean Mfg. Co.,* 183 N.Y. 78, 75, N.E. 1,098, 2 L.R.A. (N.S.) 303, 111 Am. St. Rep. 691, 5 Ann. Cas. 124. The charge is one, not of fraud, but of negligence. The question to be determined is whether the defendant owed a duty of care and vigilance to anyone but the immediate purchaser.

The foundations of this branch of the law, at least in this state, were laid in *Thomas v. Winchester,* 6 N.Y. 397, 57 Am. Dec. 455. A poison was falsely labeled. The sale was made to a druggist, who in turn sold to a customer. The customer recovered damages from the seller who affixed the label. "The defendant's negligence," it was said, "put human life in imminent danger." A poison, falsely labeled, is likely to injure anyone who gets it. Because the danger is to be foreseen, there is a duty to avoid the injury. Cases were cited by way of illustration in which manufacturers were not subject to any duty irrespective of contract. The distinction was said to be that their conduct, though negligent, was not likely to result in injury to anyone except the purchaser. . . . *Thomas v. Winchester* became quickly a landmark of the law. In the application of its principle there may, at times, have been uncertainty or even error. There has never in this state been doubt or disavowal of the principle itself. The chief cases are well known, yet to recall some of them will be helpful. *Loop v. Litchfield,* 42 N.Y. 351, 1 Am.

Rep. 513, is the earliest. It was the case of a defect in a small balance wheel used on a circular saw. The manufacturer pointed out the defect to the buyer, who wished a cheap article and was ready to assume the risk. The risk can hardly have been an imminent one, for the wheel lasted five years before it broke. In the meanwhile the buyer had made a lease of the machinery. It was held that the manufacturer was not answerable to the lessee. *Loop v. Litchfield* was followed in *Losee v. Clute,* 51 N.Y. 494, 10 Am. Rep. 638, the case of the explosion of a steam boiler. That decision has been criticized (Thompson on Negligence, 233; Shearman & Redfield on Negligence [6th Ed.] sec. 117); but it must be confined to its special facts. It was put upon the ground that the risk of injury was too remote. The buyer in that case had not only accepted the boiler, but had tested it. The manufacturer knew that his own test was not the final one. The finality of the test has a bearing on the measure of diligence owing to persons other than the purchaser. Beven, Negligence (3d Ed.) pp. 50, 51, 54; Wharton, Negligence (2d Ed.) sec. 134.

These early cases suggest a narrow construction of the rule. Later cases, however, evince a more liberal spirit. First in importance is *Devlin v. Smith*, 89 N.Y. 470, 42 Am. Rep. 311. The defendant, a contractor, built a scaffold for a painter. The painter's servants were injured. The contractor was held liable. He knew that the scaffold, if improperly constructed, was a most dangerous trap. He knew that it was to be used by the workmen. He was building it for that very purpose. Building it for their use, he owed them a duty, irrespective of his contract with their master, to build it with care.

From *Devlin v. Smith* we pass over intermediate cases and turn to the latest case in this court in which *Thomas v. Winchester* was followed. That case is *Statler v. Ray Mfg. Co.,* 195 N.Y. 478, 480, 88 N.E. 1,063. The defendant manufactured a large coffee urn. It was installed in a restaurant. When heated, the urn exploded and injured the plaintiff. We held that the manufacturer was liable. We said that the urn "was of such a character inherently that, when applied to the purposes for which it was designed, it was liable to become a source of great danger to many people if not carefully and properly constructed."

It may be that *Devlin v. Smith* and *Statler v. Ray Mfg. Co.* have extended the rule of *Thomas v. Winchester.* If so, this court is committed to the extension. The defendant argues that things imminently dangerous to life are poisons, explosives, deadly weapons — things whose normal function it is to injure or destroy. But whatever the rule in *Thomas v. Winchester* may once have been, it has no longer that restricted meaning. A scaffold (*Devlin v. Smith, supra*) is not inherently a destructive instrument. It becomes destructive only if imperfectly constructed. A large coffee urn (*Statler v. Ray Mfg. Co., supra*) may have within itself, if negligently made, the potency of a danger, yet no one thinks of it as an implement whose normal function is destruction.

What is true of the coffee urn is equally true of bottles of aerated water. *Torgesen v. Schultz,* 192 N.Y. 156, 84 N.E. 956, 18 L.R.A. (N.S.) 726, 127 Am. St. Rep. 894. We have mentioned only cases in this court. But the rule has received a like extension in our courts of intermediate appeal. In *Burke v. Ireland,* 26 App. Div. 487, 59 N.Y. Supp. 369, in an opinion by Cullen, J., it was applied to a builder who constructed a defective building; in *Kahner v. Otis Elevator Co.,* 96 App. Div. 169, 89 N.Y. Supp. 185, to the manufacturer of an elevator; in *Davies v. Pelham Hod Elevating Co.,* 65 Hun, 573, 20 N.Y. Supp. 523 affirmed in this court without opinion, 146 N.Y. 363, 41 N.E. 88, to a contractor who furnished a defective rope with knowledge of the purpose for which the rope was to be used. We are not required at this time either to approve or to disapprove the application of the rule that was made in these cases. It is enough that they help to characterize the trend of judicial thought.

Devlin v. Smith was decided in 1882. A year later a very similar case came before the Court of Appeal in England (*Heaven v. Pender,* 11 Q.B.D. 503). We find in the opinion of Brett, M. R., afterwards Lord Esher, the same conception of a duty, irrespective of contract, imposed upon the manufacturer by the law itself:

> "Whenever one person supplies goods or machinery, or the like, for the purpose of their being used by another person under such circumstances that every one of ordinary sense would, if he thought, recognize at once that unless he used ordinary care and skill with regard to the condition of the thing supplied, or the mode of supplying it, there will be danger of injury to the person or property of him for whose use the thing is supplied, and who is to use it, a duty arises to use ordinary care and skill as to the condition or manner of supplying such thing."

He then points out that for a neglect of such ordinary care or skill whereby injury happens, the appropriate remedy is an action for negligence. The right to enforce this liability is not to be confined to the immediate buyer. The right, he says, extends to the persons or class of persons for whose use the thing is supplied. It is enough that the goods "would in all probability be used at once . . . before a reasonable opportunity for discovering any defect which might exist," and that the thing supplied is of such a nature "that a neglect of ordinary care or skill as to its condition or the manner of supplying it would probably cause danger to the person or property of the person for whose use it was supplied, and who was about to use it." On the other hand, he would exclude a case "in which the goods are supplied under circumstances in which it would be a chance by whom they would be used or whether they would be used or not, or whether they would be used before there would probably be means of observing any defect," or where the goods are of such a nature that "a want of care or skill as to their condition or the manner of supplying them would not probably produce danger of injury to person or property." What was said by Lord Esher in that case did not command the full assent of his associates. His opinion has been criticized "as requiring every man to take affirmative precautions to protect his neighbors as well as to refrain from injuring them." Bohlen, Affirmative Obligations in the Law of Torts, 44 Am. Law Reg. (N.S.) 341. It may not be an accurate exposition of the law of England. Perhaps it may need some qualification even in our own state. Like most attempts at comprehensive definition, it may involve errors of inclusion and of exclusion. But its tests and standards, at least in their underlying principles, with whatever qualification may be called for as they are applied to varying conditions, are the tests and standards of our law.

We hold, then, that the principle of *Thomas v. Winchester* is not limited to poisons, explosives, and things of like nature, to things which in their normal operation are implements of destruction. If the nature of a thing is such that it is reasonably certain to place life and limb in peril when negligently made, it is then a thing of danger. Its nature gives warning of the consequences to be expected. If to the element of danger there is added knowledge that the thing will be used by persons other than the purchaser, and used without new tests, then, irrespective of contract, the manufacturer of this thing of danger is under a duty to make it carefully. That is as far as we are required to go for the decision of this case. There must be knowledge of a danger, not merely possible, but probable. It is possible to use almost anything in a way that will make it dangerous if defective. That is not enough to charge the manufacturer with a duty independent of his contract. Whether a given thing is dangerous may be sometimes a question for the court and sometimes a question for the jury. There must also be knowledge that in the usual course of events the danger will be shared by others than the buyer. Such knowledge may often be inferred from the nature of the transaction. But it is possible that even knowledge of the danger and of the use will not always be enough. The proximity or remoteness of the relation is a factor to be considered. We are dealing now with the liability of the manufacturer of the finished product, who puts it on the market to be used without inspection by his customers. If he is negligent, where danger is to be foreseen, a liability will follow.

. . . From this survey of the decisions, there thus emerges a definition of the duty of a manufacturer which enables us to measure this defendant's liability. Beyond all question, the nature of an automobile gives warning of probable danger if its construction is defective. This automobile was designed to go fifty miles an hour. Unless its wheels were sound and strong, injury was almost certain. It was as much a thing of danger as a defective engine for a railroad. The defendant knew the danger. It knew also that the car would be used by persons other than the buyer. This was apparent from its size; there were seats for three persons. It was apparent also from the fact that the buyer was a dealer in cars, who bought to resell. The maker of this car supplied it for the use of purchasers from the dealer just as plainly as the contractor in *Devlin v. Smith* supplied the scaffold for use by the servants of the owner. The dealer was indeed the one person of whom it might be said with some approach to certainty that by him the car would not be used. Yet the defendant would have us say that he was the one person whom it was under a legal duty to protect. The law does not lead us to so inconsequent a conclusion. Precedents drawn from the days of travel by stagecoach do not fit the conditions of travel today. The principle that the danger must be imminent does not change, but the things subject to the principle do change. They are whatever the needs of life in a developing civilization require them to be.

In reaching this conclusion, we do not ignore the decisions to the contrary in other jurisdictions. It was held in *Cadillac Co. v. Johnson, 221* Fed. 801, 137 C.C.A. 279 L.R.A. 1,915E, 287, that an automobile is not within the rule of *Thomas v. Winchester.* There was, however, a vigorous dissent. Opposed to that decision is one of the Court of Appeals of Kentucky, *Olds Motor Works v. Shaffer,* 145 Ky. 616, 140 S.W. 1,047, 37 L.R.A. (N.S.) 560, Ann. Cas. 1913B, 689. The earlier cases are summarized by Judge Sanborn in *Huset v. J. I. Case Threshing Machine Co.,* 120 Fed. 865, 57 C.C.A. 237, 61 L.R.A. 303. Some of them, at first sight inconsistent with our conclusion, may be reconciled upon the ground that the negligence was too remote, and that another cause had intervened. But even when they cannot be reconciled, the difference is rather in the application of the principle than in the principle itself. Judge Sanborn says, for example, that the contractor who builds a bridge, or the manufacturer who builds a car, cannot ordinarily foresee injury to other persons than the owner as the probable result. 120 Fed. 865, at page 867, 57 C.C.A. 237, at page 239, 61 L.R.A. 303. We take a different view. We think that injury to others is to be foreseen not merely as a possible, but as an almost inevitable, result. See the trenchant criticism in *Bohlen, supra,* at page 351. Indeed, Judge Sanborn concedes that his view is not to be reconciled with our decision in *Devlin v. Smith, supra.* The doctrine of that decision has now become the settled law of this state, and we have no desire to depart from it.

. . .

We think the defendant was not absolved from a duty of inspection because it bought the wheels from a reputable manufacturer. It was not merely a dealer in automobiles. It was a manufacturer of automobiles. It was responsible for the finished product. It was not at liberty to put the finished product on the market without subjecting the component parts to ordinary and simple tests. *Richmond & Danville R. R. Co. v. Elliott,* 149 U.S. 266, 272, 13 Sup. Ct. 837, 37 L.Ed. 728. Under the charge of the trial judge nothing more was required of it. The obligation to inspect must vary with the nature of the thing to be inspected. The more probable the danger the greater the need of caution.

There is little analogy between this case and *Carlson v. Phoenix Bridge Co.,* 132 N.Y. 273, 30 N.E. 750, where the defendant bought a tool for a servant's use. The making of tools was not the business in which the master was engaged. Reliance on the skill of the manufacturer was proper and almost inevitable. But that is not the defendant's situation. Both by its relation to the work and by the nature of its business, it is charged with a stricter duty.

Other rulings complained of have been considered, but no error has been found in them.

The judgment should be affirmed, with costs.

SUMMARY

This chapter has attempted to explain the role that individual cases and their holdings play in the precedent-oriented American legal system.

These cases are found in books called case reporters published by the government (as in the case of *United States Supreme Court Reports*) or by a private publisher (as is the case with the *Supreme Court Reporter*). The paralegal must become familiar with these reporters, their official abbreviations, and the citation system that locates cases.

Most written opinions contain several distinct elements, usually beginning with an overview of the basic facts of the case. A judicial history section summarizes the actions of the various inferior courts. After reviewing this introductory material, the opinion then usually identifies the issues being decided, reports the court's decision, and provides a carefully reasoned legal justification for that decision. The manner in which these individual issues are answered will ultimately determine the final disposition of the case — it may be either affirmed or reversed. Often the reversals are sent back to the lower courts to be reconsidered in light of the legal principles which the appellate court has just decided.

The individual case holding is the basic unit of legal analysis in the precedent system. It is as important in the areas of constitutional and statutory law as it is in situations involving the common law. The principle of *stare decisis* holds that courts should decide cases in ways that will be consistent with previous court interpretations of the same legal principle and thus provide stability and continuity to human affairs.

Individual judges, however, often have much discretion in the selection and interpretation of the precedent to be applied. There are often conflicting precedents that may be considered as either mandatory or persuasive authority. In addition, judges do have the power to overrule precedent decisions of their own or inferior courts. Most of the time, however, judges choose to sidestep negative precedents by emphasizing the differences in the factual situations between the precedent case and the case being decided.

When analyzing the precedent value of any given case, the paralegal should remember this advice from William Zelermyer:

> Take one case for what it is — a decision given by certain men, at a certain time, in a certain place, on the basis of certain reasoning applied to certain questions arising out of certain happenings under certain circumstances. We cannot tell with certainty what the same or other men would decide, at the same or another time, in the same or another place, on the basis of the same or other reasoning applied to the same or other questions arising out of other happenings under the same or other circumstances. One case does not provide an answer to a legal problem — it is but a clue to be used in the attempt to find an answer by the process of legal reasoning.[8]

KEY TERMS

appellant	persuasive authority
appellee	petitioner
affirmed	precedent
case citation	*ratio decidendi*
case reporter	reasoning
disposition	remanded
facts of the case	respondent
holding	reversed
issue	sidestepping precedent
mandatory authority	*stare decisis*
obiter dictum	syllogism
parallel citation	written opinion

REVIEW QUESTIONS

1. What are the differences between official case reporters and unofficial ones? Give an example or two of each.

2. Explain the meaning of each part of the following case citation: *Pines v. Perssion*, 14 Wis.2d 590, 111 N.W.2d 409 (1961).

3. In which reporters would one find the following cases?

   93 S. Ct. 2071   551 P.2d 398

   18 F.R.D. 107   213 N.J. 652

4. If Robert Barrett sued the First National Bank of Congerville, what would be the name by which the case would be cited? Would the name change if the bank took the case to an appellate court after Barrett had won a victory in the trial court?

5. Is a decision of the 4th Cir. Court of Appeals mandatory authority for a federal district court in the 7th Circuit? Is a decision of the Georgia Supreme Court persuasive authority for an appellate court in Minnesota?

DISCUSSION QUESTIONS

1. While courts ordinarily abide by the principle of *stare decisis*, they can overturn or refuse to follow precedents when they think the law should be changed. Do you agree that judges should have such powers? What factors should a judge consider when determining whether a precedent should be followed?

2. In *Flood v. Kuhn* the majority opinion took the position that it was up to the legislative branch to overturn the principle established in the precedent cases. On the other hand, in both the dissenting opinion in *Flood* and in the *Holytz v. City of Milwaukee* opinion, the judges took the position that the court should change the law without waiting for legislative action. When should the courts require legislative action and when should they take it upon themselves to make the change?

3. What should be the role of persuasive authority? To what extent should the courts of Washington take into consideration the manner in which the courts of Alabama have resolved similar legal problems? Why should they give them any consideration at all?

4. In *Texas v. White* the justices of the United States Supreme Court disagreed among themselves about the true nature of the court's holding in *Chambers v. Maroney*. Which group of justices properly interpreted the original decision? Why do you take that position?

PROJECTS

1. Locate, read, and then brief *Larsen v. General Motors Corporation*, 391 F.2d 495 (8th Cir. 1968). What is the broadest, most expansive principle of law for which this case could properly be cited as precedent? What is the narrowest, most limited principle? Identify the types of authorities utilized in the reasoning. Which did the court choose to follow?

2. Locate, read, and then brief *Skinner v. Whitley*, 281 N.C. 476, 189 S.E.2d 239 (1972). Now respond to the same questions listed in number one above.

3. Locate, read, and then brief *Renslow v. Mennonite Hospital*, 67 Ill.2d 348, 367 N.E.2d 1250 (1977). Respond to the questions listed in number one above.

REFERENCES

1. *A Uniform System of Citation* (Cambridge: Harvard Law Review Association, periodically revised).
2. 423 U.S. 67, 96 S. Ct. 304, 46 L.Ed.2d 209 (1975).
3. *Ibid.*, at 68, S. Ct. at 305.
4. *Ibid.*, at 69–71, S.Ct. at 305–306.
5. *Flood v. Kuhn,* at 284, S.Ct. at 2,112–2,113.
6. *Ibid.*, at 292–293, S.Ct. at 2,117.
7. 423 U.S. 67, 96 S.Ct. 304, 46 L.Ed.2d 209 (1975).
8. William Zelermyer, *The Process of Legal Reasoning* (Englewood Cliffs: Prentice-Hall, 1963), p. 112.

CHAPTER 6

Statutory, Administrative, and Constitutional Law

We began our discussion of finding and interpreting the law with an analysis of court cases because court opinions are important in the interpretation of statutes, administrative regulations, and constitutions, as well as the common law. Once a court has interpreted a provision of some statute or constitution in a certain way, that interpretation becomes precedent in the same way that a court's interpretation of the common law becomes precedent. Moreover, it is court decisions which have established the various principles that govern the interpretation of statutes, regulations, and constitutions. This chapter focuses on those principles.

FINDING THE STATUTE

The Publication of Statutes

State and federal statutes are usually published in three primary forms: individual slip laws, periodic compilation of new laws passed within a certain time period, and unified codes. Paralegals need to be familiar with these publications.

When laws are first officially enacted, they are usually published individually as slip laws. Federal slip laws are available at libraries designated as official depositories and can be ordered directly from the United States Government Printing Office. State slip laws are usually available at larger libraries in the various states and from the state governments themselves.

At the end of a legislative term the federal and most state governments have the laws passed during that term published together as one or more volumes in a continuing set. They are usually arranged in chronological order by date of passage and are referred to as either statutes-at-large or sessions laws.

New federal statutes also appear in several other publications. West Publishing's *U.S. Code Congressional and Administrative News* and the Lawyers' Co-operative Publishing Company's *Current Public Laws and Administrative Service* both contain the full text of public laws along with information about the legislative history. These publications come out in pamphlet form on a monthly or semimonthly basis. *United States Law Week* is a weekly loose-leaf service that also includes the text of many of the more important laws passed during that particular week. Similar loose-leaf and pamphlet services exist in some states.

The publications discussed here are arranged chronologically by date of passage; however, codes* arrange the laws by subject matter. While the above publications contain only those laws passed during a particular time period, codes contain all public laws currently in force in a particular area. The *United States Code* is the official codification of federal statutes and is printed and distributed by the U.S. Government Printing Office. The *United States Code Annotated* and the *United States Code Service* (formally known as the *Federal Code Annotated*) are published by West and Lawyers' Co-operative respectively. In addition to the text of the laws themselves, these two annotated versions of the code have information about the legislative history and references to court decisions which have interpreted the statutes. Some state statutes are also published by West in an anno-

*The formal names for these codes differ from one state to another. In addition to being called codes, they may be labeled as revised statutes, consolidated statutes, or compiled statutes.

tated form. Table 6.1 lists the most common publications and abbreviations.

Local ordinances are usually published as individual slip laws and then kept in a loose-leaf binder. They are usually found in local libraries and at the administrative offices of the governmental unit involved.

Statutory Citations

Whenever possible, statutory citations should include the name of the statute and the section as it was originally enacted. Statutes currently in force are usually cited to the code. For example:

Administrative Procedure Act, 5 U.S.C. §552(b)(3) (1974)

Cannabis Control Act, Ill. Rev. Stat. ch. 56½, §701 (1973)

The number 5 preceding the U.S.C. designation indicates that it is Title 5. The § symbol stands for section and ch. for chapter.

If the act does not appear in the code (either because it has been repealed or it was passed too recently to be included in the code), it is cited to the statutes-at-large (session laws) or simply to the public law number and its date of passage. For example:

Clayton Act §7, ch. 25, §7, 38 Stat. 631 (1914) Pub. L. No. 95-221, §1 (March 14, 1978)

When session laws are cited, the year of enactment is usually shown in parentheses. When codes are cited, the year of codification is usually given.

Local ordinances follow the same general format:

Portland, Ore., Police Code art. 30 (1953)

INTERPRETING STATUTES

Court decisions are based on a specific set of facts and establish legal rules that ostensibly apply to a relatively narrow set of similar circumstances. Statutes are generally written in a more universalistic format and are designed to apply to a more com-

TABLE 6.1
Common Publications Containing the Texts of Statutes

Publication	Abbreviation	Coverage
United States Code	U.S.C.	Codified federal statutes
United States Code Annotated	U.S.C.A.	Codified federal statutes with annotations
United States Code Service	U.S.C.S.	Codified federal statutes with annotations (same as F.C.A.)
Federal Code Annotated	F.C.A.	Codified federal statutes with annotations (same as U.S.C.S.)
United States Statutes-at-Large	Stat.	Federal statutes enacted at a particular time
U.S. Code Congressional and Administrative News	None[a]	Federal statutes enacted at a particular time
Current Public Laws and Administrative Service	None[a]	Federal statutes enacted at a particular time
United States Law Week	U.S.L.W.	Federal statutes enacted at a particular time
Alabama Code[b]	Ala. Code	Codified Alabama statutes
Arizona Revised Statutes Annotated[b]	Ariz. Rev. Stat. Ann.	Codified Arizona statutes with annotations
California Business and Professions Code[c]	Cal. Bus. & Prof. Code	Codified California statutes relating to business and the professions
New York Domestic Relations Laws[c]	N.Y. Dom. Rel.	Codified New York statutes relating to domestic relations

[a]Since these publications are not used in formal citations, no abbreviation is given.
[b]These are typical of the format used in most states and are used to illustrate this pattern.
[c]A few states publish their laws in separate publications according to the subject.

prehensive set of circumstances. While judges interpret legal rules in a specific factual context, legislatures formulate rules that are supposed to apply to a variety of future situations.

The formulation of such future-oriented rules is frequently a very difficult task, and statutes often end up fraught with ambiguity. Sometimes the ambiguity is the result of sloppy draftsmanship, but more often it is merely the result of being applied to unanticipated circumstances. On the other hand, the ambiguity may have been purposely included in order to provide a basis for compromise by glossing over conflicts among the legislators. For a combination of all of these reasons, statutes often contain ambiguous sections.

As an example, §1715 of Title 18 of the *United States Code* declares that:

> Pistols, revolvers, and other firearms capable of being concealed on the person are non-mailable and shall not be deposited in or carried by the mails or delivered by any postmaster, letter carrier, or other person in the Postal Service.
>
> . . .
>
> Whoever knowingly deposits for mailing or delivery, or knowingly causes to be delivered by mail according to the direction thereon, or at any place to which it is directed to be delivered by the person to whom it is addressed, any pistol, revolver, or firearm declared non-mailable by this section, shall be fined not more than $1,000 or imprisoned not more than two years, or both.

To illustrate the ambiguity of statutes such as this, we see that no mention is made of size. Thus, would a person who mailed a sawed-off shotgun be in violation of this statute if the overall length of the weapon was 22 inches? What if it was 12 inches in length — or 32 inches?

Section 31-1 of the Illinois Criminal Code declares that:

> . . . A person who knowingly resists or obstructs the performance by one known to the person to be a police officer of any authorized act within his official capacity commits a Class A misdemeanor.[1]

But is an unlawful arrest an authorized act? Is a person guilty of violating this law if an attempt is made to keep a police officer from conducting an illegal search of that person's house?

Or consider the meaning of the Mann Act. It declares that:

> Whoever knowingly transports in interstate or foreign commerce, or in the District of Columbia or in any Territory or Possession of the United States, any woman or girl for the purpose of prostitution or debauchery, or for any other immoral purpose, or with the intent and purpose to induce, entice, or compel such woman or girl to become a prostitute or to give herself up to debauchery, or to engage in any other immoral practice. . . .
>
> . . .
>
> Shall be fined not more than $5,000 or imprisoned not more than five years, or both.[2]

What constitutes any other immoral practices? Is it a violation of this law for a man to transport a woman from Sacramento, California to Reno, Nevada for the purpose of having her become his mistress? Is it a violation of the act to transport a prostitute to another state so that she can have a vacation (which does not involve any immoral behavior)? Is it a violation to transport that same prostitute back to the state she left so that she can voluntarily resume her work as a prostitute? Is it a violation of the act for a man to transport a woman across state lines so that she can perform a striptease number at a stag party?

These are just a few examples of the ambiguity that is often found in statutes. When questions like these arise, the courts are assigned the task of clarifying their meaning. They will, of course, look to *stare decisis* and the manner in which other courts have interpreted the same words. Often the situation is one which has not been addressed before, and the court must strike out on its own. "In the interpretation of statutes," wrote Mr. Chief Justice Hughes, "the function of the courts is easily stated. It is to construe the language so as to give effect to the intent of Congress."[3] In seeking to determine this intent the courts utilize three main approaches: literalism, intrinsic analysis, and extrinsic analysis.

Literalism

Statutory interpretation usually begins with a literal reading of the statute itself. This literalistic approach is based on the assumptions that:

1. The words used reflect the true intentions of the legislature.

2. The legislature intended that the words they used be interpreted in light of their common, ordinary meanings.

The following sections of the United States Supreme Court's opinion in *Barrett v. United States* illustrate the application of a literalistic approach. Petitioner Barrett, who had been convicted of violating part of the federal Gun Control Act of 1968, argued that the prohibition of that statute did not apply to her specific conduct (a Kentucky gun dealer selling a gun, that had been previously shipped in from another state, to a Kentucky resident who was a convicted felon). Note the manner in which the court applies a literal interpretation of the words used in the act and how it even focuses on the tense of the verbs.

Barrett v. United States

423 U.S. 212, 96 S. Ct. 498, 46 L.Ed.2d 45 (1976)

Mr. Justice Blackmun delivered the opinion of the Court.

Petitioner Pearl Barrett has been convicted by a jury in the United States District Court for the Eastern District of Kentucky of a violation of 18 U.S.C. §922(h), a part of the Gun Control Act of 1968, Pub. L. 90-618, 82 Stat. 1213, amending the Omnibus Crime Control and Safe Streets Act of 1968, Pub. L. 90-351, 82 Stat. 197, enacted earlier the same year. The issue before us is whether §922(h) has application to a purchaser's intrastate acquisition of a firearm that previously, but independently of the purchaser's receipt, had been transported in interstate commerce from the manufacturer to a distributor and then from the distributor to the dealer.

. . .

Petitioner was charged with a violation of §922(h). He pleaded not guilty. At the trial no evidence was presented to show that Barrett personally had participated in any way in the previous interstate movement of the firearm. The evidence was merely to the effect that he had purchased the revolver out of the local dealer's stock, and that the gun, having been manufactured and then warehoused in other States, had reached the dealer through interstate channels. At the close of the prosecution's case, Barrett moved for a directed verdict of acquittal on the ground that §922(h) was not applicable to his receipt of the firearm. The motion was denied. The court instructed the jury that the statute's interstate requirement was satisfied if the firearm at some time in its past had traveled in interstate commerce. A verdict of guilty was returned. Petitioner received a sentence of three years, subject to the immediate parole eligibility provisions of 18 U.S.C. §4208(a)(2).

Petitioner concedes that Congress, under the Commerce Clause of the Constitution, has the power to regulate interstate trafficking in firearms. Brief for Petitioner 7. He states, however, that the issue before us concerns the scope of Congress' exercise of that power in this statute. He argues that, in its enactment of §922(h), Congress was interested in "the business of gun traffic," Brief for Petitioner 11; that the Act was meant "to deal with *businesses,* not individuals per se" (emphasis in original), *id.,* at 14, that is, with mail-order houses, out-of-state sources, and the like; and that the Act was not intended to, and does not, reach an isolated intrastate receipt, such as Barrett's transaction, where the handgun was sold within Kentucky by a local merchant to a local resident with whom the merchant was acquainted, and where the transaction "has no apparent connection with interstate commerce," despite the weapon's manufacture and original distribution in States other than Kentucky. *Id.,* at 6.

We feel, however, that the language of §922(h), the structure of the Act of which §922(h) is a part, and the manifest purpose of Congress are all adverse to petitioner's position.

Section 922(h) pointedly and simply provides that it is unlawful for four categories of persons, including a convicted felon, "to receive any firearm or ammunition which has been shipped or transported in interstate or foreign commerce." The quoted language is without ambiguity. It is directed unrestrictedly at the felon's receipt of any firearm that "has been" shipped in interstate commerce. It contains no limitation to a receipt which itself is part of the interstate movement. We therefore have no reason to differ with the Court of Appeals' majority's conclusion that the language "means exactly what it says." 504 F.2d, at 632.

It is to be noted, furthermore, that while the proscribed act, "to receive any firearm," is in the present tense, the interstate commerce reference is in the present perfect tense, denoting an act that has been completed. Thus, there is no warping or stretching of language when the statute is applied to a firearm that already has completed its interstate journey and has come to rest in the dealer's showcase at the time of its purchase and receipt by the felon. Congress knew the significance and meaning of the language it employed. It used the present perfect tense elsewhere in the same section, namely, in §922(h)(1) (a person who "has been convicted"), and in §922(h)(4) (a person who "has been adjudicated" or who "has been committed"), in contrast to its use of the present tense ("who is") in §§922(h)(1), (2), and (3). The statute's pattern is consistent and no unintended misuse of language or of tense is apparent.

Had Congress intended to confine §922(h) to direct interstate receipt, it would have so provided, just as it did in other sections of the Gun Control Act. See §922(a)(3) (declaring it unlawful for a nonlicensee to receive in the State where he resides a firearm purchased or obtained "by such person outside that State"); §922(j) (prohibiting the receipt of a stolen firearm (moving as . . . interstate . . . commerce")); and §922(k) (prohibiting the receipt "in interstate . . . commerce" of a firearm the serial number of which has been removed). Statutes other than the Gun Control Act similarly utilize restrictive language when only direct interstate commerce is to be reached. . . .

The literal approach is not always as easy as it appears to be above. For example, does the clause "every wife and mother" apply to all wives and all mothers or just to everyone who is both a wife and a mother? To deal with these types of ambiguities, the courts have developed several principles to guide their interpretation. The last antecedent doctrine declares that relative and qualifying words and phrases are applied to the words and phrases immediately preceding them and not to those which are more remote. The express mention, implied exclusion rule states that if some idea is not expressly stated, the legislature intended that it be excluded. The *ejusdem generis** principle holds that when a series of specific enumerations is followed by a catchall phrase such as "and others," it is to be interpreted to be limited to matters which are like the ones specifically listed.

An interesting application of *ejusdem generis* appears in the following Supreme Court application of the Mann Act. Go back to page 185 and reread the words of the act itself. Then note the manner in which the opinions of Justices Day and McKenna differ in their application of the principle of *ejusdem generis* to a situation in which someone had transported a woman across state lines so that she could become his mistress.

Caminetti v. United States

242 U.S. 470, 37 S. Ct. 192 (1917)

Mr. Justice Day delivered the opinion of the Court:

It is contended that the act of Congress is intended to reach only "commercialized vice," or the traffic in women for gain, and that the

*This Latin phrase is translated as "of the same class."

conduct for which the several petitioners were indicted and convicted, however reprehensible in morals, is not within the purview of the statute when properly construed in the light of its history and the purposes intended to be accomplished by its enactment. In none of the cases was it charged or proved that the transportation was for gain or for the purpose of furnishing women for prostitution for hire, and it is insisted that, such being the case, the acts charged and proved, upon which conviction was had, do not come within the statute.

. . .

In *United States v. Bitty,* 208 U.S. 393, 52 L.Ed. 543, 28 Sup. Ct. Rep. 396, it was held that the act of Congress against the importation of alien women and girls for the purpose of prostitution "and any other immoral purpose" included the importation of an alien woman to live in concubinage with the person importing her. In that case this court said:

"All will admit that full effect must be given to the intention of Congress as gathered from the words of the statute. There can be no doubt as to what class was aimed at by the clause forbidding the importation of alien women for purposes of 'prostitution.' It refers to women who, for hire or without hire, offer their bodies to indiscriminate intercourse with men. The lives and example of such persons are in hostility to 'the idea of the family, as consisting in and springing from the union for life of one man and one woman in the holy estate of matrimony; the sure foundation of all that is stable and noble in our civilization; the best guaranty of that reverent morality which is the source of all beneficent progress in social and political improvement.' *Murphy v. Ramsey,* 114 U.S. 15, 45, 29 L.Ed. 47, 57, 5 Sup. Ct. Rep. 747. . . . Now the addition in the last statute of the words, 'or for any other immoral purpose,' after the word 'prostitution,' must have been made for some practical object. Those added words show beyond question that Congress had in view the protection of society against another class of alien women other than those who might be brought here merely for purposes of 'prostitution.' In forbidding the importation of alien women 'for any other immoral purpose,' Congress evidently thought that there were purposes in connection with the importations of alien women which, as in the case of importations for prostitution, were to be deemed immoral. It may be admitted that, in accordance with the familiar rule of *ejusdem generis,* the immoral purpose referred to by the words 'any other immoral purpose' must be one of the same general class or kind as the particular purpose of 'prostitution' specified in the same clause of the statute. 2 Lewis's Sutherland, Stat. Constr. §423, and authorities cited. But that rule cannot avail the accused in this case; for the immoral purpose charged in the indictment is of the same general class or kind as the one that controls in the importation of an alien woman for the purpose strictly of prostitution. The prostitute may, in the popular sense, be more degraded in character than the concubine, but the latter nonetheless must be held to lead an immoral life, if any regard whatever be had to the views that are almost universally held in this country as to the relations which may rightfully, from the standpoint of morality, exist between man and woman in the matter of sexual intercourse."

. . .

Mr. Justice McKenna, dissenting:

The transportation which is made unlawful is of a woman or girl "to become a prostitute or to give herself up to debauchery, or to engage in any other immoral practice." Our present concern is with the words "any other immoral practice," which, it is asserted, have a special office. The words are clear enough as general descriptions; they fail in particular designation; they are class words, not specifications. Are they controlled by those which precede them? If not, they are broader in generalization and include those that precede them, making them unnecessary and confusing. To what conclusion would this lead us? "Immoral" is a very comprehensive word. It means a dereliction of morals. In such sense it covers every form of vice, every form of conduct that is contrary to good order. It will hardly be contended that in this sweeping sense it is used in the statute. But, if not used in such sense, to what is it limited and by what limited? If it be admitted that it is limited at all, that ends the imperative effect assigned to it in the opinion of the court. But not insisting quite on that, we ask again, By what is it limited? By its context, necessarily, and the purpose of the statute.

. . .

In other words, it is vice as a business at which the law is directed, using interstate commerce as a facility to procure or distribute its victims.

. . .

United States v. Bitty, 208 U.S. 393, 52 L.Ed. 543, 28 Sup. Ct. Rep. 296, is not in opposition. The statute passed upon was a prohibition against the importation of alien women or girls, — a statute, therefore, of broader purpose than the one under review. Besides, the statute finally passed upon was an amendment to a prior statute, and the words construed were an addition to the prior statute, and necessarily, therefore, had an added effect. The first statute prohibited the importation of any alien woman or girl into the United States *for the purpose of prostitution* [italics mine]. The second statute repeated the words and added *"or for any other immoral purpose."* Necessarily there was an enlargement of purpose, and besides, the act was directed against the importation of foreign corruption, and was construed accordingly. The case, therefore, does not contradict the rule; it is an example of it.

Principles like *ejusdem generis* and *express mention, implied exclusion* are guidelines which the court can either apply or not apply at its discretion. There are occasions on which judges openly reject the entire literalistic approach. Observe the manner in which judges choose to ignore the literal meaning of words in the statute when they conclude that such a reading would not in fact properly reflect the true intent of the legislature. The *Holy Trinity* case involves the application of a statute prohibiting importation of aliens for a specific job. *United States v. Powell* raises the question of what constitutes a concealable firearm.*

The Church of the Holy Trinity v. United States

143 U.S. 457, 12 S. Ct. 511, 36 L.Ed. 226 (1892)

Mr. Justice Brewer delivered the opinion of the court:

Plaintiff in error is a corporation, duly organized and incorporated as a religious society, under the laws of the State of New York. E. Walpole Warren was prior to September, 1887, an alien residing in England. In that month the plaintiff in error made a contract with him, by which he was to remove to the city of New York and enter into its service as rector and pastor; and, in pursuance of such contract, Warren did so remove and enter upon such service. It is claimed by the United States that this contract on the part of the plaintiff in error was forbidden by chapter 164, 28 Stat. at L. 332, and an action was commenced to recover the penalty prescribed by that Act. The Circuit Court held that the contract was within the prohibition of the statute, and rendered judgment accordingly (36 Fed. Rep. 303); and the single question presented for our determination is whether it erred in that conclusion.

The first section describes the act forbidden, and is in these words:

"Be it enacted by the Senate and House of Representatives of the United States of America in Congress assembled, that from and after the passage of this Act it shall be unlawful for any person, company, partnership or corporation, in any manner whatsoever, to prepay the transportation, or in any way assist or encourage the importation or migration of any alien or aliens, any foreigner or foreigners, into the United States, its territories or the District of Columbia, under contract or agreement, parol or special, express or implied, made previous to the importation or migration of such alien or aliens, foreigner or foreigners, to perform labor or service of any kind in the United States, its territories or the District of Columbia."

*See the previous discussion of this statute on page 184.

It must be conceded that the act of the corporation is within the letter of this section, for the relation of rector to his church is one of service, and implies labor on the one side with compensation on the other. Not only are the general words "labor" and "service" both used, but also, as it were to guard against any narrow interpretation and emphasize a breadth of meaning, to them is added "of any kind"; and further, as noticed by the Circuit Judge in his opinion, the fifth section, which makes specific exceptions, among them professional actors, artists, lecturers, singers, and domestic servants, strengthens the idea that every other kind of labor and service was intended to be reached by the first section. While there is great force in this reasoning, we cannot think Congress intended to denounce with penalties a transaction like that in the present case. It is a familiar rule that a thing may be within the letter of the statute and yet not within the statute, because not within its spirit, nor within the intention of its makers.

United States v. Powell

423 U.S. 87, 96 S. Ct. 316, 46 L.Ed.2d 228 (1975)

Mr. Justice Rehnquist delivered the opinion for the court.

Respondent was indicted on a single count of mailing a firearm capable of being concealed on the person (the sawed-off shotgun . . .), in violation of 18 U.S.C. §1715. At trial there was evidence that the weapon could be concealed on an average person. Respondent was convicted by a jury which was instructed that in order to return a guilty verdict it must find that she "knowingly caused to be delivered by mail a firearm capable of being concealed on the person."

. . .

. . . She contends that as a matter of statutory construction, particularly in light of the doctrine of *ejusdem generis,* the language "other firearms capable of being concealed on the person" simply does not extend to sawed-off shotguns. . . .

The thrust of respondent's argument is that the more general language of the statute ("firearms") should be limited by the more specific language ("pistols and revolvers") so that the phrase "other firearms capable of being concealed on the person" would be limited to "concealable weapons such as pistols and revolvers."

We reject this contention. The statute by its terms bans the mailing of "firearms capable of being concealed on the person," and we would be justified in narrowing the statute only if such a narrow reading was supported by evidence of congressional intent over and above the language of the statute.

In *Gooch v. United States,* 297 U.S. 124, 128, 56 S. Ct. 395, 397, 80 L.Ed. 522 (1936), the Court said:

> The rule of *ejusdem generis,* while firmly established, is only an instrumentality for ascertaining the correct meaning of words when there is uncertainty. Ordinarily, it limits general terms which follow specific ones to matters similar to those specified; but it may not be used to defeat the obvious purpose of legislation. And, while penal statutes are narrowly construed, this does not require rejection of that sense of the words which best harmonizes with the context and the end in view.

Intrinsic Factors

If literalism is not followed by judges, they must rely on another method of determining the legislature's intent. Thus, when courts look beyond the literal meaning of the words themselves, they often focus on the context in which the disputed clause occurs. This intrinsic approach involves looking at the overall structure of the larger legislative package and asking the following questions: What was the title the legislature gave to the act? Are there relevant subheadings provided? Is the same term used elsewhere in the statute or in related statutes? It is usually assumed that the name chosen for the act is significant, that the clause is intended to be read as part of a larger, more comprehensive regulatory scheme and that the legislature intended to be consistent in its approaches to the problem. The following selections from the *Barrett* and the *Locken* cases illustrate this type of contextual analysis. *Barrett* has been discussed before and deals with the interpretation of a federal gun control statute. *People v. Locken* is a state case interpreting the obstruction of justice statute presented on page 184.

Barrett v. United States

423 U.S. 212, 96 S. Ct. 498, 46 L.Ed.2d 45 (1976)

Mr. Justice Blackmun:

. . .

B. The very structure of the Gun Control Act demonstrates that Congress did not intend merely to restrict interstate sales but sought broadly to keep firearms away from the persons Congress classified as potentially irresponsible and dangerous. These persons are comprehensively barred by the Act from acquiring firearms by any means. Thus, §922(d) prohibits a licensee from knowingly selling or otherwise disposing of any firearm (whether in an interstate or intrastate transaction, see *Huddleston v. United States,* 415 U.S., at 833, 94 S. Ct., at 1,273) to the same categories of potentially irresponsible persons. If §922(h) were to be construed as petitioner suggests, it would not complement §922(d), and a gap in the statute's coverage would be created, for then, although the licensee is prohibited from selling either interstate or intrastate to the designated person, the vendee is not prohibited from receiving unless the transaction is itself interstate.

Similarly, §922(g) prohibits the same categories of potentially irresponsible persons from shipping or transporting any firearm in interstate commerce, or, see 18 U.S.C. §2(b), causing it to be shipped interstate. Petitioner's proposed narrow construction of §922(h) would reduce that section to a near redundancy with §922(g), since almost every interstate shipment is likely to have been solicited or otherwise caused by the direct recipient. That proposed narrow construction would also create another anomaly: if a prohibited person seeks to buy from his local dealer a firearm that is not currently in the dealer's stock, and the dealer then orders it interstate, that person violates §922(h), but under the suggested construction, he would not violate §922(h) if the firearm were already on the dealer's shelf.

We note, too, that other sections of the Act clearly apply to and regulate intrastate sales of a gun that has moved in intrastate commerce. For example, the licensing provisions, §§922(a)(1) and 923(a), apply to exclusively intrastate, as well as interstate, activity. Under §922(d), as noted above, a licensee may not knowingly sell a firearm to any prohibited person, even if the sale is intrastate. *Huddleston v. United States,* 415 U.S., at 833, 94 S. Ct., at 1,273. Sections 922(c) and (a)(6), relating, respectively, to a physical presence at the place of purchase and to the giving of false information, apply to intrastate as well as to interstate transactions. So, too, do §922(b)(2) and (5).

Construing §922(h) as applicable to an intrastate retail sale that has been preceded by movement of the firearm in interstate commerce is thus consistent with the entire pattern of the Act. To confine §922(h) to direct interstate receipts would result in having the Gun Control Act cover every aspect of intrastate transactions in firearms except receipt. This, however, and obviously, is the most crucial of all. Congress surely did not intend to except from the direct prohibitions of the statute the very act it went to such pains to prevent indirectly, through complex provisions, in the other sections of the Act.

People v. Locken

59 Ill.2d 459, 322 N.E.2d 51 (1974)

Justice Davis:

Andy Locken, then age twenty, and his mother, Mrs. Erma Anderson, gave a party in honor of the Harper College wrestling team, of which Andy was a member, at their home at 907 Sigwalt Street, Arlington Heights. When one of the detectives, who was with the other peace officers, asked to be let into the house, the defendant, Andy Locken, asked if he had a warrant, and the officer replied, "We don't need any." The officer then tried to force his way into the Anderson/Locken home without a warrant and Andy Locken resisted his entrance. A scuffle ensued, and, after being sprayed with Mace, Andy was subdued, handcuffed, and placed under arrest. When Mrs. Anderson later called at the police station to inquire about her son, she was booked and placed under arrest.

The aggravated-assault charged against Andy Locken was withdrawn by the prosecution prior to trial, and the battery charge against him was disposed of in his favor, and Mrs. Anderson was acquitted on all charges.

. . .

Section 31-1 of the Criminal Code (Ill. Rev. Stat. 1971, ch. 38, par. 31-1), under which Andy Locken was charged, provides:

A person who knowingly resists or obstructs the performance by one known to the person to be a peace officer of any authorized act within his official capacity shall be fined not to exceed $500 or imprisoned in a penal institution other than the penitentiary not to exceed one year, or both.

As indicated by the Committee Comments upon §31-1, a complete understanding of §31-1 can be reached only by reading it in conjunction with §7-7:

. . . Note that the offense covers only resistance or obstruction to 'authorized' acts of the officer. *However, if the act resisted or obstructed is the making of an arrest, a private person is not authorized to resist such arrest with force even though he knows the arrest is unlawful* (§7-7). (Emphasis added.) S.H.A., ch. 38, §31-1, Committee Comments at 735 (1970).

Section 7-7 of the Criminal Code (Ill. Rev. Stat. 1971, ch. 38, par. 7-7) provides:

(a) A person is not authorized to use force to resist an arrest which he knows is being made either by a police officer or by a private person summoned and directed by a peace officer to make the arrest, even if he believes that the arrest is unlawful and the arrest in fact is unlawful.

It appears that the legislature, by adopting §7-7, intended that the making of an unlawful arrest is to be considered an "authorized act" for purposes of §31-1. Consequently, resistance of even an unlawful arrest by a known officer is a violation of §31-1.

Just as the courts can decide not to follow literal interpretations, they can decide not to follow this type of intrinsic analysis. Returning to the *Caminetti* case, one can see how the dissenters used intrinsic analysis to support their conclusion that the Mann Act applied only to commercialized vice. The majority opinion, of course, rejects this approach in favor of a literal reading of the text itself.

Caminetti v. United States

242 U.S. 470, 37 S. Ct. 192 (1917)

Mr. Justice McKenna, dissenting:

For the context I must refer to the statute; of the purpose of the statute Congress itself has given us illumination. It devotes a section to the declaration that the "act shall be known and referred to as the 'White Slave Traffic Act.' " And its prominence gives it prevalence in the construction of the statute. It cannot be pushed aside or subordinated by indefinite words in other sentences, limited even there by the context. It is a peremptory rule of construction that all parts of a statute must be taken into account in ascertaining its meaning, and it cannot be said that §8 has no object. Even if it gives only a title to the act, it has especial weight. *United States v. Union P. R. Co.,* 91 U.S. 72, 82, 23 L.Ed. 224, 229. But it gives more than a title; it makes distinctive the purpose of the statute. The designation "white slave traffic" has the sufficiency of an axiom. If apprehended, there is no uncertainty as to the conduct it describes. It is commercialized vice, immoralities having a mercenary purpose, and this is confirmed by other circumstances.

Mr. Justice Day for the majority:

But it is contended that though the words are so plain that they cannot be misapprehended when given their usual and ordinary interpretation, and although the sections in which they appear do not in terms limit the offense defined and punished to acts of "commercialized vice," or the furnishing or procuring of transportation of women for debauchery, prostitution, or immoral practices for hire, such limited purpose is to be attributed to Congress and engrafted upon the act in view of the language of §8 and the report which accompanied the law upon its introduction into and subsequent passage by the House of Representatives.

In this connection, it may be observed that while the title of an act cannot overcome the meaning of plain and unambiguous words used in its body (*United States v. Fisher,* 2 Cranch, 358, 386, 2 L.Ed. 304, 313; *Goodlett v. Louisville & N. R. Co.,* 122 U.S. 391, 408, 30 L.Ed. 1230, 1233, 7 Sup. Ct. Rep. 1,254; *Patterson v. The Eudora,* 190 U.S. 169, 172, 47 L.Ed. 1002, 1003, 23 Sup. Ct. Rep. 821; *Cornell v. Coyne,* 192 U.S. 418, 430, 48 L.Ed. 504, 509, 24 Sup. Ct. Rep. 383; *Lapina v. Williams,* 232 U.S. 78, 92, 58 L.Ed. 515, 520, 34 Sup. Ct. Rep. 196), the title of this act embraces the regulation of interstate commerce "by prohibiting the transportation therein for immoral purposes of women and girls, and for other purposes." It is true that §8 of the act provides that it shall be known and referred to as the "White Slave Traffic Act," and the report accompanying the introduction of the same into the House of Representatives set forth the fact that a material portion of the legislation suggested was to meet conditions which had arisen in the past few years, and that the legislation was needed to put a stop to a villainous interstate and international traffic in women and girls. Still, the name given to an act by way of designation or description, or the report which accompanies it, cannot change the plain import of its words. If the words are plain, they give meaning to the act, and it is neither the duty nor the privilege of the courts to enter speculative fields in search of a different meaning.

Extrinsic Factors

In their search for legislative intent, courts will occasionally look beyond the literal meaning of the clause in question and beyond the statutory context in which that clause is located. In these cases they look for evidence of legislative intent that can be found outside of the statute itself. This type of analysis examines the act's legislative history.

The exact nature of the materials included in a legislative history will vary depending on the importance of the statute and the type of legislative body involved. This section will review the various types of documents that are usually available for federal legislation. Some types of similar documents will also be available in state cases.

Statutes begin as bills. A legislator introduces a draft of what the proposed law should look like. Prior to passage there may be amendments that change various sections of the bill. The pattern that emerges from an examination of multiple bills and amendments can sometimes provide insight into the legislative intent of the final act. The court, for example, would probably not read the act to apply to a particular situation if the legislative history showed that an amendment to do precisely that had been defeated.

Before bills are presented on the floor of the legislative body they are usually sent to a committee. Committees will often hold public hearings where interested parties can testify about the proposed law. The proceedings of these hearings are published and the transcript becomes a part of the statute's legislative history. More importantly, the committee will sometimes issue an official report discussing the nature of the proposed legislation and what they expect it to accomplish. This, too, becomes part of the history.

When the bill is debated on the floor of the legislative body, proponents and opponents often make statements about what they expect the bill to do or not to do. The transcripts of these debates become another source of information about legislative intent.

In determining legislative intent, courts may quote from any of these sources. Note the Supreme Court's use of legislative history in the *Holy Trinity* case.

The Church of the Holy Trinity v. United States

143 U.S. 457, 12 S. Ct. 511, 36 L.Ed. 226 (1892)

Mr. Justice Brewer:
Again, another guide to the meaning of a statute is found in the evil which it is designed to remedy; and for this the court properly looks at contemporaneous events, the situation as it existed, and as it was pressed upon the attention of the legislative body. *United States v. Union Pac. R. Co.* 91 U.S. 72, 79 [as: 224, 228]. The situation which called for this statute was briefly but fully stated by *Mr. Justice* Brown when, as district judge, he decided the case of *United States v. Craig,* 28 Fed. Rep. 795, 798: "The motives and history of the Act are matters of

common knowledge. It had become the practice for large capitalists in this country to contract with their agents abroad for the shipment of great numbers of an ignorant and servile class of foreign laborers, under contracts, by which the employer agreed, upon the one hand, to prepay their passage, while, upon the other hand, the laborers agreed to work after their arrival for a certain time at a low rate of wages. The effect of this was to break down the labor market, and to reduce other laborers engaged in like occupations to the level of the assisted immigrant. The evil finally became so flagrant that an appeal was made to Congress for relief by the passage of the Act in question, the design of which was to raise the standard of foreign immigrants, and to discountenance the migration of those who had not sufficient means in their own hands, or those of their friends, to pay their passage."

It appears, also, from the petitions, and in the testimony presented before the committees of Congress, that it was this cheap unskilled labor which was making the trouble, and the influx of which Congress sought to prevent. It was never suggested that we had in this country a surplus of brain toilers, and, least of all, that the market for the services of Christian ministers was depressed by foreign competition. Those were matters to which the attention of Congress, or of the people, was not directed. So far, then, as the evil which was sought to be remedied interprets the statute, it also guides to an exclusion of this contract from the penalties of the Act.

A singular circumstance, throwing light upon the intent of Congress, is found in this extract from the report of the Senate Committee on Education and Labor, recommending the passage of the bill: "The general facts and considerations which induce the committee to recommend the passage of this bill are set forth in the report of the Committee of the House. The committee report [sic] the bill back without amendment, although there are certain features thereof which might well be changed or modified, in the hope that the bill may not fail of passage during the present session. Especially would the committee have otherwise recommended amendments, substituting for the expression, 'labor and service,' whenever it occurs in the body of the bill, the words 'manual labor' or 'manual service,' as sufficiently broad to accomplish the purposes of the bill, and that such amendments would remove objections which a sharp and perhaps unfriendly criticism may urge to the proposed legislation. The committee, however, believing that the bill in its present form will be construed as including only those whose labor or service is manual in character, and being very desirous that the bill become a law before the adjournment, have reported the bill without change." (Page 6,059, *Congressional Record*, 48th Congress.) And referring back to the report of the Committee of the House, there appears this language: "It seeks to restrain and prohibit the immigration or importation of laborers who would have never seen our shores but for the inducements and allurements of men whose only object is to obtain labor at the lowest possible rate, regardless of the social and material well-being of our own citizens and regardless of the evil consequences which result to American laborers from such immigration. This class of immigrants care nothing about our institutions, and in many instances never even heard of them; they are men whose passage is paid by the importers; they come here under contract to labor for a certain number of years; they are ignorant of our social condition, and that they may remain so they are isolated and prevented from coming into contact with Americans. They are generally from the lowest social stratum, and live upon the coarsest food and in hovels of a character before unknown to American workmen. They, as a rule, do not become citizens, and are certainly not a desirable acquisition to the body politic. The inevitable tendency of their presence among us is to degrade American labor, and to reduce it to the level of the imported pauper labor." (Page 5,359, *Congressional Record,* 48th Congress.)

We find, therefore, that the title of the Act, the evil which was intended to be remedied, the circumstances surrounding the appeal to Congress, the reports of the committee of each house, all concur in affirming that the intent of Congress was simply to stay the influx of this cheap unskilled labor.

Note also that there is often a great deal of ambiguity in the legislative history. It is not uncommon for both sides to quote sections of the legislative history that favor their positions. This ambiguity is demonstrated in the *Powell* case.

United States v. Powell

423 U.S. 87, 96 S. Ct. 316, 46 L.Ed.2d 228 (1975)

Mr. Justice Rehnquist for the majority:

The legislative history of this particular provision is sparse, but the House report indicates that the purpose of the bill upon which §1715 is based was to avoid having the Post Office serve as an instrumentality for the violation of local laws which prohibited the purchase and possession of weapons. H. R. Rep. No. 610, 69th Cong., 1st Sess. (1926). It would seem that sawed-off shotguns would be even more likely to be prohibited by local laws than would pistols and revolvers. A statement by the author of the bill, Representative Miller of Washington, on the floor of the House indicates that the purpose of the bill was to make it more difficult for criminals to obtain concealable weapons. 66 Cong. Rec. 726 (1924). To narrow the meaning of the language Congress used so as to limit it to only those weapons which could be concealed as readily as pistols or revolvers would not comport with that purpose. Cf. *United States v. Alpers,* 338 U.S. 680, 682, 70 S. Ct. 352, 354, 94 L.Ed. 457 (1950).

We therefore hold that a properly instructed jury could have found the 22-inch sawed-off shotgun mailed by respondent to have been a "[firearm] capable of being concealed on the person" within the meaning of 18 U.S.C. §1715. Having done so, we turn to the Court of Appeals' holding that this portion of the statute was unconstitutionally vague.

Mr. Justice Stewart in dissent:

The legislative history of the bill on which §1715 was based contains persuasive indications that it was not intended to apply to firearms larger than the largest pistols or revolvers. Representative Miller, the bill's author, made it clear that the legislative concern was not with the "shotgun, the rifle, or any firearm used in hunting or by the sportsman." 66 Cong. Rec. 727. As a supporter of the legislation stated: "The purpose . . . is to prevent the shipment of pistols and revolvers through the mails." 67 Cong. Rec. 12,041. The only reference to sawed-off shotguns came in a question posed by Representative McKeown: "Is there anything in this bill that will prevent the citizens of Oklahoma from buying sawed-off shotguns to defend themselves against these bank-robbing bandits?" Representative Blanton, an opponent of the bill, responded: "That may come next. Sometimes a revolver is more necessary than a sawed-off shotgun." 66 Cong. Rec. 729. In the absence of more concrete indicia of legislative intent, the pregnant silence that followed Representative Blanton's response can surely be taken as an indication that Congress intended the law to reach only weapons of the same general size as pistols and revolvers.

Sometimes the legislative history can include the failure of the legislative body to react to administrative or judicial interpretations. This aspect of the judicial reasoning process is well illustrated in the continuing controversy over the antitrust status of professional sports. In *Federal Baseball Club v. National League*[4] and *Toolson v. New York Yankees, Inc.*[5] the Supreme Court held that professional baseball was not covered by federal antitrust laws. The Court went on in other cases to rule that other professional sports (such as football, hockey, and boxing) were covered. Then in 1972 when the Court was forced to justify this inconsistency in the Curt Flood case,[6] the majority asserted that since Congress did not pass a specific law to include baseball, the Congress must have approved the Court's earlier position excluding it.

In addition to the legislative history materials discussed above, the courts may also consider interpretations which have been given by administrative agencies. Unless there is a clear reason to the contrary, the courts are expected to sustain the interpretations established by agencies set up to administer the law.

Finally, the courts will also consider the statute's relationship to the common law. Except where there is a clear intent to the contrary, statutes are interpreted in a manner consistent with common law.

Conclusion

When courts are asked to interpret the meaning of statutes, they can use several techniques. They can utilize a dictionary and a grammar book to give a literal interpretation or they can study committee hearings and floor debates from the legislature. Figure 6.1 provides a summary of the major principles of statutory interpretation. The legislative intent is not always clear and sometimes application of these principles can lead to contradictory results. Indeed, Table 6.2 demonstrates the way in which these principles can be set off against each other.

When the legal advocate is attempting to persuade a court to interpret case law in a way that will be favorable to the client, that advocate presents case precedents favorable to the client's interests and attempts to distinguish the case at hand from the fact situations of cases presented by the opposition. Likewise, when the legal advocate is attempting to persuade a court to interpret a statute in a way favorable to a particular client, that advocate urges the court to adopt the method of interpretation which favors the client. The paralegal, therefore, needs to develop the ability to work comfortably with each of the approaches (literalism, intrinsic factors, and extrinsic factors).

ADMINISTRATIVE LAW

Administrative law materials will generally consist of rules and regulations similar in format to statutes as well as agency opinions and decisions that closely resemble court opinions. In either case the interpretation techniques utilized are similar to those discussed above and in chapter 5.

FIGURE 6.1
Summary of the Principles of Statutory Interpretation

Many writers have assembled lists of principles of statutory construction and have presented them at varying levels of specificity. This list attempts to summarize the primary approaches. It is not designed to be exhaustive and the principles are not mutually exclusive.

1. Statutes should always be interpreted to be consistent with the intent of the legislators who enacted them.

2. Statutes should be read literally with the words given meanings that were commonly used at the time the statutes were written.

   a. When modifying words and phrases are used, they should be assumed to modify the words and phrases to which they are closest.

   b. When a list of specific items is followed by a general catch-all like "and others," it is to be interpreted as including only items that are of the same class or type as those specifically listed. (This rule is usually referred to by the Latin phrase *ejusdem generis*.)

   c. If something is not expressly mentioned, it should be assumed that the legislature did not want it included. (This rule is often referred to as express mention, implied exclusion.)

3. Individual parts of a statute should be interpreted so that they will be consistent with the other parts of the statute.

4. Unless the legislative intent is clearly to the contrary, statutes should be interpreted to be consistent with other statutes and with the common law.

5. Statutes should be interpreted to be consistent with committee reports, floor debates, and other aspects of the legislative history.

Federal administrative regulations and decisions are published in the *Federal Register* (Fed. Reg.). This publication is issued daily (except Sundays, Mondays, and the days following holidays). The *Code of Federal Regulations* (C.F.R.) is analogous to the *United States Code* in that it contains only those regulations which are of a general permanent nature and currently in force. It is organized on the basis of the same fifty titles as the *United States Code*.

Some states publish codes of regulations that correspond to the *Code of Federal Regulations*. In other states the regulations must be obtained from each individual agency. At both the state and

TABLE 6.2
An Assemblage of Contrasting Canons of Construction

The following sets of thrusts and parries demonstrate the manner in which the canons of construction can be used on either side of an argument.

Canons of Construction

Thrust	*Parry*
1. A statute cannot go beyond its text.	1. To effect its purpose a statute may be implemented beyond its text.
2. Statutes in derogation of the common law will not be extended by construction.	2. Such acts will be liberally construed if their nature is remedial.
3. Statutes are to be read in the light of the common law and a statute affirming a common law rule is to be construed in accordance with the common law.	3. The common law gives way to a statute which is inconsistent with it. When a statute is designed as a revision of a whole body of law applicable to a given subject it supersedes the common law.
4. Where a foreign statute which has received construction has been adopted, previous construction is adopted too.	4. It may be rejected where there is conflict with the obvious meaning of the statute or where the foreign decisions are unsatisfactory in reasoning or where the foreign interpretation is not in harmony with the spirit or policy of the laws of the adopting state.
5. Where various states have already adopted the statute, the parent state is followed.	5. Where interpretations of other states are inharmonious, there is no such restraint.
6. Statutes *in pari materia* must be construed together.	6. A statute is not *in pari materia* if its scope and aim are distinct or where a legis-

Canons of Construction

Thrust	*Parry*
	lative design to depart from the general purpose or policy of previous enactments may be apparent.
7. A statute imposing a new penalty or forfeiture, or a new liability or disability, or creating a new right of action will not be construed as having a retroactive effect.	7. Remedial statutes are to be liberally construed and if a retroactive interpretation will promote the ends of justice, they should receive such construction.
8. Where design has been distinctly stated no place is left for construction.	8. Courts have the power to inquire into real — as distinct from ostensible — purpose.
9. Definitions and rules of construction contained in an interpretation clause are part of the law and binding.	9. Definitions and rules of construction in a statute will not be extended beyond their necessary import nor allowed to defeat intention otherwise manifested.
10. A statutory provision requiring liberal construction does not mean disregard of unequivocal requirements of the statute.	10. Where a rule of construction is provided within the statute itself the rule should be applied.
11. Titles do not control meaning; preambles do not expand scope; section headings do not change language.	11. The title may be consulted as a guide when there is doubt or obscurity in the body; preambles may be consulted to determine rationale, and thus the true construction of terms; section headings may be looked upon as part of the statute itself.

(Continued)

TABLE 6.2 — Continued

Canons of Construction

Thrust	*Parry*
12. If language is plain and unambiguous it must be given effect.	12. Not when literal interpretation would lead to absurd or mischievous consequences or thwart manifest purpose.
13. Words and phrases which have received judicial construction before enactment are to be understood according to that construction.	13. Not if the statute clearly requires them to have a different meaning.
14. After enactment, judicial decision upon interpretation of particular terms and phrases controls.	14. Practical construction by executive officers is strong evidence of true meaning.
15. Words are to be taken in their ordinary meaning unless they are technical terms or words of art.	15. Popular words may bear a technical meaning and technical words may have a popular signification and they should be construed to agree with evident intention or to make the statute operative.
16. Every word and clause must be given effect.	16. If inadvertently inserted or if repugnant to the rest of the statute, they may be rejected as surplusage.
17. The same language used repeatedly in the same connection is presumed to bear the same meaning throughout the statute.	17. This presumption will be disregarded where it is necessary to assign different meanings to make the statute consistent.
18. Words are to be interpreted according to the proper grammatical effect of their arrangement within the statute.	18. Rules of grammar will be disregarded where strict adherence would defeat purpose.

Canons of Construction

Thrust	Parry
19. Exceptions not made cannot be read in.	19. The letter is only the "bark." Whatever is within the reason of the law is within the law itself.
20. Expression of one excludes another. [Quite typically: not "*the* other."]	20. The language may fairly comprehend many different cases where some only are expressly mentioned by way of example.
21. General terms are to receive a general construction.	21. They may be limited by specific terms with which they are associated or by the scope and purpose of the statute.
22. It is a general rule of construction that where general words follow an enumeration they are to be held as applying only to persons and things of the same general kind or class specifically mentioned (*ejusdem generis*).	22. General words must operate on something. Further, *ejusdem generis* is only an aid in getting the meaning and does not warrant confining the operations of a statute within narrower limits than were intended.
23. Qualifying or limiting words or clauses are to be referred to the next preceding antecedent.	23. Not when evident sense and meaning require a different construction.
24. Punctuation will govern when a statute is open to two constructions.	24. Punctuation marks will not control the plain and evident meaning of language.
25. It must be assumed that language has been chosen with due regard to grammatical propriety and is not interchangeable on mere conjecture.	25. "And" and "or" may be read interchangeably whenever the change is necessary to give the statute sense and effect.

(Continued)

TABLE 6.2 — Continued

Canons of Construction	
Thrust	*Parry*
26. There is a distinction between words of permission and mandatory words.	26. Words imparting permission may be read as mandatory and words imparting command may be read as permissive when such construction is made necessary by evident intention or by the rights of the public.
27. A proviso qualifies the provision immediately preceding.	27. It may clearly be intended to have a wider scope.
28. When the enacting clause is general, a proviso is construed strictly.	28. Not when it is necessary to extend the proviso to persons or cases which come within its equity.

Source: Karl Llewellyn, *The Common Law Tradition* (Boston: Little, Brown, 1960), Appendix C.

federal levels some private publishers issue loose-leaf reporters that contain administrative regulations in specialized areas like taxes and labor law.

Citations for administrative regulations follow a form that is analogous to statutes, for example:

Atomic Energy Comm. Rules of Practice §2.701, 21 Fed. Reg. 805 (1956)

49 C.F.R. §6.1 (Supp. 1966)

Adjudicative decisions are cited in the following manner:

Electric Bond and Share Co., 11 S.E.C. 1,146 (1942)

The abbreviation stands for the agency involved — in this case the Securities and Exchange Commission.

CONSTITUTIONAL LAW

Just as ambiguity can be found in statutes and administrative regulations, it can be found in constitutions. Indeed, the broader and more general the document the greater the likelihood that ambiguity will occur. Consider, for example, the following clauses contained in the United States Constitution:

> The Congress shall have Power to regulate *Commerce* with foreign Nations, and among the several States, and with the Indian Tribes (art. I, §8). The Congress shall have Power to make all Laws which shall be *necessary and proper* for carrying into Execution the foregoing Powers, and all other Powers vested by this Constitution in the Government of the United States, or in any Department or Officer thereof (art. I, §8).

> The *executive Power* shall be vested in a President of the United States of America (art. II, §1).

> The President, Vice-President, and all civil Officers of the United States, shall be removed from Office on Impeachment for, and Conviction of, Treason, Bribery, or other *high Crimes and Misdemeanors* (art. II, §4).

> Congress shall make *no law* respecting an *establishment of religion,* or prohibiting the *free exercise thereof;* or abridging the *freedom of speech,* or *of the press;* or the right of the people peaceably to assemble, and to petition the Government for a redress of grievances (amd. I).

> *Excessive* bail shall not be required, nor *excessive* fines imposed, nor *cruel and unusual* punishment inflicted (amd. VIII).

> No State shall make or enforce any law which shall abridge the *privileges or immunities* of citizens of the United States; nor shall any State deprive any person of life, liberty, or property, without *due process of law:* nor deny to any person within its jurisdiction the *equal protection of the laws* (amd. XIV).

The italicized words are not italicized in the Constitution itself but have been italicized here to draw attention to the ambiguity of various words and phrases.

Over the years the courts have been asked to interpret these and other parts of the Constitution. In approaching this task the courts generally utilize the same approaches discussed in the section on statutory construction. They attempt a literal reading of the words themselves, consider the relationship of the clause in question in conjunction with similar ones located elsewhere in the document, and go back to the minutes of the Constitutional Convention and to the legislative history of amendments.*

Once a court has formally interpreted the meaning of a particular clause of the Constitution, that court decision takes on precedent value and becomes the basis for a case law on the meaning of the Constitution. Therefore, rather than going back and starting again, succeeding courts follow the leads of previous courts and gradually a series of cases develops which explains that "no law" as it is used in the First Amendment really does not mean that the government cannot pass a law restricting obscene materials or punishing libelous statements. As the case law expands, one begins to understand when something is to be considered obscene and when it is not — or when a search is a reasonable search and when it is not.

It is important to realize that the courts (particularly the United States Supreme Court) have the greatest freedom in exercising discretion in the area of constitutional law. This is due not only to the great ambiguity involved but also to the view that the Constitution is a "living" document. The Supreme Court is thus legitimately able to change its interpretations to meet the needs of a changing society. As the great Oliver Wendell Holmes once declared: "[a] word is not a crystal, transparent and unchanged, it is the skin of a living thought and may vary greatly in color and content according to the circumstances and the time in which it is used."[7]

SUMMARY

Statutes are published in the form of individual slip laws, statutes-at-large or sessions laws, and codes. In addition to pro-

---

*James Madison took particularly extensive notes on the debates at the Philadelphia convention which created the United States Constitution. These notes and other important documents relating to the federal Constitution are available in several forms. One particularly good source is Max Farrand, ed., *The Records of the Federal Convention of 1787* (New Haven: Yale University Press, 1937). Records of state constitutional conventions will differ from state to state. In states such as Illinois, where the constitutions were revised fairly recently, the records are in general very good.

viding the actual text of the legislation, annotated codes contain information about the legislative history and references to court decisions which have interpreted the legislation. The format of a legislative citation will depend on whether it is being cited by its public law number, its popular name, the statutes-at-large, or the code.

Where judicial decisions focus on the resolution of a particular conflict that has already occurred between specific parties, statutes ordinarily address future situations for general categories of people, business entities, governments, and so forth. For many reasons, these statutes often contain great ambiguity with respect to their application to a specific event.

In the process of applying the statute in a specific case, the courts must resolve at least part of the ambiguity. The court must decide what the statute means in the context of specific facts presented in the litigation. Whenever possible the court will look to previous court decisions which have interpreted that same statute. However, judges are sometimes asked to interpret statutes in situations where no other courts have done so or where appellate courts must review the interpretations of lower courts.

Under the fundamental principle of statutory interpretation, the judge should construe the language to be consistent with the intent of legislators who enacted the statute. One can do this by giving ambiguous words their most common dictionary meaning. Judges have also developed principles like *ejusdem generis* and express mention, implied exclusion to guide them in utilizing this literalistic approach. Sometimes, however, the courts will reject the outcome of such literal analysis and choose instead to focus on the context of the disputed section in the larger act. This intrinsic approach considers titles assigned to sections and consistency with other sections. At other times the court will look completely beyond the statutory text and use extrinsic analysis or what is commonly called the legislative history. Administrative interpretations and even the common law can be considered as part of this extrinsic analysis.

The interpretation of administrative regulations is similar to that of statutes. At the federal level the regulations are first published in the *Federal Register* and then in the *Code of Federal Regulations*. The methods for publishing state regulations vary widely. Agency opinions and decisions are also published and interpreted like judicial cases.

The interpretation of constitutions also involves the use of literalism, and intrinsic and extrinsic analysis. The legislative history of a constitutional provision involves examination of the notes from the constitutional convention (where available), or the regular legislative hearings, committee reports, and debates that accompany the ratification of a constitutional amendment. Once a court has formally interpreted a constitutional provision, those cases take on precedent value and influence future interpretations of the same clause.

KEY TERMS

annotated codes

codes

contextual analysis

ejusdem generis

express mention, implied exclusion

extrinsic analysis

intrinsic analysis

last antecedent doctrine

legislative history

legislative intent

literalism

sessions laws

slip laws

statutes-at-large

REVIEW QUESTIONS

1. What is the difference in the way in which statutes-at-large and codes are organized?

2. What is the official codification of federal statutes?

3. In what ways does the form of a statute differ from the form of a judicial decision?

4. What is the difference between the *Federal Register* and the *Code of Federal Regulations*?

5. What do *ejusdem generis*, express mention, implied exclusion, and the last antecedent doctrine have in common?

DISCUSSION QUESTIONS

1. Why are statutes sometimes ambiguous? Could careful drafting remove all aspects of this ambiguity? Is it desirable to reduce the amount of ambiguity that usually occurs in drafting legislation?

2. What should be the criteria for rejecting a literalistic approach in favor of an intrinsic or extrinsic analysis?

PROJECTS

1. Locate and then read 15 U.S.C. §1601-1611. Now answer the following questions: (a) Is the statute directed at a particular class or type of person (e.g., government officials, businesses with over twenty-five employees, and so on) or to the general public? (b) What behavior is being regulated (e.g., people are required to file a tax return or are prohibited from using a certain type of drug)? (c) Are there any special conditions which must occur before the statute becomes operative (e.g., the president must declare a national emergency)? (d) Are there any specific exceptions or exclusions? (e) Is there a penalty for failure to comply? If so, what is it? Now locate 12 C.F.R. §226.4, 226.6, and 226.8 and note the relationship of these sections to the statute.

2. Read and then brief *McBoyle v. United States,* 283 U.S. 25 (1931). What principles of statutory construction were used in this case? Do you agree with their conclusion? Why or why not?

3. Read and then brief *National R.R. Passenger Corp. v. National Assn. of R.R. Passengers,* 414 U.S. 453, 94 S. Ct. 690, 38 L.Ed.2d 646 (1974). What techniques of analysis are used to interpret the statute in this case?

4. Read and then brief *Richardson v. Ramirez,* 418 U.S. 24, 94 S. Ct. 2655, 41 L.Ed. 2d 551 (1974). What techniques of analysis are used to interpret the 14th Amendment?

REFERENCES

1. *Ill. Rev. Stat.*, ch. 38, §31-1.
2. 18 U.S.C., §2,421.
3. *United States v. American Trucking Ass'ns,* 310 U.S. 534, 542, 60 S. Ct. 1,059, 1,063 (1940).
4. 259 U.S. 200, 42 S. Ct. 465, 66 L.Ed. 898 (1922).
5. 346 U.S. 356, 74 S. Ct. 78, 98 L.Ed. 64 (1953).
6. *Flood v. Kuhn,* 407 U.S. 258, 92 S. Ct. 2,099, 32 L.Ed. 2d 728 (1972).
7. *Towne v. Eisner,* 245 U.S. 418, 425, 38 S. Ct. 158, 159, 62 L.Ed. 372 (1918).

CHAPTER 7

Legal Research

To fully understand the law, the paralegal must research the constitutions, statutes, and administrative regulations which form the basis of the law in any particular area. Chapters 5 and 6 discussed the location and interpretation of basic source materials and court decisions. Both chapters explained that the paralegal can locate the proper material by its legal citation. But, what if one does not know the proper citation? What if one does not even know whether there is a relevant statute or a case on point? When situations such as these arise, the paralegal needs to utilize one or more of the research strategies discussed in this chapter.

Paralegals are fortunate to be dealing with one of the best organized and indexed sets of knowledge anywhere. In most situations there are at least two alternative methods of seeking the same item. The materials are widely cross-indexed and one piece of information usually leads to several others. When the proper resource materials are available, legal research can be both challenging and rewarding.

ANALYZING THE PROBLEM

Legal research is not conducted in a vacuum. It is undertaken to answer a specific legal problem. Therefore, the first step in the research process is to analyze the problem itself. What are the specific legal issues involved? Are there any statutes known to be involved? Is the problem primarily a matter of local or state law or is it primarily a matter of federal law? What general substantive areas of the law are involved — contract, torts, criminal?

Let us suppose, for example, that a paralegal working for a legal aid agency in Peoria, Illinois, is brought into the following landlord-tenant problem. A client has arrived at the office with a written notice from her landlord stating that if she has not paid the $250.00 she owes in back rent within five days, she will be evicted from her apartment. The client has explained that the landlord left the notice with her nine-year-old son while she was shopping at the grocery store. While she was very unhappy with the apartment and wanted to move out, she had been unable to find suitable housing which she could afford. She wanted to move because the place was overrun by cockroaches and the apartment's temperature during the winter never rose above 60°F. The client does not have a lease and makes monthly rent payments to the building manager. The attorney handling the case has instructed the paralegal to write a memorandum analyzing the client's options.

The ability to recognize the legal issues in this situation strongly depends on knowledge of landlord-tenant law. If the paralegal is generally familiar with this type of law, it will be immediately apparent that the research should focus on the implied warranty of habitability, the tenant's right to repair and offset, the procedural requirements for eviction, and the right to raise affirmative defenses in various types of eviction actions. The paralegal will also know that the research will involve state statutes, local ordinances, and the common law.

If the researcher is not familiar with the law in this area, he or she must learn some of the basic principles of landlord-tenant law to decide where to direct the research.

Since the paralegal's knowledge will differ from topic to topic, this chapter begins with a research strategy which assumes that the researcher knows very little about the particular area involved. A paralegal who comes to a legal problem with a more complete background can eliminate some of the earlier stages in the research process.

DISCOVERING BASIC PRINCIPLES

General overviews of various areas of the law are found in encyclopedias, treatises, articles in periodicals, and annotations. Since treatises, periodical articles, and annotations are usually more specialized and less comprehensive, it is wise to begin with an encyclopedia. An encyclopedia can introduce the basic language and principles and provide a frame of reference for further research.

American Jurisprudence 2d

American Jurisprudence 2d or simply *Am. Jur. 2d,* as it is formally cited and usually referred to, is one of two general encyclopedias which summarizes the entire body of American case law as well as significant federal and common state statutory laws. The encyclopedia is divided into 443 separate topics, ranging from abandoned property to zoning and planning. The treatment of these topics takes up fifty-eight volumes of textual materials. Each topic is broken down into numerous subtopics and each of the subtopics contains a narrative description of the general rules which have emerged from various court decisions. Wherever conflicting decisions are found, the authors point out the conflict and briefly explain both positions. Figure 7.1 shows the manner in which the authors discuss the habitability of an apartment.

In addition to this type of general narrative discussion, *Am. Jur. 2d* also provides various types of cross-references with the citations to specific court cases, annotations in *American Law Reports, Annotated,** selected law review articles, other sections of *Am. Jur. 2d,* and parallel sections of *American Jurisprudence. American Jurisprudence (Am. Jur.)* is an earlier version of *Am. Jur. 2d* that has been gradually replaced by the newer volumes.

*This set is abbreviated as *A.L.R.* and is discussed in greater detail on pages 234–235.

§ 769   LANDLORD AND TENANT   49 Am Jur 2d

accordingly been held that a letting of premises equipped as a motion-picture theater carries with it an implied warranty that they are fit for immediate occupation and use as a theater, which is broken where the heating apparatus proves inadequate to heat the theater during the winter months.[18]

§ 769. Habitability of dwelling or apartment.

Although there are a few decisions to the contrary,[19] the general rule supported by nearly all the authorities on the subject is that in the absence of statute, there is no warranty, covenant, or condition implied in the letting of an unfurnished house or tenement that it is reasonably fit for habitation, and uninhabitability does not warrant abandonment or constitute a constructive eviction,[20] unless there are some special terms in the lease which will raise an implied covenant or condition that the premises shall be fit for occupancy as a dwelling.[1] Nor is there any implied warranty that premises habitable at the time of the demise will continue habitable during the term.[2] These rules apply equally to the case of the letting of several rooms in a tenement or apartment house, if they pass out of the control of the landlord into the exclusive possession of the tenant.[3]

Responsibility of the landlord for the habitable condition may rest upon an express provision in the lease, but a warranty that a house is habitable is not a warranty that it will continue to be habitable.[4] While a recital in a lease that the premises are in good condition has been held in some cases to have the effect of a warranty of habitability,[5] in other cases such a recital has not been deemed to have that effect.[6] Representations as to

---

18. Davey v Christoff, 36 **Ont** L 123, 28 DLR 447.

As to furnished houses, see § 770, infra.

19. Leonard v Armstrong, 73 **Mich** 577, 41 NW 695. See also Buckner v Azulai, 251 **Cal** App 2d Supp 1013, 59 Cal Rptr 806, 27 ALR3d 920, discussed infra this section, at note 15.

Annotation: 27 ALR3d 924, 931, § 3 (vermin infestation); 4 ALR 1453, s. 13 ALR 818, 29 ALR 52, 34 ALR 711.

20. Doyle v Union P. R. Co. 147 **US** 413, 37 L Ed 223, 13 S Ct 333; Webel v Yale University, 125 **Conn** 515, 7 A2d 215, 123 ALR 863; Purcell v English, 86 **Ind** 34; Young v Povich, 121 **Me** 141, 116 A 26, 29 ALR 48; Hopkins v Murphy, 233 **Mass** 476, 124 NE 252, 13 ALR 816; York v Steward, 21 **Mont** 515, 55 P 29; Faber v Creswick, 31 NJ 234, 156 A2d 252, 78 ALR2d 1230; Daly v Wise, 132 **NY** 306, 30 NE 837; Franklin v Brown, 118 **NY** 110, 23 NE 126; Moore v Weber, 71 **Pa** 429; Pines v Perssion, 14 **Wis** 2d 590, 111 NW2d 409 (recognizing rule).

Annotation: 27 ALR3d 924, 931 et seq., §§ 4, 6, 8 (vermin infestation); 4 ALR 1453, 1454, s. 13 ALR 818, 29 ALR 52, 34 ALR 711.

The reason for the fact that in the absence of statute there is no warranty that leased property is habitable, as stated by Baron Parke in Hart v Windsor, 12 Mees & W 68, 152 **Eng** Reprint 1114, is that "there would be no limit to the inconvenience which would

708

ensue. It is much better to leave the parties in every case to protect their interests themselves by proper stipulations, and if they really mean a lease to be void by reason of any unfitness in the subject for the purpose intended, they should express that meaning."

1. Wolfe v Arrott, 109 **Pa** 473, 1 A 333.

Annotation: 4 ALR 1453, 1455, s. 13 ALR 818, 29 ALR 52, 34 ALR 711.

2. York v Steward, 21 **Mont** 515, 55 P 29; Blake v Dick, 15 **Mont** 236, 38 P 1072; Moore v Weber, 71 **Pa** 429.

Annotation: 4 ALR 1453, 1455, s. 13 ALR 818, 29 ALR 52, 34 ALR 711.

3. St. George Mansions v Hetherington, 42 Ont L 10, 4 ALR 1450, 41 DLR 614.

Annotation: 4 ALR 1453, 1455, s. 13 ALR 818, 29 ALR 52, 34 ALR 711.

4. Wolfe v Arrott, 109 **Pa** 473, 1 A 333.

Annotation: 4 ALR 1453, 1455, 1459, s. 13 ALR 818, 29 ALR 52, 34 ALR 711.

5. Curran v Cushing, 197 Ill App 371 (abstract); Tyler v Disbrow, 40 **Mich** 415.

Annotation: 4 ALR 1453, 1459, 1460, s. 13 ALR 818, 29 ALR 52, 34 ALR 711.

6. Foster v Peyser, 9 Cush (**Mass**) 242, holding that where a lease of a dwelling house provided that the lessor should not be called upon to make any repairs during the term, "the house being now in perfect order," the latter provision related to the state of

---

FIGURE 7.1

Sample *Am. Jur. 2d* Page Regarding Habitability of Dwelling or Apartment

Am. Jur. 2d volumes supersede the corresponding *Am. Jur.* books.*

Like most secondary legal reference books, *Am. Jur. 2d* is kept current with the publication of pocket part supplements. New material is organized to correspond with the numbering system used in the bound volume and then inserted in a special pocket at the back of that volume. Figure 7.2 shows the pocket part materials which supplement the material discussed in the main text in Figure 7.1. When these pocket supplements get too thick and unwieldy, the publisher issues a replacement volume.

There are two primary methods for locating the appropriate sections to research. The paralegal's ability to find the most relevant sections of the textual material will depend on prior knowledge of the law in that particular area.

The person who is totally unfamiliar with a particular area should start with the subject analysis method. Each general topic in *Am. Jur. 2d* begins with a short narrative description of what will be discussed in that section as well as a review of related topics which are covered elsewhere. (*See* Figure 7.3.) This is followed by an outline of the major topics covered in that section and a detailed outline of each subtopic. Figure 7.4 shows the amount of detail contained in the outlines of the subtopics. A careful review of the entire outline for the landlord and tenant area will help the researcher locate all potentially relevant sections.

An alternative method of finding the relevant sections of *Am. Jur. 2d* involves using the indexes in separate volumes at the end of the series and those at the back of each substantive volume. The procedure is similar to that used in reading any normal index. The key is to determine the correct words to locate. Figure 7.5 demonstrates that once the researcher has looked up "uninhabitability" several sections appear to be quite promising. But how does the researcher know that one should look up "uninhabitability"? There is no secret formula. The researcher should compile a list of potential key words to be researched. If the words cannot be located in an index, the researcher should attempt to identify several synonyms and then try to find them in an index. If none of these efforts work, the subject analysis method described previously would probably be the best approach.

---

*A table of parallel references between *Am. Jur.* and *Am. Jur. 2d* can be found at the beginning of each *Am. Jur. 2d* volume.

LANDLORD AND TENANT § 769

liability for injury or death of tenant or third person caused by dangerous condition of premises. 64 ALR3d 339.

Love, Landlord's Liability for Defective Premises: Caveat Lessee, Negligence, or Strict Liability? 1975 Wisconsin L Rev 19.

Additional case authorities for section:

Covenant of habitability is implied in residential but not business leases. Van Ness Ind., Inc. v Claremont Plainting & Decorating Co., NJ Super 507, 324 A2d 102.

p 706, n 6—

See, however, Marini v Ireland, 56 **NJ** 130, 265 A2d 526, 40 ALR3d 1356, holding that a covenant is implied, at least in residential letting, that there are no latent defects, at inception of lease, in facilities vital to use of premises for residential purposes, and that these facilities will remain in usable condition during entire term of lease.

To the same effect, see Mease v Fox, — **Iowa** —, 200 NW2d 791.

Doctrine of implied warranty of habitability did not apply to corporate tenant taking premises "as is" under commercial lease. Coulston v Teliscope Productions, Ltd (Sup App T) 378 NYS2d 553.

Court will not reject common law doctrine of caveat emptor in landlord-tenant relationships; no implied warranty of habitability arises from residential lease. Blackwell v Del Bosco (**Colo**) 558 P2d 563 (court noted that implied warranty theory involves social and economic complexities better suited to legislative research, and explained that embracing the theory might cause landlords to raise rents significantly or abandon run-down premises, leaving the poor without any place to live.

§ 769. Habitability of dwelling or apartment

Practice Aids: Modern status of landlord's tort liability for injury or death of tenant or third person caused by dangerous condition of premises. 64 ALR3d 339.

Line, Implied Warranties of Habitability and Fitness for Intended Use in Urban Residential Leases. 26 Baylor L Rev 161, Spring 1974.

Moskovitz, The Implied Warranty of Habitability: A New Doctrine Raising New Issues. 62 California L Rev 1444, December 1974.

Meyers, The Covenant of Habitability and the American Law Institute. 27 Stanf L Rev 879, Feb., 1975.

p 708, n 19—Lemle v Breeden, 51 **Hawaii** 426, 478, 462 P2d 470, 40 ALR3d 637.

Mease v Fox, — **Iowa** —, 200 NW2d 791.

Marini v Ireland, 56 **NJ** 130, 265 A2d 526, 40 ALR3d 1356.

Annotation: 40 ALR3d 646, 652, 653, §§ 4[b], 5[a].

p 708, n 2—

See, however, Javins v First Nat. Realty Corp.

138 App **DC** 369, 428 F2d 1071, cert den 400 US 925, 27 L Ed 2d 185, 91 S Ct 186, in which under the Housing Regulations for the District of Columbia a warranty to maintain the leased premises in habitable condition was held implied by operation of law into leases of urban dwelling units covered by the Regulations; Marini v Ireland, 56 **NJ** 130, 265 A2d 526, 40 ALR3d 1356, stating that even though lease of apartment did not include specific covenant to repair, landlord should, in residential letting, be held to implied covenant against latent defects, whether designated as covenant "to repair" or as covenant "of habitability and livability fitness," which is a covenant that at inception of lease there are no latent defects in facilities vital to use of premises for residential purposes as well as a covenant that these facilities will remain in usable condition during entire term of lease, in performance of which covenant the landlord is required to maintain those facilities in condition that renders premises livable.

p 709, n 13—

Annotation: Landlord and tenant: Constructive eviction based on flooding, dampness, or the like. 33 ALR3d 1356.

Uniform Laws:

A landlord is required to make all repairs and do whatever is necessary to put and keep the premises in a fit and habitable condition. Uniform Residential Landlord and Tenant Act § 2.104(a)(2).

Hirsch, Hirsch & Margolis, Regression Analysis of the Effects of Habitability Laws Upon Rent: An Empirical Observation on the Ackerman-Komesar Debate. 63 Cal L Rev 1098, Sept. 1975.

In the light of the implied warranty of habitability in an apartment lease agreement, it was error to refuse the tenant's application for a judicial declaration that she was obliged to make rental payments only after the landlord complied with his duty to substantially obey the housing codes and make the premises habitable where the court found that the premises developed defects, not caused by the tenant, during her occupancy which constituted substantial violations of the governing municipal housing code. Hinson v Delis, 26 **Cal** App 3d 62, 102 Cal Rptr 661.

In general, there is no implied warranty of habitability given to a tenant, but rather, he takes the premises as he finds them and bears the risk of any defective conditions which are within the area under his exclusive possession and control. Thomas v Roper, 162 **Conn** 343, 294 A2d 321 (no finding that alleged defect existed at the beginning of the tenancy).

p 709, n 15—

See Lemle v Breeden, 51 **Hawaii**, 426, 478, 462, P2d 470, 40 ALR3d 367, in applying an implied warranty of habitability and fitness for use in the lease of a dwelling and observing that the application of such a warranty in leases of rented dwellings recognizes changes in the

[49 Am Jur 2d Supp]

FIGURE 7.2

Sample Pocket Part Supplement Page from *Am. Jur. 2d*

AMERICAN JURISPRUDENCE

SECOND EDITION

Volume 49

LANDLORD AND TENANT

Scope of Topic: This article discusses the principles and rules of law applicable to and governing the relation of landlord and tenant. In general, it embraces the creation and existence of the relation through a formal lease, or otherwise, and the rights, duties, and liabilities arising out of the relationship, including the rights and liabilities of third persons such as assignees of the leasehold, subtenants, and transferees of the landlord's reversion, and including the liability of the landlord and tenant for injuries sustained on, or as a result of the use of, the demised premises. The article also includes ground rents and permanent leaseholds.

Treated elsewhere are the following: the responsibility as between landlord and tenant for injuries to persons upon highways, streets, or sidewalks adjacent to the leased premises (see 39 Am Jur 2d, HIGHWAYS, STREETS, AND BRIDGES §§ 369, 370, 499, 502, 521, 522, 537, 544); the liability of a landlord or tenant for injuries sustained in the use of elevators on the leased premises (see 26 Am Jur 2d, ELEVATORS AND ESCALATORS §§ 18–20, 28, 29, 40, 49); the taking of leased property in eminent domain, compensation and damages therefor, and apportionment thereof between landlord and tenant (see 26, 27 Am Jur 2d, EMINENT DOMAIN §§ 79, 177, 250, 352 et seq.); a property owner's duty and liability to a prospective tenant (see NEGLIGENCE); the status and rights of cotenants (see 20 Am Jur 2d, COTENANCY AND JOINT OWNERSHIP); estates and tenancies generally, including estates for life created by leases with reservation of rent, and estates less than freehold (see 28 Am Jur 2d, ESTATES §§ 9 et seq., 56 et seq., 130, 131); the power of corporations to lease their realty (see 19 Am Jur 2d, CORPORATIONS §§ 1023, 1024); leases involving persons of a particular status or in a particular relationship or under disability (see 3 Am Jur 2d, ALIENS AND CITIZENS § 23; 31 Am Jur 2d, EXECUTORS AND ADMINISTRATORS §§ 249, 250; 39 Am Jur 2d, GUARDIAN AND WARD §§ 113–117; 41 Am Jur 2d, HUSBAND AND WIFE §§ 154, 164 et seq.; 42 Am Jur 2d, INFANTS §§ 69, 75, 111; LIFE TENANTS AND REMAINDERMEN; MORTGAGES; MUNICIPAL CORPORATIONS, COUNTIES AND OTHER POLITICAL SUBDIVISIONS; PARTNERSHIP; TRUSTS); leases of particular kinds of property or for particular purposes (see 38 Am Jur 2d, GARAGES, AND FILLING AND PARKING STATIONS §§ 153 et seq.; 38 Am Jur 2d, GAS AND OIL §§ 54 et seq., 103 et seq., 164 et seq.; LOGS AND TIMBER; MINES AND MINERALS; RAILROADS; SCHOOLS); leases of personal property (see 8 Am Jur 2d, BAILMENTS §§ 28 et seq., 91, 96 et seq., 149 et seq., 225, 251) or

1

FIGURE 7.3
Sample *Am. Jur. 2d* Topic Analysis Page

§ 768. Tenantability and fitness; implied warranty or covenant
§ 769. Habitability of dwelling or apartment
§ 770. — Furnished house or apartment
§ 771. Liability for injuries resulting from defective premises
§ 772. — Under statutes
§ 773. — Possession in common by tenants

b. Duty to Make or Pay for Repairs or Improvements

§ 774. Generally
§ 775. Reservation of right to enter or making repairs as creating duty to repair
§ 776. Duty to improve
§ 777. Duty to pay for improvements made by lessee
§ 778. Statutory duty to repair
§ 779. Alterations or improvements required by statute or public authorities

c. Liability for Injuries to Persons on Premises in Right of Tenant

§ 780. Generally
§ 781. Subtenants
§ 782. Lease for public purposes; liability to tenant's business patrons; "public purpose" rule
§ 783. — Bases or rationale of liability under "public purpose" rule
§ 784. — Application of "public purpose" rule; requisites
§ 785. — Particular purposes
§ 786. Responsibility for danger caused by tenant or for his misuse or negligent use of premises

d. Representations, Misrepresentations, Fraud, Concealment, or Nondisclosure

§ 787. Generally; representations
§ 788. Nondisclosure or concealment of defects
§ 789. — Prevailing view as to extent of liability and duty of disclosure
§ 790. — Minority view; duty to discover and disclose defects
§ 791. Nondisclosure, concealment, misrepresentation, or fraud as to habitability
§ 792. — Infected houses

e. Liability for Damages in Making Repairs or Improvements

§ 793. Generally
§ 794. Negligence as basis of liability; causal relationship
§ 795. Where landlord's undertaking is gratuitous or voluntary
§ 796. Damage to property
§ 797. Who may recover
§ 798. Contributory negligence; assumption of risk

2. As to Property Not Included in the Lease

a. In General

§ 799. Generally
§ 800. Grounds of liability, generally
§ 801. Failure to repair
§ 802. Change or alteration in physical conditions
§ 803. Permissive character of use
§ 804. Premises leased to other tenants

28

FIGURE 7.4

Format for *Am. Jur. 2d* Subject Analysis Outline

INDEX

1159

FIGURE 7.5
Sample Index Page for *Am. Jur. 2d* Landlord and Tenant Volume

Corpus Juris Secundum

Corpus Juris Secundum is the other general encyclopedia. It too is usually referred to by its standard abbreviation — *C.J.S.* It is acclaimed as "the most exhaustive and comprehensive legal encyclopedia ever written," and "a complete restatement of the entire body of American law based upon all reported cases from 1658 to date."[1] *C.J.S.* is divided into 433 topics spread over 101 textual volumes. These topics are in turn subdivided into many specific subtopics.

Figure 7.6 demonstrates the similarity in approach between *Am. Jur. 2d* and *C.J.S.* Both summarize the sometimes contradictory decisions of various state and federal courts and include citations to these cases and to law review articles. While *Am. Jur. 2d* includes cross-references to *Am. Jur.* and to *A.L.R.*, *C.J.S.* includes cross-references to *Corpus Juris* (an earlier version of *C.J.S.*), and to the key number system used in West's digests.* *C.J.S.* also uses pocket supplements to update the material as shown in Figure 7.7 and issues replacement volumes when the supplements become too unwieldy. On the other hand, *C.J.S.* begins each subtopic with a summary statement in boldface type but *Am. Jur. 2d* does not.

As with *Am. Jur. 2d* the researcher can use either the subject analysis or the index methods to locate relevant textual materials in *Corpus Juris Secundum.* Figures 7.8, 7.9, and 7.10 show the similarities in makeup of the subject analysis and index sections in *Am. Jur. 2d* and *C.J.S.* Both individual volume indexes and a multivolume general index at the end of the set are included in *C.J.S.* Note that in *Am. Jur. 2d* information about the implied warranty of habitability was found under the index heading of "uninhabitability." However, the *C.J.S.* index has no such heading. In the *C.J.S.* index the heading is "habitable condition." The general index contains a law chart designed to help select the correct topic areas, as shown in Figure 7.11. It divides all of the more than 400 topics into subcategories under the general areas of persons, property, contracts, torts, crimes, remedies, and government.

---

*See pages 251–256 for an explanation of key numbers and the digest system.

not excuse the lessor from his obligation to deliver the building in a sound condition as to structural parts,[61] or exclude the lessor's warranty against essential defects.[62] Under a statute requiring the lessor to maintain a thing in condition such as to serve for the use for which it was hired, where a room is rented for the storage of goods, the lessor is liable for damages to the goods due to the condition of the room.[63]

Compliance with ordinances. The general rule of no implied warranty of suitability of property for the purpose for which it was leased has been applied where property cannot be used for the purpose for which it was leased because such use would consti-

§ 305. —— Dwellings

a. In general
b. Furnished dwellings

a. In General

Ordinarily there is no implied covenant or warranty on the part of a landlord that property leased for dwelling purposes is habitable or fit for habitation, or that it is free from vermin; but such a covenant or warranty may be implied where the lease is of an apartment in a multiple dwelling.

Library References

Landlord and Tenant ⊂⇒125.

It is generally recognized that there is no implied warranty or covenant on the part of a landlord

---

that property leased for dwelling purposes is habitable or fit for habitation,[69.50] or that it is safe, tenantable, or fit for the purposes of the lease,[70] at least where the dwelling is unfurnished.[71] The rule applies equally to the case of the letting of several rooms in a tenement house if they pass out of the control of the landlord into the exclusive possession of the tenant.[72]

Some authorities hold that, in the absence of fraud,[73] there is no implied covenant or representation by the landlord that a house or apartment is free from vermin or disease germs;[74] while other authorities are to the effect that, unless there is a provision to the contrary in the lease of an apartment in a multiple dwelling, the landlord impliedly covenants that the premises will be habitable,[75] free from vermin,[76] and suitable for the dwelling

purposes for which they are leased,[77] and that the landlord is under a duty to maintain a leased apartment in a reasonably safe condition.[78]

A fraudulent concealment of defects or conditions making the premises unfit for residence may justify an abandonment thereof,[79] or may be waived by the tenant.[80] A mere expression of opinion on the part of the landlord does not amount to a warranty that a dwelling is fit for habitation.[81] In any event, the scope of a warranty does not extend beyond the terms of the representation.[82]

An express covenant that the lease of a dwelling is subject to the landlord obtaining a certificate of occupancy may be waived by the tenant where he takes possession and remains for a substantial period of time although the landlord has not obtained the required certificate.[82.5]

69.50 U.S.—State of Md., for Use of Pumphrey v. Manor Real Estate & Trust Co., C.A.Md., 176 F.2d 414.
Ill.—Ciskoski v. Michalsen, 152 N.E. 2d 479, 19 Ill.App.2d 327.
Pa.—De Raczynski v. Mack, Com.Pl., 25 Monroe L.R. 15.

Safe for habitation
Normally, there is no implied covenant that leased premises are safe for habitation and use or that they will remain in that condition.
Del.—Brandt v. Yeager, Super., 199 A.2d 768.

Implication
Although no covenant of habitability shall be implied from a landlord-tenant relationship, such a covenant may be implied from the terms of a lease.
N.Y.—Heissenbuttel v. Comnas, 177 N.Y.S.2d 850, 14 Misc.2d 509.

Abandonment for uninhabitability
Tenant should inspect premises before taking them, or he should secure an express warranty, and he is not entitled to abandon premises be-

will not be implied, there being no such express covenant.
N.Y.—Mulligan v. Fioravera, 239 N.Y. S. 438, 228 App.Div. 270, affirmed 175 N.E. 304, 255 N.Y. 539.
Shea v. Dyas, 12 N.Y.S.2d 951.

Under oral lease of apartment in multiple dwelling, landlord does not impliedly warrant that demised premises are in a reasonably safe condition.
Conn.—Bentley v. Dynarski, 186 A.2d 791, 150 Conn. 147—Torre v. De Renzo, 122 A.2d 25, 143 Conn. 302.

71. Del.—**Corpus Juris cited in** Leech v. Husbands, 152 A. 729, 731, 4 W.W.Harr. 362.
36 C.J. p 47 note 8.
Furnished dwellings see infra subdivision b of this section.

72. Mass.—McKeon v. Cutter, 31 N. E. 389, 156 Mass. 296.
36 C.J. p 47 note 9.

73. Del.—Leech v. Husbands, 152 A. 729, 4 W.W.Harr. 362.

74. U.S.—**Corpus Juris cited in**

76. Cal.—Buckner v. Azulai, supra.
Minn.—Delamater v. Foreman, 239 N. W. 148, 184 Minn. 428.

77. Cal.—Buckner v. Azulai, Super., 59 Cal.Rptr. 806.
Ill.—Allmon v. Davis, 248 Ill.App. 350.

Heat
Landlord leasing modern apartment containing apparently modern heating system impliedly warrants it will maintain reasonably comfortable temperature.
La.—Purnell v. Dugue, 129 So. 178, 14 La.App. 137.

Lack of plumbing and sewage system
Where leased house did not contain proper plumbing and sewage disposal system as required by state and parish law, mere showing that no application or plans for sewage system had been submitted, without further proof that premises were in fact unsanitary and uninhabitable, did not render lease void ab initio.
La.—Hancock v. Sliman, App., 175 So. 2d 437.

FIGURE 7.6
Sample Page from Text of *Corpus Juris Secundum*

CORPUS JURIS SECUNDUM

———•———

LANDLORD AND TENANT

This Title includes nature and incidents of estates for years and tenancies from year to year, at will, or at sufferance; leases and agreements for the occupation of real property in general, the relation between the parties thereto, and their rights and liabilities as between themselves and as to others incident to such relation; and remedies relating thereto.

Excluded are leases of property of particular classes of persons (Infants; Insane Persons; Corporations; and other specific titles); leases of particular species of property (Railroads; Mines and Minerals; Waters; and other specific titles); rent charges and ground rents (Ground Rents); and implied liabilities for use and occupation of real property (Use and Occupation).

Analysis

See also descriptive word index in volume containing end of this Title

51C C.J.S.—1

1

FIGURE 7.7

Page of Updated Material from *Corpus Juris Secundum*, Pocket Supplement

§ 303 LANDLORD & TENANT

51C CJS 48

Pages 771-777

27.5 Del.—Brown v. Robyn Realty Co., Super., 367 A.2d 183.
D.C.—Kanelos v. Kettler, C.A., 406 F.2d 951, 132 U.S.App.D.C. 133.

Statute not retroactive
N.Y.—Kaplan v. Coulston, 381 N.Y.S.2d 634, 85 Misc.2d 745.

Implied warranty of habitability
Iowa—Duke v. Clark, 267 N.W.2d 63.
Tex.—Johnson v. Highland Hills Drive Apartments, 568 S.W.2d 661.

page 772

27.10 La.—Reed v. Classified Parking System, App., 232 So.2d 103, writ ref. 234 So.2d 194, 255 La. 1097, writ ref. 234 So.2d 194, 255 La. 1098.
29. Ill.—Longenecker v. Hardin, 264 N.E.2d 878, 130 Ill.App.2d 468.
La.—McCrory Corp. v. Latter, App., 331 So.2d 577, writ den. 334 So.2d 229.
N.Y.—Houston Realty Corp. v. Castro, 404 N.Y.S.2d 796, 94 Misc.2d 115.
Ohio—Glyco v. Schultz, 289 N.E.2d 919, 35 Ohio Misc. 25.

Statute held inapplicable to business property
N.J.—Van Ness Industries, Inc. v. Claremont Painting & Decorating Co., 324 A.2d 102, 129 N.J.Super. 507.

Untenantable conditions not found
Conn.—Thomas v. Roper, 294 A.2d 321, 162 Conn. 343.
N.J.—Park Hill Terrace Associates v. Glennon, 369 A.2d 938, 146 N.J.Super. 271.

Statutory provision breached
N.Y.—Kekllas v. Saddy, 389 N.Y.S.2d 756, 88 Misc.2d 1042.
35. Mo.—Henderson v. W. C. Haas Realty Management, Inc., App., 561 S.W. 2d 382.

§ 304. Suitability of Premises for Purpose for Which They Were Leased

page 773

43. U.S.—Pointer v. American Oil Co., D.C.Ind., 295 F.Supp. 573.
Ala.—Martin v. Springdale Stores, Inc., Civ., 354 So.2d 1144, cert. den. Ex parte Martin, 354 So.2d 1146.
N.J.—Conroy v. 10 Brewster Ave. Corp., 234 A.2d 415, 97 N.J.Super. 75—Coleman v. Steinberg, 253 A.2d 167, 54 N.J. 58.
Academy Spires, Inc. v. Jones, 261 A.2d 413, 108 N.J.Super. 395.
N.Y.—Refrigeration for Science, Inc. v. Deacon Realty Corp., 334 N.Y.S.2d 418, 70 Misc.2d 500, affd. 344 N.Y.S. 2d 1018, 42 A.D.2d 691.
Tex.—Cameron v. Calhoun-Smith Distributing Co., Civ.App., 442 S.W.2d 815.

page 774

44. Kan.—Service Oil Co., Inc. v. White, 542 P.2d 652, 218 Kan. 87.

47. Suitability assured
Ga.—Warner v. Arnold, 210 S.E.2d 350, 133 Ga.App. 174.
48.10 Minn.—Vermes v. American Dist. Tel. Co., 251 N.W.2d 101.
N.J.—Academy Spires, Inc. v. Jones, 261 A.2d 413, 108 N.J.Super. 395.

page 775

49. Kan.—Service Oil Co., Inc. v. White, 542 P.2d 652, 218 Kan. 87.
N.J.—Reste Realty Corp. v. Cooper, 251 A.2d 268, 53 N.J. 444, 33 A.L.R.3d 1341.
51. Kan.—Service Oil Co., Inc. v. White, 542 P.2d 652, 218 Kan. 87.
52.5 N.H.—Goglia v. Rand, 319 A.2d 281, 114 N.H. 252.

Lessee's knowledge of difficulties immaterial
N.Y.—Henderson Development Co., Inc. v. Commenco Corp., 355 N.Y.S.2d 859, 44 A.D.2d 889, affd 337 N.E.2d 130, 37 N.Y.2d 728, 374 N.Y.S.2d 618.
53. La.—Evans v. Does, App., 283 So.2d 804.

Intended as protection for lessee
N.Y.—Henderson Development Co., Inc. v. Commenco Corp., 355 N.Y.S.2d 859, 44 A.D.2d 889, affd. 337 N.E.2d 130, 37 N.Y.2d 728, 374 N.Y.S.2d 618.

54. Language not ambiguous
Ga.—Gilreath v. Argo, 219 S.E.2d 461, 135 Ga.App. 849.
55. Iowa—C.J.S. quoted in Osterling v. Sturgeon, 156 N.W.2d 344, 348, 261 Iowa 836.

page 776

58. Del.—Brown v. Robyn Realty Co., Super., 367 A.2d 183.
60.10 La.—Add Chemical Co. v. Gulf-Marine Fabricators, Inc., App., 345 So.2d 216, writ den., Sup., 347 So.2d 263.

§ 305. ——— Dwellings

page 777

69.50 Colo.—Blackwell v. Del Bosco, 536 P.2d 838, 35 Colo.App. 399, affd. Sup.
N.Y.—Graham v. Wisenburn, 334 N.Y. S.2d 81, 39 A.D.2d 334.
Or.—Cook v. Salishan Properties, Inc., 569 P.2d 1033, 279 Or. 333.

Statutory tenants no action based on contract
N.Y.—Committee For Preservation of Fresh Meadows, Inc. v. Fresh Meadows Associates, 403 N.Y.S.2d 839, 62 A.D.2d 529.

70. Would not be implied under circumstances
Colo.—Blackwell v. Del Bosco, 536 P.2d 838, 35 Colo.App. 399, affd. Sup., 558 P.2d 563.

There is other authority that in a lease of a dwelling house there is an implied warranty of habitability and fitness for use intended,[72.5] which exists in unfurnished as well as furnished dwellings.[72.10] In determining whether there exists a breach of this implied warranty each case must depend on its own facts and circumstances.[72.15]

72.5 Cal.—Hinson v. Delis, 102 Cal.Rptr. 661, 26 C.A.3d 62.
Hawaii—Lemle v. Breeden, 462 P.2d 470, 51 Haw. 426, 478, 40 A.L.R.3d 637.
Iowa—Mease v. Fox, 200 N.W.2d 791.
Minn.—Fritz v. Warthen, 213 N.W.2d 339, 298 Minn. 54.
N.J.—Berzito v. Gambino, 308 A.2d 17, 63 N.J. 460.
N.Y.—Tonetti v. Penati, 367 N.Y.S.2d 804, 48 A.D.2d 25.
Hall v. Fraknoi, 330 N.Y.S.2d 637, 69 Misc.2d 470.

Substantial compliance with building code
Ill.—Jack Spring, Inc. v. Little, 280 N. E.2d 208, 50 Ill.2d 351.
Mo.—King v. Moorehead, App., 495 S.W. 2d 65.
N.Y.—Morbeth Realty Corp. v. Velez, 343 N.Y.S.2d 406, 73 Misc.2d 996.

Protection does not coincide with State Sanitary Code
Mass.—Boston Housing Authority v. Hemingway, 293 N.E.2d 831, 363 Mass. 184.

Oral or written lease
Wash.—Foisy v. Wyman, 515 P.2d 160, 83 Wash.2d 22.

Provisions of housing code part of lease
Kan.—Steele v. Latimer, 521 P.2d 304, 214 Kan. 329.

Bare living requirements to be maintained
Cal.—Green v. Superior Court of City and County of San Francisco, 111 Cal.Rptr. 704, 517 P.2d 1168, 10 C. 3d 616.

Implied warranty created by ordinance
N.Y.—401 Boardwalk Corp. v. Gutzwiller, 368 N.Y.S.2d 122, 82 Misc.2d 84.

Object
N.Y.—401 Boardwalk Corp. v. Gutzwiller, 368 N.Y.S.2d 122, 82 Misc.2d 84.

Breach of warranty
N.Y.—Cohen v. Werner, 368 N.Y.S.2d 1005, 82 Misc.2d 295, affd. 378 N.Y.S. 2d 868, 85 Misc.2d 341.

Read into leases
N.Y.—Kipsborough Realty Corp. v. Goldbetter, 367 N.Y.S.2d 916, 81 Misc.2d 1054.

Statute held not retroactive
N.Y.—Francais v. Cusa Bros. Enterprises, Inc., 385 N.Y.S.2d 183, 53 A.D.2d 24.

Applicable to rent control or stabilized buildings
N.Y.—Park West Management Corp. v. Mitchell, 404 N.Y.S.2d 115, 62 A.D. 2d 291.

Statute retroactive
N.Y.—Park West Management Corp. v. Mitchell, 404 N.Y.S.2d 115, 62 A.D. 2d 291.

Same remedies as for breach of express warranty
Pa.—Pugh v. Holmes, 384 A.2d 1234.

72.10 Hawaii—Lund v. MacArthur, 462 P.2d 482, 51 Haw. 473.

72.15 Relevant factors to be considered
Cal.—Hinson v. Delis, 102 Cal.Rptr. 661, 26 C.A.3d 62.
Hawaii—Lemle v. Breeden, 462 P.2d 470, 51 Haw. 426, 478, 40 A.L.R.3d 637—Lund v. MacArthur, 462 P.2d 482, 51 Haw. 473.
Iowa—Mease v. Fox, 200 N.W.2d 791.
Mo.—King v. Moorehead, App., 495 S.W. 2d 65.
N.J.—Timber Ridge Town House v. Dietz, 338 A.2d 21, 133 N.J.Super. 577.
Wash.—Foisy v. Wyman, 515 P.2d 160, 83 Wash.2d 22.

Presence of rats in dwelling
Hawaii—Lemle v. Breeden, 462 P.2d 470, 51 Haw. 426, 478, 40 A.L.R.3d 637.

Complaint held to state cause of action
Ill.—Gillette v. Anderson, 282 N.E.2d 149, 4 Ill.App.3d 838.
Mich.—Borman's Inc. v. Lake State Development Co., 230 N.W.2d 363, 60 Mich.App. 175.

Constructive eviction as material breach
Mass.—Boston Housing Authority v. Hemingway, 293 N.E.2d 831, 363 Mass. 184.

Right to negotiate better terms is no defense
N.Y.—Morbeth Realty Corp. v. Velez, 343 N.Y.S.2d 406, 73 Misc.2d 996.

Notice of defects by other tenants is sufficient
Mass.—Boston Housing Authority v. Hemingway, 293 N.E.2d 831, 363 Mass. 184.

Reasonable time for correction of defect
Mo.—King v. Moorehead, App., 495 S.W. 2d 65.

Breach must be of substantial nature
Cal.—Green v. Superior Court of City and County of San Francisco, 111 Cal.Rptr. 704, 517 P.2d 1168, 10 C. 3d 616.
Iowa—Mease v. Fox, 200 N.W.2d 791.
Mass.—McKenna v. Begin, App., 362 N. E.2d 548.

Abandonment not essential element of cause of action
N.Y.—401 Boardwalk Corp. v. Gutzwiller, 368 N.Y.S.2d 122, 82 Misc.2d 84.

Mail delivery
Tex.—Johnson v. Highland Hills Drive Apartments, Civ.App., 552 S.W.2d 493.

Notice of breach
Ill.—Jarrell v. Hartman, 363 N.E.2d 626, 6 Ill.Dec. 812, 48 Ill.App.3d 985.

FIGURE 7.8

Sample Topic Summary Page from *C.J.S.*

LANDLORD & TENANT 51C C.J.S.

IX. LANDLORD'S TITLE AND REVERSION—Continued

B. Estoppel of Tenant to Deny Title—Continued

See also descriptive word index in volume containing end of this Title

12

FIGURE 7.9
Sample Topic Outline Page from *C.J.S.*

LANDLORD & TENANT

Guests—Continued
Repairs,
Covenant to repair as applying to, § 418(5), p. 128
Multiple dwellings, duty of owner to keep premises in repair, § 418(1), p. 110, n. 6
Gun club, lease of agricultural land for recreational purposes, limitation of term, § 227, n. 50
Habendum clause,
Assignment of lease, necessity, § 40
Term, effect, § 29, n. 68
Habitable condition,
Duty of lessor to put or keep premises in, § 367, p. 936 ; § 417(3), p. 35
Implied covenant, § 305
Public officials ordering premises vacated as unfit, dispossession proceedings, § 758, p. 92
Termination of lease by lessee, § 112, p. 357
Hail insurance, sharecroppers,
Apportionment, § 805, p. 338, n. 66
Liens, § 817, n. 64
Halls and hallways,
Common use, liability of landlord,
Hallways reserved for common use, § 423(4), p. 171
Personal injuries, § 417(7), p. 58
Guests or invitees, liability of landlord for personal injuries to, § 418(2), p. 118
Insurer of safety, landlord, § 417(7), p. 60
Lights and lighting,
Assumption of risk of injury as result of failure to provide, § 417(20), p. 109
Duty or obligation of landlord, § 297 ; § 417(7), p. 64
Multiple dwellings, duty of landlord to repair, § 366(1), p. 927, n. 78
Premises used by several tenants in common, landlord's duty to repair, § 366(2), p. 932
Right to use as passing under lease, § 295(1)
Handicapped persons,
Rent control, eviction, § 792.13, n. 55
Sharecroppers, termination of lease, § 807
Handrails,
Exterior stairways, duty to provide lighting, § 417(7), p. 66
Tenant factories, duty of maintaining stairs, § 367, p. 937
Hanging clothes, defective appliances for, liability for injuries, § 417(11), p. 77
Harassment, dispossession proceedings, § 792
Hardship,
Forfeiture of lease, relief against, § 102, p. 333
Rent control, § 792.15
Harvesting crops. Agricultural products. ante
Harvesting ice, entry on premises before time for purpose of, § 308
Hay, reservation of title to, § 348, p. 881
Hazardous use of premises, increased insurance rates, liability of lessee, § 384
Health,
Ejectment, exemplary damages, § 727, n. 88
Rent control, compelling necessity, § 792.15, n. 86
Health officer, removal from premises precluded by order, failure to surrender possession, § 316, p. 800
Hearings. Rent control, post

52A C.J.S.—59

Heat and heating,
Breach of covenant,
Admissibility of evidence, action for rent, § 564
Damages, § 301, p. 765
Implied covenant, action, § 300
Liability for personal injury or illness resulting, § 417(4), p. 43
Breakdown, untenantable premises, termination of lease, § 99(2), p. 320, n. 5
Construction of contracts to furnish, § 299, p. 759
Constructive eviction, failure to furnish, § 458, p. 313
Pleading as defense in action for rent, § 561(2), p. 706
Covenant running with land, § 299, p. 758
Covenant to furnish heat as obligating lessor to repair, § 368(1), p. 943
Criminal liability for failure to furnish, § 302
Defects in appliances, liability of landlord, § 423(3)
Express agreement to furnish, § 298
Implied agreement to furnish, § 298
Action for breach, § 300
Obligation of landlord to furnish, § 297
Property damage caused by negligence, § 423(4), p. 175
Rent, failure to furnish, § 485, p. 410
Heirs,
Adverse possession by heirs of tenant, § 286
Dispossession proceedings,
Defendants, § 763
Right to maintain after death of lessor, § 762, p. 120
Distress, right to distrain, § 679
Estoppel of tenant to deny title, assertion by, § 273, pp. 709, 710
Lease of real property as affecting interest, § 252
Rent control, § 792.9, n. 81
Herbage, lease of authorized, § 207
Hidden dangers, duty of tenant to keep premises safe, § 435, p. 208
Hidden defects, duty to disclose, § 303, p. 771
Landlord's duty to repair, § 366(1), p. 926
High heels, contributory negligence of person injured, § 434, n. 96
Highways, distress, property on, § 681, p. 878
Hinges, entry by removing door from as forcible, § 723
Hiring contract, distress, property hired or bailed, § 681, p. 875
Holding over,
Acts constituting, § 75
Adverse possession of tenant holding over, § 285
Assignee of lease, liability of lessee, § 316, p. 800
Breach of implied covenant of possession under another lease, § 310
Condition of premises,
Right of tenant to complain, § 319
Termination of lease, liability on covenant, § 410
Consent,
Evidence, § 744, n. 24
Extension or renewal by, § 74
Justification for failure to surrender possession, § 316, p. 800
Tenancies at sufferance, § 177

FIGURE 7.10

Sample Index Page for *C.J.S.* Landlord and Tenant Volume

THE LAW CHART

A Practical Working Index of the Standard Law
Titles Under the Seven Grand Divisions:

1. PERSONS
2. PROPERTY
3. CONTRACTS
4. TORTS
5. CRIMES
6. REMEDIES
7. GOVERNMENT

ALL RELATED TITLES ARE HERE GROUPED
Enabling Comparison and Discrimination in the Selection of the Right One.

DIRECTIONS

FIRST: Select the Grand Division that Covers Your Question.
SECOND: Select its Pertinent Subhead.
THIRD: Under the Subhead Select the Most Specific Title.

1. PERSONS

INCLUDING ASSOCIATIONS, PARTNERSHIPS, AND
CORPORATIONS

Classes of Natural Persons in General

Absentees
Adjoining Landowners
Aliens
Ambassadors and Consuls
Amicus Curiæ
Bastards
Citizens
Convicts
Drunkards
Indians
Infants
Innkeepers
Insane Persons
Paupers
Principal and Surety
Slaves
Spendthrifts

Family and Domestic Relations

Adoption of Children
Apprentices
Divorce
Guardian and Ward
Husband and Wife
Marriage
Master and Servant
Parent and Child

Fiduciary and Representative Relations

Agency
Attorney and Client
Brokers
Depositaries
Executors and Administrators
Factors

C.J.S.General Index A   *1*

FIGURE 7.11
Sample Page from the General Index for *C.J.S.*

Local Reference Encyclopedias

American Jurisprudence 2d and *Corpus Juris Secundum* cover cases from all fifty states. Sometimes it helps to compare and contrast the differences between laws of various states. At other times only the laws of one particular state will be relevant. In these cases one should use a local encyclopedia specifically geared to the laws of that state. (Unfortunately, such local encyclopedias are not published in all states.)

These local encyclopedias carry names such as *California Jurisprudence 2d, Michigan Law and Practice,* and *Pennsylvania Law Encyclopedia.* They are usually arranged by topics that parallel those in the national encyclopedias. They have subject analysis sections, indexes, and supplements that also closely resemble those in *Am. Jur. 2d* and *C.J.S.* Figures 7.12 and 7.13 show the manner in which *Illinois Law and Practice* handles the implied warranty of the habitability question.

Special Subject Encyclopedias, Treatises, and Restatements

In addition to the types of encyclopedias discussed above, there are encyclopedias which focus on a single broad topic such as contracts or evidence. They bear names like *Fletcher's Cyclopedia of the Law of Private Corporations.* Such encyclopedias closely resemble multivolume treatises — *Corbin on Contracts* and *Wigmore on Evidence,* for example.

There are differences between an encyclopedia and a treatise — an encyclopedia simply summarizes the law while a treatise summarizes, interprets, and evaluates the law. Although some treatises are published as multivolume sets, most look just like a standard library book. In addition to the standard table of contents, text, and index, legal treatises usually also contain a table of cases, and many are also supplemented with pocket parts. They are given regular library call numbers and can be found in the standard library card catalog.

Restatements represent still another source of general background information. In 1923 a group of prominent law professors, judges, and lawyers founded the American Law Institute and began a series of books to summarize the basic principles of the common law in several major areas. Recognizing that there was disagreement among some courts on the meaning of some of

§ 237. Tenantable Condition and Suitability for Purposes of Lease

While it has been stated that there is no implied covenant on the part of a landlord that the premises are, or will remain, in a tenantable condition fit for the purposes for which rented, it has also been stated that there is a legal duty resting on the landlord in the first instance to have the premises in such condition.

It has been stated that in the absence of express agreement the tenant takes the premises as he finds them without implied covenants that they are fit for habitation or in any particular condition of repair,[36] and that there is no implied contract on the part of the landlord that the leased premises are tenantable or that they will continue so during the term.[37] It has also been stated that ordinarily there is no implied covenant that the premises demised are reasonably fit for the purposes for which they are rented.[38]

However, in the case of Allmon v. Davis, 1928, which was an action involving liability for rent, it was said that it is the duty of the landlord to furnish to the tenant premises which may be used for the purpose for which they are leased, since otherwise the object for which the contract is made entirely fails.[39]

---

36. Farmer v. Alton Building & Loan Ass'n, 1938, 13 N.E.2d 652, 294 Ill. App. 206.

Express covenant as excluding implied covenant

Where the lease contains an express covenant by the landlord to put the house on the leased premises in habitable condition, this excludes any implied covenant on the same matter.—Rubens v. Hill, 1904, 72 N.E. 1127, 213 Ill. 523.

Prior inspection

There is no implied covenant on part of landlord that premises at time of letting are in tenantable condition or that physical condition of premises shall remain unchanged during the term, and especially so when tenant inspects them before executing lease, except in case of fraudulent concealment of hidden defects.—Russell v. Clark, 1912, 173 Ill.App. 461.

37. Carpenter v. Stone, 1904, 112 Ill. App. 155.

Watson v. Moulton, 1901, 100 Ill.App. 560.

McCoull v. Herzberg, 1889, 33 Ill.App. 542.

Blake v. Ranous, 1887, 25 Ill.App. 486.

38. Long v. Joseph Schlitz Brewing Co., 1919, 214 Ill.App. 517.

Cohen v. Plumtree, 1912, 170 Ill.App. 311.

Rubens v. Hill, 1904, 115 Ill.App. 565, affirmed 72 N.E. 1127, 213 Ill. 523.

Lazarus & Cohen v. Parmly, 1904, 113 Ill.App. 624.

39. Allmon v. Davis, 1928, 248 Ill. App. 350 (adequate supply of water is necessary in order to make premises used as dwelling tenantable and habitable).

FIGURE 7.12
Sample Page from *Illinois Law and Practice*

LANDLORD AND TENANT § 252

§ 237. Tenantable Condition and Suitability for Purposes of Lease

Library References

C.J.S. Landlord and Tenant §§ 303–305. Landlord and Tenant ⊂∽125 (1, 2).
Modern Legal Forms ch. 42, Leases.

36. Ciskoski v. Michalsen, 1958, 152 N.E.2d 479, 19 Ill.App.2d 327.
Contract law and the form lease. See 71 N.W.L.Rev. 204 (1976).
Leaseholds and warranty of habitability, see 47 Chicago-Kent L.Rev. 53 (1970).

37. Dapkunas v. Cagle, 1976, 356 N.E. 2d 575, 1 Ill.Dec. 387, 42 Ill.App.3d 644 (tenant could not recover against landlord for injuries sustained in fall

Caveat vendor—a trend in the law of real property see 5 De Paul L.Rev. 263 (1956).
A tort remedy for slum tenant see 58 Ill.Bar. J. 204 (1969).

from back steps of single unit dwelling under theory of implied warranty of habitability and fitness for intended purpose).

The Supreme Court in a 1972 case has held that an implied warranty of habitability is deemed included in contracts, oral and written, governing tenancies in multiple dwellings,[37.5] which is fullfilled by substantial compliance with the provisions of the applicable building code.[37.10]

37.5 Jack Spring, Inc. v. Little, 1972, 280 N.E.2d 208, 50 Ill.2d 351.
Jarrell v. Hartman, 1977, 363 N.E.2d 626, 6 Ill.Dec. 812, 48 Ill.App.3d 985.
Gillette v. Anderson, 1972, 282 N.E.2d 149, 4 Ill.App.3d 838 (complaint by tenant against former landlord alleging that defendant failed to provide bathtub or shower in violation of city ordinances stated cause of action based on theory of implied warranty of habitability).
Implied warranty of habitability see 20 De Paul L.Rev. 955 (1971); 66 N.W.L.Rev. 790 (1972).

37.10 Jack Spring, Inc. v. Little, 1972, 280 N.E.2d 208, 50 Ill.2d 351.

38. Hendricks v. Socony Mobil Oil Co., 1963, 195 N.E.2d 1, 45 Ill.App.2d 44

(use to which lessee may intend to put premises).

Violations of ordinance

In absence of showing that lessors knew of existence of violations of ordinance when lease was executed and failed to disclose such knowledge to lessees who were ignorant of violations or showing as to whether violations occurred during period when lessees were in occupancy or were prior thereto, lessees were not entitled to recover from lessors on ground that lessees had expended sums to correct violations and lost rentals because city prohibited use of certain portions of property.
Eskin v. Freedman, 1964, 203 N.E.2d 24, 53 Ill.App.2d 144.

B. POSSESSION, ENJOYMENT, AND USE

§ 251. In General

2. People v. Goduto, 1961, 174 N.E.2d 385, 21 Ill.2d 605, cert. den. 82 S.Ct. 361, 368 U.S. 927, 7 L.Ed.2d 190 (lessee of property used as parking lot for lessee's customers and employees had right to demand that union organizers, who were not employees or prospective customers, but who were on parking lot for sole purpose of distributing leaflets, leave premises).
People v. DeFilippis, 1964, 203 N.E.2d 627, 54 Ill.App.2d 137, revd. on oth. grds. 214 N.E.2d 897, 34 Ill.2d 129.

§ 252. Delivery of Possession

3. People v. DeFilippis, 1964, 203 N.E. 2d 627, 54 Ill.App.2d 137, revd. on oth. grds. 214 N.E.2d 897, 34 Ill.2d 129.

Possessory ownership

At common law, tenant becomes possessory owner of an estate for a period of time during which term primary indicia of ownership passes to him.
People v. May, 1970, 262 N.E.2d 908, 46 Ill.2d 120.

FIGURE 7.13
Sample Page from *Illinois Law and Practice*, Pocket Part

these principles, the Institute sought to present what its experts thought were the best rules. These are printed in boldface type as relatively short statements. Each principle is then followed by an explanation of the situations in which it should be applied. Restatements have been published in the areas of agency, conflict of laws, foreign relations, torts, and trusts.

Legal Periodicals

Law reviews and other types of legal periodicals represent still another source on the meaning of the law. Law reviews contain a wealth of thoroughly researched information about a specific area of the law. The lead articles are usually expansive pieces, often written by law professors. The comments or notes section contains contributions of the student editors. Because the law review staffs are traditionally made up of the brightest students, their work has generally enjoyed a high reputation. Other periodicals are often more specialized and practitioner oriented, but can also contain articles of great value.

The subject index of the *Index to Legal Periodicals* provides an efficient method of locating relevant articles. In this index the articles are grouped together by common subjects. The listing includes author, title, and citation information needed to locate the correct issue and page of the periodical in which it was published. An example is shown in Figure 7.14. (The *Index to Legal Periodicals* also contains an author index.) Index sets are also available for foreign, specialized, and very old periodicals.

American Law Reports, Annotated

The *American Law Reports, Annotated* is published in four groups of volumes: *A.L.R., A.L.R.2d, A.L.R.3d,* and *A.L.R.Fed.* All four reprint important court cases, summarize the briefs of counsel, and give cross-references to *Am. Jur. 2d, Proof of Facts,* and the *A.L.R. Digest.* In addition, they provide an encyclopedia-type essay of one or more of the key issues raised by the reported case and include a discussion of related cases and an analysis of any trends that appear to be developing. If one can find a pertinent *A.L.R.* annotation, one will obtain a fairly accurate overview of the law in that given area.

LANDAU, Jack C.
Due process (F)
Freedom of the press (F)

LANDAU, Norman J.
Ind diseases (D)

LANDERS, Jonathan M.
Consumer protect (D, S, T)
Credit (D, S, T)
Loans (T)
Mortgages (T)

LANDERS, Joseph W., Jr
Adm agencies—Fla (R)
Environ law (R)

LANDES, William M.
Courts (I)
Economics (E, L)
Judicial stat (L)
Pol sci (E)
Precedents (L)

LANDLORD and tenant
Adjusting the economic relationship of landlord and tenant—rent alteration remedies. Urban L Ann 11:155-85 '76
Application of the principle of mitigation of damages to landlord-tenant law. A. J. Bradbrook. Sydney L Rev 8:15-30 Ja '77
Balancing act: strengthening South Dakota's landlord-tenant law. M. A. Wolff. SD L Rev 22:15-40 Wint '77
Can distraint stand up as a landlord's remedy? Real Estate L J 5:242-59 Wint '77
Civil remedies available to residential tenants in Ontario: the case for assertive action. Osgoode Hall L J 14:65-91 Je '76
Constitutional law—action under color of state law—legislative authorization of private action resembling public function constitutes action under color of state law. Vand L Rev 29:851-9 Ap '76
Contract law and the form lease: can contract law provide the answer? D. V. Kirby. Nw U L Rev 71:204-37 My-Je '76
Contracting out of the landlord and tenant act. E. A. Weidberg. Modern L Rev 39:337-42 My '76
Distributive impact, allocative efficiency, and overall desirability of ideal housing codes: some theoretical clarifications. R. S. Markovits. Harv L Rev 89:1815-46 Je '76
Droits et recours des parties à un contrat de bail devant la Commission des loyers. L. Robert. McGill L J 22:380-414 Fall '76
"Equal justice under the law": the evolution of a national commitment to legal services for the poor and a study of its impact on New Jersey landlord-tenant law. J. B. Ventantonio. Seton Hall L Rev 7:233-97 Wint '76
Examination of some of the recent amendments to the Ontario landlord and tenant act. M. Gorsky. Dalhousie L J 3:663-705 Ja '77
Kentucky uniform residential landlord and tenant act: tenants' new lease on life? J Family L 14:597-624 '75-'76
Landlord and tenant—landlord may be liable for theft after suitable notice of defective lock. Seton Hall L Rev 7:683-702 Spr '76
Landlord and tenant—prohibition of retaliatory eviction in landlord-tenant relations: a study of practice and proposals. NC L Rev 54:861-84 Je '76
Landlord control of tenant behavior: an instance of private environmental legislation. J. A. Humbach. Fordham L Rev 45:223-334 N '76
Landlord-tenant—caveat emptor—implied warranty of habitability in residential leases. NY L F 21:613-33 Spr '76
Landlord-tenant—commercial landlord's liability for criminal acts of third party. Wayne L Rev 22:1483-91 S '76
Landlord-tenant—due process—tenant of federally subsidized housing may not be evicted upon expiration of lease absent a showing of good cause. Md L Rev 36:255-69 '76
Landlord-tenant: proving motive in retaliatory eviction—Minnesota's solution. Minn L Rev 61:523-41 F '77
Landlord-tenant—repairs—landlord could be liable under covenant to repair for injuries to tenant's invitees caused by breach of such agreement. Fordham Urban L J 5:165-73 Fall '76
Landlord-tenant: the medieval concepts of feudal property law are alive and well in leases of commercial property in Illinois. John Marshal J 10:338-58 Wint '77
Landlords' notices to quit. D. C. S Phillips. Sol J 120:596-8 S 3 '76
Lessor's bankruptcy: the draftsman's response to the tenant's plight. L. H. Jacobson. Real Estate L J 1:152-62 Fall '72

Neither seen nor heard: keeping children out of Arizona's adult communities under Arizona revised statutes section 33-1317(B) Ariz St L J 1975:813-40 '75
New act is a step toward landlord-tenant equality in Georgia. Mercer L Rev 28:351-70 Fall '76
New look at law of landlord and tenant. G. C. Hawkins. Ala Law 38:71-80 Ja '77
Overview of the Tennessee residential landlord and tenant act. Memphis St L Rev 7:109-28 Fall '76
Reassessment of the laws relating to the determination of tenancies. A. J. Bradbrook. Adelaide L Rev 5:357-81 N '76
Repair obligations of landlords and tenants: a plea for reform. A. J. Bradbrook. UWAL Rev 12:437-66 D '76
Residential tenant's security deposit—a protected interest worth litigating. St Mary's L J 8:829-52 '77
Responsibility of landlords for conditions of habitability. J. G. Rose. Real Estate L J 1:53-80 Summ '72
Retaliatory eviction in California—a common law defense or a semantical exercise? T. G. Treece. Orange County B J 3:237-42 Fall '76
Role of the judiciary in reforming landlord and tenant law. A. J. Bradbrook. M U L R 10:459-80 S '76
State housing commissions and their tenants: the need for legislative control. A. J. Bradbrook. M U L R 10:409-41 Je '76
Texas landlord-tenant law and the deceptive trade practices act—affirmative remedies for the tenant. St Mary's L J 8:807-28 '77
Uniform residential landlord and tenant act and its potential effects upon Maryland landlord-tenant law. S. G. Davison. U Balt L Rev 5:247-98 Spr '76
See also
Eviction
Fixtures
Leases
Notice
Possession
Rents and rent control

Cases
Anastasia v. Cosmopolitan Natl Bank. 527 F 2d 150
U Cin L Rev 45:301-4 '76
Liverpool City Council v. Irwin [1976] Q B 619
Camb L J 36:15-17 Ap '77
Putnam v. Stout (NY) 345 N E 2d 319
Brooklyn L Rev 43:206-8 Summ '76

LANDO, Ole
Compar law (S)
Conflict of laws: contracts (S)

LANDRETH, Duane P.
City planning (F)
Grants-in-aid (F)
Housing (F)
Regional planning (F)

LANDRIEU, Moon
Mun corps (I)

LANDRUM, Charles, Jr
Biog (Lively)
Judges (F)

LANDRY, James E.
Air law (I)
US: CAB (I)

LANDS. See Public lands

LANDY, Craig A.
Commerce clause (T)
Corp: consol and merger (T)
Fed preemption (T)
Securities: state reg (T)

LANDYNSKI, Jacob W.
Biog (Black)
Search and seizure (I)

LANE, Bruce S.
Bonds (N)
Inc tax: exemptions—US (N)
Interest (N)

LANE, Horace C.
Automob insur (A)

LANG, Jonathan
Collective bargaining (T)
Due process (T)
Unions (T)

LANGBEIN, John H.
Banks and banking (M)
Investments (M)
Stocks (M)
Trusts and trustees (M)

FIGURE 7.14
Sample Page from *Index to Legal Periodicals*

Figure 7.15 shows how the annotation is organized. Note that both an outline of the topics covered and an extensive index are included at the beginning of the annotation. A table of the jurisdictions represented shows the state courts cited. After listing the content of related annotations, citations are included for relevant periodical articles. Figure 7.16 provides an example of the text of the annotation and demonstrates a more detailed discussion of individual cases than would be found in encyclopedias.

The *A.L.R.3d* and *A.L.R.Fed.* are supplemented with pocket parts in the same manner as the other publications mentioned previously. The *A.L.R.* and *A.L.R.2d,* on the other hand, are supplemented through the *Blue Book* and *Later Case Service* respectively. The *A.L.R. Blue Book of Supplemental Decisions* consists of three volumes that list related annotations appearing in later volumes as well as new cases. This supplements the *A.L.R. The A.L.R. Later Case Service* consists of volumes of similar content which supplement the *A.L.R.2d.* These permanent volumes are in turn supplemented by pamphlet supplements.

Many other publications contain cross-references to one of the *A.L.R.* series. If, however, the paralegal does not have such a reference, research should begin with the *A.L.R. Quick Index.* This convenient reference provides citations to annotations in both *A.L.R.2d* and *A.L.R.3d.* Figure 7.17 shows that the *Quick Index* identifies two annotations related to the habitability question. Annotations in *A.L.R.* and *A.L.R.2d* can also be found by consulting the *A.L.R. Word Index to Annotations* and the *A.L.R.2d Word Index to Annotations.*

FINDING STATUTES AND REGULATIONS

Once there is a general understanding of the applicable legal principles in a problem, an effort should be made to determine if there are any relevant statutes or administrative regulations in force. This may involve federal, state, and/or local legislation. There will undoubtedly be times when the researcher already knows about pertinent legislation and may even have obtained the citation through the general reading discussed above. For a thorough search, however, one should begin with a subject index.

646

ANNOTATION

MODERN STATUS OF RULES AS TO EXISTENCE OF IMPLIED WARRANTY OF HABITABILITY OR FITNESS FOR USE OF LEASED PREMISES

by

Jonathan M. Purver, LL.B.

INDEX

TOTAL CLIENT-SERVICE LIBRARY® REFERENCES

49 Am Jur 2d, Landlord and Tenant §§ 309, 768–772
22 Am Jur Proof of Facts 17, Eviction of Tenant
ALR Digests, Landlord and Tenant §§ 41, 44, 45
ALR Quck Index, Landlord and Tenant

Consult POCKET PART in this volume for later case service

FIGURE 7.15

Sample Pages Showing the Scope of an *A.L.R.3d* Annotation

FIGURE 7.15 — Continued

40 ALR3d   LEASE—IMPLIED WARRANTY—FITNESS   647
                             40 ALR3d 646   § 1[a]

TABLE OF JURISDICTIONS REPRESENTED
Consult POCKET PART in this volume for later case service

---

§ 1. Introduction

[a] Scope

This annotation[1] discusses those decisions which have expressly recognized that there exists, in today's modern leasing transactions, an implied warranty of habability or fitness for use of the premises which are the subject matter of

---

1. Attempting merely to show the modern status of the rules, this annotation does not purport exhaustively to collect all of the cases within its scope.

the lease. Also included, as appearing to reflect a transitional stage in the common law of leasing arrangements, is a representative selection of decisions creating some limited exceptions to the heretofore nearly universal doctrine of no implied warranty, or caveat emptor.[2]

Excluded are cases wherein a statutory provision was relied upon as giving rise to an implied warranty of habitability or fitness for use, the thrust of the collection of cases herein being to show how some courts have judicially carved and remolded the old common law pertaining to landlord and tenant in regard to warranties, in an attempt to bring the common law into line with the economic realities of modern leasing law.

Treated elsewhere is the queston as to the tenant's remedies where his premises are untenantable or unfit for the purposes for which they were leased as a result of the landlord's breach of an express covenant, or lease provision, to repair the leased premises.[3]

[b] Related matters

Tenant's right, where landlord fails to make repairs, to have them made and set off cost against rent. 40 ALR3d 1369.

Validity and construction of statute or ordinance authorizing withholding or payment into escrow of rent for period during which premises are not properly maintained by landlord. 40 ALR3d 821.

Retaliatory eviction of tenant for reporting landlord's violation of law. 40 ALR3d 753.

Landlord and tenant: constructive eviction based on flooding, dampness, or the like. 33 ALR3d 1356.

Infestation of leased dwelling or apartment with vermin as entitling tenant to abandon premises or as constructive eviction by landlord, in absence of express covenant of habitability. 27 ALR3d 924.

Who, as between landlord and tenant, must make, or bear expense of, alterations, improvements, or repairs ordered by public authorities. 22 ALR3d 521.

Implied covenant or obligation of lessor to furnish water or water supply for business needs of the lessee. 65 ALR2d 1313.

Rights and remedies of tenant upon landlord's breach of covenant to repair. 28 ALR2d 446.

Breach of covenant to furnish heat for building or room other than dwelling or apartment as an eviction. 69 ALR 1093.

Liability of landlord for damage to tenant because of infection from contagious or infectious disease. 26 ALR 1265.

Effect of nonhabitability of leased dwelling or apartment. 4 ALR 1453, 13 ALR 818, 29 ALR 52, 34 ALR 711.

✦

Skillern, Implied Warranties in Leases: The Need For Change. 44 Denver LJ 387 (1967).

Quinn & Phillips, The Law of Landlord-Tenant: A Critical Evaluation of the Past With Guidelines For the Future. 38 Fordham L Rev 225 (1969).

Schoshinski, Remedies of the Indigent Tenant: Proposal for Change. 54 Georgetown LJ 519 (1966).

Recent decision, landlord and tenant —application of implied warranty. 45 Marquette L Rev 630 (1962).

Sax & Hiestand, Slumlordism as a Tort. 65 Mich L Rev 869 (1967).

Lesar, Landlord and Tenant Reform. 35 NYU L Rev 1279 (1960).

---

2. Not discussed are cases wherein there existed an express warranty by a lessor to provide particular services, equipment, or facilities, and the question before the court was whether, based upon the express undertaking, there necessarily followed the implied warranty or understanding that the service or facility promised would be reasonably adequate to meet the expressly stated needs.

3. 49 Am Jur 2d, Landlord and Tenant § 616. As to rights and remedies of tenant upon landlord's breach of covenant to repair, see 28 ALR2d 446.

Pointing out that herein it clearly appeared that the parties contemplated the use of a building for a furniture store, the court said that since there was no showing that the construction had progressed to such an extent as to afford the lessee an opportunity to judge the suitableness of the building, it could not be said that he took the building at his peril. Accordingly, it was recognized that the lessee in such circumstance would not be liable for the rent of a building which when constructed was leaky and failed completely to keep rainwater from entering the store.

§ 5. Rejection of doctrine of caveat emptor

[a] Recognition of implied warranty of habitability or fitness for use

In the past 10 years some courts, instead of creating exceptions to the rule, have proceeded to expressly reject the doctrine of caveat emptor with respect to modern leasing agreements, and have recognized the existence of an implied warranty of habitability or fitness for use of leased premises.

Hence, in Javins v First Nat. Realty Corp. (1970) 138 App DC 369, 428 F2d 1071, cert den 400 US 925, 27 L Ed 2d 185, 91 S Ct 186, an action by a landlord for nonpayment of rent, wherein the tenants alleged numerous violations of the District of Columbia housing regulations, the court held that the common law itself "must recognize the landlord's obligation to keep his premises in a habitable condition." Saying that the housing code must be read into housing contracts, the court explained that under contract principles (which are to be applied), the tenant's obligation to pay rent is dependent upon the landlord's performance of his obligations, and that in order to determine whether any rent is owed therein, the tenant must be given an opportunity to prove the alleged housing code violations as a breach of the landlord's warranty. At trial, said the court, the finder of fact must make two findings: (1) whether the alleged violations existed during the period for which past-due rent is claimed, and (2) what portion, if any or if all, of the tenant's obligation to pay rent was suspended by the landlord's breach. The court did state, however, that the jury should be instructed that one or two minor violations standing alone which do not affect habitability are de minimis and would not entitle the tenant to a reduction in rent.

In Lemle v Breeden (1969) 51 **Hawaii** 426, 478, 462 P2d 470, 40 ALR3d 637, the court affirmed a judgment in favor of a lessee who sued to recover the deposit and rent payment for a leased home upon discovering severe rat infestation, and upheld the trial judge's grounds for recovery that there was a material breach of an implied warranty of habitability and fitness for the use intended which justified the lessee's rescinding the rental agreement and vacating the premises. Significantly stating that it need not consider the ruling of the trial court that the plaintiff was constructively evicted in light of the holding that there was an implied warranty of habitability in the case, the court pointed out that the doctrine of constructive eviction, "as an admitted judicial fiction designed to operate as though there were a substantial breach of a material covenant in a bilateral contract," no longer serves its purpose when the more flexible concept of implied warranty of habitability is legally available. Saying that it was a decided advantage of the implied warranty doctrine that there were a number of remedies available, the court pointed out that under the constructive eviction analysis the lessee must always abandon the premises at the risk of establishing sufficient facts to constitute constructive eviction or he will be liable for breach of the rental

FIGURE 7.16

Sample Page from the Text of an *A.L.R.3d* Annotation

Habeas Corpus ALR2d-3d

Sanity: existence of other remedy as affecting habeas corpus on ground of restoration to sanity of one confined as an incompetent other than in connection with crime, 21 ALR2d 1004

§ 2. Grounds for relief and matters reviewable.

Absence of counsel for accused at time of sentence as requiring vacation thereof or other relief, 20 ALR2d 1240

Anticipatory relief in federal courts against state criminal prosecutions growing out of civil rights activities, 8 ALR3d 301

Appeal, habeas corpus on ground of deprivation of right to, 19 ALR2d 789

Charge: determination whether crime is charged, 40 ALR2d 1151

Child support: court's power in habeas corpus proceedings relating to custody of child to adjudicate questions as to child's support, 17 ALR3d 764

Court martial: review by habeas corpus of court-martial convictions, 15 ALR2d 387

Custody of child
– illegitimate child, proceedings to obtain custody of, 98 ALR2d 421
– modification: child custody provisions of divorce or separation decree as subject to modification on habeas corpus, 4 ALR3d 1277
– nonresidence as affecting one's right to custody of child in habeas corpus proceedings, 15 ALR2d 432
– support: court's power in habeas corpus proceedings relating to custody of child to adjudicate questions as to child's support, 17 ALR3d 764

Identity: right of prisoner held under extradition warrant to raise question of identity in habeas corpus proceeding, 93 ALR2d 916

Insanity of accused at time of commission of offense [not raised at trial] as ground for habeas corpus after conviction, 29 ALR2d 703

Parolee's right to habeas corpus, 92 ALR2d 682

Race as factor in custody proceeding, 57 ALR2d 678

Sanity: habeas corpus on ground of restoration to sanity of one confined as an incompetent other than in connection with crime, 21 ALR2d 1004

Service of process: attack, by petition for writ of habeas corpus, on personal service as

having been obtained by fraud or trickery, 98 ALR2d 600

Sexual psychopaths, habeas corpus to test validity of confinement under statutes relating to, 24 ALR2d 376

Speedy trial: waiver or loss of accused's right to speedy trial as affecting right to habeas corpus, 57 ALR2d 339

Subsequent proceedings: discharge on habeas corpus of one held in extradition proceedings as precluding subsequent extradition proceedings, 33 ALR3d 1443

Suppression of evidence by prosecution in criminal case as ground for habeas corpus, 33 ALR2d 1421

HABENDUM CLAUSE

Conflict between granting and habendum clauses as to estate conveyed, 58 ALR2d 1374

What amounts to development or operation for oil or gas within terms of habendum clause extending primary term while the premises are being "developed or operated", 96 ALR2d 322

HABITABILITY

Implied warranty: modern status of rules as to existence of implied warranty of habitability or fitness for use of leased premises, 40 ALR3d 646

Infestation of leased dwelling or apartment with vermin as entitling tenant to abandon premises or as constructive eviction by landlord, in absence of express covenant of habitability, 27 ALR3d 924

HABITS

Custom and Usage (this index)

HABITUAL CRIMINALS

Chronological or procedural sequence of former convictions as affecting enhancement of penalty for subsequent offense under habitual criminal statutes, 24 ALR2d 1247

Felony: determination of character of former crime as a felony, so as to warrant punishment of an accused as a second offender, 19 ALR2d 227

Form and sufficiency of allegations as to time, place, or court of prior offenses under habitual criminal act or statute enhancing punishment for repeated offenses, 80 ALR2d 1196

Identity: evidence of identity for purposes of

398 **Consult POCKET PART for later annotations**

FIGURE 7.17
Sample Page from *A.L.R. Quick Index*

Subject Index

A paralegal should begin a search of the federal statutes with one of the subject indexes in the *United States Code (U.S.C.)*, the *United States Code Annotated (U.S.C.A.)*, the *Federal Code Annotated (F.C.A.)*, or the *United States Code Service (U.S.C.S.).** These indexes provide relatively easy access to both the Constitution and federal laws of a general and permanent nature that are currently in force. (See Figure 7.18.) General laws no longer in force can be located by using the subject indexes in each volume of the *Statutes at Large.* State codifications also have subject indexes. When looking for local legislation the researcher can simply scan the table of contents in the front of the volume.

Popular-Name Tables

Many pieces of legislation are commonly referred to by the names of the sponsors (the Taft-Hartley Act) or a descriptive title (the Truth in Lending Act). *U.S.C., U.S.C.A.,* and *U.S.C.S.* all contain popular-name tables that give the formal citations for these acts. In addition, *Shepard's Acts and Cases by Popular Names, Federal and State* provides a convenient source for both federal and state legislation. The *U.S. Supreme Court Reports Digest* also contains a popular-name table.

Checking for Subsequent Legislative or Judicial Action

Once the applicable statutes have been located, the researcher needs to verify that they have not been repealed or amended into other forms. One can do this by consulting the pocket part or the separate paperbound supplemental volumes that accompany the codifications. Figure 7.19 indicates the type of entry found in such a supplement.†

---

*The *United States Code Service* replaces the *Federal Code Annotated.* It comes in both an F.C.A. Edition and a Lawyers' Edition. The Lawyers' Edition contains a research aids section that includes references to *Am. Jur., Am. Jur. Trials, Am. Jur. Proof of Facts, A.L.R.,* and law reviews.

†Here, as in several other figures used later in the chapter, the substantive area of the law involved in the illustration is not related to the

41	LANDS

LANDLORD AND TENANT
Definition of tenant,
 Rent supplement payments for lower income families, 12 § 1701s
 Slum clearance and urban renewal, 42 § 1452b
Displaced persons, relocation assistance, replacement housing for tenants, 42 § 4624
Farm Tenancy, generally, this index
Income tax, improvements on subdivided realty by lessee deemed made by taxpayer, 26 § 1237
Leases, generally, this index
Lower Income Housing, generally, this index
Migratory birds, hunting stamp tax as not required of tenants, 16 § 718a
National Aeronautics and Space Administration, reimbursement, owners and tenants of land and interests in land acquired for use by, 42 § 2473
Rent, generally, this index
Rice, sharing in certificates, 7 § 1380g
Slum clearance and low-rent housing project, persons eligible, 42 § 1410
Soil conservation, distribution of payments or grants of aid among, 16 § 590h
Tenant programs and services, defined, slum clearance and low-rent housing, 42 § 1402
Water carriers in interstate and foreign commerce,
 Accounts, records and reports of lessor, 49 § 913
 Lessee's disclosing information prejudicial to consignee or shipper, penalty, 49 § 917
Wire interception, etc., furnishing applicant information, etc., to accomplish interception, 18 § 2518

LANDMARKS
Preservation of historic landmarks as national monuments, 16 § 431
Sites, erection on, cession of jurisdiction to United States, 33 §§ 727, 728

LANDS
 See, also, specific index headings
Acquisition,
 See, also, specific index headings
 Policy for,
  Declaration, 33 § 596
  Public works projects, payment of just and reasonable consideration to property owners, 33 § 596
  Short title of act, 33 § 596 **note**
  Water resources development projects, information as to probable timing for acquisition, etc., 33 § 597
Advance acquisition for future public purposes, 42 § 3104
 Appropriations, authorization, 42 § 3108
 Authority of Secretary to make grants, 42 § 3104
 Congressional declaration of purpose, 42 § 3101
 Definitions, 42 § 3106
 Diversion of land, 42 § 3104
 Eligibility for other federal loans or grant programs, 42 § 3104
 Interim use as not constituting diversion, 42 § 3104
 Labor standards, 42 § 3107
 Maximum amount of grants, 42 § 3104
 Powers and duties of Secretary, 42 § 3105
 Repayment of grants, diversion of land, 42 § 3104
 Utilization of land within reasonable period of time, 42 § 3104
Airports and Landing Areas, this index
Anadromous and Great Lakes fisheries, cooperative agreements, conservation, etc., 16 §§ 757a to 757c
Conservation. Land and Water Conservation Fund, generally, this index
Correctional institutions and facilities, grants for construction, etc., acquisition prohibited, 42 § 3750d
Definitions, this index
Executive orders and proclamations, descriptions of tracts of land, 44 § 1505 **note, Ex.Ord.No.11030**

FIGURE 7.18
Sample Page from *U.S.C.A.* Subject Index

21 § 823 FOOD AND DRUGS

(A) security of stocks of narcotic drugs for such treatment, and (B) the maintenance of records (in accordance with section 827 of this title) on such drugs; and

(3) if the Secretary determines that the applicant will comply with standards established by the Secretary (after consultation with the Attorney General) respecting the quantities of narcotic drugs which may be provided for unsupervised use by individuals in such treatment.

As amended Pub.L. 93–281, § 3, May 14, 1974, 88 Stat. 124; Pub.L. 95–633, Title I, § 109, Nov. 10, 1978, 92 Stat. 3773.

1978 Amendment. Subsec. (f). Pub.L. 95–633 added provision relating to the construction of the Convention on Psychotropic Substances.

1974 Amendment. Subsec. (g). Pub.L. 93–281 added subsec. (g).

Effective Date of 1978 Amendment. Amendment by Pub.L. 95–633 effective on the date the Convention on Psychotropic Substances enters into force in the United States, see section 112 of Pub.L. 95–633, set out as a note under section 801a of this title.

Legislative History. For legislative history and purpose of Pub.L. 93–281, see 1974 U.S.Code Cong. and Adm.News, p. 3029. See, also, Pub.L. 95–633, 1978 U.S. Code Cong. and Adm.News, p. 9496.

Code of Federal Regulations

Registration provisions, see 21 CFR 1301.01 et seq.

§ 824. Denial, revocation, or suspension of registration—Grounds

(a) A registration pursuant to section 823 of this title to manufacture, distribute, or dispense a controlled substance may be suspended or revoked by the Attorney General upon a finding that the registrant—

(1) has materially falsified any application filed pursuant to or required by this subchapter or subchapter II of this chapter;

(2) has been convicted of a felony under this subchapter or subchapter II of this chapter or any other law of the United States, or of any State, relating to any substance defined in this subchapter as a controlled substance; or

(3) has had his State license or registration suspended, revoked, or denied by competent State authority and is no longer authorized by State law to engage in the manufacturing, distribution, or dispensing of controlled substances.

A registration pursuant to section 823(g) of this title to dispense a narcotic drug for maintenance treatment or detoxification treatment may be suspended or revoked by the Attorney General upon a finding that the registrant has failed to comply with any standard referred to in section 823(g) of this title.

[See main volume for text of (b) and (c)]

Suspension of registration in cases of imminent danger

(d) The Attorney General may, in his discretion, suspend any registration simultaneously with the institution of proceedings under this section, in cases where he finds that there is an imminent danger to the public health or safety. A failure to comply with a standard referred to in section 823(g) of this title may be treated under this subsection as grounds for immediate suspension of a registration granted under such section. A suspension under this subsection shall continue in effect until the conclusion of such proceedings, including judicial review thereof, unless sooner withdrawn by the Attorney General or dissolved by a court of competent jurisdiction.

[See main volume for text of (e) and (f)]

As amended Pub.L. 93–281, § 4, May 14, 1974, 88 Stat. 125.

1974 Amendment. Subsec. (a). Pub.L. 93–281, § 4(a), provided for revocation or suspension of a registration pursuant to section 823(g) of this title for failure of a registrant to comply with standards referred to in such section 823(g).

Subsec. (d). Pub.L. 93–281, § 4(b), substituted in second sentence "A suspension under this subsection" for "Such suspension".

Legislative History. For legislative history and purpose of Pub.L. 93–281, see

22

FIGURE 7.19

Sample Page from *U.S.C.A. Pocket Part Supplement*

One can also locate amendments by using *Shepard's Citations*. *Shepard's* puts out both statute and case editions that relate to both federal and state law. At the federal level, the statute and department reports edition of *Shepard's United States Citations* contains material on the United States Constitution and federal statutes as well as various decisions of federal regulatory agencies and specialized courts such as the court of customs and patent appeals. It reports legislative changes and cites court cases which have interpreted the statutes. The type of format used in these volumes is shown in Figure 7.20. An explanation of the abbreviations used in *Shepard's* is found in the beginning of each volume.

State legislation and constitutions are included in the *Shepard's* volumes published separately for each state. These state volumes also include local charters and ordinances. Citations to state cases which interpret federal statutes are also included in the *United States Citations*.

Court interpretations of statutes can also be found through the statutes construed tables in volumes of the *National Reporter System** or the table of laws cited and construed in the *Digest of the United States Supreme Court Reports*.†

Locating the Legislative History

The annotated codes usually contain some basic information about the law's legislative history. A sample page from the *U.S.C.A.* is shown in Figure 7.21. Note that in addition to printing the text of section 1292 of chapter fifteen of the code, it also provides its public law numbers and dates of passage for both the original 1961 act and a 1966 amendment. It then briefly identifies the nature of that 1966 amendment and gives cross-references to the *United States Code Congressional and Administrative*

---

landlord–tenant problem described at the chapter's beginning. In this case it is done because there are no materials in *U.S.C.A.* relevant to the landlord problem. In other cases, it may be done to illustrate a feature of the research tool that could not be illustrated as easily with landlord–tenant materials.

*See the discussion of the *National Reporter System* in chapter 5, page 142.

†See pages 251–256 for a further discussion of the use of digests.

UNITED STATES CODE '70 Ed. & '75 Supp. T. 5 § 704

				§ 703	422US690	370FS362
§§ 702 to 705	510F2d703	556F2d903	387FS977	414FS186	A90St2721	371FS734
538F2d938	511F2d1271	557F2d286	387FS1086	414FS217	51LE196	371FS1374
§§ 702 to 704	512F2d573	558F2d1153	388FS381	414FS299	97SC982	374FS162
	512F2d775	559F2d730	388FS494	414FS985	45LE466	374FS450
519F2d682	512F2d889	559F2d1016	389FS87	414FS1106	45LE483	374FS759
551F2d1056	512F2d1190	561F2d402	389FS287	415FS653	48LE468	375FS203
391FS12	512F2d1354	561F2d632	389FS690	415FS1237	51LE196	375FS437
396FS281	513F2d1143	363FS1053	389FS1152	416FS288	53LE522	376FS249
428FS1103	514F2d812	364FS227	390FS357	416FS811	490F2d1369	376FS1102
436US854	514F2d1165	364FS424	390FS928	416FS865	491F2d1143	377FS832
	515F2d368	364FS750	391FS710	417FS136	493F2d141	380FS369
§ 702	515F2d398	364FS1013	392FS74	417FS299	501F2d1369	380FS744
L88St1978	515F2d468	365FS478	392FS133	418FS183	97SC982	382FS323
[§321	516F2d1009	366FS58	392FS1247	418FS890	507F2d768	385FS435
A90St2721	519F2d936	366FS261	393FS367	418FS1243	507F2d1110	386FS685
412US685	519F2d1161	366FS607	393FS601	419FS223	510F2d798	388FS651
418US177	520F2d54	366FS1233	393FS1116	419FS683	515F2d659	388FS830
421US560	520F2d457	367FS1377	393FS1369	419FS810	519F2d936	389FS87
422US690	521F2d1151	368FS721	394FS653	419FS859	527F2d593	389FS292
425US829	523F2d730	369FS741	394FS767	420FS1221	528F2d1051	389FS690
426US38	523F2d1346	369FS1040	394FS900	420FS1302	531F2d1398	389FS1152
41LE681	524F2d9	370FS325	394FS980	421FS80	538F2d513	390FS357
44LE379	524F2d242	370FS946	394FS1224	421FS385	539F2d788	390FS532
45LE483	524F2d407	370FS1195	395FS516	421FS848	543F2d707	391FS847
48LE409	525F2d145	371FS734	395FS923	422FS355	544F2d333	392FS1246
48LE460	525F2d269	371FS1141	396FS637	423FS407	547F2d243	393FS1116
51LE196	526F2d231	373FS589	396FS1108	423FS1065	548F2d1142	393FS1335
53LE522	527F2d721	373FS591	397FS41	424FS108	551F2d1280	394FS980
94SC2947	527F2d786	374FS162	397FS1018	425FS72	554F2d1212	396FS1108
95SC1852	527F2d1302	374FS450	397FS1050	425FS332	559F2d730	397FS360
95SC2599	528F2d46	374FS759	398FS3	426FS990	364FS1013	398FS3
96SC1924	528F2d1140	374FS874	398FS187	426FS1025	366FS1241	400FS892
96SC1962	528F2d1296	374FS1286	399FS58	427FS226	367FS893	400FS1050
97SC982	529F2d191	375FS199	399FS340	427FS1370	370FS325	401FS1072
97SC2423	529F2d537	375FS437	400FS706	428FS118	372FS539	402FS1067
485F2d180	530F2d1087	376FS249	400FS851	428FS389	374FS759	403FS1207
485F2d738	530F2d1223	376FS328	400FS1050	428FS711	374FS1286	404FS365
485F2d782	531F2d687	376FS615	401FS524	428FS938	375FS305	404FS1091
489F2d1212	533F2d416	376FS889	401FS943	429FS143	375FS437	405FS507
490F2d719	533F2d478	377FS257	401FS1078	429FS415	376FS249	405FS1227
490F2d886	534F2d1138	377FS531	401FS1383	429FS691	376FS1100	407FS1201
490F2d1360	535F2d216	377FS832	402FS582	429FS1140	377FS244	408FS281
491F2d856	537F2d29	377FS1226	402FS988	430FS426	377FS776	410FS68
492F2d413	537F2d289	377FS1285	402FS1067	430FS701	384FS219	411FS1222
492F2d489	537F2d578	378FS212	402FS1204	430FS856	385FS1217	412FS283
492F2d539	537F2d946	378FS243	403FS633	431FS106	386FS668	414FS186
494F2d1324	538F2d1149	378FS286	403FS1005	431FS469	387FS299	414FS935
495F2d274	539F2d837	378FS1288	403FS1206	431FS487	390FS216	414FS976
497F2d430	539F2d1015	379FS1170	404FS221	431FS722	390FS928	415FS212
498F2d386	539F2d1075	380FS206	404FS365	432FS564	392FS74	415FS800
498F2d1211	540F2d866	380FS365	404FS894	433FS838	393FS1116	415FS1086
498F2d1303	541F2d151	380FS744	404FS927	433FS1326	397FS1126	415FS1237
498F2d1352	541F2d250	381FS295	405FS512		401FS1001	416FS865
501F2d757	542F2d1264	381FS305	405FS1227	61FRD175	403FS633	416FS1144
502F2d480	543F2d529	381FS1147	406FS1025	64FRD565	405FS512	417FS366
504F2d156	547F2d47	382FS323	406FS1258	73FRD620	406FS1258	417FS876
504F2d259	547F2d184	382FS363	407FS794	74FRD387	407FS1201	417FS1070
504F2d268	547F2d311	383FS1249	408FS142	10ARF802s	409FS28	417FS1365
505F2d499	648F2d102	384FS188	408FS280	17ARF33s	420FS27	418FS92
506F2d234	549F2d1115	384FS219	408FS893	17ARF116n	423FS1065	419FS223
507F2d768	551F2d16	384FS626	408FS1325	23ARF303n	426FS1001	421FS80
507F2d1107	551F2d322	384FS1295	408FS1358	30ARF358n	426FS1027	421FS848
507F2d1169	551F2d448	384FS1355	409FS28	30ARF718n	429FS683	423FS1085
508F2d493	552F2d824	385FS435	409FS1192	31ARF797n	429FS837	425FS332
508F2d1040	554F2d462	386FS573	410FS68	32ARF380n	18ARF620n	427FS327
509F2d243	554F2d885	386FS668	411FS5	33ARF63n	§§ 704 to 706	428FS118
509F2d247	554F2d1212	386FS945	411FS1364	33ARF91n	518F2d306	428FS711
509F2d1080	555F2d970	386FS1347	412FS171		528F2d125	429FS691
510F2d351	556F2d358	387FS292	413FS186	§ 703		
	556F2d451	387FS673	413FS827	555F2d1114	§ 704	*Continued*
		387FS948		et seq.	421US560	

FIGURE 7.20
Sample Page from *Shepard's United States Citations*

Ch. 32 PROFESSIONAL SPORTS CONTESTS 15 § 1293

Cross References

Federal Trade Commission Act, definition of antitrust acts, see section 44 of this title.

§ 1292. Area telecasting restriction limitation

Section 1291 of this title shall not apply to any joint agreement described in the first sentence in such section which prohibits any person to whom such rights are sold or transferred from televising any games within any area, except within the home territory of a member club of the league on a day when such club is playing a game at home.

Pub.L. 87–331, § 2, Sept. 30, 1961, 75 Stat. 732; Pub.L. 89–800, § 6(b) (2), Nov. 8, 1966, 80 Stat. 1515.

Historical Note

1966 Amendment. Pub.L. 89–800 substituted "described in the first sentence of such section" for "described in such section".

Legislative History. For legislative history and purpose of Pub.L. 87–331, see 1961 U.S.Code Cong. and Adm.News, p. 3042. See, also, Pub.L. 89–800, 1966 U.S. Code Cong. and Adm.News, p. 4327.

Notes of Decisions

Championship games 1
Injunctions 2

___

1. Championship games

This chapter, which authorized a league composed of professional sports teams to sell to broadcasting companies package deals for exclusive televising of games of its various teams and to restrict area televising of a game within home territory of a team on a day when such club was playing at home, applied not only to regularly scheduled season at-home games but also to championship games, and plaintiffs were not entitled to an injunction restraining professional football league from blacking out the televising of championship football game within home territory of one of teams participating in championship game. Blaich v. National Football League, D.C. N.Y.1962, 212 F.Supp. 319.

2. Injunctions

Plaintiffs, who resided in area which was blacked out for televising of championship football game of professional football league, did not suffer irreparable injury which would entitle them to an injunction which in effect would require televising of the game. Blaich v. National Football League, D.C.N.Y.1962, 212 F. Supp. 319.

§ 1293. Intercollegiate and interscholastic football contest limitations

The first sentence of section 1291 of this title shall not apply to any joint agreement described in such section which permits the telecasting of all or a substantial part of any professional football game on any Friday after six o'clock postmeridian or on any Saturday during the period beginning on the second Friday in September and ending on the second Saturday in December in any year from any telecasting station located within seventy-five miles of the game site of any intercollegiate or interscholastic football contest scheduled to be played on such a date if—

FIGURE 7.21
Sample Page from *U.S.C.A.*

News. This historical note is then followed by brief summaries of two federal court cases which interpreted this section. Figure 7.22 demonstrates a similar approach taken in the annotated code of one of the states. It is of special interest because it contains a quotation from the committee which drafted the legislation.

At the federal level the *United States Code Congressional and Administrative News* provides an excellent source for more complete information on legislative history. In addition to the verbatim text of the act a committee report from either the House or the Senate is included. Several very useful tables provide dates for certain actions. These dates allow the researcher to trace floor debates and committee testimony through the *Congressional Record* and published hearings. The *Commerce Clearing House Congressional Index* provides yet another excellent method for cross-referencing bills and identifying key dates in the legislative process.

Administrative Actions

Once the researcher has analyzed a statute, an effort should be made to identify how it has been interpreted and applied by administrative agencies. The *Code of Federal Regulations* contains a table of all those sections of *C.F.R.* which have been promulgated under the authority of a particular statute. (One can also go from the *C.F.R.* citation back to the statutes by looking for the authority section found in the textual discussion of the regulation itself.) Other tables in *C.F.R.* allow the paralegal to relate statutes to presidential proclamations and executive orders.

The paralegal can trace back the historical development of administrative regulations by using a table in *C.F.R.*'s list of sections affected. Research can begin with the subject index, in the same way the subject index of a statutory code would be used. Figure 7.23 presents a sample of the actual text of the *Code of Federal Regulations.* In order to be as up to date as possible, one should also check the latest issues of the *Federal Register.*

Unfortunately there is no clear pattern for the publication of agency rulings. The *American Digest System* covers court decisions on administrative law questions but not the agency decisions themselves. As is the case with state administrative regulation questions, the paralegal is advised to consult directly with

38 § 7–8   CRIMINAL CODE OF 1961
Crim.Code § 7–8

§ 7–8.   Force Likely to Cause Death or Great Bodily Harm

(a) Force which is likely to cause death or great bodily harm, within the meaning of Sections 7–5 and 7–6 includes:

> (1) The firing of a firearm in the direction of the person to be arrested, even though no intent exists to kill or inflict great bodily harm; and

> (2) The firing of a firearm at a vehicle in which the person to be arrested is riding.

Laws 1961, p. 1983, § 7–8, eff. Jan. 1, 1962.

Committee Comments—1961

Revised by Charles H. Bowman

This section is intended to make clear the status of a rather common police practice of firing in the direction of a person fleeing from arrest, either on foot or in a vehicle, although the circumstances are not such that the officer is authorized to use deadly force to prevent defeat of the arrest. While firing into the air, without endangering the offender's safety, undoubtedly is permissible, firing so close to him that his safety is endangered is the use of deadly force, which can be justified only in the circumstances in which the officer is authorized to use deadly force, as stated in sections 7–5 and 7–6. (See Perkins, "The Law of Arrest," 25 Iowa L.Rev. 201 at 270, 288, 289 (1940); Note, "Use of Deadly Force in Preventing Escape of Fleeing Minor Felon," 34 N.Car.L.Rev. 122 (1955).)

Several Illinois cases illustrate this point; and the Supreme Court has approved a trial court's refusal to admit evidence that the defendant's firing at a car in which an offender was riding, was in accordance with a common police practice: "Such a custom has never been approved and cannot be too severely condemned." (People v. Klein, 305 Ill. 141 at 149, 137 N.E. 145 (1922). See also People v. Cash, 326 Ill. 104, 157 N.E. 76 (1927); and Miller v. People, 216 Ill. 309, 74 N.E. 743 (1905)—a "horse and buggy" case.)

Cross References

Method of arrest, use of force, see section 107–5 of this chapter.

Law Review Commentaries

Force in making arrest. Marvin E. Aspen. 1966 Law Forum 247.

Library References

Arrest ⚮68.
Assault and Battery ⚮64.
Homicide ⚮105.
C.J.S. Arrest § 11 et seq.
C.J.S. Assault and Battery § 97.
C.J.S. Homicide §§ 102, 137.

I.L.P. Arrest § 5.
I.L.P. Assault and Battery § 44.
I.L.P. Homicide § 51.
Illinois Pattern Jury Instructions —
IPI Criminal, 24.15.

Notes of Decisions

See, also, Notes of Decisions relative to Deadly Force following section 7–1 of this chapter.

1. In general

In prosecution for murder, defended on ground that defendant police officer was

426

FIGURE 7.22

Smith-Hurd Annotated — An Annotated Version of the *Illinois Revised Statutes*

in type of the same style and not less than half of the point size of that used for the words "peanut butter." This statement shall immediately precede or follow the words "peanut butter," without intervening written, printed, or graphic matter.

(e) The label of peanut butter shall name, by their common names, the optional ingredients used, as provided in paragraph (c) of this section. If hydrogenated vegetable oil is used, the label statement of optional ingredients shall include the words "Hydrogenated ——————— oil" or "Hardened ——————— oil", the blank being filled in either with the names of the vegetable sources of the oil or, alternatively, with the word "vegetable"; for example, "Hydrogenated peanut oil" or "Hardened peanut and cottonseed oils" or "Hydrogenated vegetable oil".

PART 165—NONALCOHOLIC BEVERAGES

Subpart A—[Reserved]

Subpart B—Requirements for Specific Standardized Nonalcoholic Beverages

§ 165.175 Soda water.

(a) *Description.* Soda water is the class of beverages made by absorbing carbon dioxide in potable water. The amount of carbon dioxide used is not less than that which will be absorbed by the beverage at a pressure of one atmosphere and at a temperature of 60° F. It either contains no alcohol or only such alcohol, not in excess of 0.5 percent by weight of the finished beverage, as is contributed by the flavoring ingredient used. Soda water designated by any name which includes the word "cola" or "pepper" shall contain caffeine from kola nut extract and/or other natural caffeine-containing extracts. Caffeine may also be added to any soda water. The total caffeine content in the finished food shall not exceed 0.02 percent by weight. Soda water may contain any safe and suitable optional ingredient, except that vitamins, minerals, and proteins added for nutritional purposes and artificial

sweeteners are not suitable for food encompassed by this standard.

(b) *Nomenclature.* (1) The name of the beverage for which a definition and standard of identity is established by this section, which is neither flavored nor sweetened, is soda water, club soda, or plain soda.

(2) The name of each beverage containing flavoring and sweetening ingredients shall appear as "——————— soda" or "——————— water" or "——————— carbonated beverage", the blank to contain the word or words that designate the characterizing flavor of the soda water as prescribed in § 101.22 of this chapter.

(3) If the soda water is one generally designated by a particular common name; for example, ginger ale, root beer, or sparkling water, that name may be used in lieu of the name prescribed in paragraph (b) (1) and (2) of this section. For the purposes of this section, a proprietary name that is commonly used by the public as the designation of a particular kind of soda water may be used in lieu of the name prescribed in paragraph (b) (1) and (2) of this section.

(c) *Label declaration.* Each of the optional ingredients used shall be declared on the label as required by the applicable sections of Part 101 of this chapter.

(Secs. 401, 701, 52 Stat. 1046 as amended, 1055-1056 as amended by 70 Stat. 919 and 72 Stat. 948 (21 U.S.C. 341, 371))

[42 FR 14477, Mar. 15, 1977]

PART 166—MARGARINE

Subpart A—General Provisions

Sec.
166.40 Labeling of margarine.

Subpart B—Requirements for Specific Standardized Margarine

166.110 Margarine.

Subpart A—General Provisions

§ 166.40 Labeling of margarine.

The Federal Food, Drug, and Cosmetic Act was amended by Pub. L. 459, 81st Congress (64 Stat. 20) on colored

393

FIGURE 7.23

Sample Page from the *Code of Federal Regulations,* Title 21, 1979, page 393.

the agency on the most convenient source for this type of information. Some loose-leaf services provide administrative regulations and rulings in such special interest areas as taxation and commerce. When available, they are a particularly useful source.

FINDING COURT DECISIONS

Whether dealing with the common law or with statutes, the researcher must be sure to identify all relevant court decisions. Under normal circumstances the review of encyclopedias, treatises, annotations and the like will reveal several significant case citations. Similarly, the annotated statutes also contain citations to court decisions. The researcher should, of course, locate these decisions in the reporters discussed in chapter 5, and study them carefully. However, one cannot rely on these citations alone. The researcher must utilize the methods described here to ensure a truly exhaustive search.

Digests

The reader may recall that court decisions frequently consider several different specific points of law. Chapter 5 indicated how one must determine the different issues raised in the case. When court decisions are published in reporters, the editors of the reporter usually provide an analysis of their own which identifies and summarizes these points of law. Figure 7.24 presents the type of introductory material contained in one of the West reporters. Following the syllabus (a narrative summary or abstract of the case), there are several key number designations and short summaries of the court's holdings on those particular points of law.

The West Publishing Company has divided the entire body of American law into a uniform classification system based on what they call key numbers. These key numbers consist of a topic title (for example, Appeal and Error) followed by the key number symbol (⚷) and the proper numerical designation. Cases printed in West reporters will always contain this listing of the key numbers involved. The numbers are aids for understanding the nature of the case and are a connecting link to the West digest system.

him. None of these matters are privileged because the privilege applies only to communications made by Miss Walker to defendant. It cannot be determined from the record and briefs whether there were in fact privileged matters communicated to the defendant, and if so, in whose presence, and for what purpose, nor can it be determined whether Miss Walker testified to any such communications. Whether a series of questions might have covered matters, some privileged and some not, is pure conjecture. Under the circumstances, in refusing to answer the question in the form in which it was propounded, we are unable to say defendant was in contempt.

For the reasons herein set forth the petition for a writ of *habeas corpus* is denied. The judgment of the circuit court of Cook County adjudging the defendant guilty of contempt for refusal to answer questions 1 and 3 is affirmed, and as to question 2 is reversed and remanded for further proceedings.

Affirmed in part, and reversed in part and remanded, and writ quashed.

50 Ill.2d 351
JACK SPRING, INC., Appellee,

v.

Emma LITTLE, Appellant.

SUTTON & PETERSON, INC., Appellee,

v.

Zeleta PRICE, Appellant.

Nos. 41730, 41739.

Supreme Court of Illinois.

Jan. 28, 1972.

Separate actions by landlords against tenants seeking to recover possession of rented premises for nonpayment of rent. The Circuit Court, Cook County, Robert C.

Buckley, J., entered judgments for plaintiffs, and defendants' appeals were consolidated. The Supreme Court, Goldenhersh, J., held that insofar as section of Forcible Entry and Detainer Act required furnishing of bond as prerequisite to prosecuting appeal, it was violative of Fourteenth Amendment of the United States Constitution and of articles of State Constitution containing due process and equal protection clauses and governing appellate court jurisdiction. The Court further held that included in oral and written contracts governing tenancies of tenants in multiple unit dwellings occupied by them was implied warranty of habitability which would be fulfilled by substantial compliance with pertinent provisions of city building code, and that affirmative defenses alleging breach of implied warranty of habitability were germane to question whether defendants were indebted to plaintiffs for rent and thus should not have been struck.

Reversed and remanded.

Kluczynski, J., dissented and filed opinion in which Underwood, C. J., joined.

Ryan, J., dissented and filed opinion.

I. Appeal and Error ⬳373(I)

Having created right of appeal, statutes adopted and rules promulgated in implementation of such right may not serve to discriminate against appellants by reason of inability to furnish an appeal bond.

2. Constitutional Law ⬳249, 316
Forcible Entry and Detainer ⬳2

Insofar as section of Forcible Entry and Detainer Act required furnishing of bond as prerequisite to prosecuting appeal, it was violative of Fourteenth Amendment of the United States Constitution and of articles of State Constitution containing due process and equal protection clauses and governing appellate court jurisdiction. S.H.A.Const.1970, art. 1, § 2; art. 6, § 6; U.S.C.A.Const. Amend. 14; S.H.A. ch. 57, § 19.

FIGURE 7.24
Syllabus and Key Number Analysis from *North Eastern Reporter, Second Series*

JACK SPRING, INC. v. LITTLE
Cite as 280 N.E.2d 208
Ill. **209**

3. Forcible Entry and Detainer ⬅43(4)

In view of invalidation of Forcible Entry and Detainer Act section requiring furnishing of bond as prerequisite to prosecuting appeal, Supreme Court rule purporting to embody such section for time and method of appeal in forcible entry and detainer cases is no longer operative. S.H.A. ch. 57, § 19; Supreme Court Rules, rule 303(b), S.H.A. ch. 110A, § 303(b).

4. Forcible Entry and Detainer ⬅45

Stay of judgment pending appeal is governed by Supreme Court rule, and its provisions supersede those contained in Forcible Entry and Detainer Act section governing conditions of defendant's appeal bond. S.H.A. ch. 57, § 20 ; Supreme Court Rules, rule 305, S.H.A. ch. 110A, § 305.

5. Forcible Entry and Detainer ⬅45

Right to an appeal is matter separate and apart from right to supersedeas during pendency of the appeal, and in being required to furnish a bond as condition to staying judgment, appellant in an action in forcible entry and detainer is in no different situation than an appellant who seeks a stay of judgment in any other type of appeal. S.H.A. ch. 57, § 20; Supreme Court Rules, rule 305, S.H.A. ch. 110A, § 305.

6. Landlord and Tenant ⬅285(7)

Supersedeas conditioned upon payment by appealing tenants of rental installments as they became due was within contemplation of Supreme Court rule governing stay of judgments pending appeal. .S.H.A. ch. 57, § 20; Supreme Court Rules, rule 305, S.H.A. ch. 110A, § 305.

7. Landlord and Tenant ⬅196

Liability for rent continues so long as tenant is in possession.

8. Landlord and Tenant ⬅48(1), 223(2)

Tenant may bring action against landlord for breach of a covenant or may recoup for damages in an action brought to recover rent.

9. Landlord and Tenant ⬅284(2)

Tenants' affirmative defenses, in landlords' actions to recover possession of rented premises because of nonpayment of rent, alleging breach of express covenants to repair were germane to issue whether tenants were indebted to landlords for rent and thus should not have been struck.

10. Landlord and Tenant ⬅125(1)

Included in oral and written contracts governing tenancies of tenants in multiple unit dwellings occupied by them was implied warranty of habitability which would be fulfilled by substantial compliance with pertinent provisions of city building code.

11. Landlord and Tenant ⬅284(2)

Tenants' affirmative defenses, in separate actions by landlords to recover possession of rented premises for nonpayment of rent, alleging breach of implied warranty of habitability were germane to question whether tenants were indebted to landlords for rent and thus should not have been struck.

12. Landlord and Tenant ⬅284(2)

Tenant's affirmative defense, in action by landlord to recover possession of rented premises for nonpayment of rent, insofar as it presented issue of whether lease provision governing examination and acceptance by tenant of condition of premises precluded implied warranty of habitability and proof of breach of alleged express agreements to repair premises was germane to issue whether rent was due and owing and thus should not have been struck.

Kleiman, Cornfield & Feldman, Chicago (Gilbert A. Cornfield and Barb J. Hillman, Chicago, of counsel), for appellants.

Irving Goodman and Nathan Einhorn, Chicago, for appellee Sutton and Peterson, Inc.

Stephen J. Epstein, Chicago, for appellee Jack Spring, Inc.

A digest is an index tool with short summaries of the points of law decided in different cases. These digest statements are arranged so that all cases on the same point of law are grouped together. If a given case involves five different points of law, it will be listed in five different parts of the digest. In West digests cases are arranged on the basis of the key numbers. In other digests they are arranged under similar classification schemes. Figure 7.25 demonstrates how entry number ten from the preliminary analysis of the *Jack Spring* case (see Figure 7.24) appears verbatim in the digest listing for Illinois cases under Landlord and Tenant ⊙═125(1).

The *American Digest System* covers both federal and state court decisions from 1658 to the present time. Cases decided between 1658 and 1896 are covered in the fifty-volume set *Century Digest*. The cases decided between 1897 and 1976 are divided into 10-year periods and published as part of the *Decennial* series. The *First Decennial* covers the years of 1897 to 1906, the *Second Decennial* covers 1907 to 1916 and so forth up to the *Eighth Decennial* for 1967 to 1976. Cases decided after 1976 appear in the *General Digest.*

In the *Century Digest* or in one of the *Decennials* all cases from that ten years (or more in the case of the *Century Digest*) relating to the same key number are grouped together in one volume. In the *General Digest,* however, each volume is a self-contained unit covering all the key numbers for a period of less than one year. Thus in working with the *Decennials* one can find all of the cases dealing with landlord and tenant ⊙═125(1) for a 10-year period in one volume. However, the researcher must look up landlord and tenant ⊙═125(1) in every single volume of the *General Digest* if the search is to be complete.

In addition to the inclusive digest system described above, West publishes a series of specialized digests that correspond to the regional reporters, state reporters, and federal reporters. Thus if one is only looking for California cases the paralegal can go to either the *California Digest* or the *Pacific Digest* to avoid searching the entire *American Digest System.* The *U.S. Supreme Court Digest* covers only Supreme Court decisions while the *Modern Federal Practice Digest* covers all federal cases reported since 1939. Lawyers' Co-op Publishing Company also publishes a digest covering the United States Supreme Court — the *U.S. Supreme Court Reports Digest.*

ing condition at inception of lease, tenant was not relieved of generally imposed burden of bearing risk of any defect in conditions within area under his exclusive possession and control by exception rendering general rule inapplicable to defects which are result of faulty design or disrepair and which existed at beginning of tenancy, were not discoverable by tenant on reasonable inspection, and were known, either actually or constructively, to the landlord.—Id.

D.C.App. 1968. In absence of statute or express covenant in lease, landlord does not impliedly covenant or warrant that leased premises are in habitable condition.—Saunders v. First Nat. Realty Corp., 245 A.2d 836.

Hawaii 1969. Implied warranty of habitability exists in unfurnished as well as furnished dwellings.—Lund v. MacArthur, 462 P.2d 482, 51 Haw. 473.

Seriousness of defects in rented dwelling and length of time during which they persist are both relevant factors to be considered in determining materiality of breach of implied warranty of habitability.—Id.

Hawaii 1969. Application of implied warranty of habitability and fitness in leases of dwellings recognizes changes in history of leasing transactions and takes into account contemporary housing realities.—Lemle v. Breeden, 462 P.2d 470, 51 Haw. 426, 478, 40 A.L.R.3d 637.

A "lease" is in essence as well as a transfer of estate in land and is, more importantly, a contractual relationship from which warranty of habitability and fitness is a just and necessary implication.—Id.

In lease of dwelling house, there is an implied warranty of habitability and fitness for use intended.—Id.

Where plaintiff leased dwelling from defendant for immediate occupation and after taking possession was forced with his family to sleep in living room rather than proper quarters because of presence of rats in dwelling, there was breach of implied warranty of habitability and fitness for use in lease.—Id.

Doctrine of constructive eviction, as an admitted judicial fiction designed to operate as though there were a substantial breach of material covenant in bilateral contract, no longer serves its purpose when more flexible concept of implied warranty of habitability is available.—Id.

Under doctrine of implied warranty of habitability and fitness in every lease of dwelling, there are a number of remedies available for breach in contrast to doctrine of constructive eviction which requires that tenant abandon premises within reasonable time after giving notice that premises are uninhabitable or unfit for his purposes.—Id.

Under doctrine that a lease is essentially a contractual relationship with an implied warranty of habitability and fitness, available remedies for breach of warranty include damages, reformation and rescission.—Id.

Under doctrine of implied warranty of habitability and fitness in leases of dwellings, seriousness of claimed defect and length of time it persists are relevant factors in considering materiality of the alleged breach.—Id.

In determining whether there exists a breach of implied warranty of habitability and fitness in lease of dwelling, each case must turn on its own facts.—Id.

Ill. 1972. Included in oral and written contracts governing tenancies of tenants in multiple unit dwellings occupied by them was implied warranty of habitability which would be fulfilled by substantial compliance with pertinent provisions of city building code.—Jack

Spring, Inc. v. Little, 280 N.E.2d 208, 50 Ill.2d 351.

Ill.App. 1970. Assertion of tenants, sued by landlord for past due rent under written lease, that premises violated city of Chicago housing code presented a valid affirmative defense to action since violations of the code would invalidate lease, and tenants were entitled to present evidence that the premises were in substantial violation of code.—Longenecker v. Hardin, 264 N.E.2d 878, 130 Ill. App.2d 468.

Ind.App. 1976. Apartment residential lease is essentially contractual in nature and carries with it mutually dependent covenants including implied warranty of habitability and full range of remedies for breach of contract. (Per Buchanan, P. J., with one Judge specially concurring.)—Old Town Development Co. v. Langford, 349 N.E.2d 744.

Prior notice, either actual or constructive, and opportunity to repair are prerequisites to landlord's breach of implied warranty of habitability. (Per Buchanan, P. J., with one Judge specially concurring.)—Id.

Iowa 1972. Question of whether landlord's breach of implied warranty of habitability is of such substantial nature as to render premises unsafe or unsanitary and, thus, unfit for habitation will usually be fact question to be determined by circumstances of each case. I.C.A. §§ 413.1 et seq., 413.9, 413.106.— Mease v. Fox, 200 N.W.2d 791.

When tenant vacates premises because of landlord's breach of implied warranty of habitability, condition of premises loses relevance in determining tenant's damage; measure of tenant's damages after vacation of premises is difference between fair rental value of premises if they had been as warranted and the promised rent computed for balance of term. I.C.A. §§ 413.1 et seq., 413.9, 413.106, 554.-2715.—Id.

Tenant is under obligation to give landlord notice of deficiency or defect not known to landlord.—Id.

Iowa 1967. Generally, subject to express contractual provisions and some fairly well defined exceptions, a tenant takes the demised premises as he finds them; the rule of caveat emptor ordinarily applies as between lessor and lessee.—Fetters v. City of Des Moines, 149 N.W.2d 815.

Kan. 1974. Provisions of city housing code relating to minimum housing standards were, by implication, read into and became part of rental agreement.—Steele v. Latimer, 521 P.2d 304.

Provisions of municipal housing code prescribing minimum housing standards are deemed by implication to become a part of a lease of urban residential property, giving rise to an implied warranty that the premises are habitable and safe for human occupancy in compliance with the pertinent code provisions and will remain so for the duration of the tenancy.—Id.

Where a breach of an implied warranty of habitability has occurred, traditional remedies for breach of contract are available to the tenant, including the recovery of damages.— Id.

La.App. 1976. Lease provision, whereby landlord agreed to make all repairs on premises due to leaks from plumbing or utility lines within or without leased premises, constituted covenant to repair; however, additional lease provision, whereby landlord agreed to at all times keep basement of leased premises waterproof, was not mere covenant to repair, but was instead obligation to keep basement

waterproof.—McCrory Corp. v. Latter, 331 So.2d 577.

La.App. 1973. Tenant's complaint, which alleged that landlord leased property to her which was unfit for purpose for which it was let, stated a cause of action for damages for emotional discomfort, loss of convenience, humiliation, etc.—Evans v. Does, 283 So.2d 804.

La.App. 1970. Sublessee accepting demised premises in condition in which they are is still entitled to warranty protection afforded him by statute. LSA–C.C. arts. 2692, 2695. —Reed v. Classified Parking System, 232 So.2d 103, writ denied 234 So.2d 194, 255 La. 1097, writ refused 234 So.2d 194, 255 La. 1098.

La.App. 1968. A tenant seeking damages under statute providing that lessor guarantees the lessee against all the vices and defects of the thing, which may prevent its being used, even in case it should appear he knew nothing of the existence of such vices and defects, must establish his claim by fair preponderance of the evidence. LSA–C.C. art. 2695.—Long v. McMichael, 219 So.2d 810.

Negligence on part of owner or lessor is not an indispensable prerequisite to recovery by tenant for a loss under statute providing that lessor guarantees the lessee against all the vices and defects of the thing, which may prevent its being used, even in case it should appear he knew nothing of the existence of such vices and defects, at time the lease was made. LSA–C.C. art. 2695.—Id.

Knowledge on part of lessor of existence of defect is not required for tenant's recovery for loss under statute providing that lessor guarantees lessee against all the vices and defects of thing, which may prevent its being used even in case it should appear he knew nothing of the existence of such vices and defects, at time lease was made, for it suffices if the defect exists and it is established as the cause of the loss, damage or injury. LSA–C.C. art. 2695.—Id.

The preponderance of evidence exacted of the tenant or lessee under statute providing lessor guarantees lessee against all vices and defects of the thing, which may prevent its being used even in case it should appear he knew nothing of the existence of such vices and defects at time lease was made, does not mean proof beyond a reasonable doubt but contemplates evidence sufficient to establish tenant's claim to reasonable certainty and beyond the realm of mere possibility, speculation or conjecture. LSA–C.C. art. 2695.—Id.

Md.App. 1974. Implied warranty of merchantability is inapplicable to leases, as title does not pass in such transactions. Code 1957, art. 95B, §§ 2–105(1), 2–314.—Sheeskin v. Giant Food, Inc., 318 A.2d 874, 20 Md.App. 611.

Mass. 1973. In rental of any premises for dwelling purposes, under a written or oral lease, for a specified time or at will, there is an implied warranty of habitability, that is, that the premises are fit for human occupation; such warranty means that at inception of rental there are no latent or patent defects in facilities vital to use of premises for residential purposes and that such facilities will remain during the entire term in a condition which makes the property livable; such warranty, insofar as it is based on the State Sanitary Code and local health regulations, cannot be waived by any provision of the lease or rental agreement. M.G.L.A. c. 111 § 5.— Boston Housing Authority v. Hemingway, 293 N.E.2d 831.

Since tenant's covenant to pay rent is dependent on the landlord's implied warranty of

For references to other topics, see Descriptive-Word Index

FIGURE 7.25

Sample Page from the *Eighth Decennial Digest*

Now if the researcher has already found one or more cases relevant to the problem, those cases can be looked up in a West reporter to find the appropriate key number and a summary of what that key number involves (as in Figure 7.24). One can also find the proper key number by using the table of cases which identifies the key numbers in each indexed case.

Alternatively, one can also use the descriptive-word index to locate appropriate key numbers. Figure 7.26 shows a page from one of these descriptive-word indexes. In using it, the researcher should look up key words associated with the case. These words can relate to the parties in the suit, the place where the action occurred, the type of action it is (e.g., negligence, defamation, and so on), the relief being sought (e.g., damages, injunction, and so on), and the defense being relied upon (e.g., assumption of risk or act of God).

One can also find the appropriate key number through the topic-analysis sections at the beginning of each major topic. Thus one can simply turn to the beginning of the landlord and tenant section of the digest and scan the list until the appropriate sub-topic is found. Figure 7.27 presents an example of part of the subject analysis section for landlord and tenant.

Shepard's Citations

Just as one can use *Shepard's* to determine if a statutory provision is still in force, one can also rely upon it to discover if a case has been overruled by subsequent judicial action. There can be little more embarrassing to a lawyer than to rely upon a case for authority only to find that it has been reversed by a higher court. *Shepard's* also provides the researcher with citations to other cases in which the case being cited was formally mentioned by another court. These types of references can be useful means of locating additional cases from the same or other jurisdictions.

Shepard's United States Citations covers decisions from *United States Reports, United States Supreme Court Reports, Lawyers' Edition,* and the *Supreme Court Reporter.* Each set has its own section with cases geared to its citation. *Federal Reporter Citations* covers the courts of appeals and district courts

LANDLORD & TENANT

LANDLORD AND TENANT—Cont'd
Fall—Cont'd
Parking area, ice, timeliness of notice. **Land & Ten 169(11)**
Salesman, rain water covering concrete porch. **Land & Ten 167(8)**
Side steps, handrails lacking. **Land & Ten 169(11)**
Sidewalk, ice, landlord normally removing in past. **Land & Ten 162**
Sidewalk, water dripping from air conditioner. **Land & Ten 169(8)**
Special use of driveway, landlord not clearing snow. **Indem 13.2(5)**
Fee received to permit early termination of lease, consideration. **Damag 78(6)**
Fire, landlord's act or omission not connected. **Land & Ten 164(1)**
Fires, liability of tenant. **Land & Ten 55(1)**
Fuses, landlord inducing tenants to continue using high amperage fuses, fire damage. **Land & Ten 169(7)**
Glass in doors, building code met, running child. **Land & Ten 164(1)**
Gold clause, repeal of individual gold ownership prohibition. **Land & Ten 213(1)**
Habitability, warranty, conditions beyond landlord's control. **Land & Ten 125(1)**
Hole in floor of apartment, constructive notice, tenant suffering personal injuries. **Land & Ten 169(6)**
Hurricane, flood damaging vehicles, tenant unwarned of peril. **Land & Ten 166(10)**
Indemnity, exculpatory clauses, public policy. **Land & Ten 164(1)**
Independent contractors, damages to tenant, vicarious liability. **Land & Ten 169(11)**
Injunction—
Unconstitutional termination practices, consent of landlord rendering case moot and plaintiff not representative for class action. **Fed Civ Proc 181**
Insurance agents and brokers, percentage lease agreements, licenses. **Land & Ten 200.1**
Lien—
Notice, month-to-month rent arrearage. **Land & Ten 244**
Locking tenants out of apartments, exemplary damages. **Land & Ten 180(4)**
Minorities, requiring landlords to report on, validity. **Const Law 220.5(1)**
Mortgages—
Foreclosure—
Intervention, tenants, subsidy program. **Fed Civ Proc 331**
Mugging, landlord's employee, stairway. **Land & Ten 169(6)**
Municipal appropriations, tenant's union, public purpose. **Mun Corp 861**
Negro, rental application rejection, race. **Civil R 13.13(3)**
Noise, impairment of warranty of habitability. **Land & Ten 298(1)**
Personal injuries to tenant in course of criminal action, liability of landlord. **Land & Ten 162**
Personal injuries, warranty of habitability. **Land & Ten 164(1)**
Possession of leased premises—
Rent, consistent failure to pay when due. **Land & Ten 278.9(3)**
President, tenants' association, slipping letters under tenants' doors. **Nuis 3(1)**
Property tax, rebate to tenants—
Const Law 148, 229(1), 283
Tax 37.11
Race discrimination, rental records, government inspection for year. **Civil R 13.16**
Rack, bolting to wall without landlord's consent. **Fixt 15**

LANDLORD AND TENANT—Cont'd
Rape, security allegedly inadequate. **Land & Ten 169(3)**
Relocation assistance, rehabilitation project forcing tenant out. **Const Law 242.3(1)**
Relocation expenses, former owner as port authority's tenant. **States 123**
Renewal, equitable relief, timely written notice not sent. **Decl Judgm 318**
Repairs, massive repairs to bring building in compliance with building code, obligation of landlord. **Land & Ten 152(4)**
Res ipsa loquitur, fire, landlord owning defective stove. **Land & Ten 55(3)**
Retaliatory eviction, defenses, intent to demolish building. **Land & Ten 284(1)**
Security—
Advance refurbishing fee. **Land & Ten 184(2)**
Attorney fees—
Damage deposit improperly retained. **Costs 172, 252**
Damage deposits recovery, attorney fees, limitations—
Assumpsit 14
Lim of Act 35(1)
Deposits, income status, food stamps. **Agric 2**
Security deposit, deduction of attorneys fees for recovery of property. **Land & Ten 184(2)**
Security deposit, wrongful withholding, attorney fees—
Princ & A 123(11)
Release 57(1)
Security deposits, action for recovery, attorney fees. **Land & Ten 184(2)**
Security deposits, wrongful withholding, attorney fees. **Land & Ten 216**
Senior citizens, rent freeze—
Const Law 208(3), 228.3
Em Dom 2(1)
Land & Ten 200.11
Shooting-robbery, common hallway, security inadequacy. **Land & Ten 169(11)**
Shortage of low income housing inducing tenant to sign lease against public policy. **Land & Ten 164(1)**
Smoking causing fire in apartment, negligence of tenant. **Land & Ten 55(3)**
Social guests drinking on premises, dram shop liability. **Int Liq 306**
Solicitors of tenants, license. **Const Law 230.3(1), 287**
Stairways, loose bricks on back stairway, tort liability. **Land & Ten 164(7)**
Summary proceeding for possession—
Attorney fees, rent unpaid, lease authorizing legal fees. **Land & Ten 310(1)**
Fine, proceeding unsuccessful. **Land & Ten 278.17(4)**
Stay of execution, rent arrearage, several prior arrearages. **Land & Ten 311**
Summary seizure, tenant's property, contractual lien—
Civil R 13.5(4)
Const Law 254
Tax escalation clauses, additional rent. **Land & Ten 200.46**
Taxation—
Leasehold, tax-exempt property—
Const Law 229(1)
Tax 40(6)
Unfair trade practice, personalty converted, tenants temporarily moving out. **Trade Reg 861**
Union of tenants, standing to sue, housing development. **Fed Civ Proc 115**
Water charge, application only to multiple unit tenants. **Const Law 242**
Window guards, apartments containing children under 10. **Mun Corp 601.3**

LANDLORD AND TENANT—Cont'd
Wrongful death of tenant, premature release of inmate from state psychiatric hospital, tort liability. **States 184.7**

LANDMARK PRESERVATION
Railroad terminal, office building, construction on top. **Const Law 278(1)**

LAND-USE CASE
Environmental control agency, estoppel. **Health & E 25.5**

LANGUAGE
Briefs, English. **Fed Cts 712**
Interpreters, appointment, non-English-speakers represented by counsel. **Trial 22**
Miranda warnings, Spanish translation not made. **Infants 16.8**
Unemployment compensation, fault or misconduct. **Social S 393**
Voir dire, prospective jurors' fluency in Spanish. **Jury 131(10)**

LAP
Drunken driving, stopped vehicle, woman on lap of man behind wheel. **Autos 355(6)**

LAPAROTOMY
Exploratory operation, wife kicked, death. **Homic 236(1)**

LAPAROTOMY PADS
Abdominal surgery, pad left in, assistant surgeon not determining. **Phys 15(14)**
Automobile insurance, term unspecified, premium unpaid. **Insurance 310(2)**

LARCENY
Altenative abetting theory, little evidence of second participant. **Const Law 265**
Attorney—
Conviction, moral turpitude. **Atty & C 39**
Conviction, third degree grand larceny. **Atty & C 39**
Deception, class A misdemeanor. **Atty & C 39**
Grand larceny conviction. **Atty & C 39**
Grand theft conviction. **Atty & C 58**
Guilty plea, theft from savings and loan association. **Atty & C 39**
Boat, marina employees and others conspiring, policy excluding employee dishonesty. **Insurance 435.22(1)**
Broker, client's funds, commingling a misdemeanor. **Crim Law 29**
Burglary alarm service companies employees, perpetration, respondeat superior. **Mast & S 307**
CB radio, complaint of theft, freedom of information. **Records 14**
Coffee bags, checker dismissed. **Offic 69.7**
Confession, corroboration, similar offenses. **Mil Jus 172**
Continuing larceny doctrine, jacket stolen off base, transportation on base. **Mil Jus 58**
Contractors, building materials after termination of contract, insurance liability. **Insurance 417.5(1)**
Counsel for accused, withdrawal, indictment not alleging value. **Crim Law 1077.3**
Court-room crowded, confidential communications difficult. **Crim Law 1166.11**
Credit card, handwriting exemplar, accused's twin giving. **Obst Just 5**
Credit cards, street value, evidence. **Larc 46**
Emergency assistance, destitution. **Social S 10**
Enhanced punishment, petty theft with prior felony conviction. **Crim Law 1201**
Evidence—
Military offenses. **Mil Jus 181**

FIGURE 7.26
Sample Page from Descriptive-Word Index of the *General Digest*

LANDLORD & TENANT

28-8th D—806

VI. TENANCIES AT WILL AND AT SUFFERANCE.—Cont'd

119. Creation of tenancy at sufferance.
   (1). In general.
   (2). Tenant holding over after expiration of term.
120. Termination.
   (1). In general.
   (2). Necessity and sufficiency of notice to quit in general.
   (3). Waiver by tenant of right to notice.
   (4). Surrender and abandonment.

VII. PREMISES, AND ENJOYMENT AND USE THEREOF.

(A) DESCRIPTION, EXTENT, AND CONDITION.

⇐121. Sufficiency of description.
122. Extent of premises.
123. Property included in general.
124. Appurtenances.
   (1). In general.
   (2). Means of entrance or exit.
   (3). Power and light.
125. Tenantable condition of premises.
   (1). In general.
   (2). Suitability of premises for the purpose for which they were leased.

(B) POSSESSION, ENJOYMENT, AND USE.

⇐126. Duty of tenant to take possession.
127. Right of entry and possession of tenant.
128. Delivery of possession.
   (1). In general.
   (2). Waiver of failure to deliver possession.
129. Actions for failure to deliver possession.
   (1). In general.
   (2). Pleading.
   (3). Evidence.
   (4). Damages.
   (5). Questions for jury.
130. Covenants for quiet enjoyment.
   (1). Implied covenant.
   (2). What constitutes breach of covenant.
   (3). Actions for breach of covenant in general.
   (4). Damages.
131. Disturbance of possession of tenant.
132. —— By landlord.
   (1). In general.
   (2). Actions in general.
   (3). Damages.
133. —— By third persons.
   (1). In general.
   (2). Liability of landlord.
   (3). Actions.
134. Mode and purposes of use of premises in general.
   (1). Mode of use in general.
   (2). Restrictions in lease as to mode of use.
   (3). Purpose for which premises may be used.
   (4). Rights, duties, and liabilities of sub-lessees or assignees.
   (5). Interference with use by landlord or others.
   (6). Actions by landlord.
135. Cultivation of land under farm leases.
136. —— Rights and duties of tenant in general.
137. —— Timber.
138. —— Manure.
139. —— Crops.
   (1). Right or title to crops in general.
   (2). Right to way-going crop.
   (3). Tenant of land subject to judgment lien.
   (4). Injury to crop.
   (5). Action to recover value.
140. Injuries to premises.
141. —— By landlord.
142. —— By third persons.
   (1). In general.
   (2). Injuries to grass and crops.
   (3). Obstruction of light.
   (4). Obstruction of way.
   (5). Liability of landlord.
   (6). Actions in general.
   (7). Damages.
   (8). Right of tenant to abate nuisance.
144. Duty of tenant to surrender on termination of lease.

(C) INCUMBRANCES, TAXES, AND ASSESSMENTS.

⇐145. Incumbrances on leasehold in general.
146. Covenants against incumbrances.
147. Duty to remove or discharge incumbrances.
148. Covenants and agreements as to taxes and assessments.
   (1). In general.
   (2). What taxes or assessments are within the covenant.
   (3). Liability of assignees.
   (4). Actions for breach of covenant.
149. Liabilities for taxes and assessments.

(D) REPAIRS, INSURANCE, AND IMPROVEMENTS.

⇐150. Right and duty to make repairs in general.
   (1). In general.
   (2). Duty to rebuild on destruction of property.
   (3). Landlord's right of entry to make repairs.
   (4). Rights of subtenants.
   (5). Right of tenant to repair at landlord's cost.
151. Statutory provisions.
152. Covenants and agreements as to repairs and alterations.
   (1). In general.
   (2). Consideration for agreement.
   (3). Construction and operation of covenants in general.
   (4). Nature of repairs included in covenant or agreement.
   (5). Duty to rebuild on destruction of property.
   (6). Right of landlord to notice that repairs are necessary.
   (7). Agreement by landlord to pay for repairs.
   (8). Rights and liabilities of assignees and subtenants.

FIGURE 7.27
Sample of Topic Analysis from Landlord and Tenant Section of the *Eighth Decennial Digest*

as well as such specialized material as decisions of the commissioner of patents. In addition to these sets, *Shepard's* also publishes sets that correspond to each of the regional reporters and to the state reporters. They carry names such as *Shepard's Atlantic Reporter Citations* and *Shepard's Michigan Citations*.

Citations for *Jack Spring, Inc. v. Little*, 280 N.E.2d 208 (Illinois, 1972) (*see* Figure 7.24) are presented in Figure 7.28. To locate the proper citation, the researcher must find the page or pages which cover the relevant volume. The volume numbers located in the top corners of the pages help speed this process. Once the correct page is found, one must read up and down the columns until the volume number is found within the column (in this case near the bottom of the first column). The boldface numbers that follow reflect the page numbers upon which the case begins. Thus the researcher looks up and down the columns until the number 208 is found near the top of the fifth column. The actual citation information is located under number 208 in that column.

The citation information will ordinarily begin by listing any parallel cites for the same case in parentheses. Thus it can be seen that *Jack Spring* was also published at 50 Ill.2d 351. In this case the decision was not reviewed by a higher court. If it had been, there would also be a citation for that same case at the higher court level. (The designation in the citations for 280 N.E.2d 205 reports that the U.S. Supreme Court denied *certiorari* at 409 U.S. 948.) After reviewing any actions on the same case by other courts, *Shepard's* lists other cases in which the judges formally cited *Jack Spring* in their opinions. These citations are grouped together by the states in which they were decided. The small letters f, j, d, and e stand for followed, dissenting opinion, distinguished, and explained. Other commonly used abbreviations are explained in the front of each *Shepard's* volume. The small superior number appearing after the reporter abbreviation (e.g., the 10 in 282NE[10]151) corresponds to the point of law which was listed as number 10 in the syllabus analysis in *Jack Spring* (in this case, the issue of implied warranty of habitability). In addition to citing cases, *Shepard's* may also include citations to law review articles and *American Law Reports, Annotated*. See, for example, the *A.L.R.3d* citation under 280 N.E.2d 300 in Figure 7.28.

Column 1

–878–
(29◎S99)
(58℗p194)
s269NE²53
15A2.1428s
–884–
(29◎S135)
(58℗p323)
–886–
(29◎S123)
(58℗p317)
–889–
(29◎A189)
(58℗p328)
–892–
(29◎A187)
(58℗p327)
–894–
(31M34)
(58℗p188)
288NE²307
–901–
287NE⁴461
287NE⁵461
–902–
279NE343
279NE³909
297NE²519
–906–
279NE343
f279NE⁵905
280NE¹679
280NE²679
280NE³679
280NE⁴679
–915–
281NE¹573
282NE380
282NE⁴80
296NE¹202
Ill
287NE²129
DC
302A2d754
Me
294A2d689

Vol. 280
–1–
(31IA1063)
290NE⁴418
–3–
(41IA97)
–4–
(31IA1059)
–7–
(31IA1055)

Column 2

–10–
(31IA1050)
281NE⁴426
304NE¹16
–13–
(31IA1078)
–14–
(41IA23)
–16–
(41IA90)
–17–
(31IA1047)
285NE²252
292NE42
e301NE²302
–19–
(41IA391)
305NE¹638
–23–
(31IA1065)
299NE²42
–29–
Case 1
(41IA85)
–29–
Case 2
(41IA6)
cc280NE42
279NE¹732
–42–
(41IA4)
cc280NE29
–43–
(31IA1085)
–46–
(31IA1074)
–49–
(41IA65)
284NE⁴74
302NE³432
–52–
(41IA369)
–57–
j280NE¹316
281NE¹802
282NE¹862
j282NE¹869
d285NE¹683
294NE¹821
301NE¹238
–59–
284NE⁴91
–64–
297NE⁴440
–69–
s285NE₂830

Column 3

–81–
283NE⁴387
283NE³388
283NE³389
e285NE⁴827
291NE¹902
291NE²902
291NE⁵902
–88–
s198NE233
282NE⁶553
282NE⁷553
283NE⁶585
285NE841
286NE⁷851
287NE⁶366
287NE⁶574
287NE⁵900
289NE⁵300
289NE¹²333
291NE⁵578
298NE²32
301NE⁶206
–95–
Case 1
(29NY930)
(329S2d321)
s313S2d189
337S2d338
–95–
Case 2
(29NY931)
(329S2d322)
s321S2d200
344S2d458
–96–
(29NY933)
(329S2d323)
–97–
Case 1
(29NY934)
(329S2d323)
–97–
Case 2
(29NY935)
(329S2d324)
s291S2d829
286NE¹732
304NE¹366
335S2d¹296
349S2d¹669
–98–
(29NY937)
(329S2d325)
286NE¹716
j286NE²735
294NE¹206
331S2d337
335S2d¹273
j335S2d²300
340S2d240
341S2d¹619
–99–
(29NY938)
(329S2d326)
s326S2d191

Column 4

–100–
(29NY939)
(329S2d327)
s324S2d426
–101–
(29M190)
–106–
(29M190)
(57℗p361)
–110–
(29M190)
(58℗p129)
–129–
cc141NE269
cc233NE730
cc293NE260
cc393US5
cc21LE5
cc89SC35
297NE501
NH
293A2d767
–144–
285NE⁹784
–149–
349S2d562
–152–
23A2.932s
–155–
284NE⁶926
291NE424
296NE⁴475
296NE²475
296NE³475
–166–
296NE⁴495
f296NE⁶501
298NE²156
298NE⁷159
–171–
cc225NE921
–174–
298NE²878
–183–
287NE⁵463
303NE⁶738
–187–
289NE886
294NE382
–199–
282NE86
–201–
(51Il2d14)
s397US95
s25LE78
s90SC818
cc263NE833

Column 5

–203–
(51Il2d35)
f284NE²431
302NE³217
302NE⁴217
–205–
(51Il2d46)
US cert den
in409US948
–208–
(50Il2d351)
282NE¹⁰151
290NE⁵590
f298NE⁸175
f298NE⁹175
j298NE¹¹176
j298NE¹²176
d301NE¹²11
j301NE⁸12
j301NE¹²13
e302NE¹⁰209
e302NE¹⁰211
467F2d1273
468F2d²798
Mass
293NE⁶841
293NE¹²841
j293NE¹⁰850
j293NE¹²850
Calif
517P2d1169
Iowa
200NW796
Mo
495SW71
NJ
291A2d582
308A2d22
Wash
515P2d163
–224–
(50Il2d379)
j278NE249
e303NE6
–230–
(50Il2d390)
279NE¹⁵531
289NE23
295NE¹⁵552
298NE³220
301NE²274
–234–
(31IA1014)
r294NE267
s298NE7
L305NE¹584
–236–
(41IA34)
–239–
(41IA45)
s305NE308
288NE¹535
292NE¹754
293NE¹629
293NE²734
293NE²766
d297NE²362

Column 6

–240–
(41IA55)
–242–
(41IA48)
303NE¹504
–244–
(41IA38)
–249–
(41IA118)
–253–
(41IA51)
f298NE²63
301NE²341
–256–
(41IA113)
289NE⁶117
–260–
(41IA46)
–262–
Case 1
(41IA112)
–262–
Case 2
(41IA59)
–264–
(41IA123)
f288NE³632
–266–
(41IA881)
–268–
(41IA60)
–269–
(41IA494)
298NE²415
d299NE¹103
–276–
(41IA90)
–281–
(41IA89)
–283–
(41IA86)
–286–
(31IA1090)
296NE¹91
304NE518
d304NE¹519
–288–
(41IA26)
–291–
(41IA29)
–294–
(41IA106)
s295NE266
–297–
(41IA111)

Column 7

–298–
(41IA109)
–300–
s270NE764
288NE²184
j288NE³567
NC
189SE756
RI
298A2d531
25A2.383s
–307–
f283NE⁸804
285NE⁷683
286NE⁹704
286NE⁶704
286NE⁷704
286NE⁸843
286NE⁸843
286NE⁸843
f288NE⁷553
289NE³320
292NE595
292NE⁷615
296NE¹664
298NE⁴464
298NE³508
300NE³136
301NE¹180
301NE²180
301NE⁵190
301NE¹521
–313–
j281NE¹803
j282NE837
282NE⁸860
285NE⁸683
286NE⁸669
300NE372
301NE⁹238
301NE³670
303NE297
303NE¹683
–327–
299NE219
304NE⁶829
–336–
289NE¹⁰177
289NE303
–359–
(29NY457)
(329S2d569)
s282NE625
s321S2d132
s331S2d672
–362–
(29NY939)
(329S2d574)
s312S2d35
–371–
(29◎S139)
(58℗p342)
s285NE763
–374–
(29◎S144)
(58℗p344)

Column 8

–364–
Case 2
(29NY944)
(329S2d577)
s320S2d943
–365–
Case 1
(29NY946)
(329S2d578)
s318S2d670
–365–
Case 2
(29NY947)
(329S2d579)
s304S2d147
s316S2d393
–366–
Case 1
(29NY949)
(329S2d579)
s316S2d238
338S2d970
347S2d418
348S2d621
–366–
Case 2
(29NY950)
(329S2d580)
s323S2d527
s331S2d780
329S2d82
338S2d401
344S2d994
–367–
Case 1
(29NY952)
(329S2d581)
s314S2d137
–367–
Case 2
(29NY952)
(329S2d582)
s315S2d768
s336S2d781
–368–
Case 1
(29NY953)
(329S2d583)
s305S2d434
–368–
Case 2
(29NY954)
(329S2d584)
s322S2d843
s322S2d849
337S2d843

FIGURE 7.28
Sample Page from *Shepard's North Eastern Reporter Citations*

COMPUTER-ASSISTED RESEARCH

While the computer has not revolutionized the field of law, it has begun to make inroads. It has been primarily used in time-keeping and billing procedures, but now there are two major computer systems for legal research: Lexis and Westlaw.

Both systems are based on the same general principles. The full text of court decisions (and in some circumstances other legal documents as well) are stored in a computer's memory bank. Then, with the use of a video display terminal unit (connected to the computer by a telephone line), a researcher can instruct the computer to locate and reproduce all decisions that have certain key words in them. For example, the terminal operator can request that the computer identify all Oregon cases which somewhere in their text use the words "promissory estoppel." The text of these cases can then be displayed on the video screen so that the researcher can determine what are going to be useful cases. If any are useful, the researcher can obtain a paper copy from the printing unit attached to the terminal.

The systems can also be used to obtain quick copies of cases for which the researcher already has a citation and to check if the case has been acted on by a higher court.

The systems have been designed for easy operation. While there are certain terms and formats that must be learned, the operation does not require any knowledge of fortran or other computer languages. If paralegals have an opportunity to use such a system, they should certainly take advantage of it. The small investment of time in learning to operate the terminal will easily be made up by the efficiency of the system.

The computer is simply an aid. Just as when one uses a digest or any other legal research tool, the individual must supply the initial words that are the basis for the search. Once the computer has located the cases, it is still up to the individual to interpret them properly.

ADDITIONAL RESEARCH AIDS

If the various steps described above are followed, the researcher should have both a general understanding of the relevant legal principles and an exhaustive list of statutes and cases that apply to a particular problem. Hopefully, the background knowledge of the paralegal will be sufficient to properly analyze the effects of these statutes and cases. If, however, problems of interpretation persist, one should return to the encyclopedias, annotations, treatises, and periodicals mentioned at the beginning of this chapter. After having read through the additional cases and statutes, the researcher may gain a new level of understanding from these more analytical materials.

At many of these stages the paralegal may come across an unfamiliar word or Latin phrase. When that occurs, either a legal dictionary or the general index of *Am. Jur. 2d* or *C.J.S.* is useful to refer to. Legal dictionaries not only provide precise definitions but also contain illustrations and case authority. Similar definitions of words and phrases (such as *expressio unius est exclusio alterius*) are also defined in the text of the encyclopedias. The general index can be used to find the location of these definitions.

In many states the continuing legal education division of the bar association publishes excellent loose-leaf material on certain areas of the law. If these materials are available, they should be reviewed in addition to the other source materials.

CITATIONS FOR SECONDARY SOURCES

The proper formats for the citation of cases and statutory materials were discussed in chapters 5 and 6. The paralegal should also become familiar with citations for the secondary sources discussed in this chapter.

Encyclopedias are usually cited by both the volume number and topic. For example, the section on habitability, which is presented in Figure 7.1 would be cited as:

49 *Am. Jur. 2d*, Landlord and Tenant, 769 (1970)

The material covered in Figures 7.6 and 7.12 would be cited as:

51C *C.J.S.*, Landlord and Tenant, 305 (1968)

24 *I.L.P.*, Landlord and Tenant, 237 (1956)

The year is included in parentheses to avoid confusion that might result after replacement volumes have been issued.

Treatises are cited by author, title, page, and year of publication while restatements are simply cited by the section and the year. Examples of these would be:

Nowak, Rotunda, and Young, *Constitutional Law*, 419 (1978)

Restatement, Contracts, 287 (1932)

Periodical citations include the author's last name, title of the article, volume number, abbreviation for the periodical, page number on which the article begins, and the date. If a specific page within the article is cited, the reference follows the page on which the article begins.

Brickman, *Expansion of Lawyering Process Through a New Delivery System*, 71 COLUMBIA L. REV. 1, 21 (1971)

References to annotations in *American Law Reports* are cited in a format that parallels a case citation. For example, one would find Figure 7.16 cited either as:

Lemle v. Breeden, 40 ALR 3d 637 (1969)

or simply:

Annotation, 40 ALR 3d 646, 653

Since the digests and *Shepard's Citations* are only indexing aids and do not make any statements about the law itself, these resource books would not be cited in legal writing.

REPORTING THE RESEARCH

Once all of the relevant materials discussed above have been reviewed, they must be synthesized into a concise analysis that will explore and evaluate the options available to the client. In evaluating the various statutes, regulations, and cases, the paralegal must apply the principles discussed in chapters 5 and 6. The *ratio decidendi* must be separated from the *obiter dicta* and the hierarchy of law utilized. Mandatory authority must be separated from persuasive authority.

Purpose of the Legal Memorandum

The legal memorandum is designed to carefully analyze a specific legal problem. It identifies and summarizes the relevant cases, statutes, and other sources of law; evaluates the probable application of these legal principles to the specific set of facts; and weighs the strengths and weaknesses of alternative courses of action.

The memorandum should be objective about the strengths and weaknesses of a client's position because it provides the raw materials upon which an appellate brief or an argument in support of a motion can later be built.

Format for a Legal Memorandum

A legal memorandum is written on a particular problem, for a particular person or group of persons. Usually the paralegal prepares it for a specific attorney, so it is important to obtain clear instructions on the nature of the legal problem and also the format desired by the attorney. There is no single correct or incorrect format to use, and lawyers and law firms have their own specifications.

Most memorandums tend to include the same general sections, so a paralegal should be familiar with the elements included in Figure 7.29. If one does not obtain specific instructions, follow these directions.

In restating the facts the paralegal should remember the discussion in chapter 5 on analysis of facts in court cases, because he needs to include only the legally relevant facts. When analyzing a case, the paralegal simply reports the facts as the court pronounced them. In writing a legal memorandum the facts may be disputed and there may not have been any court decision that has formally accepted one version of the facts over another. In cases such as these the writer must report both parties' versions

FIGURE 7.29
Format for a Legal Memorandum

Section 1 — Facts
State the relevant facts in the legal problem being researched.

Section 2 — Issues
Identify the legal issues in the problem.

Section 3 — Analysis
On an issue by issue basis:
A. Identify and explain the probable effect of any constitutional provisions, statutes, or administrative regulations applicable to this situation. Include proper citations.
B. Identify and discuss relevant cases. Include the proper citations.
   1. State the holding of the case.
   2. Discuss the similarities and the differences between the facts of the case being cited and the facts involved in the problem being researched.
   3. Discuss the impact of this case if applied to your client's situation.

Section 4 — Summary
Summarize the strengths and weaknesses of your client's case as objectively as possible. Specify which courses of action appear most promising.

Section 5 — Additional Research
Discuss the nature of any needed additional research. What facts need to be clarified? What additional legal materials should be examined?

---

of the facts or at least emphasize those aspects that are in dispute. If a court of law has already ruled on some aspect of the case, its findings and actions should also be reported as part of the fact section of the memorandum.

The identification of the legal issues can also be related back to the discussion of issues in chapter 5. This is a key stage in the research process because the rest of the memorandum is organized around these issues.

The third part identifies and analyzes the statutes, regulations, and cases that apply to each issue. This section is the main one in the memorandum and will be three-quarters or more of the length of the document. The analysis proceeds on an issue by issue basis, and careful attention is given to the applicability of the factual situations found in the cases that are cited.

The fourth section provides an evaluative summary of the materials covered in the third part. While the paralegal should strive for clarity and economy throughout the memorandum, this section should be particularly brief and concise.

The last section highlights needed additional work. It may involve using more legal research materials, or it may simply point out the need for further information about the facts.

Application of the Format

This final section applies some of the research materials used as figures in earlier sections of this chapter to the legal memorandum format discussed above and thus provides selected examples of the way in which these and other materials would be treated in a legal memorandum.

Section 1 — Facts

Our client rents an apartment in Peoria, Illinois on a month-to-month basis without a lease. She has received a written notice that she owes $250.00 in back rent and that if this back rent is not paid within five days, she will be evicted. The notice was left with her nine-year-old son while she was out. The apartment has had a problem with cockroaches and is never heated above 60° in the winter. The client has been unable to find alternative housing at a price she can afford.

The section above is a simple statement of the facts as they have been reported to the paralegal. While the facts may be incomplete, they do provide a basis for research on the general problem. Research will undoubtedly reveal areas in which additional facts will be needed before the client's position can be completely evaluated.

Section 2 — Issues

1. Does the poor condition of the apartment relieve the client of her obligation to pay the rent?

2. Can the client utilize the implied warranty of habitability as a defense against the threatened eviction?

3. Did delivery of the notice to her nine-year-old son constitute adequate notice of her delinquency?

4. What additional procedures must the landlord undertake in order to retake possession of the apartment?

As stated previously there is no magic formula for determining the issues in a case. It takes experience and some knowledge of the law. The paralegal should consult with the attorney about the issues before beginning the research process.

Section 3 — Analysis

ISSUE 1 — Does the poor condition of the apartment relieve the client of her obligation to pay the rent?

A. There are no applicable provisions of federal or state constitutions, statutes, or regulations.

Chapter 10, section 8 of the local ordinances provide as part of the building code that either all dwelling units must be equipped with a heating system that is capable of maintaining a minimum temperature of 68° Fahrenheit in the unit or the landlord must provide through a central heating system enough heat to maintain a minimum temperature of 68° Fahrenheit in each unit.

The client's landlord seems to be in violation of this provision. The ordinances do not say anything about cockroaches.

B. *Jack Spring, Inc. v. Little,* 50 Ill.2d 351, 280 N.E.2d 208 (1972) held that there was an implied warranty of habitability which must be filled by substantially complying with the provisions of the building code. If this warranty is not fulfilled, the tenant is relieved of the obligation to pay rent.

This case is similar to our client's case in that it involves a tenant who had not paid all of her rent, there was no written lease involved, the rental unit was an apartment in a larger complex, the apartment was not in compliance with the local building code, and she had sought but been unable to obtain suitable alternative housing. On the other hand, in this case, the city had already filed a formal complaint against the landlord and the landlord had repeatedly ignored the tenant's requests that repairs be made. While the record does not reveal the exact nature of the violations, we are led to believe that they were numerous and repeated.

If this case were to be applied to our client (that is if it is not distinguished on the basis of the differences discussed above) it would establish that the landlord had violated an implied warranty of habitability and that our client would therefore be relieved of her obligation to pay rent.

The researcher often finds citations to relevant cases while doing the general background reading in encyclopedias, annotations, and other general reference works. In this case the researcher could have come across the citation for *Jack Spring* in the pocket supplement for *C.J.S.* (Figure 7.7) or the pocket supplement for *Illinois Law and Practice* (Figure 7.13). If the researcher had not taken note of the citation in the general readings, the citation would have been found in the *Eighth Decennial Digest* (Figure 7.25).

After reading the case, the researcher summarizes the holding relevant to the issue (not the holdings that relate to such subjects as the bond requirement under the Forcible Entry and Detainer Act). Note that in comparing the facts of the cited case with the facts of the situation being researched, one often finds that more knowledge is needed about the client's situation. These gaps in the facts should be mentioned prominently in section 5 of the memorandum.

While there are other cases that are related to Issue 1 and these would be discussed in the same manner that the *Jack Spring* case was, this sample legal memorandum will now skip ahead to show part of the treatment given to Issue 2.

ISSUE 2 — Can the client utilize the implied warranty of habitability as a defense against the threatened eviction?

A. There are no applicable provisions of the federal Constitution or statutes.

Chapter 80, section 8, of the *Illinois Revised Statutes* authorizes a landlord to take action for possession of the owned apartment under the procedures of the Forcible Entry and Detainer Act if a tenant fails to pay back rent after being notified in writing that the lease will be terminated if the rent is not received in 5 days.

Chapter 80, section 6 authorizes a landlord to terminate a month-to-month tenancy with 30 days written notice and then maintain an action for forcible detainer and ejectment after that 30 days.

These two provisions establish the basis for a landlord taking possession after having given the appropriate written notice. The notice received by the client would appear to meet the requirements of section 8.

B. *Jack Spring, Inc. v. Little,* 50 Ill.2d 351, 280 N.E.2d 208 (1972) held that tenant could assert affirmative defense based on implied warranty of habitability in action by landlord for possession of rented premises because of nonpayment of rent.

In this case, the landlord's complaint alleged that rent for the premises for a period of two months was due and owing, and that plaintiff claimed possession of the property and for damages equal to the amount of rent owed. While the client's landlord has not yet filed a complaint, it is likely that this too would be for possession based on nonpayment of rent.

If this case is followed, it will allow the client to use the violation of the building code as a defense against the landlord's probable forcible entry and detainer action.

Fredman v. Clore, 13 Ill.App.3d 903, 301 N.E.2d 7 (1973) held that tenants could not raise a defense based on implied warranty of habitability where landlord brought action for possession only after having given notice under chapter 80, section 6.

In this case, the landlord simply gave the tenant one month's notice that the month-to-month tenancy was to end and that he intended to take possession when it ended. Our client's landlord's notice indicates that he is acting under section 8 rather than section 6.

If the landlord sues for possession based on overdue rent, then this case would not apply. If he were to switch tactics and give the notice called for in section 6, this case would definitely work against our client's position.

Clore v. Fredman, 59 Ill.2d 20, 319 N.E.2d 18 (1974) held that tenants could raise a defense of retaliatory eviction under a forcible entry and detainer action based on notice given under chapter 80, section 6.

When the Illinois Supreme Court reviewed the appellate court decision discussed above, it did allow the tenants to introduce a defense based on retaliatory eviction. The tenants in this case had reported building code violations to the city inspections department and had begun making their rent payments to an escrow account rather than to the landlord. As far as we know, our client has not made any complaint to a public official about the potential violation existing in her apartment.

While this case allows the tenant to raise a retaliatory eviction defense that ultimately comes back to the implied warranty of habitability, it is doubtful that our client could use such a defense if she had not in fact made a formal complaint with the city.

The *Jack Spring* case is discussed again because it is also related to the resolution of Issue 2. Note that the holding and relevant facts differ from the holding and facts discussed in relationship to the first issue. *Fredman v. Clore* shows how courts can use what may seem to be a very insignificant difference in the facts as basis for reaching an opposite conclusion. It also shows how the basis for a holding can shift from one level of appellate court to another.

Section 4 — Summary

Our client appears to be in a pretty good position. Since the lack of heat is in violation of the building code, she can assert an implied warranty of habitability. This implied warranty can be used to defeat a forcible entry and detainer action by the landlord for possession based on overdue rent.

On the other hand, if the landlord were to simply give our client a month's notice that her tenancy was being terminated, he would be able to retake possession under a forcible entry and detainer action without her being able to assert the implied warranty defense. On the other hand, if our client reports the violation to city officials, she may then be able to assert a defense based on retaliatory action.

Since the notice was delivered to someone under the age of 10, it is not considered a valid notice. Thus our client could also defend against an eviction action on the basis that the notice was defective.

If the landlord is to retake possession of the apartment, he will have to serve proper notice by delivering a written or printed copy to the client personally, sending it by certified mail with return receipt requested, or leaving it with someone else residing in the client's apartment who is over the age of 10. Then he will have to take the client to court under the Forcible Entry and Detainer Act.

Section 5 — Additional Research

There are several factual questions that need to be answered before our client's case can be completely evaluated. The most important questions are:

1. Has there been any inspection of the apartment's heating system by the city inspections department?

2. What kind of evidence is there as to the actual temperature in the apartment?

3. Do other apartments in the same building have the same problem?

4. Is the landlord aware of the problem and has he made any attempt to resolve it?

5. Just how extensive have been our client's efforts to locate alternative housing?

Additional research should also be done with respect to the infestation by cockroaches. If it could be established that they permeated the entire building, only the landlord would be in a position to correct it. There are some cases which hold that such infestation is grounds for constructive eviction. This aspect thus deserves further research.

SUMMARY

Legal research is one of the most important tasks a paralegal can perform because the findings will form the basis for advising the client and preparing the case. It involves skills developed through experience, imagination, ingenuity, patience, and perseverance.

This chapter has sought to identify and describe the resource materials ordinarily available in a good law library and their use in various legal research strategies.

While there is no single correct way to approach a legal research problem, all the alternatives must begin with a careful examination of the nature of the legal issues involved. If the paralegal's substantive background is not developed well enough to recognize the key words and basic principles involved, general background reading in a legal encyclopedia should be undertaken. The subject analysis section provides a quick overview of the subtopics to help locate relevant sections. The encyclopedia will not only provide knowledge on key terms that should be indexed in other sources, but also cross-references to specific cases, law review articles, and annotations. The treatises, restatements, legal periodicals, and annotations also offer the general background usually needed before focusing on a specific problem.

The search for relevant legislation usually begins with the subject index of the codes. Popular-name tables can also be very helpful. Once a specific statute has been located, the researcher must check to be sure that it has not been repealed or amended. This check is usually made through the use of pocket supplements in the code volumes and *Shepard's Citations*.

Valuable information about an act's legislative history can be located in the annotated codes. The *United States Code Congressional and Administrative News* is an even better source for such information because it allows the researcher to easily locate appropriate floor debates and committee testimony.

After the relevant statutes have been analyzed, the researcher should check on any administrative regulations or decisions interpreting those statutes. At the federal level, consult the *Code of Federal Regulations* and the *Federal Register*. There is a wide variation in reporting this information at the state level.

Relevant case citations can be located in several ways. Usually the background reading in encyclopedias, law reviews, and so forth will yield references to promising cases. By reading and then Shepardizing those cases the paralegal will find additional cases. However, the researcher cannot rely exclusively on this cross-reference technique. The digests should be used to systematically identify relevant cases. Either the descriptive word index or the subject analysis sections of a digest will indicate the appropriate key numbers for the principles of law involved. These key numbers lead to the sections of the digest with short summaries of what each case decided with respect to that particular principle of law.

After locating and analyzing the relevant statutes, administrative regulations, and cases, the researcher may wish to return again to (or perhaps read for the first time) the general reference works (encyclopedias, annotations, law review articles, and so forth) to better understand the impact of those statutes and cases.

There is no single correct way of approaching a legal research problem. Indeed, the availability of alternatives is one of the major features of legal research. The same topic can usually be approached under several different index headings. If the explanation offered in *C.J.S.* seems confusing, turn to *Am. Jur. 2d* for a slightly different approach to the same topic. If digests are not available, use citators. Each researcher should develop a personal style.

The end result must show thorough research and accuracy. It must also be communicated in a clear concise manner to the lawyer working on the case. While this communication may occasionally take place in a short personal conversation, it is usually best done in a written memorandum. While the format may vary from one law office to another, the basic elements usually include: identification and summary of the relevant cases, statutes, and other sources of law; analysis of the probable application of these legal principles to specific facts of the case at hand; and evaluation of the strengths and weaknesses of several alternative courses of action.

While legal research is a very time-consuming task, it is also very challenging and rewarding.

KEY TERMS

American Jurisprudence 2d	legal encyclopedia
American Law Reports	legal memorandum
Corpus Juris Secundum	pocket part
digests	Popular-name Table
index method	restatements
Index to Legal Periodicals	subject analysis method
key number	treatise
law review	

REVIEW QUESTIONS

1. What methods are used to keep legal reference books up to date?
2. What are the differences between *Am. Jur. 2d* and *C.J.S.*?
3. What is the difference between an encyclopedia, a treatise, and an annotation?
4. What is the coverage of each of the following digests: *Century Digest, Decennial Digest, General Digest,* and a state digest?
5. What should be contained in a good legal memorandum?

DISCUSSION QUESTIONS

1. What are the advantages and disadvantages of the West key number system?
2. Why is it better to utilize a variety of approaches to legal research rather than relying on a single method?
3. To what extent should a paralegal include one's own conclusions about the meaning of the law as part of a memorandum reporting on the research that was done?

PROJECTS

1. Does a husband have the right to administer corporal punishment to his wife when she does not obey his reasonable requests? Find the answer in both *Am. Jur. 2d* and *C.J.S.* What is the answer? Now compare the features of each and indicate which encyclopedia you prefer. Why?

2. Use the *U.S. Code Congressional and Administrative News* to find answers to the following questions about the legislative history of Public Law Number 95-222.

   a. What was the difference between the House and Senate bills with respect to their handling of abortions?

   b. How was this difference resolved in the final statute?

   c. What is the relationship of this act to the Hatch Act?

   Now use the legislative history table to find:

   a. What was the number assigned to this act when it was introduced as a bill in the House?

   b. When was it considered on the floor of the Senate?

   c. What is its citation in the *Statutes-at-Large*?

3. Locate references to 557 of the Administrative Procedure Act in *Shepard's United States Citations*. (Use the 1972 *Supplement to Statutes* edition.) Then give the citation for a United States Supreme Court case interpreting subsection a.

4. Use the descriptive word index of the *General Digest* to find the key number dealing with a landlord's obligation to remove snow and ice from the sidewalk leading up to his apartment building. What is the appropriate key number? Under what index heading did you find this number?

5. Use the *Index to Legal Periodicals* to find a citation for a 1977 law review article on paying expert witnesses on a contingent fee basis. What was the citation?

6. Assume that the hypothetical landlord-tenant problem discussed in this chapter had occurred in your city. Research the law of your state and write a memorandum on your research.

REFERENCE

1. *West's Law Finder* (St. Paul: West Publishing Company, 1978), p. 34.

PART IV

PREPARING THE CASE

The preceding two sections have presented various research approaches on the legal and factual aspects of a client's situation. In this section we will examine the role of the paralegal in preparing a case for litigation.

There are, of course, many activities in law offices that are not directed toward litigation: Wills are prepared, contracts written, and businesses incorporated. As mentioned in chapter 2, paralegals have important functions in many of these activities and there are specialized texts available on these areas.

The rules of civil and criminal procedure are very complex and differ from one state to the next. These chapters therefore are not designed to train the reader to be a litigation specialist, but to provide a general understanding of the paralegal's role in litigation and to present the different types of documents used.

Chapter 8 is an overview of the paralegal's role in a trial case. It covers preparation of the legal documents involved, witnesses, and exhibits. The paralegal may work closely with the attorney to gather and organize notes and other materials that the attorney will use during the trial itself.

Since paralegals are allowed to represent clients in some administrative hearings, chapter 9 discusses the basic principles of administrative law and the administrative hearing process. This information, combined with that in the preceding chapters, provides a basic understanding of the approaches and skills required.

Chapter 10 reviews the appellate process and emphasizes those tasks most relevant to the paralegal's needs. In addition to filing notices of appeal and ordering copies of the transcript and record, the paralegal can help digest the court record and prepare appellate briefs.

CHAPTER 8

Commencing Litigation

Litigation is a dispute that has been turned into a formal lawsuit. The stages in both civil and criminal litigation were presented in chapter 1 and the reader should carefully review these materials before proceeding with this chapter.

Litigation is a very complex process involving pleadings and motions. Prior to the trial interrogatories are prepared and digested, exhibits assembled, and trial materials organized. It is a process that offers many opportunities for paralegals, so this chapter discusses some of the tasks paralegals may perform. The division of responsibility among attorney, paralegal, and secretary will of course vary.

Since the paralegal is more likely to be involved in civil than in criminal litigation, this chapter is organized around the preparation of a civil case. The illustrations have been drawn from *Renslow v. Mennonite Hospital*, a malpractice case involving the transfusion of Rh positive blood to a patient who was Rh negative.* Even though the focus here is on civil actions, appropriate references to the criminal process have been included.

There will, of course, be some variation in procedures from one state to another, so one must always consult the statutes and court rules for the particular tribunal. Local federal district court rules are available in pamphlets from the district court office. Federal court rules are also found in the annotated codes and Supreme Court digests as well as some specialized loose-leaf services. Complete texts of the court decisions which construe the federal rules of civil and criminal procedure are in *Federal Rules Service* and *Federal Rules Decisions.†*

At the state level jurisdictional requirements of the courts are also made clear in constitutions and in state statutes. Paralegals should become thoroughly familiar with the civil practice act of the state in which they are employed. The rules established by the courts themselves are usually available in pamphlets from the courts involved. In addition, rules of the state's appellate courts are usually published in either the annotated statutes, the case reporters, or specialized publications on court rules.

FILING THE SUIT

The attorney decides if and when litigation is to begin. The decision to litigate involves not only a determination of who will be sued and the legal grounds for that suit but also in which court the suit will be brought. The paralegal can make an important contribution to this decision by researching some of the available options, tracing corporate ownerships, or finding the location of parties to the suit.

---

*The Illinois Supreme Court decision in this case was assigned as part of one of the projects listed at the end of chapter 5.

†The jurisdiction of the federal courts is dealt with in 18 U.S.C. §1332 and 28 U.S.C. §§1331-1346. *Federal Rules Service* is published by Callaghan and Company. It contains a single loose-leaf volume of the rules currently in force as well as other volumes reporting the court decisions which interpret these rules. West Publishing Company produces *Federal Rules Decisions* as a unit of its National Reporter System. It reports district court decisions involving the rules of procedure which are not published in the *Federal Supplement*. West also publishes a multivolume treatise by Wright and Miller entitled *Federal Practice and Procedure*.

Parties to the Suit

The first step in filing a lawsuit is deciding who is going to be sued. The party who has allegedly been wronged sues the party who is allegedly responsible for that wrong. However, the party one might assume to be the logical defendant may not be worth suing (i.e., the party may not have money to pay the damages a court might award).* Often there is more than one possible defendant and the plaintiff will want to make sure the one with the "deepest pocket" is included. In other words, the plaintiff goes after the defendant with the most assets. Therefore, a defendant's employer is often brought into the suit on the basis of agency law and the doctrine of *respondeat superior.*† In an automobile accident case the plaintiff may sue the manufacturer of the auto or the governmental unit responsible for maintaining the roadway.

One must also be certain that the named parties of a lawsuit are legally capable of suing and being sued. While corporations can generally sue and be sued, there may be some limitations on their access to the courts in states in which they are not incorporated. In some states, partnerships and unincorporated associations lack the capacity to sue or be sued. In those cases the suit must be brought by or against all of its individual members. In many states a minor must sue or be sued through a named guardian or "next friend."‡ Additional complications can arise when executors, trustees, bailees, or assignees are involved.§ Here the

*This is referred to as being judgment proof.

†Agency law covers situations in which one person acts as the representative of another. The doctrine of *respondeat superior* holds that an employer is responsible for the actions of employees when the act is done during their employment.

‡A guardian is a person who has the legal right and duty to take care of another's property where that person is a child or is otherwise incompetent of taking care of it. A next friend may not be the legal guardian but is a responsible party the court recognizes as being a legitimate representative of the party's interests. See James, Civil Procedure §9.9 (1965) for a more complete discussion of the competency to sue.

§An executor is a person appointed to handle the property of a deceased person. A trustee holds money or property for the benefit of someone else through a trust arrangement. A bailee is one who has responsibility for the property someone else has loaned to them (such as when a person leaves his car with a mechanic). An assignee is one to whom certain property or other rights have been transferred by the legal owner (such as when a business assigns a promissory note to a bank or a collection agency).

question is simply whether they can sue in their own name or whether they must act through the legal owner.

When compulsory joinder rules apply, the plaintiff cannot sue one potential defendant without including the others as well. Where such rules do not apply, the plaintiff may be selective in deciding who will be included in the suit and who will not.* The plaintiff may also wish to consider the possibility of a class action suit. Here the named plaintiff brings the suit on behalf of a large class of additional plaintiffs who are in a similar situation with respect to having been wronged by the defendant.

In the *Renslow v. Mennonite Hospital* case, the selection of the parties was fairly straightforward. The young woman who had received the wrong blood sued individually on her own behalf and as the "mother and next friend" of her daughter. The daughter was included as a plaintiff because she had been born prematurely in a jaundiced condition and suffered from hyperbiluminemia because her mother's blood had been sensitized by the faulty transfusion. It was further alleged that the daughter suffered permanent damage to various organs, brain, and nervous system. The hospital at which the transfusion took place and the doctor who headed the hospital laboratory were named as parties in the suit.

Selection of the Court

Once the parties of the suit have been decided, the plaintiff's attorney must decide where the case should be filed. As discussed in chapter 1, specific courts have limited authority to hear only particular types of cases. The plaintiff must therefore take the litigation to a court with the proper jurisdiction.

Sometimes both the federal and state courts may have concurrent jurisdiction. In such cases the plaintiff can search for the best available forum. In deciding which court to choose, an attorney will usually consider such matters as filing requirements, deadline dates, the current backlog of cases, discovery procedures, the rules of evidence, and the personalities of the judges.

---

*A defendant may later file a cross-claim to bring in the defendant the plaintiff left out.

The convenience of the physical location of the court may also be a factor.

In the *Renslow* case both the plaintiffs and the defendants were residents of Illinois and the allegedly negligent acts took place in Illinois. Thus, in this situation, the plaintiff's attorney had little choice but to file in the circuit courts of Illinois.

Notice

Before a court will hear a lawsuit it must be convinced that the defendant(s) have received proper notice that the suit has been filed against them. Proper notice usually requires that the local sheriff (or a United States marshal in federal cases) personally deliver a summons to the defendant(s). There are occasions where proper notice can be satisfied by mailing the summons to the defendant's last known address, publishing copies of the summons in newspapers of general circulation, or delivering it to an authorized agent. Once again the paralegal must consult the state's civil practice act on the type of service required in the case. Local court rules indicate proper format.

Proper notice should include the name(s) of the party or parties to the suit, the court in which suit has been filed, statement of the plaintiff's claim, and the number of days within which the defendant must respond. In most jurisdictions a copy of the complaint is delivered along with the summons as a means of notifying the defendant of the nature of the claim. The summons then provides the party with information relating to the required response. Figure 8.1 shows the style of a typical summons. The caption for our model malpractice case would be:

> EMMA M. RENSLOW, Individually and as mother and next friend of LEAH ANN RENSLOW, a minor
> Plaintiffs,
>
> – vs –
>
> MENNONITE HOSPITAL, a corporation, and HANS STROINK, M.D.,
> Defendants.

FIGURE 8.1
Sample Summons

[Page one of the sample summons is presented below.]

In the Circuit Court   No. _____
of the 11th Judicial Circuit
McLean County, Illinois

[Official caption of case goes here]

SUMMONS

To each defendant:

You are summoned and required to file an answer in this case, or other-wise file your appearance, in the office of the clerk of this court within 30 days after service of this summons, not counting the day of service. IF YOU FAIL TO DO SO, A JUDGMENT OR DECREE BY DEFAULT MAY BE TAKEN AGAINST YOU FOR THE RELIEF ASKED IN THE COMPLAINT.

To the officer:

This summons must be returned by the officer or other person to whom it was given for service, with indorsement of service and fees, if any, im-mediately after service. If service cannot be made, this summons shall be re-turned so indorsed.

This summons may not be served later than 30 days after its date.

Plaintiff's Attorney_____   Witness_____ , 19__

Address_____

City_____   _____

Telephone _____   Clerk of Court
                                                   (Seal of Court)

                                             Date of Service_____ , 19__
                                             (To be inserted by officer on copy left
To: _____   with defendant or other person.)

[Page two of the sample summons, to be filled in by the Sheriff and court, is presented below.]

SHERIFF'S FEES

Service and return . . . . $_____

Miles . . . . _____

    Total . . . . $_____

Sheriff of _____ County

I certify that I served this summons on defendant as follows:

(a) (Individual defendants — personal):
By leaving a copy and a copy of the complaint with each individual defendant personally, as follows:
    Name of Defendant   Date of Service

(b) (Individual defendants — abode):
By leaving a copy and a copy of the complaint at the usual place of abode of each individual defendant with a person of his family, of the age of 10 years or upwards, informing that person of the contents of the summons, and also by sending a copy of the summons and of the complaint in a sealed envelope with postage fully prepaid, addressed to each individual defendant at his usual place of abode, as follows:
    Name of Defendant   Person With Whom Left
    Date of Service   Date of Mailing

(c) (Corporation defendants):
By leaving a copy and a copy of the complaint with the registered agent, officer, or agent of each defendant corporation, as follows:
    Defendant Corporation
    Registered Agent, Officer or Agent
    Date of Service

(d) (Other service):

Sheriff of _____ County
By _____, Deputy

The Criminal Context

In the criminal context the prosecuting attorney must decide who to charge and which sections of the criminal code will be involved. It is highly unlikely that paralegals would be involved at this stage. In felonies proper notice is made through arrests, and in misdemeanors it may take the form of a summons or notice to appear. The defendant must be brought into court and personally informed of the charges.

THE PLEADINGS

Pleadings are formal written statements filed with the court at the beginning of a lawsuit. They may include the complaint, the answer, the cross-complaint, and the demurrer, and are designed to narrow and focus the issues involved.

The Complaint

The complaint states the allegations that form the basis of the plaintiff's case. Figure 8.2 presents the first three counts of the medical malpractice suit under discussion. It lists the facts which the plaintiff claims entitles her to more than $500,000 in damages.

Complaints must begin with a caption section that identifies the parties, the court, and the docket number. Emma and Leah Renslow are identified as the plaintiffs while Mennonite Hospital and Dr. Stroink are the defendants. The suit was filed in McLean County in the Circuit Court of the Eleventh Judicial District of Illinois. At the time it was filed, the clerk of the courts assigned the docket number of 75-L-8. The number in this case means that the suit was the eighth case to be filed in the law division during 1975.

The body of the complaint consists of the allegation of facts which constitute a cause of action.* In most states the facts being pleaded must be ultimate facts as opposed to conclusions of law or mere evidentiary matter. It is often quite difficult to make the distinction between these three concepts, and the paralegal drafting complaints will probably need to consult with the attorney at this point.

The federal rules allow for notice pleading. Here the complaint must simply identify the transaction from which the plaintiff's

---

*In order to present a cause of action, the facts must present a situation for which the law provides a remedy.

FIGURE 8.2
Sample Complaint

IN THE CIRCUIT COURT OF THE ELEVENTH JUDICIAL
CIRCUIT OF
ILLINOIS
McLEAN COUNTY

Caption

EMMA M. RENSLOW, Individually
and as mother and next friend of
LEAH ANN RENSLOW, a minor,
              Plaintiffs,

              vs   AT LAW NO. 75 L 8

MENNONITE HOSPITAL, a corporation, and HANS STROINK, M.D.,
              Defendants.

COMPLAINT

COUNT I

EMMA M. RENSLOW, by her attorneys, LAW OFFICES OF
STRODEL & KINGERY, ASSOC., for cause of action against
MENNONITE HOSPITAL, a corporation, states that:

1. On or about October 8, 1965 Defendant hospital owned,
operated, managed and maintained and controlled a certain
hospital, located in the city of Bloomington, County of Mc-
Lean, and State of Illinois, wherein it treated persons suffering from various ailments, and provided rooms, laboratories,
drugs, and various medical devices and services for patients
admitted to said hospital for medical care and treatment in
said hospital.

Allegations

2. On or about October 8, 1965 through and including October 14, 1965, DR. HANS STROINK, Defendant herein, was
an agent or employee of said hospital, and was in fact the Director of Laboratories for said hospital, and had under his
supervision and control various laboratory technicians who,
among other duties, were charged from time to time, and including the period mentioned herein, with the typing of blood
for use in transfusion of patients in said hospital.

3. On or about October 8, 1965 the Plaintiff, EMMA M.
RENSLOW, then known as EMMA MURPHY, a minor age 13,
and born April 16, 1952, was admitted as a patient in said
hospital by Dr. Seymour R. Goldberg, a duly licensed physician and surgeon in the State of Illinois, and member of the
medical staff of said Defendant hospital.

(Continued)

FIGURE 8.2 — Continued

Allegations

4. At all times mentioned herein the Plaintiff was in the exercise of all due care and caution for her own personal well being commensurate with her age and experience.

5. On October 8, 1965, pursuant to the order of Dr. Seymour Goldberg, said minor Plaintiff was infused with 500 c.c. of whole blood as part of the care and treatment for her condition of ill-being. Additionally, on or about October 9, 1965, by order of Dr. Seymour Goldberg, an additional 500 c.c. of whole blood was infused in said minor Plaintiff as part of the treatment for her condition of physical ill-being. On both said dates of blood infusion, the Plaintiff was and still is blood type A Rh negative, and the blood infused aforesaid was in fact type A Rh positive.

6. On October 8, 1965, and October 9, 1965, said Defendant hospital, acting through its agent or employee, DR. HANS STROINK, as Director of Laboratories, and acting through its agents, certain laboratory technicians, the exact names of whom are not presently known, selected the blood units to be transfused into the Plaintiff, exercised blood typing techniques, and went through procedures to compare the Plaintiff's blood type with the blood types about to be transfused into the Plaintiff, said acts all occurring in the course of care and treatment of the Plaintiff while a patient in Defendant hospital and in the course of the professional supervision and responsibility of the said DR. HANS STROINK and the laboratory technicians aforesaid, all of said persons being agents or employees of Defendant hospital.

7. As a direct and proximate result of the foregoing the mis-typed blood was in fact transfused into the Plaintiff, permanently injuring her by sensitizing her blood.

8. At the time of the transfusions aforesaid up through and including November 15, 1973, the Plaintiff had no adverse reactions known by her to said blood transfusions, had no knowledge whatsoever of the medical consequences of being transfused with the wrong blood and first became aware of her blood sensitization from said transfusions in December, 1973, as a result of routine antibody screening of her blood during the course of prenatal visitation with Dr. A. K. Patel, a duly licensed physician and surgeon in the State of Illinois specializing in obstetrics and gynecology, who attended the Plaintiff for and during a state of pregnancy at said time.

9. Subsequently, during the course of her pregnancy, the

Plaintiff developed increasing medical and blood chemistry signs of sensitization to such an extent that definite jeopardy to her unborn child was diagnosed by the said Dr. A. K. Patel, resulting in the Plaintiff being hospitalized at Brokaw Hospital, Normal, Illinois, on or about March 25, 1974, where labor was induced leading to the live birth of a premature infant female child, now known as LEAH ANN RENSLOW, a minor, who was in fact jaundiced and required an immediate and complete exchange transfusion of her blood at said Brokaw Hospital and subsequent transfer to St. Francis Hospital, Peoria, Illinois, to the premature facility located therein for additional care and treatment as a premature infant, and a second complete exchange transfusion of her blood.

10. The selection, transfusion, and management of the infusion of blood in the Plaintiff at MENNONITE HOSPITAL in October of 1965 as aforesaid was exclusively and solely within the control, direction, management, and maintenance of said Defendant hospital and its agents or employees, DR. HANS STROINK, and various laboratory technicians as aforesaid.

Allegations

11. During the selection and typing of the blood aforesaid and the transfusing of same the Plaintiff exercised no control, direction, or management whatsoever over the entire process aforedescribed.

12. During the transfusion of blood aforesaid in October, 1965, the entire process of selection of the blood, typing, comparing, and transfusing was exclusively managed and maintained and controlled by Defendant hospital and its agents or employees aforesaid at the time of the injury thereby committed on the Plaintiff.

13. The occurrence speaks for itself; that is, the occurrence would not have taken place in the ordinary course of things if Defendant hospital acting through its agents or employees aforesaid had not negligently failed to use proper care in the selection, typing, comparing, transfusing and other techniques of the blood infused into the Plaintiff aforesaid; and the control, management, and maintenance of said transfusion process and blood selection and typing process was at all times under the exclusive control, direction, and management of the Defendant hospital, DR. HANS STROINK, as Director of its Laboratories, and the various laboratory technicians involved in the procedure aforesaid.

14. As a direct and proximate result of the aforesaid neg-

(Continued)

FIGURE 8.2 — Continued

Allegations

ligence by Defendant hospital, acting by and through its agent or employee, Defendant DR. HANS STROINK, and the laboratory technicians aforesaid, the Plaintiff sustained severe and permanent personal injuries by virtue of her blood being sensitized, resulting in the premature birth of her child, LEAH ANN RENSLOW, and will in the future incur difficult and abnormal pregnancies and medical problems with the birth of any subsequent children, arising from any and all subsequent pregnancies.

AND FURTHER, the Plaintiff has expended or become obligated to expend large sums of money for hospital care and treatment, medical bills and drug bills, endeavoring to be cared for as a result of her pregnancy and the premature birth of her child aforesaid, and will in the future incur additional unusual and extra expenses for any medical care and attention and hospitalization from any future pregnancies or birth of any future child borne by the Plaintiff.

AND FURTHER, the Plaintiff has suffered great mental anguish following her diagnosis as a blood sensitized person; and throughout the pregnancy and delivery of her child aforesaid, she suffered great mental anguish for her own well being and for the well being of her child. Additionally, she will in the future suffer great fear for her physical well being and the physical well being of any child in gestation as a result of future pregnancies.

15. At all times mentioned herein, at and subsequent to November, 1973, the Plaintiff is and was the duly married spouse of Steven Renslow, and the child born aforesaid, LEAH ANN RENSLOW, is a product of the marriage of Steven Renslow to the Plaintiff.

Prayer

WHEREFORE, the Plaintiff, EMMA M. RENSLOW, prays judgment against MENNONITE HOSPITAL, a corporation, in the sum of FIVE HUNDRED THOUSAND DOLLARS ($500,000) plus costs of this suit.

Jury Demand

Plaintiff demands trial of this Count by Jury.

COUNT II

Allegations

EMMA M. RENSLOW, by her attorneys, LAW OFFICES OF STRODEL & KINGERY, ASSOC., for additional cause of action against Defendant hospital, states that:

1–12. The Plaintiff repeats and realleges the allegations

contained in paragraphs (1)–(12) of Count I as and for paragraphs (1)–(12) of this Count.

13. On October 8, 1965 and October 9, 1965, the Defendant, MENNONITE HOSPITAL, acting by and through its agents or employees, DR. HANS STROINK and various laboratory technicians as aforesaid, was then and there guilty of one or more or all of the following negligent and careless acts or omissions:

Allegations

(a) The Defendant hospital negligently and carelessly failed to properly select the proper blood to be transfused into the Plaintiff.

(b) The Defendant hospital negligently and carelessly mis-typed the blood selected by it to be infused into the Plaintiff.

(c) The Defendant hospital negligently and carelessly improperly compared the blood type of the blood to be transfused into the Plaintiff with the Plaintiff's blood type.

(d) The Defendant hospital negligently and carelessly caused the wrong blood to be infused into the Plaintiff.

14–15. Plaintiff repeats and realleges the allegations contained in paragraphs (14) and (15) of Count I as and for paragraphs (14) and (15) of this Count.

Prayer

WHEREFORE, the Plaintiff, EMMA M. RENSLOW, prays judgment against MENNONITE HOSPITAL, a corporation, in the sum of FIVE HUNDRED THOUSAND DOLLARS ($500,000) plus costs of this suit.

Jury Demand

Plaintiff demands trial of this Count by Jury.

COUNT III

Allegations

EMMA M. RENSLOW, by her attorneys, LAW OFFICES OF STRODEL & KINGERY, ASSOC., for additional cause of action against MENNONITE HOSPITAL, a corporation, and HANS STROINK, M.D., states that:

1–15. Plaintiff repeats and realleges the allegations of paragraphs (1) through (15) of Count II as and for paragraphs (1) through (15) of this Count.

16. Subsequent to the transfusing of the wrong type blood into the Plaintiff as aforesaid, Defendant hospital, by and through its Director of Laboratories, HANS STROINK, M.D., discovered that the wrong type blood had in fact been administered to the Plaintiff, but, notwithstanding such dis-

(Continued)

FIGURE 8.2 — Continued

Allegations	covery, at no time subsequent to said transfusion did said hospital or said HANS STROINK, M.D., in any way or manner advise the minor Plaintiff or her family that she in fact had been infused with the wrong typed blood or the future consequences of such infusion of the wrong typed blood into the Plaintiff as she matured, married, and became subject to pregnancy. 17. The aforesaid failure of said hospital and its said Director of Laboratories, HANS STROINK, M.D., in deliberately failing to advise the Plaintiff or her family of the infusion of the wrong typed blood aforesaid, was in fact a wilful and wanton and reckless act of misconduct on the part of said hospital and said HANS STROINK, M.D.
Prayer	WHEREFORE, Plaintiff prays judgment against MENNO-NITE HOSPITAL, a corporation, and HANS STROINK, M.D., jointly and severally, in the sum of FIVE HUNDRED THOUSAND DOLLARS ($500,000) as compensatory damages and the sum of FIVE HUNDRED THOUSAND DOLLARS ($500,000) in punitive damages, plus costs of this suit.
Jury Demand	Plaintiff demands trial of this Count by Jury.

claim arises. The distinction between ultimate facts, conclusions of law, and evidentiary material loses its importance and the discovery process is used to provide more complete information about the facts.

The Renslow complaint was divided into several different counts, each count presenting a separate legal claim and able to stand by itself. For purposes of illustration, only the first three counts of the complaint have been reproduced. The first six paragraphs in Count I identify the individuals and the basic events leading to the transfusion of the blood. Paragraph seven asserts that these actions were the direct and proximate cause of the plaintiff's injuries. Numbers eight and nine describe the nature of plaintiff's injuries and the manner in which they were discovered. Then paragraphs ten through thirteen attempt to fix the blame firmly on the defendants' negligence.

Paragraph fourteen sets the stage for the requested relief. It does so by elaborating on the consequences of her injuries (physical, financial, and mental). Fifteen relates to a side issue. It happened that Leah Renslow had been conceived before her mother had married her father. This final paragraph establishes that Emma was married to Leah's father prior to her birth.

The allegations section is followed by the prayer for relief. Here the plaintiff indicates what action it wants the court to take. While the relief is usually in monetary damages, it can be a restraining order or some other equitable action. In Count I the plaintiff requests $500,000 plus costs of the suit. Note that the complaint also makes a demand for a jury trial.

This same pattern is then repeated with regard to the remaining counts. Count II essentially repeats Count I except that paragraph thirteen alleges four specific instances in which the defendant acted negligently and carelessly. Count III, on the other hand, introduces the additional charges that the defendants committed a wilful and wanton and reckless act of misconduct by not informing Emma Renslow of her condition after they had discovered their error. On this count the plaintiff requests $500,000 as compensatory damages and another $400,000 as punitive damages.*

While that section is not reproduced here the complaint ends with a signature section which in some cases must be verified (i.e., accompanied by an affidavit that the plaintiff has read the complaint and that its contents are correct).

In drafting a complaint the paralegal should draw upon the format and some of the language used either in form books or in model complaints kept in the pleadings file of their office. Various publishers have produced books with sample forms geared to the rules of civil procedure in that state and there are several major sets of form books published that may be used as guidelines for federal procedure.† In addition to showing the proper format, they

---

*Compensatory damages compensate the victim for actual losses. Punitive damages punish or make an example of the person who was responsible. Sometimes called exemplary damages, punitive damages are reserved for cases in which the defendant acted in a malicious or wilful manner.

†*Am. Jur. Legal Forms 2d* (Lawyers' Cooperative), *Bender's Federal Practice Forms* (Mathew Bender), *Nichols Cyclopedia of Federal Procedure Forms* (Callaghan), and *West's Federal Forms* (West) are the most commonly used federal form books.

contain sample clauses for use in accomplishing such items as filing against a party who is as yet unknown or including the possibility that the defendant was an agent for some larger entity. These clauses have been tested in other cases and found to be valid. Figure 8.3 shows sample pages from a standard form book.

It should also be noted that a single complaint can allege more than one cause of action. Each cause of action, however, must be alleged in a separate section or count. Furthermore, separate counts can allege contradictory facts. (This is known as pleading in the alternative.) Thus, if the plaintiff were not sure which of two passengers had been driving an automobile involved in an accident, the first count of the complaint might allege that one person was driving while the second count might allege that it was the other person who had been driving.

The Defendant's Response

There are five basic options available to a defendant in a civil lawsuit: (1) deny the facts which the plaintiff says took place; (2) admit the facts but assert that those facts do not provide the plaintiff with a legal remedy; (3) assert that there are procedural defects in the complaint; (4) assert a claim of his or her own against either the plaintiff or another defendant; or (5) simply not respond at all. With the exception of not responding at all, these options are generally not considered mutually exclusive. Specific techniques to assert these options differ from one state to the next.

Failure to take any action, however, is viewed as an admission of the allegations contained in the complaint and creates a situation in which the plaintiff can seek a default judgment. While a judgment for the plaintiff is not automatic in such cases (plaintiff must still convince a judge that the claim is legitimate), the defendant has no right either to challenge the evidence presented or to present contrary evidence.*

The first line of defense usually involves a technical challenge

---

*In a default judgment the judge awards the judgment against a party who failed to appear in court to contest the matter. While it is possible to have a default judgment set aside, it is a very difficult task — especially if more than 30 days have elapsed.

to the wording of the complaint. In some jurisdictions this takes the form of a demurrer. The modern trend, however, involves instituting a technical challenge through a motion to dismiss. A general demurrer asserts that even if the alleged facts were true, no cause of action would exist. It is considered a special demurrer when the defendant challenges the complaint on the basis of such circumstances as a failure to join an indispensable third party, lack of jurisdiction, the plaintiff's legal capacity to sue, or existence of another suit involving the same matter. Note in Figure 8.4 the multitude of procedural attacks being made on the complaint shown in Figure 8.2.

If a general demurrer is rejected, in many jurisdictions the defendant must take a default judgment before the decision can be appealed. It is considered a waiving of the demurrer if the defendant goes ahead and answers the complaint after an unfavorable ruling by the trial judge. In the federal system, on the other hand, the defendant is not precluded from raising the issue again both at the trial and on appeal, even though an answer was filed. If the demurrer (or motion to dismiss) is accepted, the plaintiff is usually allowed to amend the complaint so that it will be acceptable to the court.

In the Renslow case the trial court judge accepted the assertion contained in paragraph three of the defendant's motion and dismissed that portion of the complaint which sought damages for the daughter. It did so on the basis of a conclusion that the law did not provide that a child who had not been conceived at the time could sue for negligent acts committed against the mother. The plaintiff then appealed the case on this narrow issue. Action on the mother's case was suspended until the appellate courts resolved the issue of the daughter's right to sue. Then after the Illinois Supreme Court declared that the daughter could sue, the action returned to the trial court and the suit advanced normally.

Where the complaint has been found to be technically sound, the defendant must choose to admit or deny the facts that have been alleged in the complaint. Note that in Figure 8.5 Mennonite Hospital's answer admits that Emma Renslow was admitted as the hospital's patient on October 8, 1965, but denies all the rest. When the facts are denied, the conflicting versions must eventually be settled by the trial process.

In some cases the defendant may admit the facts as they have been alleged but go on to assert additional facts which would lead concise statement of defendant's defense or defenses,[29] and (3) set up any counterclaim or counterclaims that he may have.[30] If new matter by way of defense is pleaded in the answer, the plaintiff should file a reply [31] admitting or denying each allegation of such new matter.[32]

II. FORMS

A. Complaints

§ 151.02. General form.[33]

[Caption as in § 2.02.]

Plaintiff ———, by his [or, her] attorney ———, complaining of defendant ——— [, a corporation], alleges as follows:

1. At the time of the occurrence [or, accident] hereinafter complained of [or, described], and prior thereto, defendant ——— was, and still is, a resident of [or, a corporation organized and existing under the laws of the state of Illinois and having its principal office and place of business in] ———, ——— county, Illinois; and said defendant then and there owned or possessed and controlled, and [, by his (or, its) agents and employees,] was operating ——— [state what defendant owned, etc.] [or, said defendant (, by his [or, its] agents and employees,) was then and there ——— (state what defendant was doing)].

2. [Allege duty of defendant as in § 151.04.]

3. [Allege exercise of due care by plaintiff as in § 151.05.]

4. On or about ———, 19—, at approximately ——— —.m., in [or, near] ———, ——— county, Illinois, disregarding his [or, its] aforementioned duty, defendant [, by his (or, its) said agents and employees,] negligently ——— [state what defendant did or omitted to do in violation of his or its duty, and, if breach of a statutory duty is alleged, cite the statute]; and, as a direct and

---

[29] Ill Rev Stats c 110, § 33, subd (1).

[30] Ill Rev Stats c 110, § 38.
Law governing answers and counterclaims in automobile accident cases, see §§ 56.03, 56.04.

[31] Ill Rev Stats c 110, § 32.

[32] Ill Rev Stats c 110, § 40, subd (1).

Law governing replies in automobile accident cases, see § 56.05.

[33] Composite complaint in automobile accident case, see § 56.07.
Allegations as to damages in personal injury actions, see §§ 30.64–30.172.
Allegations as to property damage, see §§ 30.173–30.191.

FIGURE 8.3
Sample Form Book Pages

proximate result thereof, ———— [describe occurrence or accident] ; whereby plaintiff then and there sustained injuries to his [or, her] person [and/or, plaintiff's aforementioned property was then and there damaged] as hereinafter alleged.

5. [Allege damages as in § 151.12.]

Wherefore, plaintiff demands judgment against defendant for the sum of ———— dollars ($————) and his [or, her] costs of suit.

————, Plaintiff's attorney

[Name, address and telephone of plaintiff's attorney.]

§ 151.03. Golfer struck by other player's ball.[34]

[Caption and commencement as in § 151.02.]

1. At the time of the occurrence hereinafter mentioned, and prior thereto, defendant ———— was engaged in playing golf upon a certain golf course commonly known as "————" and located adjacent to ———— street, near the intersection thereof with ———— avenue, in [or, near] the city [or, village] of ————, ———— county, Illinois.

2. As defendant then and there well knew, or in exercise of ordinary care would have known, various other players and persons were then lawfully present upon and about said course; wherefore it became, and was, the duty of defendant to exercise ordinary care, in conducting himself and playing upon said course, to guard against injury to such other players and persons, including plaintiff.

3. At said time, and immediately prior thereto, plaintiff was lawfully present and playing golf upon said course, and was in the exercise of due care for the safety of his [or, her] own person.

4. On or about ————, 19—, at approximately ———— —.m., defendant negligently drove his golf ball, as hereinafter specified, and, as a direct and proximate result thereof, said ball struck plaintiff with great force and violence, and greatly injured him [or, her] as hereinafter alleged.

[34] Adapted from Hampson v. Simon, 345 Ill App 582, 104 NE2d 112. Allegations as to damages in personal injury actions, see §§ 30.64–30.172.

FIGURE 8.4
Sample of Motion to Dismiss

IN THE CIRCUIT COURT OF THE ELEVENTH JUDICIAL CIRCUIT
OF ILLINOIS
McLEAN COUNTY
TRIAL DIVISION

EMMA M. RENSLOW, Individually
and as mother and next friend of
LEAH ANN RENSLOW, a minor,
                          Plaintiffs,

                  vs.   AT LAW NO. 75 L 8

MENNONITE HOSPITAL, a corporation, and HANS STROINK, M.D.,
                          Defendants.

MOTION TO DISMISS

NOW COMES the defendant MENNONITE HOSPITAL and files this its Motion to Dismiss the Complaint of the plaintiff and states:

1. The Complaint fails to state a cause of action against this defendant.
2. The Complaint was not filed within the time limited by law.
3. That the plaintiff has no standing to sue in behalf of the plaintiff, LEAH ANN RENSLOW, a minor, for the reason that said minor was not a person contemplated or in being at the time of the allegedly injurious occurrences and thus is not one of the persons who might be entitled to sue for damages allegedly incurred.
4. That the plaintiff attempts to assert several different types of causes of action within a single count in some of the counts respecting this hospital, and thus fails to comply with the Illinois Civil Practice Act, and particularly Section 33 thereof, by failing to state her alleged causes of action in separate counts and in separate paragraphs.
5. That there are no facts alleged which are sufficient to show an employer–employee relationship between Dr. Hans Stroink and this hospital, and the court may take judicial notice that doctors are not ordinarily employees of hospitals in the absence of some peculiar relationship or the allegation sufficient to show the same.
6. That there are no facts alleged sufficient to bring this plaintiff within any exceptions to the Statute of Limitations requiring that plaintiff file her claimed cause of action within two years next following the actions complained about.
7. That there is no cause of action in the plaintiff for the alleged mental anguish and no right to recover for the same.
8. That the allegations of the Complaint are insufficient in law to sustain a charge of willful and wanton misconduct or a claim for punitive damages.

9. That there are no facts alleged which are sufficient to show that the alleged injury could have taken place only through negligence on the part of this defendant or any other defendant, and thus the doctrine of *res ipsa loquitur* has no application to the allegations of the Complaint.

10. That the alleged damages complained about are too speculative and conjectural to be such as to accord plaintiff a right to sue for the same.

11. That the allegations of Count II are conclusionary in nature and do not allege actionable misconduct on the part of this hospital or any of its agents and servants.

12. That the charge that the hospital caused "wrong blood" to be infused into the plaintiff is a sheer conclusion, unsupported by any factual allegations and ought to be stricken, as should all charges respecting the same.

13. That there are no facts alleged which are sufficient to sustain the allegations in Count III to the effect that this hospital "discovered that the wrong typed blood had been administered."

14. That the allegations that the hospital or its agents failed to "properly select" the "proper blood" constitute nothing other than conclusions and are insufficient to sustain charges of negligence.

15. That the Complaint in this cause is barred in its entirety by the provisions of Chapter 91, Section 181, et seq. of the Illinois Revised Statutes, it being the public policy of Illinois to promote the health and welfare of the people by limiting the legal liability arising out of such procedures as the transfusing of whole blood.

WHEREFORE, for want of a sufficient Complaint, this defendant prays judgment that the Complaint of the plaintiff may be dismissed at plaintiff's cost.

TRIAL BY JURY IS DEMANDED.

HEYL, ROYSTER, VOELKER & ALLEN

By: *Denis J. Heyl*

Attorneys for Defendant
MENNONITE HOSPITAL, a
Corporation

18th February 15
Denis J. Heyl

HEYL, ROYSTER, VOELKER & ALLEN
Suite 300 The Central Building
Peoria, Illinois 61602
Phone: (309) 676-6184

FIGURE 8.5
Sample of an Answer to a Complaint

IN THE CIRCUIT COURT OF THE ELEVENTH JUDICIAL CIRCUIT OF
ILLINOIS
McLEAN COUNTY
TRIAL DIVISION

EMMA M. RENSLOW, individually
and as Mother and Next Friend of
LEAH ANN RENSLOW, a minor,
                    Plaintiffs,

          vs.   AT LAW NO. 75 L 8

MENNONITE HOSPITAL, a corporation,
                    Defendant.

ANSWER TO COMPLAINT

NOW COMES the defendant, MENNONITE HOSPITAL, a corporation, and its Answer to the Complaint of the plaintiff states:

COUNT I

1. This defendant denies each and all of the allegations of Paragraph 1.
2. This defendant denies each and all of the allegations of Paragraph 2.
3. This defendant admits the allegations of Paragraph 3.
4. This defendant denies each and all of the allegations of Paragraph 4.
5. This defendant denies each and all of the allegations of Paragraph 5.
6. This defendant denies each and all of the allegations of Paragraph 6.
7. This defendant denies each and all of the allegations of Paragraph 7.
8. This defendant denies each and all of the allegations of Paragraph 8.
9. This defendant denies each and all of the allegations of Paragraph 9.
10. This defendant denies each and all of the allegations of Paragraph 10.
11. This defendant denies each and all of the allegations of Paragraph 11.
12. This defendant denies each and all of the allegations of Paragraph 12.
13. This defendant denies each and all of the allegations of Paragraph 13.
14. This defendant denies each and all of the allegations of Paragraph 14.
15. This defendant has no knowledge sufficient to form a belief with respect to the truth of the allegations of Paragraph 15 and therefore denies the same.

WHEREFORE, this defendant prays judgment that the plaintiff take nothing by her complaint and that this defendant may recover its costs.

TRIAL BY JURY IS DEMANDED.

COUNT II

---

to a decision in the defendant's favor even if all of the plaintiff's allegations were correct. Such affirmative defenses might include assumption of risk, contributory negligence, estoppel (a legal concept that prevents a person from proving something in court because of an action taken at an earlier date), consent, fraud, or the running of the statute of limitations.

In addition to denying facts and asserting defenses, the defendant can either counterclaim or file a cross-complaint. In a counterclaim the defendant asserts a cause of action against the plaintiff, while in a cross-claim (or third party action, as it is often called) one defendant asserts a cause of action against another defendant.

Paralegals are often asked to prepare drafts of the answers, motions to dismiss, and other documents which make up the defendant's response to the complaint. The paralegal must consult closely with the supervising attorney and may wish to use form books.

Additional Responses

When the defendant raises an affirmative defense,* presents a demurrer, or files a counterclaim, the plaintiff has the opportunity to respond to those arguments. After the court has ruled on demurrers and motions to strike or dismiss, the parties are usually permitted to amend their pleadings. Through this give-and-take of the pleadings the case is either thrown out or the issues are narrowed and sharpened for trial.

The "Tickler" System

Once the defendant has been served with the summons, there is a set period of time within which to respond. Every time a motion is

---

*In an affirmative defense the defendant asserts additional facts that provide a legally acceptable justification for the actions that form the basis of the complaint. If a valid affirmative defense is established, the defendant can admit to the plaintiff's allegations and still win the lawsuit. Examples of an affirmative defense include assumption of risk and contributory negligence.

filed or an answer is received, another time period begins and another deadline approaches. If any of these deadlines is missed, one may have to go back and start the process all over again or face having a default judgment rendered against the client.

Since these deadline dates are so important, most offices maintain a well-developed system for monitoring important dates, often referred to as a "tickler" system because it supposedly tickles one's memory. The system can range from recording each deadline date on a special calendar to filing duplicate copies of the document or special forms in a file based on dates.

When paralegals work in the litigation area, they must understand their firm's monitoring system and what the deadline dates mean because they may be given the primary responsibility for making sure that the appropriate dates are entered into the system at each stage in the process.

The Criminal Context

In criminal cases the criminal complaint and the indictment (or information) provide the defendant with notice of the crime. The prosecuting attorney (or in some cases the grand jury) will determine the particular sections of the criminal code with which the person is to be charged. Unlike civil procedure the defendant responds to the charges verbally in open court at the arraignment; therefore, paralegals are not usually involved in this stage of the criminal process.

DISCOVERY DEVICES

Discovery devices are vehicles which can give the suit's parties important information about the identification of the witnesses, the nature of the testimony, and possibly such details as the existence and location of potential witnesses. Indeed, they can even be used to inquire about a person's financial status and insurance coverage. These discovery devices include interrogatories, depositions, requests for admissions, motions to produce documents, and motions for a physical or mental exam.

Interrogatories

Interrogatories are written questions sent to one of the other parties in the lawsuit to obtain written answers in return. They are usually used by both parties after the complaint and initial responses have been filed. Figure 8.6 shows the first page of the interrogatories which the defendants sent to Emma Renslow. In addition to locating potential witnesses, interrogatories are often

FIGURE 8.6
Sample Page from Interrogatories

B 7514   DJW:th

IN THE CIRCUIT COURT OF THE ELEVENTH JUDICIAL CIRCUIT
OF ILLINOIS
McLEAN COUNTY
TRIAL DIVISION

EMMA M. RENSLOW, Individually
and as mother and next friend of
LEAH ANN RENSLOW, a minor,
                    Plaintiff,
            vs.   AT LAW NO. 75 L 8
MENNONITE HOSPITAL, a corpo-
ration, and HANS STROINK, M.D.,
                    Defendants.

INTERROGATORIES

The Plaintiff, EMMA M. RENSLOW, Individually and as mother and next friend of LEAH ANN RENSLOW, a minor, is hereby notified to answer the following interrogatories separately and fully in writing, under oath and within twenty-eight (28) days after service of these interrogatories, all in accordance with Supreme Court Rule 213(c); these interrogatories may be answered on these interrogatories in the space provided and, if necessary, the reverse side hereof:

1. State your full name, age, and place of birth.
2. Have you ever been known by any other name? If so, give the other name or names and state where and when you used such names.
3. State your present residence address and the period during which you have resided at said address.
4. Are you married at the present time? If so, state: (a) Your spouse's full name.

---

used to establish dates, determine a person's medical or financial condition, and inquire about the existence of documentary evidence.

Paralegals often have major roles in drafting and digesting these interrogatories. At the drafting stage it is often useful to consult office files on previous similar cases as well as a variety of specialized trial practice books. *American Jurisprudence Trials,** for example, includes ideas for interrogatories in its discussions of trial preparation (see Figure 8.7). Continuing legal education publications may also provide useful resource materials.

When a law office receives interrogatories directed at its client, the client is usually instructed to write out the answers as fully as possible. A paralegal may then edit these answers and prepare the formal responses that will be returned to the other party's attorney. Figure 8.8 provides an example of the form for responses to an interrogatory. Note that for ease of reading the questions are repeated verbatim as they were in the defendant's document. These responses are accompanied by a sworn statement that the answers provided are true and correct to the best of one's information, knowledge, and belief (see Figure 8.9). When answers to a firm's interrogatories are received from the other party, the paralegal may help in analyzing and organizing them.

Depositions

Depositions are witness statements taken under oath prior to the trial itself. They generally are in the same format as a courtroom testimony where one attorney questions the witness and the opposition has an opportunity to cross-examine. The judge is not present but a court reporter is there to administer the oath and to record testimony.

Where interrogatories can only be directed at other parties to the suit, any witness can be deposed. Depositions are used primarily to preserve the testimony of a witness who may not be available for the trial (as in the case of a physician) or when the

*This is a multivolume series published by Lawyers' Co-operative Publishing Company. Each volume contains several essays on preparation for trials involving different types of legal problems. There are of course many individual treatises that seek to do the same thing.

attorney wants to make sure the deposing individual's story cannot be changed. Since a person can be subpoenaed to be deposed, a statement may be obtained from a witness unwilling to give another form of statement to the attorney or to an investigator.

While the attorney will ask the questions, the paralegal may be involved in drafting them and analyzing and organizing the answers.

Requests for Admissions

Requests for admissions can only be directed at other parties to the suit and are used primarily to establish the genuineness of documents and to eliminate the necessity of proving more routine matters. Aside from preparing a routine request and organizing the answers, the paralegal would probably not be very involved.

Motions on Documents and Physical Examinations

The motion to produce documents provides access to relevant documentary evidence so that the party requesting the material can inspect and copy the documents. Whereas this procedure is limited to the obtaining of documents in the possession of one of the other parties to the suit, other documents can be obtained through a subpoena *duces tecum* issued at the time of a deposition. The motion for a physical examination is usually used in personal injury cases or other situations where the health of one of the parties is at issue.

Enforcing Discovery Rights

Parties in a suit have an obligation to respond to interrogatories and requests for admissions, to attend depositions, undergo physical examinations, and produce documents. On the other hand, there are limits to the materials that must be supplied. If the judge can be convinced that discovery attempts have gone beyond the bounds of reasonableness and amount to an undue burden or harassment, a protective order can be issued to allow the party to refuse to comply with certain types of discovery actions.

---

names and respective duties of all persons making entries on such records.[4]

All autopsy reports should be examined with particular attention to the dates of the reports and the cause of death stated. The persons who made the reports should be questioned to determine to what extent they relied upon information given to them by the doctor or hospital personnel.[5] Depositions should be taken of hospital personnel who have since left the employ of the defendant hospital. These persons may give information more freely than if they were still employed there.

§ 32. INTERROGATORIES TO PARTIES[6]

Interrogatories should be used to discover each defendant's part in the mishap, and to determine relationships of agency, employment, or partnership. All interrogatories should request that the party produce whatever records or reports he may have in his possession.

The following are suggested lines of inquiry to be pursued in interrogatories to particular defendants. The list of queries is not necessarily exhaustive.

Referring Physician
1. Explain the purpose of the history that was taken of the patient.
2. State what complaints the patient had and what symptoms you discovered.
3. Explain in detail your diagnosis of the patient's symptoms.
4. State what treatments or medications you prescribed.
5. State what recommendations you made about surgery, anesthesia, or a particular surgeon or hospital.
6. State to what extent you informed the surgeon, obstetrician, or hospital personnel of the plaintiff's history, treatment, and medication.

---

4. How to Handle an Anesthesia Injury Case, by Albert Averbach. Clev-Mar L Rev vol 15 no 3 p 404 (Sept 1966).

5. How to Handle an Anesthesia Injury Case, by Albert Averbach. Clev-Mar L Rev vol 15 no 3 p 403 (Sept 1966).

6. See, generally, 4 AM JUR TRIALS, DISCOVERY—WRITTEN INTERROGATORIES, p. 1.

FIGURE 8.7
Sample Discussion on Interrogatories from *American Jurisprudence Trials*

7. Did you inform the surgeon or hospital personnel as to the patient's known allergies, or any other contraindications to the use of spinal anesthesia?

8. State any partnership arrangements you have with any other medical practitioner.

Surgeon or Obstetrician

9. State in detail what preanesthetic history was taken of the patient.

10. State any information you have as to who prescribed saddle block anesthesia to be given.

11. Describe in detail the scope of your responsibilities to the patient.

12. Describe in detail what control you exercised over the anesthetist or other attendants.

13. State who furnished the anesthetist, the anesthetic agents, and anesthetic apparatus for this particular patient.

14. In the course of the operation, did you assist at all in the administration of anesthesia or did you make any recommendations?   Describe.

15. Describe in detail the events that took place from the start of the operation until the patient left your supervision.

16. State any partnership arrangements you have with any other individual in the practice of medicine.

Anesthetist

17. Explain in detail the taking of the preanesthetic history of the patient.

18. State who determines the type of anesthesia to be used and how this decision is made known to the anesthetist.

19. What anesthetic agent or agents were used on the patient?

20. Describe in detail how you administered anesthesia to this patient.

21. Describe the events from the time you first began administration of anesthesia.

22. Give a chronological history of the patient's vital signs during this time.

23. Describe employment or other arrangements resulting in your engagement to administer anesthesia to this patient.

FIGURE 8.8
Sample Interrogatory with Responses

---

14. State whether you have made any statement or statements in any form to any person regarding any of the events or happenings referred to in your complaint. If so, state:
    (a) The names and addresses of the person or persons to whom such statements were made;
    (b) The date such statements were made;
    (c) The form of the statement, whether written, oral, by recording device, or to a stenographer;
    (d) Whether such statements, if written, were signed;
    (e) The names and addresses of the persons presently having custody of such statements.
ANSWER: No statements have been made other than to my attorneys.

15. State the full name and last known address, giving the street, street number, city and state, of every witness known to you or to your attorneys who claims to have seen or heard the defendant make any statement or statements pertaining to any of the events or happenings alleged in your complaint.
ANSWER: Attorney Robert C. Strodel, 900 First National Bank Building, Peoria, Illinois, had a telephone conversation with Hans Stroink, M.D., on December 26, 1974, in which Dr. Stroink admitted that the blood transfused was mistyped by the laboratory technicians and stated that he (Dr. Stroink) learned of the error sometime later. Also in the possession of Mr. Strodel is a signed note from Dr. Stroink stating that the two technologists were employees of Mennonite Hospital. The note is undated, but was written in response to an inquiry of Mr. Strodel dated December 28, 1974.

16. Supply the following information with respect to each individual whose name you have given in the answer to the preceding interrogatory:
    (a) The location or locations where the defendant made any such statement or statements;
    (b) The name and address of the person or persons in whose presence the defendant made any such statement or statements;
    (c) The time and date upon which the defendant made any such statement or statements;
    (d) The full name and address of any other person who was present at the time and place the defendant made such statement or statements;
    (e) Whether you or anyone acting on your behalf obtained statements in any form from any persons who claim to be able to testify to the statement or statements made by the defendant.

ANSWER: See answer to #15 above.

17. If the answer to paragraph (e) above is in the affirmative, then state:
   (a) The names and addresses of the persons from whom any such statements were taken;
   (b) The date upon which said statements were taken;
   (c) The names and addresses of the employers of the persons who took such statements;
   (d) The names and addresses of the persons having custody of such statements;
   (e) Whether such statements were written, oral, by recording device, or by court reporter or stenographer.

ANSWER: See answer to #15 above.

18. State whether you, your attorney, your insurance carrier or anyone acting on your or their behalf obtained statements in any form from any persons regarding any of the events or happenings that occurred at the scene of the incident referred to in the complaint immediately before, at the time of, or immediately after said incident. If so, state:
   (a) The name and address of the person from whom any such statements were taken;
   (b) The dates on which such statements were taken;
   (c) The names and addresses of the persons and employers of such persons who took such statements;
   (d) The names and addresses of the persons having custody of such statements;
   (e) Whether such statements were written, by recording device, by court reporter, or stenographer.

ANSWER: Other than the information provided in answer to question #15, no such statements have been obtained.

19. State the names and addresses of any and all proposed expert witnesses, and the technical field in which you claim they are an expert.

ANSWER: Unknown at this time, information will be provided upon determination.

20. Do you intend to rely upon any medical text in your cross-examination of this Defendant's medical experts? If so, state:
   (a) The exact title of each medical text upon which you intend to rely;
   (b) The name and address of the publisher of each such medical text;
   (c) The date upon which each such medical text was published;
   (d) The name of the author of each such medical text.

ANSWER: Unknown at this time, information will be provided upon determination.

FIGURE 8.9
Sworn Statement Which Accompanies Interrogatory

STATE OF ILLINOIS ⎤
⎟ SS
COUNTY OF McLEAN ⎦

EMMA MURPHY RENSLOW, having first been duly sworn, deposes and states that she has read the foregoing Answers to Interrogatories by her Subscribed, both individually and on behalf of the minor Plaintiff, LEAH ANN RENSLOW, and that the answers contained herein are true and correct to the best of her information, knowledge, and belief.

Emma Murphy Renslow

EMMA MURPHY RENSLOW, Individually and as mother and next friend of LEAH ANN RENSLOW, minor

Subscribed and sworn to before me this _____ day of May, 1975.

Edna O. Kilroy

Notary Public

ROBERT C. STRODEL
LAW OFFICES OF STRODEL & KINGERY, ASSOC.
900 First National Bank Building
Peoria, Illinois 61602
Phone: (309) 676-3612

If one of the parties refuses to respond to certain questions or to supply certain documents, an attorney can seek a court order for their compliance. A plaintiff's failure to follow such a court order can be sanctioned by a prohibition against using certain evidence, dismissal of some counts, and on rare occasions a dismissal "with prejudice" of the entire case.*

The Criminal Context

While the rights of discovery are not quite as broad in the criminal context as they are in the civil context, most jurisdictions provide a significant degree of discovery in criminal cases. The defense usually has rights that are broader than those of the prosecution.

*Dismissal with prejudice means that the case cannot be refiled.

Prosecutors often use preliminary hearings and grand juries to place a key witness's testimony on the record. Both sides must make available a list of the persons to be called as witnesses and the documents to be submitted as evidence.

PREPARING FOR THE TRIAL

Organization and preparation are keys to successful litigation. Paralegals can play important roles in assembling and organizing trial materials and preparing witnesses and draft motions.

Pretrial Motions

During the discovery process, both sides are likely to make a variety of motions. The motion to dismiss in Figure 8.4 is just one example. If a count of the complaint is dismissed, the plaintiff will probably move to amend the complaint. A motion to quash the summons provides a method for contesting a court's jurisdiction. The defense may also move to require the plaintiff to make its complaint more specific. A motion for judgment on the pleadings is similar to a demurrer because it asserts that even if the facts alleged in the complaint were true, there would be no cause of action present. A motion for summary judgment, on the other hand, asserts that since there are no material facts in dispute, the judge should decide the case without holding a trial.

Other pretrial motions are designed to affect how the trial will be conducted. For example, Renslow's attorney filed a motion in limine* (Figure 8.10) to prevent the defendants' attorneys from disclosing that Leah Ann had been conceived before her parents were married and to disallow anyone other than Dr. Stroink from presenting medical testimony for the defendants. The plaintiff's attorney also filed the motion shown in Figure 8.11 requesting that the judge inquire and permit the attorneys to inquire into certain areas during the *voir dire*.†

In the criminal context a defendant might file motions calling for the reduction of bond, the setting aside of an indictment, or

---

*A motion in limine is a motion seeking to prevent reference to specific information in the presence of the jury.

†The *voir dire* is the portion of the trial during which potential jurors are questioned to determine if they are fit to serve on a case.

FIGURE 8.10
Motion in Limine

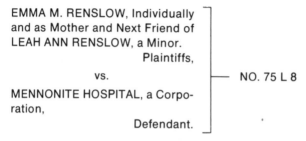

IN THE CIRCUIT COURT OF THE ELEVENTH JUDICIAL CIRCUIT
OF ILLINOIS
McLEAN COUNTY

EMMA M. RENSLOW, Individually
and as Mother and Next Friend of
LEAH ANN RENSLOW, a Minor.
　　　　　　　　　Plaintiffs,

vs.　　　　　　　　　　　　　　── NO. 75 L 8

MENNONITE HOSPITAL, a Corporation,
　　　　　　　　　Defendant.

MOTION IN LIMINE

Plaintiffs in the above cause, by their attorneys, LAW OFFICES OF
STRODEL & KINGERY, ASSOC., move this court to enter a protective order
prior to the trial of the above cause as follows:

1. Forbidding the Defendant and/or its counsel from in any manner questioning, commenting, or otherwise disclosing that EMMA MURPHY, now
known as EMMA MURPHY RENSLOW, was, in fact, pregnant with LEAH ANN
RENSLOW prior to the time of her marriage to STEVEN RENSLOW.

2. Forbidding the Defendant and/or its counsel from offering the expert
testimony of any persons other than HANS STROINK, M.D., by virtue of the

the severing of multiple defendants. Motions to suppress evidence allegedly seized in an illegal manner are also quite common.

While the decision on which pre-trial motions should be filed
belongs to the attorney, the paralegal may have the major responsibility for drafting them. They are generally straightforward
and form books offer samples.

Pleadings Folder

When an attorney goes into a trial, information must be readily
available in a usable form. A paralegal can perform a valuable
service by assembling and organizing that information into a trial
notebook with several sections. Sometimes these sections consist
of a series of specialized files.

answer of Defendant's counsel in the attached letter of May 15, 1978, that the only professional person to be called as a witness would be DR. STROINK.

3. Directing Defendant and/or Defendant's counsel to refrain from asking any questions of any witness at the trial of this cause pertaining to possible Rh blood factor sensitization of EMMA MURPHY RENSLOW, other than the infusion of Rh-positive blood, unless such questioning is, in fact, supported by competent medical testimony that such Rh sensitization could or might occur to a reasonable degree of medical certainty other than by the blood infusion claimed to have been given the Plaintiff by Defendant Hospital in October, 1965.

EMMA M. RENSLOW, Individually and as Mother and Next Friend of LEAH ANN RENSLOW, a Minor,

Plaintiffs,

By. *Robert C. Strodel*

One of Their Attorneys

ROBERT C. STRODEL
LAW OFFICES OF STRODEL & KINGERY, ASSOC.
900 First National Bank Building
Peoria, Illinois 61602
Phone: (309) 676-3612

The pleadings file should contain copies of the original and amended complaints, answers, demurrers, motions to dismiss, and similar documents. In criminal cases it should include the police report. In addition to assembling these documents, the paralegal should prepare a cover sheet that summarizes the complaint and the responses and then cross-references these summaries to the original documents. This sheet should also identify the factual allegations that remain in dispute and must therefore be settled through the trial.

Witness Folder

Proper discovery devices will yield the names of those who will be called to testify and in most cases interrogatories and depositions

FIGURE 8.11
Motion Regarding Jury Selection

IN THE CIRCUIT COURT OF THE ELEVENTH JUDICIAL CIRCUIT
OF ILLINOIS
McLEAN COUNTY

EMMA M. RENSLOW, Individually
and as Mother and Next Friend of
LEAH ANN RENSLOW, a Minor,
                    Plaintiffs,

          vs.   No. 75 L 8

MENNONITE HOSPITAL, a Corporation,
                    Defendant.

MOTION REGARDING JURY VOIR DIRE

The Plaintiffs in the above cause, by their attorneys, LAW OFFICES OF STRODEL & KINGERY, ASSOC., state to the Court that:

1. There has been extensive newspaper, newsmagazine, radio news reporting, television news reporting and special events programming, legislative debate, together with public forum discussion of what has generally been termed to be a "malpractice crisis" in the United States, and expressly including Illinois.

2. Extensive paid advertising in news media by the American Medical Association and its state subsidiaries, expressly including Illinois, has steadfastly concentrated a campaign well calculated to mold public opinion against holding physicians, hospitals, and other health-care providers to the same standards of accountability in tort as other segments of society.

   (a) Extensive legislative lobbying in all fifty (50) states, including Illinois, has sought limitations on recovery, attempts to make new public policy regarding attorney fees, and other matters germane to medical negligence litigation.

3. Because of the enormity of public issue emphasis of problems relevant to medical malpractice, it is paramount within the framework of the concept of a "fair trial" that both Court and counsel inquire in depth of prospective jurors beyond the normal course of inquiry in existing tort litigation.

4. With the advent of Supreme Court Rule 234, broad discretion is placed in a trial Judge to determine and limit the extent to which attorneys will be allowed *voir dire* examination, in addition to such examination as may be initiated by the Court. Unless such examination in malpractice litigation is extensive and probing by both Court and counsel, it becomes increasingly improbable that a plaintiff in a malpractice case can, in fact, obtain a fair trial by an impartial jury. Accordingly, *Plaintiff requests this court to inquire on its own*

motion under Rule 234, and to permit counsel for both parties extensive supplemental inquiry relevant to the following specific questions:

(a) Are any prospective jurors, their relatives, close friends, or business
associates *employed:*

(1) By a physician, chiropractor, osteopathic physician, dentist, or
other practitioner of the healing arts?

(2) By any hospital in any capacity whether medical, paramedical,
or administrative?

(3) By any nursing home or similar care facility in any capacity
whether medical or administrative?

(4) As a nurse, nurse's aid, licensed practical nurse, or orderly by
any hospital, clinic, physician's office, dental office, or any other practitioner of the healing arts?

(5) As a medical technician, laboratory technician, blood bank
technician, therapist, x-ray technician, or any other paramedical occupation allied with the healing arts?

(b) Do any prospective jurors, members of their families, close friends,
or business associates suffer from any chronic or disabling illness that requires regular or periodic medical care, examination, treatment, or
therapy of any kind?

reveal what they will say. This information should be used as the
basis for a witness folder.

The paralegal should prepare a summary sheet for each witness with some details about the background and what that witness is expected to prove. The paralegal should then abstract the
responses the witness has given to interrogatories and depositions. Special attention should be given to those sections which
show internal inconsistencies or which contradict other information. These abstracts in turn should be cross-referenced to copies
of the interrogatories or the transcript of the deposition so the
attorney can quickly turn to the appropriate section. Copies of the
appropriate sections should then be included in the witness file.

For each witness the file should also contain a list of key questions the attorney will need to ask that witness. In both civil and
criminal cases there are various facts which the plaintiff or the
prosecutor must prove in court in order to win the case. If the
attorney fails to establish one of these key elements, the case can
be lost before the defendant's evidence is even presented. (When

an affirmative defense is being offered, the burden of proving certain elements shifts to the defendant.) Since the rules of evidence require that certain foundations be laid before particular questions can be asked, and since the rules of evidence are very particular about the precise form of the question, it is wise for the attorney to have firmly in mind: (1) the elements that must be proved, (2) the foundation that must be laid, and (3) the form of the questions themselves. It is even better if this information is recorded in the witness file.

While the attorney will select the questions, the paralegal can again provide assistance. For example, a paralegal might be told to research *American Jurisprudence, Proof of Facts** or some other specialized practice aid to find the elements that need to be proved as well as sample questions. An example of such material is found in Figure 8.12.

In situations involving an expert witness, it is useful for the paralegal to prepare a glossary of technical terms likely to be used during that expert's testimony.

Preparing Witnesses

Closely related to organizing a witness folder is preparation of the witnesses. This is very important, and either the attorney or the paralegal should meet with witnesses friendly to their side prior to trial. Such a meeting can serve several important purposes. First, the attorney can discover more about what the witness can or cannot actually testify to and what the witness's demeanor may be at the trial. Equally important, it can give the witness a better insight into what may occur at the trial. Witnesses should be introduced to the types of questions they will be asked and the difference between direct and cross-examination. While it is not ethical to suggest that witnesses alter the content of their testimony, it is appropriate to highlight the most critical parts and to explain how this information must be brought out in the context of direct examination (where leading questions are not allowed). Witnesses should also be prepared for the antagonistic questions

---

*This multivolume series is published by Lawyers' Co-operative Publishing Company and specifies the elements needed to prove various types of lawsuits. It also provides questions the attorney can ask witnesses to elicit the proper information.

they are likely to receive on cross-examination. The witnesses should be told not to answer questions they do not understand and not to volunteer information beyond the scope of the question.

Evidence Folder

An evidence folder should be prepared for any documents, charts, photographs, or other evidence the attorney plans to present. These materials should be clearly identified and arranged in the order in which they will be introduced.

Jury Folder

If the trial is going to be conducted before a jury, a special folder should be prepared to aid in the jury selection process. This folder should contain as much information as possible about the individuals who will be on jury duty at the time the case is filed. In large important cases a firm may use the services of organizations that specialize in obtaining information about potential jurors. Some of these firms even interview neighbors and co-workers to obtain information about life styles and attitudes.

Regardless of how much information has been obtained in advance, the file should contain a list of questions the attorney would like to see asked on *voir dire*. In some jurisdictions the attorneys are allowed to ask their own questions, while in others they must be content with submitting requests to the judge.

A jury folder should also contain a list of the instructions the attorney would like the judge to read to the jury at the end of the trial. The early organization of these instructions can assist the attorney in preparing a case by highlighting the type of evidence that must be presented. Sample instructions can usually be found in books that specialize in printing varieties of jury instructions. In many states the courts have approved specific sets of instructions which must be followed when applicable.

Legal Issues File

The legal issues file should contain any motions the attorney might wish to make during the course of the trial as well as legal

MALPRACTICE   **Proof 6**

PROOF NO. 6

STANDARD OF CARE—TESTIMONY OF EXPERT

ELEMENTS OF PROOF

Proof by an expert witness that the defendant-physician's conduct has not conformed to the standard fixed by law is an essential element in any medical malpractice case in which the question of the defendant's negligence is not a matter of common knowledge or the subject of a presumption or inference arising out of the doctrine of res ipsa loquitur. Proof of the following facts and circumstances tends to establish that defendant-physician has breached the duty of care owed to the plaintiff:

— Witness and defendant belong to same school of medicine

— Witness and defendant practice same specialty

— Witness and defendant practice in same locality

— Familiarity of witness with skill and knowledge of average practitioner in locality

— Familiarity of witness with amount of care exercised by average practitioner in locality

— Basis of witness' familiarity with skill, knowledge, and care of average practitioner in locality

  — length of time witness has practiced in locality

  — discussion with others

  — association with others

  — local medical literature

— Opinion of witness as to whether defendant-physician's conduct conformed to standard

— Opinion of witness as to how practitioner in same locality possessing average skill and knowledge and exercising an average amount of care would have treated patient

School of medical thought. A defendant-doctor is entitled to be judged according to the tenets of the school he holds himself out as following. It has consequently been held that

595

FIGURE 8.12

Sample Proof from *American Jurisprudence, Proof of Facts*

Proof 6   MALPRACTICE

the conduct of naturopaths, homeopaths, chiropractors, and osteopaths among others is to be measured by the standards of their own school and not those of licensed medical doctors. The particular school followed, however, must be a recognized one of definite principles, as distinguished from a cult or quackery. Regardless of the school defendant belongs to, where he holds himself out as capable of treating a bodily ill he will be held to certain minimum requirements of skill and knowledge. Where defendant professes a skill he does not in fact have, he will nevertheless be held to the standards of those possessing such skill. In this proof it has been established that defendant held himself out as a medical doctor.

Q. What kind of a doctor are you?

A. A medical doctor.

Q. What degree do you hold in this regard?

A. That of doctor of medicine.

> **Locality in which defendant practices.** Historically the conduct of the physician has been judged according to the norm in his particular community. Many courts today have broadened the geographical area in the belief that such a limitation is unrealistic in an age of mass communication and rapid transportation. Some courts accordingly make only a general urban-rural distinction. Other courts have made the state the pertinent locality.

Q. Where is your office?

A. On .... Street in the Town of ...., State of
....

Q. Is your practice confined to this town?

A. Yes.

> **Particular medical specialty.** The defendant-physician holding himself out as a specialist is held to the standards of that specialty. It has already been established in this case that defendant is a general practitioner.

Q. Do you practice a particular medical specialty?

596

memorandums in support of the desired position on matters involving interpretation of the law. These memorandums should cite appropriate statutes, cases, or court rules to support the attorney's position. The attorney can then bring these citations to the attention of the judge if his position is challenged during the trial. If the legal issue is particularly complex, the judge may ask for a written brief on the subject. The paralegal may prepare drafts of both the motions and the memorandums.

Notes for Opening and Closing Statements

The attorney will probably also have a file with notes for the oral presentations that must be made as part of the opening and closing arguments in the case. While these notes will undoubtedly be the personal product of the attorney, the paralegal may be consulted and should be familiar with its content.

In nonjury cases, the judge may reserve his decision and request written briefs on the case. These briefs may argue the legal issues in much the same way that an appellate brief does (see chapter 10) or they may argue the evidence in a manner that closely resembles an attorney's closing argument to the jury.

AT THE TRIAL

The legal and ethical restrictions discussed in chapter 3 prohibit a paralegal from directly representing a client in the courtroom. A paralegal cannot examine potential jurors or witnesses or argue motions. There are, however, several valuable functions the paralegal can serve during the trial.

For one, the paralegal can coordinate the witnesses, matching the schedule of the court with those of the witnesses. The paralegal is responsible for notifying the witnesses as to when they will be needed and for contacting them on short notice if the schedule is changed.

The paralegal may be asked to take notes and locate materials in the various folders. The paralegal who has been working extensively with the case and has digested the interrogatories and depositions may be in a better position to find the appropriate materials or to catch contradictions in witness testimony than either a secretary or another attorney.

SUMMARY

This chapter provides an overview of the functions a paralegal can perform in the litigation process. Since the specific documents and procedures discussed here vary, the reader is reminded to consult the statutes and court rules that apply to the tribunal involved.

The decision to bring a lawsuit begins with deciding who will be named as parties to the action. There are many considerations that go into the naming of both plaintiffs and defendants. Paralegals are often given major responsibilities for investigating the financial and legal status of potential litigants. They may also be assigned to research jurisdictional requirements of state and federal courts to determine the most favorable forum.

The lawsuit is officially begun when the plaintiff files a complaint with the court and then provides the defendant with proper notice of this action. This notice is usually achieved by having the local sheriff personally deliver a summons directly to the defendant although the law often provides for alternatives.

The body of the complaint consists of the allegations of facts which constitute a cause of action and a request for specific relief. In situations where notice pleading is allowed, one need only identify the transaction from which the plaintiff's claim arises. Pleadings on file from similar cases and form books can help in drafting these complaints.

There are four common responses to a complaint. The defendant can: (1) deny the facts which the plaintiff says took place, (2) admit the facts but assert those facts do not provide the plaintiff a legal remedy, (3) assert that there are procedural defects in the complaint, or (4) assert a claim against either the plaintiff or another defendant. These responses are not mutually exclusive.

Discovery devices such as interrogatories and depositions provide attorneys with information about the identity of the witnesses and the material about which they will testify. Interrogatories are written questions to which the other side provides written responses. Depositions are oral testimonies under oath prior to the trial itself. In both cases the paralegal may help draft the questions. The paralegal will most likely also draft responses to interrogatories and digest and abstract the answers to both. The paralegal will also keep track of deadlines and due dates in the filing of pleadings and motions.

As the trial itself approaches, the paralegal may assist in preparing documents and witnesses. The attorneys must know what to expect from the witnesses and the witnesses must know what to expect from the attorneys. Documentary evidence must be organized so that it is available when needed. At the trial itself the paralegal can coordinate witnesses, quickly locate appropriate documents and notes, and take notes on the witnesses' testimony.

Throughout the litigation process, the paralegal serves a number of very important functions. The division of labor among the attorney, the paralegal, and the secretary will, of course, vary. Ultimately the quality of the paralegal's work determines the delegation of these responsibilities.

KEY TERMS

affirmative defense	executor
agency	guardian
assignee	interrogatories
bailee	judgment proof
cause of action	jurisdiction
class action suit	litigation
compensatory damages	motion in limine
compulsory joinder	notice
count	punitive damages
counterclaim	request for admissions
cross-claim	*respondeat superior*
default judgment	summons
demurrer	"tickler" system
depositions	trustee
discovery	*voir dire*

REVIEW QUESTIONS

1. What tasks are likely to be undertaken by a paralegal who is assisting an attorney in preparing a complaint and filing a lawsuit?

2. What is the paralegal's role in the discovery process?

3. The paralegal cannot represent a client in a court of law but can serve other functions in the courtroom. What are those functions?

DISCUSSION QUESTIONS

1. What factors should be most influential in the selection of one court over another?

2. What is the difference between legitimately preparing a witness and unethically coaching that witness? Give some examples of both the legitimate and the nonlegitimate.

PROJECTS

1. Consult your state's civil practice act to determine the requirements for serving a summons. List the various methods available and the conditions under which each can be used.

2. Under what circumstances does your state court have jurisdiction over a party who is not a resident of your state and who is not physically in the state?

3. Draft a complaint on behalf of a client who was injured in a traffic accident. Assume that the plaintiff was a passenger in an automobile operated by the defendant, and that while traveling at a speed of 65 mph the auto went through a stop sign on a country road and collided with another. Plaintiff suffered a cerebral concussion in the accident and later developed a seizure disorder that made it difficult for him to maintain a job. Assume that both parties are residents of your state and that the accident occurred in your state.

4. Assume that you worked for a law firm representing the defendant in the situation described in question number three. Draft a set of interrogatories to be sent to the plaintiff.

CHAPTER 9

Involvement in Administrative Proceedings

At both federal and state levels the executive branch contains numerous departments, bureaus, and agencies assigned the tasks of administering the law in specialized areas.* Sometimes these agencies are placed outside the executive branch to make them more independent of the chief executive. In addition to enforcing the statutes and ordinances passed by the legislative branch, these administrative units often make their own laws (administrative regulations) and issue interpretations of the meaning of statutes. In summary, these administrative units issue regulations, authorize special privileges (through licensing, grants, and government contracts), prosecute violators, and adjudicate disputes. The powers, procedures, and judicial review of these agencies constitute the subject matter of administrative law.

A paralegal's involvement with administrative law is likely to come at two different levels: advocacy on behalf of a client at the

---

*The same is also true at the local level.

agency level and preparation for judicial review of an agency's action. In the latter case, the paralegal's duties will include researching the law and preparing for litigation as we have discussed in chapters 7 and 8. When the matter is before the agency itself, however, the paralegal can often provide direct representation.*

This chapter will first present some of the basic principles relating to formation and limitations of administrative regulations. It will then discuss the basic procedures utilized in administrative determinations. Since these procedures vary from one agency to another (there is even wide variation within federal agencies, to say nothing of variations from one state to another), the presentation is kept at a fairly general level, but it should help the reader understand the process utilized in any specific agency.

THE NATURE OF ADMINISTRATIVE LAW

When a court evaluates the validity of an administrative regulation, order, or interpretation, it must consider not only whether it is consistent with a statute that authorizes it, but also whether the proper procedures were utilized in its formation and whether the legislature could constitutionally assign such a task to the agency.

Delegation of Authority

As our society has grown more complex, Congress has generally limited itself to developing general outlines of national policy, then delegating the formulation of specific rules to specialized administrative agencies. Congress has neither the time, the energy, nor the expertise to develop specific criteria for such areas as licensing radio stations or setting rates for interstate truckers. It certainly does not have the time to be constantly updating these types of rules every time the economy changes or there is a new technological development. Table 9.1 contrasts the wording of a statute with that of an administrative regulation on

*See the discussion of paralegal participation in administrative hearings on pages 69–72 in chapter 3.

TABLE 9.1

Comparison of Specificity in Statutes and Administrative Regulations

Statutes

42 U.S.C. 423(d)(1)(A) defines disability as: inability to engage in any substantial gainful activity by reason of any medically determinable impairment which . . . has lasted or can be expected to last for a continuous period of not less than twelve months. . . .

42 U.S.C. 423(d)(3) declares that: a "physical or mental impairment" is an impairment that results from anatomical, physiological, or psychological abnormalities demonstrable by medically acceptable clinical and laboratory techniques.

Administrative Regulations

20 C.F.R. 1506(a)(1) lists specific impairments recognized by the agency as being "sufficient to preclude an individual from engaging in any gainful activity." Examples include:

Amputation of lower extremity (at or above the tarsal region) . . .

Inability to use prosthesis effectively, without other assistive devices, due to stump complications, persisting or expected to persist, for at least twelve months from the onset of disability.

---

the same subject. Note the manner in which the regulation provides operational definitions for the terms used in the statute.

Since the United States Constitution specifically assigns the power to legislate to the Congress, it has been argued that the delegation of legislative power to the executive branch violates the principle of separation of powers. In 1935 the United States Supreme Court invalidated two acts of congress on such a theory.[1] Those two cases were aberrations, however, and the high court has not struck down a statute on delegation grounds since then.

In upholding delegations to administrative agencies, the courts have traditionally discussed filling in details, or delegation consistent with legislatively determined standards.[2] In reality the delegations have involved much more than filling in details and the standards provided have often been rather ambiguous.*

---

*The courts have held that terms such as "just and reasonable," "unfair methods of competition," and "in the public interest" supply

According to Kenneth Culp Davis, preeminent scholar in the administrative law field:

> The non-delegation doctrine in the federal courts has failed. It has not prevented the delegation of power, and it has not accomplished the later purpose of assuring meaningful standards. Delegation without meaningful standards is a necessity in any modern government.[3]

The state courts face delegation questions similar to those of the federal courts and Davis reports that state courts will still occasionally invalidate statutes on nondelegation grounds.[4]

Recognizing the insufficiency of statutory standards, some courts appear to be requiring the promulgation of administrative standards to control the use of discretion in individual cases.[5] In other words, when an agency official makes decisions involving specific parties, those decisions must be based on general standards announced by the agency prior to their application to specific situations.

In handling administrative law cases, the paralegal should be aware of the delegation question and thoroughly investigate the nature of the legislative and administrative standards which supposedly control the agency's exercise of discretion. The agency must, of course, follow those standards. The vagueness or the lack of such standards might later be used as a basis for a court challenge to an unfavorable action.

Rule Making

Administrative agencies make rules and issue orders. When they are promulgating rules they are exercising a legislative function which parallels the passing of a statute by the legislature. The rule will apply only to acts which take place after its official enactment. On the other hand, orders are issued as part of an adjudicative process which parallels decisions issued by the courts. The orders are based on the agency's judgment that a person or organization's conduct did not comply with an agency

---

sufficient standards. *Amalgamated Meat Cutters v. Connally,* 337 F. Supp. 737 (D.C. 1971) provides a particularly good example of the extent the courts are willing to stretch the concept of Congressional standards when they do not appear on the face of the legislation.

rule or statute. Ratemaking by an agency like the Interstate Commerce Commission is considered to be a form of rulemaking because of its prospective application.

Section 533 of the Administrative Procedure Act[6] requires that many federal agencies follow a rule-making process that involves publishing proposed new rules in the *Federal Register*. Following this publication the agency must give interested persons an opportunity to submit written data and arguments related to the proposal. (In some cases the opportunity for oral presentations may also exist.) The agency must then consider these comments in formulating the rule. The final rules must be published again at least 30 days before they are to become effective and include a concise general statement of their basis and purpose. This statement, in conjunction with other agency communications, should demonstrate that there was reasonable basis for rejecting suggestions that were not followed.[7]

There are various exceptions to these procedures. When the rules involve the setting of rates, for example, the agencies are often required to hold formal hearings. The Occupational Safety and Health Act calls for public hearings on proposed rules. The paralegal will need to consult both the statute creating and defining the agency in question and §553 to determine the procedures to be used. Wherever state agencies are involved, the paralegal must consult the state statutes.*

One important exception to the requirements of §553 involves interpretative rules, general statements of policy or rules of agency organization, procedure, or practice. Interpretative rules are the agency's announcements of how it interprets the meaning of statutes it must enforce. Where the legislative rules discussed in previous paragraphs presumably add to the legislative framework of regulation, interpretative rules merely clarify what the legislature included in the statute.

When the courts review such statutes they consider such interpretative rules to be "a body of experience and informed judgment to which the courts and litigants may properly resort for guidance."[8] However,

---

*As of 1976 twenty-eight states had adopted versions of a model state administrative procedure act. See Kenneth Culp Davis, *Administrative Law of the Seventies* (Rochester: Lawyers' Co-operative Publishing Company, 1976), p. 9.

The weight of such a judgment in a particular case will depend upon the thoroughness evident in its consideration, the validity of its reasoning, its consistency with earlier and later pronouncements, and all those factors which give it power to persuade. . . .[9]

In *General Electric Co. v. Gilbert,* for example, the United States Supreme Court pointedly rejected the Equal Employment Opportunity Commission's (EEOC) interpretative rules on disabilities related to pregnancy.[10] The EEOC had issued an interpretative ruling stating that Title VII of the Civil Rights Act of 1964 requires that disabilities due to pregnancy or childbirth be treated the same as other temporary disabilities in employers' disability insurance plans. After rejecting EEOC's authority to have promulgated the regulations in the first place, the opinion of the court said the rule in question contradicted an earlier interpretation by the commission. It further indicated that yet another federal agency (the Wage and Hour Administration) had adopted the opposite point of view.

When legislative rules are involved, the courts must ask if the agency had statutory power to adopt rules on that subject, if the agency used proper procedures in promulgating those rules, and, sometimes, if the statute under which the rules were established is constitutional.

ADJUDICATORY HEARINGS

Paralegals are most likely to be involved in adjudicatory hearings in situations where a client seeks some benefit from an administrative agency. A typical example is a client who applies to the Social Security Administration for disability benefits. While the initial decision is made solely on the basis of the client's application and medical records, a hearing may be held as part of the appeal from an unfavorable decision. Similarly, when a welfare agency has decided to eliminate or reduce a recipient's welfare benefits, it must provide the recipient with an opportunity to appeal.

In other cases, the agency may attempt to impose a sanction on a client for violating agency rules. For example, an employer might be accused of unfair labor practices before the National Labor Relations Board, a state agency might seek to revoke a real estate broker's license for allegedly participating in racially discriminatory practices, or a governmental body might seek to terminate a civil service employee.

A hearing is the verbal presentation of a person's case. For example, when a judge hears an attorney's motion to dismiss a lawsuit or to suppress certain evidence, that judge meets with representatives of both parties and allows them to verbally present their arguments on the motion. In the administrative context, an adjudicatory hearing is a mechanism through which parties to a dispute can present arguments and evidence about their case to an administrative decision maker. (Rule-making hearings, on the other hand, resemble legislative hearings in which interested parties present evidence and arguments about what the general law should be in the future.) While hearings are usually presided over by the individual who has been given at least the initial responsibility for rendering a decision, on some occasions the hearing officer is there solely to record what will be reviewed by the actual decision makers.

The procedures for a hearing will vary according to the agency and the type of problem. At one extreme, the procedures at a hearing may be almost identical to those used at a nonjury trial. At the other extreme, the person may merely tell the story in an administrator's office in a rather informal manner. The exact nature of the hearing will depend on statutory requirements and how the courts have interpreted requirements of the due process clause.

Due Process Requirements

According to the Fifth and Fourteenth Amendments to the United States Constitution, the government is not allowed to deprive a person of life, liberty, or property without affording that person due process of law. This applies to federal and state governments and covers not only legislative acts but also those actions of administrative agencies, sanitary districts, public schools, and all other governmental units. The central idea behind the due process clause is that the government must act in a fair and reasonable manner. However, application of the clause involves some very sophisticated legal analysis.

First, the courts must determine if the due process clause is even applicable to the situation. The due process clause only applies when the government is seeking to deprive a person of "life, liberty, or property." It is clearly a violation of one's liberty to be placed in jail, but is it also a violation to be denied the opportunity to publish a newspaper, or to bus someone's children across town rather than allowing them to attend a neighborhood school? Is it a deprivation of property when a court garnishees a person's wages because that person owed someone money? Is the welfare department's action in reducing a person's level of benefits a denial of a property right? Each of these questions must be answered by the courts on a case-by-case basis.

After determining that the due process clause does apply, the courts then decide what the government must do to meet the standards of fairness and reasonableness. Here again the answer varies according to the situation. Procedural due process focuses on the method used to determine if the deprivation should take place. Substantive due process focuses on the government's right to make the deprivation, rather than the way in which it takes place.

The paralegal is most likely to be involved in controversies over the applicability of various due process procedures. In the administrative context, there is much variation in procedures at hearings and even in the decision to hold a hearing.

Figure 9.1 lists the elements associated with procedural due process. The paralegal must become familiar with all of them. With the exception of number 6c all have been held to be applicable to felony trial. In other types of trials, however, the government may legitimately decide not to include certain elements. For example, the Supreme Court has ruled that juvenile proceedings need not entail the right to a trial by a jury.[11]

Some administrative hearings must include adequate notice, personal appearance, representation by retained counsel (or representation by nonlawyer or self), right to present witnesses, confrontation and cross-examination, an impartial decision maker, a decision based on evidence at the hearings, and a statement of the reasons for the decision.[12] On the other hand, the courts have also upheld a procedure in which the accused had only the rights to notice and to present arguments personally.[13] In deciding which elements of due process apply to a given administrative situation, the courts appear to have balanced the relative importance of several different factors. In *Mathews v. Eldridge* the

FIGURE 9.1
Elements of Due Process

---

1. *Adequate Notice*
   a. Sufficiently clear to be able to understand the true nature of the complaint;
   b. Received long enough in advance of hearing to allow adequate time for preparation.

2. *Speedy Justice*
   a. Trial or hearing held without undue delay.

3. *Discovery*
   a. Right to see prior to the start of the trial or hearing physical and documentary evidence to be presented by the other side;
   b. Right to be informed of the identity of the witnesses to be used by the other side;
   c. Right to take depositions and/or interrogatories of witnesses;
   d. Right to subpoena relevant information prior to the start of the hearing or trial.

4. *Opportunity to Be Heard*
   a. Right to appear in person;
   b. Right to present arguments;
   c. Right to present physical and documentary evidence;
   d. Right to have witnesses testify.

5. *Compulsory Process*
   a. Right to require persons to come forth with evidence or to testify.

6. *Representation*
   a. Right to retained counsel (lawyer can speak on client's behalf);
   b. Right to appointed counsel (lawyer paid for by the government when the person cannot obtain one on his or her own);
   c. Right to nonattorney representative (paralegal or other nonlawyer can speak for participant);
   d. Self-representation (right to serve as one's own counsel).

7. *Confrontation*
   a. Participant has right to be present when evidence is presented.

8. *Cross-examination*
   a. Participant or proper representative can question adversarial witnesses.

9. *Nature of the Evidence*
   a. Evidence presented under oath;
   b. Only relevant evidence considered;

---

    c. "Strict" rules of evidence used (as they apply in regular court cases);

    d. Verbatim transcript made of the proceedings.

10. *Participation by the Public*

    a. Hearing or trial is open for the public to observe what takes place;

    b. Right to a jury (the public actually has a role in deciding the case).

11. *Nature and Basis of the Decision*

    a. Decision maker must be impartial;

    b. Decision must be based on evidence in the record;

    c. Application of the appropriate standard of proof (either preponderance of evidence or beyond a reasonable doubt);

    d. Decision must be in writing;

    e. Decision maker must give reasons for the decision.

12. *Right to Appeal to a Higher Authority*

United States Supreme Court emphasized the following three considerations:

> . . . First, the private interest that will be affected by the official action; second, the risk of an erroneous deprivation of such interest through the procedures used, and the probable value, if any, of additional or substitute procedural safeguards; and finally, the Government's interest, including the function involved and the fiscal and administrative burdens that the additional or substitute procedural requisites would entail.[14]

Since it is generally to the client's advantage to use these due process protections, the paralegal should determine which ones apply to the specific hearing situation. Lack of adequate procedures at a hearing can form the basis for an appeal.

Pleadings and Service

Pleadings are important in civil litigation but relatively unimportant in administrative adjudication. They serve solely to notify the parties that a hearing will be held. Service can be made through certified mail. In a Social Security disability case, for example, one need only file the request for hearing form shown in Figure 9.2.

Section 554 of the federal Administrative Procedure Act states that notice should consist of:

1. The time, place, and nature of the hearing;

2. The legal authority and jurisdiction under which the hearing is being held; and

3. The matters of fact and law asserted.[15]

The paralegal should of course consult relevant statutes and the agency's own procedures to become familiar with the type of notice requirements to be applied.

Discovery

Most agency procedures provide a limited role for discovery techniques. Lists of exhibits to be presented and witnesses who will appear are usually available from the agency. Subpoenas can usually be issued upon a showing of "general relevance and reasonable scope of the evidence sought."[16] Depositions can be taken "when the ends of justice would be served."[17]

In some cases the paralegal may be able to obtain very helpful information under the Freedom of Information Act.[18] The act declares in part that an agency shall:

> upon request by an individual to gain access to his record or to any information pertaining to him which is contained in the system, permit him and upon his request, a person of his own choosing to accompany him, to review the record and have a copy made of all or any portion thereof in a form comprehensible to him, except that the agency may require the individual to furnish a written statement authorizing discussion of that individual's record in the accompanying person's presence; . . .[19]

In preparing for the hearing, the paralegal should carefully examine the statements of policy and interpretative rules of the agency. Some of these are published in the *Federal Register*, but

DEPARTMENT OF HEALTH, EDUCATION, AND WELFARE
SOCIAL SECURITY ADMINISTRATION
BUREAU OF HEARINGS AND APPEALS

REQUEST FOR HEARING

Take or mail original and all copies to your local Social Security Office.

CLAIMANT'S NAME

WAGE EARNER'S NAME   (Leave blank if same as above)

SOCIAL SECURITY NUMBER

SPOUSE'S NAME AND SOCIAL SECURITY NUMBER
(Complete ONLY in Supplemental Security Income Case)

CLAIM FOR
(Check one or more boxes)   (Circle type of claim)

☐ Entitlement to Disability Benefits   DIB   DWB   CDB

☐ Continuance of Disability Benefits   DIB   DWB   CDB

☐ Other (Specify) _____

☐ Supplemental Security Income   Aged   Blind   Disabled

☐ Continuance of Supplemental   Aged   Blind   Disabled
Security Income

I disagree with the determination made on the above claim and request a hearing. My reasons for disagreement are:

Check one of the following:
☐ I have additional evidence to submit.
(Attach such evidence to this form or
forward to the Social Security Office
within 10 days.)
☐ I have no additional evidence to submit.

Check ONLY ONE of the statements below:
☐ I wish to appear in person.

☐ I waive my right to appear and give
evidence, and hereby request a decision
on the evidence on file.

Signed by: (Either the claimant or representative should sign. Enter addresses for both. If claimant's representative is not an attorney, complete Form SSA-1696.)

SIGNATURE OR NAME OF CLAIMANT'S REPRESENTATIVE
☐ ATTORNEY ☐ NON ATTORNEY

CLAIMANT'S SIGNATURE

ADDRESS

ADDRESS

CITY, STATE, AND ZIP CODE

CITY, STATE, AND ZIP CODE

TELEPHONE NUMBER

DATE:

TELEPHONE NUMBER

(Claimant should not fill in below this line)

TO BE COMPLETED BY SOCIAL SECURITY ADMINISTRATION

Is this request timely filed?   ☐ Yes   ☐ No
If "No" is checked: (1) Attach claimant's explanation for delay, (2) Attach any pertinent letter. material, or information in the Social Security Office.

ACKNOWLEDGMENT OF REQUEST FOR HEARING

Your request for a hearing was filed on _____ at _____
The Administrative Law Judge or the Hearing Examiner, SSI, will notify you of the time and place of the hearing at least 10 days prior to the date which will be set for the hearing.

HEARING OFFICE COPY
TO:
☐ Hearing Office _____ (Location)
☐ (Claims Involving SSI or combined SSI-RSDI) ____ (Location)
☐ Supplemental Security Income File Attached

CLAIMS FILE COPY
TO:
☐ Hearing Office _____
☐ Claim File(s) Requested by Teletype to ____ (Location)
☐ ACB (BDP)

For the Social Security Administration

By: _____
(Signature)   (Title)

(Street Address)

(City)   (State)   (Zip Code)

Interpreter Needed _____ (Language)   Servicing Social Security Office Code _____

Form HA-501
(3/74)

HEARING OFFICE COPY

FIGURE 9.2
Standardized Request for Hearing Form

others must be specifically requested under the provisions of §552(a)(2):

> Each agency, in accordance with published rules, shall make available for public inspection and copying —
> (A) final opinions, including concurring and dissenting opinions, as well as orders, made in the adjudication of cases;
> (B) those statements of policy and interpretations which have been adopted by the agency and are not published in the *Federal Register;* and
> (C) administrative staff manuals and instructions to staff that affect a member of the public; unless the materials are promptly published and copies offered for sale.

Administrative staff manuals and other instructions to field staff are particularly useful because they give explicit and detailed information on how factors are measured and evaluated. The presentation at the hearing can then be geared to meeting these criteria.

Negotiation

The Administrative Procedure Act authorizes hearing officers to "hold conferences for the settlement or simplification of the issues by consent of the parties."[20] These conferences can provide an opportunity to reach negotiated settlement. For that reason, the paralegal should be thoroughly familiar with all aspects of the case before attending the conference. It is particularly important to know the true nature of the documentary evidence and what testimony is likely to be given. Only then can one reasonably estimate the probability of winning the case. This probability of winning and probable benefits must be carefully weighed against potential costs to the client.

Preparation of a Trial Notebook

When attorneys prepare for trial, they usually use either a single trial notebook or a series of separate folders on pleadings, witnesses, jury, legal issues, opening statements, and closing arguments. These materials are discussed in chapter 8. Although paralegals entering a hearing do not need a jury folder, they do need to prepare as an attorney does for trial.

The paralegal should thoroughly organize questions for witnesses. While the rules of evidence are not as strict as they are in a trial, the paralegal will experience great difficulties if the questions have not been carefully worked out in advance. The biggest danger is failing to bring out evidence essential to elements the paralegal must prove.

After the questions have been prepared, the paralegal should meet with the client to discuss how the hearing will be conducted. During this session, the paralegal should review these questions as well as those the hearing officer or the agency representative are likely to ask the client. Other friendly witnesses should also receive a similar orientation.

The Hearing Officer

The hearing officer directs the actions of the parties involved in a hearing in much the same way that a judge does during a trial. Since hearings are usually less structured than trials, the hearing officer has more flexibility in organizing the hearing and influencing the atmosphere.

Section 3105 of the Administrative Procedure Act provides that hearing examiners be appointed by the various agencies and assigned to cases on a rotating basis. In order to help ensure their impartiality, Congress has given the Office of Personnel Management* (rather than the agency itself) control over the hearing officers' wages.[21] Similarly, the hearing officers can only be removed from office by independent procedures conducted by the commission.[22]

The hearing officers, or administrative law judges, as they have been officially designated by the Civil Service Commission,[23] have the power to:

1. Administer oaths and affirmations;
2. Issue subpoenas authorized by law;
3. Rule on offers of proof and receive relevant evidence;
4. Take depositions or have depositions taken when the ends of justice would be served;

*Formerly Civil Service Commission.

5. Regulate the course of the hearing;
6. Hold conferences for the settlement or simplification of the issues by consent of the parties;
7. Dispose of procedural requests or similar matters;
8. Make or recommend decisions in accordance with §557 of this title; and
9. Take other action authorized by agency rule consistent with this subchapter.[24]

Most states also attempt to ensure the independence of their hearing officers and give them similar types of powers.

Location and Opening Statements

Administrative hearings are held in a variety of locations. Some agencies have impressive wood-paneled hearing rooms that resemble courtrooms. In this kind of setting the hearing officer will usually sit at a desk placed above the level of the table where the hearing participants sit. Administrative hearings sometimes are also held in regular conference rooms where the hearing officer and the participants sit around the same table.

The diagram in Figure 9.3 shows a typical setting for a Social Security Administration disability hearing. A hearing assistant sits at the table, at the right hand of the administrative law judge. This assistant handles a tape recorder and takes notes about where certain testimony will appear on the tape. The claimant and the claimant's representative sit on the administrative law judge's left, across the table from the hearing assistant. The vocational expert* sits across the table from the claimant and next to the hearing assistant. Other witnesses sit in a row of chairs away from the table until it is their turn to testify in a chair at the far end of the table.

Hearing officers usually begin proceedings by introducing themselves and explaining the extent their position is independent from the agency. Opening statements by attorneys or paralegals are rare.

---

*A vocational expert is an expert witness who testifies about qualifications for certain types of jobs and the ability of persons with certain types of disabilities to find appropriate jobs.

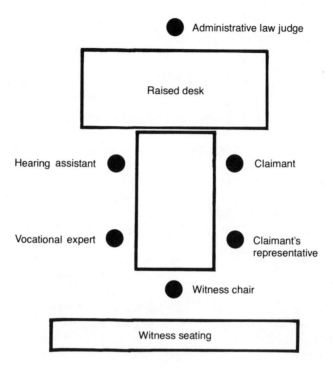

FIGURE 9.3
Typical Seating Arrangement at Social Security Administration Disability
Hearing

Presentation of Evidence

Administrative hearings do not follow the strict rules of evidence
used in trials. There is less emphasis on whether a particular type
of evidence should be admitted, and more emphasis on the weight
given to admitted evidence in reaching the final decision.[25] At the
federal level the Administrative Procedure Act provides that:

> Any oral or documentary evidence may be received, but the agency as
> a matter of policy shall provide for the exclusion of irrelevant, imma-
> terial, or unduly repetitious evidence. A sanction may not be imposed
> or rule or order issued except on consideration of the whole record or
> those parts thereof cited by a party and supported by and in accord-
> ance with the reliable, probative, and substantial evidence.[26]

Documentary evidence is usually reviewed first. Each side turns its documents over to the judge. Opposing sides each have an opportunity to review them and to raise objections. It is not necessary to use witnesses in the manner of a trial.

Testimonial evidence is taken in much the same way as during a trial. There is a relaxation of rules regarding admissible statements and the type of foundation for the case that must be laid. The hearing officer is likely to take a much more active role in questioning the witness personally and in some cases may thoroughly question the witness before the paralegal can ask questions (even when it's the paralegal's own witness).

In questioning a witness the paralegal should use the same types of questions an attorney would use in court. The testimony should begin by establishing the witness's identity and place of residence, the witness's connection with the subject of the hearing, and what the witness knows that will contribute to the client's case. If the questioning occurs after either the hearing officer or a representative for the opposing side has elicited detrimental admissions, the paralegal should attempt to neutralize or explain away the apparently harmful testimony. Even though strict rules of evidence will probably not be followed, the paralegal should avoid leading questions.

When cross-examining a witness who has testified for the opposing side, the paralegal should either seek to discredit the testimony or to bring out further information helpful to the client. Unless there is reasonable opportunity to accomplish either objective, it is probably best not even to attempt a cross-examination for a cross-examination can either reinforce already unfavorable testimony or bring out further damaging information. If the strategy involves discrediting the witness, the questions should focus on such issues as contradictions in testimony; uncertainty by the witness; physical factors that might reduce the reliability of testimony (such as poor eyesight, hearing, or a poor vantage point with dim lighting conditions); and bias against one's client. The paralegal should also indicate situations where testimony involves hearsay or mere conclusions.* Even though such tes-

---

*Expert witnesses are expected to present opinions and conclusions. If an expert witness's testimony is unfavorable, the paralegal may wish to question the basis for the witness's conclusions. There are times when it can be demonstrated that these conclusions do not logically follow from the facts that have been established.

timony may not result in excluding the statements, it does emphasize their unreliability.

Closing Arguments

In administrative hearings there is no jury to be swayed with emotional rhetoric, and the traditional closing arguments lose much of their importance. On many occasions the final argument is submitted to the hearing officer in a written memorandum rather than an oral statement. Whether in written or oral form, the closing argument should highlight the strong points of one's case and dwell on weaknesses and inconsistencies in the opponent's presentation.

PREPARING APPEALS

If the client receives a negative decision after the hearing (or is denied opportunity for a hearing), the paralegal must explore the possibilities of an appeal. In many instances there is provision for appeal within the administrative structure. If this exists, it is usually necessary to exhaust these administrative remedies before the courts will consider handling the case.* Where no such administrative appeal exists or where the remedies have already been exhausted, the case must be taken to court.

The Nature of the Decision

The format of the hearing officer's decision will vary from one agency or governmental unit to another. Section 557(c) of the federal Administrative Procedures Act requires that:

*This exhaustion of remedies concept saves the courts work and gives the agency a chance to correct its mistakes. There are some circumstances in which the administrative appeal mechanism is incapable of awarding the type of remedy being sought. In those cases it is possible to go directly to the courts. The concept of exhaustion should not be confused with that of ripeness. Under the ripeness doctrine, the courts refuse to take the case because the facts and issues have not yet been sufficiently clarified.

The record shall show the ruling on each finding, conclusion, or exception presented. All decisions, including initial, recommended, and tentative decisions, are a part of the record and shall include a statement of (A) findings and conclusions, and the reasons or basis therefor, on all the material issues of fact, law, or discretion presented on the record; and (B) the appropriate rule, order, sanction, relief, or denial thereof.

After the hearing, the hearing officer reviews the recording of the testimony, the documentary evidence, and any relevant memoranda submitted, and then drafts the written decision. In most agencies the decision is then reviewed by a staff attorney before the hearing officer signs and releases it.

The released decision usually begins by listing the date and location of the hearing and who attended. It then identifies the issues, and the relevant statutes and regulations, and offers summaries of witnesses' testimony. The three most important sections follow: The first is an evaluation of the evidence (the relative weight or credibility given to different testimony and documents); the second is the findings section in which the hearing officer states his opinion of the facts; and the third is the decision section in which the hearing officer clearly states the legal effect of the decision (i.e., the party will or will not receive disability benefits).

All aspects of this written decision should be carefully examined when considering an appeal because the substance of this document must be attacked in the appeal.

Administrative Appeal

Many agencies provide a format for an appeal to a special appeals unit but the appeal procedure is usually limited to submission of written documents — and the grounds for appeal are often quite narrow. Ordinarily the appealing party must allege either availability of new evidence, existence of an error on the face of the record, misapplication of the law, or gross abuse of discretion.

In preparing an appeal, the paralegal should examine the procedural requirements of the particular agency. If it is a federal agency one should consult both the *U.S. Code* and the *Code of*

Federal Regulations. A specific request for review form is ordinarily supplied by the agency. This document is often accompanied by an appeal brief, which is usually divided into sections that discuss the facts and history of the case, cite relevant statutes and regulations, and combine the facts and the law together in an argument section. An example of such an appeal is reproduced in Figure 9.4. Note especially the way the facts are linked with specific references to the hearing transcript, as well as other documents. Also note how court decisions are utilized in the argument section.

Before attempting to draft such an appeals document, one should read ahead to chapter 10. While there are differences between administrative appeals documents and those submitted to an appellate court, the same basic skills are required.

Taking an Appeal to the Courts

When the final administrative action results in an unfavorable decision, the paralegal, in consultation with the supervising attorney, should consider seeking judicial review of that action. The federal Administrative Procedure Act provides:

> A person suffering legal wrong because of agency action, or adversely affected or aggrieved by agency action within the meaning of a relevant statute, is entitled to judicial review thereof.[27]

Note that in order to receive this judicial review, the client must have suffered a legal wrong or otherwise be adversely affected by the agency's action. This provision thus is related to the general concept of standing. To be recognized as a legitimate party in a litigation, one must show that one is personally affected by the actions forming the basis of the lawsuit.

In addition to standing, the paralegal must consider the application of the concepts of ripeness, exhaustion, and reviewability. Ripeness requires that the facts have been sufficiently established and clarified by the agency to adequately define the legal issues. If they have not, the court may require further administrative actions before it will consider taking any actions on the merits of the claims. Exhaustion of remedies requires that all available administrative remedies be utilized prior to taking the

FIGURE 9.4
Appeal to Social Security Administration for Benefits

UNITED STATES OF AMERICA
BEFORE THE DEPARTMENT OF HEALTH, EDUCATION AND WELFARE
SOCIAL SECURITY ADMINISTRATION

In the matter of the
application of Ms. Elizabeth
Nelson for Disability ———— No. 652-29-3186
Insurance Benefits and
Supplemental Security
Income

MEMORANDUM OF FACTS, LAW, AND AUTHORITY IN SUPPORT OF
CLAIMANT'S REQUEST FOR REMAND TO PRESIDING OFFICER
FOR THE TAKING OF ADDITIONAL EVIDENCE

This memorandum is submitted pursuant to 20 C.F.R. §404.948 (b) and appellant's written request of May 9, 1978. That the record be left open for the submission of this memorandum and additional medical information.

STATEMENT OF FACTS

Ms. Nelson is a forty-year-old widow, D.O.B. (10-20-37), with a 10th grade education.[1] She has worked primarily in bars and supper clubs as a waitress and bartender.[2] She does have some limited experience as a clerical worker.[3] She quit her last job on October 13, 1977 because of a pain in her side, back, and leg.[4] She suffered a seizure on October 15, 1977, and again on November 5, 1977. She was admitted to a hopital via the emergency room for a diagnostic workup.[5] A peculiar brain scan was noted, and she was sent for a C.I.T. scan at St. James Hospital in Springfield, Illinois.[6] This scan indicated a meningioma in the left parietal region.[7] Surgery to remove the tumor was performed on November 22, 1977, by Dr. Lloyd Kissenger. It appeared successful and he told Ms. Nelson to return in a year.[8]

Since her operation, she has been treated by Dr. Herman Greenburg. His

[1] S.S.A. Form 16, Exhibit no. 1.
[2] S.S.A. Form 401, Exhibit no. 13.
[3] S.S.A. Form 401, Exhibit no. 13.
[4] S.S.A. Form 401, Exhibit no. 12, and Dr. Greenburg's case notes of September 27, 1977 and October 11, 1977.
[5] Dr. Greenburg's Admittance Notes, November 6, 1977.
[6] Dr. Greenburg's Discharge Notes, November 8, 1977.
[7] November 8, 1977 C.I.T. scan. Dr. James Andrews, St. James Hospital.
[8] Exhibit no. 18, Dr. Kissenger's report.

notes indicate that on January 13, 1978, she could not work.[9] On February 13, 1978, she was having seizures, had been weak, and unable to work.[10] On May 3rd, he notes that she was still suffering from headaches, dizziness, and had a seizure approximately ten days before. He also notes that she was nervous and jittery. He increased both her prescriptions.[11] Since that time, Ms. Nelson has been unable to work. Her right arm is still so uncoordinated that she cannot use an ashtray. She cannot lift her arm above her head, nor hold pots and pans with her right hand. She has severe headaches from above the right eye to the temple area, and is so heavily medicated that she must sleep for three to four hours after she takes her medication.[12]

Dr. Greenburg's report of July 25, 1978, indicates that he is unsure of the causes of Ms. Nelson's epilepsy, and whether it is related to the meningioma. He found her to be severely nervous; with a "flattened and aggressive personality, and near paranoia."[13] He felt she could return to work, but suggested that "an examination by a neurologist would probably be in order."[14] When asked on July 25, 1978, whether a psychiatric consultation would be in order, Dr. Greenburg replied, "It would certainly help in evaluation."[15]

That these facts indicate the need for a remand by the appeals council to the presiding officer for the taking of additional evidence will be established in the paragraphs that follow.

PROCEDURAL HISTORY OF THE CASE

Ms. Nelson applied for O.A.S.D.I. benefits on November 10, 1977, prior to her first surgery.[16] She alleges an onset date of November 5, 1977, when she was hospitalized after a seizure, during which the tumor was discovered.[17] The application was denied on December 20, 1977, although no notice of denial was ever made part of the record. She appealed this decision, and was again denied benefits although no notice of reconsideration is part of the record.[18] The "D.D.T." of January 25, 1978, states that the denial of benefits

[9]Exhibit no. 23, Dr. Greenburg.
[10]Dr. Greenburg's case notes, February 13, 1978.
[11]Dr. Greenburg's case notes, May 3, 1978.
[12]Ms. Nelson's affidavit of August 7, 1978.
[13]Dr. Greenburg's report of July 25, 1978.
[14]Dr. Greenburg's report of July 25, 1978.
[15]Smith–Greenburg letter of July 25, 1978.
[16]Exhibit no. 1.
[17]Exhibit no. 2.
[18]Decision of March 20, 1978, "jurisdiction" section.

(Continued)

FIGURE 9.4 — Continued

---

was based on Dr. Greenburg's report of January 13, 1978, and a telephone contact of January 23, 1978.[19] No copies of that phone contact are now part of the record, nor were they at the time of Administrative Law Judge, A.L.J. Hanrahan's decision.[20] She requested a hearing on February 14, 1978, and waived her right to a hearing.[21] She was afraid to appear without an attorney, could not afford one, and was not advised of the availability of free legal services in the community by employees of the Social Security Administration.[22]

A.L.J. Richard Hanrahan made a decision on the record on March 20, 1978. Although the last piece of medical evidence he had from the claimant's treating physician stated Ms. Nelson was unable to work, A.L.J. Hanrahan determined that Ms. Nelson had not established that her impairment would last the required twelve months.[23]

The appellant requested review by the appeals council on May 5, 1978. An accompanying letter of May 9, 1978, outlined several reasons for requesting review, and requested an opportunity to submit additional evidence. With this memorandum are five pieces of additional evidence: two letters and a copy of case notes from her treating physician, and two affidavits.

It is the appellant's contention that the additional evidence is new and material, and indicates the need for consultative examinations by a psychiatrist and a neurologist. That the remand of the instant case to a presiding officer is appropriate will be established in the paragraphs which follow.

STATEMENT OF THE LAW

A. Jurisdiction

The regulations which pertain to the granting of a review by the appeals council (20 CFR §404.947 (a) (b)) read in part:

> (b) Where new and material evidence is submitted with the request for review, the entire record will be evaluated and review will be granted where the appeals council finds the presiding officer's action, finding, or conclusion is contrary to the weight of evidence currently of record.

The previous section contains two other criteria which allow review by the appeals council that apply to this case:

(1) There is an abuse of discretion by the presiding officer.

(2) There is an error of law.

B. Admissibility of New Evidence

New evidence may be admitted "where it appears to the appeals council

---

[19]Exhibit no. 6.
[20]Decision of March 20, 1978, exhibit list.
[21]Decision of March 20, 1978.
[22]Ms. Nelson's affidavit of August 3, 1978.
[23]Decision of March 20, 1978, page 6.

that such evidence is relevant and material to an issue before it, thus may affect its decision." (20 CFR 404.949 (a))

If the appeals council finds that additional evidence is necessary for a sound decision "it will remand the case to a presiding officer for the receipt of additional evidence, further proceedings, and a new decision. . . ." (20 CFR 404.949 (b))

C. The Taking of Additional Evidence on Remand to the Presiding Officer
The appeals council may remand to the presiding officer for rehearing, receipt of evidence, and decision any case which it decides to review provided in 20 CFR §404.947, and §404.947a . . . the presiding officer shall initiate such additional proceedings and take such action . . . as directed . . . and may take any additional action not inconsistent with the order of remand. (20 CFR 404.950)

ARGUMENT

That the appeals council should remand the instant case for the taking of additional evidence will be established in the following paragraphs.

A) THE EVIDENCE SUBMITTED SUBSEQUENT TO THE REQUEST FOR REVIEW IS RELEVANT AND MATERIAL.

A.L.J. Hanrahan stated in his decision of March 20, 1978, that: "This decision should not be interpreted as to preclude a further consideration of a new claim . . . if it is substantiated by appropriate medical evidence *with* respect . . . to a continuance of disabling severity, actually or prospectively."[24]

The evidence submitted with this memorandum describes two types of problems. The first is that Ms. Nelson has not returned to work, has severe headaches, epileptic seizures which occur even with medication, continues to be uncoordinated and weak in her right arm, and is so heavily medicated that she sleeps a great deal.[25] Dr. Greenburg has suggested that a neurological examination "would probably be in order."[26]

The second and a new problem which surfaces in the new evidence is the question about Ms. Nelson's mental health. Dr. Greenburg stated that she was "nervous and jittery," and suffered from severe nervousness, "a tremendously flattened and aggressive personality, and near paranoia."[27]

The claimant's representative has also noted the problem. In his affidavit,

[24]Decision of March 20, 1978, page 6.
[25]Dr. Greenburg's report of July 25, 1978; Ms. Nelson's affidavit of August 7, 1978.
[26]Dr. Greenburg's report of July 25, 1978.
[27]Dr. Greenburg's report of July 25, 1978.

(Continued)

FIGURE 9.4 — Continued

---

it is noted that the claimant is depressed, cries during interviews, and believes her doctor is lying about her.[28] Dr. Greenburg, in his note of July 25th, notes that a psychiatric examination "would certainly help in evaluation."[29] The claimant also notes in her affidavit that she has been nervous and depressed.[30]

The new evidence is apparently contradictory. Dr. Greenburg states that Ms. Nelson could return to work. But, in the same letter, states she is having severe emotional problems,[31] and later he stated that she should be examined by a psychiatrist.[32] Ms. Nelson has not returned to work.[33]

Numerous cases have discussed the question of whether a remand is appropriate when new evidence is presented. The standard outlined in *U.S. v. Dorgan* §522 F 2d 969 (9th Cir 1975) was initially set out in *Wray v. Folson* 166 F Supp 390 (W.D. Ark 1958) wherein the court stated:

> "In these circumstances, courts must not require such technical and cogent showing of good cause as would justify the granting of a new trial, but where no party will be prejudiced by the acceptance of additional evidence and the evidence offered bears directly and substantially on the matter in dispute."

When the issue becomes one where a psychiatric impairment is a possible disability which has never adequately been examined, the courts have routinely remanded cases to the secretary for a consultative psychiatric examination. *McGee v. Weinberger* 518 F 2d 330 (5th Cir 1975), *Dodsworth v. Celebrezze* 349 F 2d 312 (5th Cir 1965), *Hassler v. Weinberger* 502 F 2d 172 (7th Cir 1974).

B) THE ADMINISTRATIVE LAW JUDGE FAILED TO MAKE FULL INQUIRY INTO THE FACTS AND THERE ARE ERRORS OF LAW IN THE RECORD.

On January 13, 1978, Ms. Nelson presented Social Security with a note from her doctor which said she was unable to work.[34] The state agency responsible for making the determination contacted Dr. Greenburg by telephone on or about January 23, 1978. As a result the state agency determined that Ms. Nelson was not disabled because her impairment was not expected to last twelve months.[35] No copy of, notes of, or transcription from that call is

[28]T. Smith's affidavit of August 7, 1978.
[29]Smith-Greenburg letter of July 25, 1978.
[30]Ms. Nelson's affidavit of August 7, 1978.
[31]Dr. Greenburg's report of July 25, 1978.
[32]Smith-Greenburg letter dated July 25, 1978.
[33]Affidavit of Ms. Nelson, August 7, 1978.
[34]Dr. Greenburg's statement exhibit no. 22.
[35]Exhibit no. 6.

currently available to the appellant nor was it available to A.L.J. Hanrahan when he made his decision.[36] The appellant contends this deprives her of her due process right to cross-examine guaranteed by the courts, in that it assumes that a conversation did in fact take place between someone at the state agency and Dr. Greenburg, and that Dr. Greenburg did in fact state that Ms. Nelson would not be disabled for a period of twelve months or longer. As Chief Justice Hughes once wrote in *Consolidated Edison Co. v. N.L.R.B.* 305 US at 230, "mere uncorroborated hearsay or rumor does not constitute substantial evidence." The Supreme Court distinguished that standard in the case of *Richardson v. Perales* 409 US 389 (1971). In that case, involving the right of Social Security claimants to cross-examine reporting physicians, the court ruled at 397 that the procedural integrity and fundamental fairness of the administrative process was maintained *when the reporting physician's reports admitted into evidence* were based on *actual* examinations of the claimant, based on *personal consultation* and *personal* examination.

The process by which Dr. Greenburg's opinion on the duration of Ms. Nelson's disability was sought does not even begin to comport to the standard outlined in *Perales* (supra). Indeed, it is "material without a basis on evidence having rational probative force," which is inadmissible in administrative hearings. *Perales* 407 & 408. Yet, it was upon just such questionable evidence A.L.J. Hanrahan based his conclusion. In *Rios v. Hackney* 294 F. Supp. 885 (N.D. Tx 1974), the court held that this type of process violated the appellant's due process rights to cross-examination.

Confronted with the lack of actual evidence regarding the length of time Ms. Nelson would be unable to work, the A.L.J. had the "affirmative duty to inquire into all the facts at issue." *Coulter v. Weinberger* 527 F 2d 224 (3d Cir 1975). Social Security regulations state that: "[t]he Administrative Law Judge shall inquire fully into the matters at issue." 20 C.F.R. §404.927. "[A] duty devolves on the hearing examiner to scrupulously and conscientiously probe into, inquire of, and explore for all the relevant facts surrounding the alleged claim." *Henning v. Gardner* 276 F. Supp. 662, 624-625 (N.D. Tx 1967). The failure on the part of the A.L.J. to ask Doctor Greenburg for a statement regarding the severity and longevity of Ms. Nelson's impairment and to admit that statement into evidence does not comply with the standards outlined above, and is therefore an abuse of discretion, and an error in law.

THE APPELLANT'S CLAIM SHOULD BE REMANDED TO A PRESIDING OFFICER FOR TAKING OF ADDITIONAL EVIDENCE.

20 C.F.D. 404.949 (a) states that where the appeals council has determined that additional evidence is needed to reach a sound decision, it will remand the case to a presiding officer . . . except where the appeals council can obtain the evidence more expediently. . . .

[36]Exhibit list attached to decision.

(Continued)

FIGURE 9.4 — Continued

The issue before the administration is whether Ms. Nelson is currently disabled. Ms. Nelson does not believe she can return to work.[37] Her treating physician believes a consultative psychiatric and neurological examination would be appropriate.[38]

Therefore, there are questions as to whether this is a single or multiple impairment. It is important, therefore, that Ms. Nelson be given the right to a hearing in which she be able to present evidence as to the extent of her impairments.

Respectfully Submitted

Prairie State Legal Services, Inc.
219 North Main Street — Suite 500
Bloomington, Illinois 61701
TEL: (309) 827-5021
BY: Thomas E. Smith *Thomas Smith*
     Legal Assistant

[37]Ms. Nelson's affidavit of August 7, 1978.
[38]Dr. Greenburg's reports of July 25, 1978.

matter to the courts. Finally, the litigant must also demonstrate that statutes and court decisions have provided for judicial remedies in that particular type of case. Some types of issues are considered to be totally committed to agency discretion and simply not reviewable by the courts.[28]

If review is possible, it may take place in several different forums.

The form of proceeding for judicial review is the special statutory review proceeding relevant to the subject matter in a court specified by statute or, in the absence or inadequacy thereof, any applicable form of legal action, including actions for declaratory judgments or writs of prohibitory or mandatory injunction or habeas corpus, in a court of competent jurisdiction. Except to the extent that prior, adequate, and exclusive opportunity for judicial review is provided by law, agency action is subject to judicial review in civil or criminal proceedings for judicial enforcement.[29]

In some cases the courts may delay the agency's action until they can review it.[30]

In reviewing agency decisions the courts can only set aside agency actions, findings, and conclusions in circumstances where they have been found to be:

(A) Arbitrary, capricious, an abuse of discretion, or otherwise not in accordance with law;
(B) Contrary to constitutional right, power, privilege, or immunity;
(C) In excess of statutory jurisdiction, authority, or limitations, or short of statutory right;
(D) Without observance of procedure required by law;
(E) Unsupported by substantial evidence . . . or;
(F) Unwarranted by the facts to the extent that the facts are subject to trial de novo (a new hearing) by the reviewing court.[31]

Note that conditions B, C, and D are legal. They question the proper interpretation of constitutional and statutory provisions. Conditions A, E, and F draw the court into a review of the facts of the particular dispute. In subsection E, the term "unsupported by substantial evidence" has been interpreted as being "such relevant evidence as a reasonable mind might accept as adequate to support a conclusion."[32] Thus while the courts will review factual determinations, they will seek to minimize situations in which they substitute their own judgment for that of the agency decision maker and will instead give the agency the benefit of any reasonable doubt.

In addition to the substantial evidence rule, reviewing courts have at various times applied other similar formulations to determine the scope of review over factual determinations. These alternatives have included the "clearly erroneous" test, the "no basis in fact" standard, "in the absence of substantial evidence to the contrary," and the requirement that there be a "total lack of evidence."[33] In preparing an appeal, the paralegal should check the case law to determine which formulations have been applied to the case. The appeal should then utilize these key definitions. However, one should not place too much importance on the specific test used. For as Davis so aptly puts it:

Formulas about scope of review do not always control judicial action; the formulas can be bent in any direction, in accordance with what the reviewing court deems to be the needs of justice or the public welfare.[34]

SUMMARY

A paralegal's participation in administrative law may include direct advocacy on behalf of a client as well as the same tasks involved in litigation work.

Administrative regulations flow from a delegation of legislative power from the legislature to the agency. The emphasis in the courts today is no longer on whether the subject can be properly delegated but on whether the legislature has provided adequate standards for controlling the discretionary use of the agency's power. In situations where the legislature has not provided such standards, some courts now appear to be requiring the promulgation of administrative standards to control the use of discretion in individual cases.

The federal Administrative Procedure Act specifies formal procedures that federal agencies must often follow in promulgating their rules. However, there is great variation in requirements for a given agency. The paralegal must therefore carefully research the rulemaking requirement for a specific case.

While adjudicatory hearings tend to follow the general outlines of a civil trial, they are less formal and do not involve as many due process protections. To meet requirements of the due process clause, an agency's procedures must be fair and reasonable. The courts have decided that the fair and reasonable procedures required in some agency hearings are not necessary in others.

The pleadings do not play an important role and serve simply to notify the other party that a hearing will be held. Service is usually through certified mail. The Administrative Procedure Act does provide for issuing subpoenas, and the Freedom of Information Act is often used as a supplementary discovery device. The Administrative Procedure Act also provides for prehearing conferences which may help lead to a negotiated settlement.

The hearing is presided over by a hearing officer (officially designated as an administrative law judge), who acts much as a judge would. An assistant usually records the proceedings and takes notes. While it is relatively easy to get evidence admitted into the record, the decision makers have great discretion over the weight assigned to that evidence.

When the law provides for appeal within the agency itself, the party is usually required to pursue this appeal before the courts will agree to intervene. The agency's decision must include a summary of what that agency determined as facts as well as a clear statement of the reasons for its decision. The administrative appeal is usually handled through submission of written documents with no room for oral advocacy.

If an agency appeal is either unavailable or unsuccessful, the paralegal with the supervisory attorney should consider seeking judicial review in court. In doing so the paralegal must carefully research the question of reviewability as well as those of standing, exhaustion, and ripeness.

While this chapter has focused on the federal Administrative Procedure Act, the states have adopted many of the same features. When administrative law matters arise at the state level, the paralegal should consult the state statutes and agency rules for guidance.

KEY TERMS

adjudicatory hearing	order
administrative law	procedural due process
administrative law judge	reviewability
due process of law	ripeness
exhaustion of remedies	rule
Freedom of Information Act	rule-making hearing
hearing officer	standing
interpretative rule	substantive due process
legislative rule	

REVIEW QUESTIONS

1. What types of limitations have the courts imposed on the delegation of legislative power to administrative agencies?

2. What steps must an agency usually take when it promulgates a new rule?

3. What is meant by the right to counsel? How does its application to administrative hearings differ from its application to trials?

4. What is the difference between the right to be heard, compulsory process, confrontation, and cross-examination?

5. How can the Freedom of Information Act be used as a discovery device?

6. What types of agency actions are reviewable?

7. Why should a party be required to exhaust one's administrative remedies before being able to obtain judicial review?

DISCUSSION QUESTIONS

1. What types of limitations should be placed on the delegation of power to nonelected public officials? Should bureaucrats be treated any differently than judges in this regard?

2. What should be the extent of public participation in agency rule making? Is there some way of ensuring that regulatory agencies do not become the captive of the industry they supposedly regulate?

3. Many agency decisions involve highly technical areas in which the agency personnel are presumably specialists. To what extent should their decisions be reviewed by judges? Are judges qualified to make technical decisions on such questions as the safe level of radiation or emissions from an automobile? What standard of review should be applied to such technical decisions? How much deference should the courts show the agencies?

4. Which elements of due process should be required in an administrative hearing? If you believe there should be a variable standard, what should be the maximum and minimum? In which types of hearings should the maximum and minimum apply?

PROJECTS

1. Select any federal or state agency of your choice and draw an organization chart for that agency. Which parts of the agency perform legislative functions and which parts adjudicative?

2. Compare and contrast the federal Administrative Procedure Act with the administrative procedures in your state.

3. Read *Richardson v. Perales*, 402 U.S. 390, 91 S. Ct. 1421 (1971). The application of what aspect of due process is involved in this case? Why do the dissenters disagree with the majority position in this case? With which position do you agree, and why?

REFERENCES

1. *Panama Refining Company v. Ryan*, 293 U.S. 388, 55 S. Ct. 24, 79 L. Ed. 446 (1935) and *Schechter Poultry Co. v. United States*, 295 U.S. 495, 55 S. Ct. 837, 79 L. Ed. 1570 (1935).
2. See, for example, *United States v. Grimaud*, 220 U.S. 506, 521, 31 S. Ct. 480, 484, 55 L. Ed. 563 (1911) and *United States v. Chicago, M. & St. P. R. R. Co.*, 282 U.S. 311, 324, 51 S. Ct. 159, 162, 75 L. Ed. 359 (1931).
3. Kenneth Culp Davis, *Administrative Law Text*, 3d ed. (St. Paul: West Publishing Company, 1972), p. 51.
4. *Ibid.*, p. 51.
5. See Kenneth Culp Davis, *Administrative Law in the Seventies* (Rochester: The Lawyers' Co-operative Publishing Company, 1976).
6. 5 U.S.C. §553.
7. See *Automotive Parts & Accessories Assn. v. Boyd*, 407 F. 2d 330 (D.C., 1968).
8. *Skidmore v. Swift & Co.*, 323 U.S. 134, 140, 65 S. Ct. 161, 164, 89 L. Ed. 124 (1944).
9. *Ibid.*
10. 429 U.S. 125, 94 S. Ct. 401, 50 L. Ed. 2d 343 (1976).
11. *McKiever v. Pennsylvania*, 403 U.S. 528, 91 S. Ct. 1976, 29 L. Ed. 2d 647 (1971).
12. *Goldberg v. Kelly*, 397 U.S. 254, 90 S. Ct. 1011, 25 L. Ed. 2d 287 (1970).
13. *Goss v. Lopez*, 419 U.S. 565, 95 S. Ct. 729, 42 L. Ed. 2d 725 (1975).
14. 424 U.S. 319, 335, 96 S. Ct. 893, 903, 47 L. Ed. 2d 18 (1976).
15. 5 U.S.C. §554(b).
16. 5 U.S.C. §555(d).
17. 5 U.S.C. §556(e)(4).
18. See 5 U.S.C. §§552, 552a, and 552b.
19. 5 U.S.C. §552a(d)(1).
20. 5 U.S.C. §556(c)(6).
21. 5 U.S.C. §5362.
22. 5 U.S.C. §7521.
23. 5 C.F.R. §930.203a.
24. 5 U.S.C. §556(c).
25. See chapter 14 in Davis, *Administrative Law Text*.
26. 5 U.S.C. §556(d).
27. 5 U.S.C. §702.
28. 5 U.S.C. §701.
29. 5 U.S.C. §703.

30. 5 U.S.C. §705.
31. 5 U.S.C. §706(2).
32. *Consolidated Edison Co. v. N.L.R.B.*, 305 U.S. 197, 229, 59 S. Ct. 206, 217, 83 L. Ed. 126 (1938).
33. See pages 528–530, and 535–538 in Davis, *Administrative Law Text.*
34. *Ibid.*, p. 529.

CHAPTER 10

The Preparation of Appeals

"I'll take my case all the way to the Supreme Court" is a battle cry that has been echoed by many concerned clients. It recognizes the possibility that the initial decision might not be satisfactory and represents a commitment to take the cause to a higher authority. Attorneys do not like to lose a case and the appeal represents a possible vindication for them. There are few attorneys who have not dreamed of arguing a case before the United States Supreme Court.

On the other hand, appeals consume time and money. The client's initial desire for appeal often pales because of costs. Additionally, the option to appeal may either be very limited or even nonexistent. For while almost everyone has the right to one appeal, the nature of the issues considered in that appeal may be narrow in scope and subsequent appeals are usually up to the discretion of the reviewing court.

The decision to appeal thus involves balancing predicted chances of success with costs. It is a decision which must ultimately be made by the client but the paralegal may assist with the research the lawyer undertakes to advise the client of the chances for success. It is therefore important to understand some of the basic principles of our appellate system.

THE SCOPE OF APPELLATE REVIEW

The reader will recall from chapter 1 that while both the federal and state court systems are divided into trial and appellate courts, the number of such courts, their names, and their jurisdictions vary according to the system. In preparing a specific appeal, the paralegal must carefully read the appropriate statutes and court rules to determine which court has jurisdiction and what permissible grounds for appeal exist. There are some general principles applicable in all court systems, and knowledge of them should help one in understanding a specific statute or court rule.

Cases That Can Be Appealed

Just as courts will generally refrain from hearing administrative cases until all remedies have been exhausted, so the appellate courts will refrain from reviewing trial court actions until those actions have been finalized. The appellate courts insist that an attorney must have filed a motion for a new trial and that this motion must have been rejected before the case can be elevated to the appellate level. In effect, the appellate courts want to give trial courts every opportunity to correct their own mistakes before they will review the case.

While a party must ordinarily wait until the final judgment, sometimes appellate courts will review such issues as injunctions or an order quashing a subpoena. But again, one must consult statutes and court rules in a jurisdiction to find a list of specific circumstances in which an appeal can be taken from something other than a final judgment.

Once alternative remedies have been exhausted, the person wishing to carry the case to the appellate courts must file a *timely* appeal. In the federal courts a notice of appeal must be filed within thirty days of the entry of the final judgment or order.*

---

*A party has 60 days within which to file the notice of appeal when the United States Government is one of the parties. See section 4 of the Federal Rules of Appellate Procedure.

While federal rules do allow for a thirty-day extension upon a showing of excusable neglect these time limits are strictly followed.[1] If the notice is not filed in the proper time limits in a civil case, the federal appellate courts will simply refuse to hear it.[2] Most states are equally strict about their filing requirements.*

In the criminal context, failure to meet the filing deadline is not quite as devastating because of the availability of the writ of habeas corpus. A habeas corpus action charges that officials of the state (usually the officers of the state prison system) are unlawfully holding the body of the defendant. Since the lawfulness of the person's incarceration depends on the legality of that person's conviction, the court considering the writ must review the circumstances of the original trial. The writ of habeas corpus can be sought after the time limit for filing appeals has expired. It should also be noted, however, that the trend of some recent cases has been to reduce the availability of this remedy.[3]

A Proper Foundation

As stated in chapter 1, when an appellate court hears a case it does not conduct the trial again. It simply reviews the official record of proceedings at the trial court. Moreover, it limits its review to specific appealable issues. To meet the requirements of an appealable issue the party appealing it must have laid a proper foundation for the appeal at the trial level.

As previously stated, appellate courts like to give trial courts an opportunity to correct any errors before reviewing cases. Therefore, in addition to limiting review to the final judgment, appellate courts usually limit review of issues to situations in which the attorney raised the appropriate objection at the trial level. In other words, the lawyer cannot complain later to the appellate judges about something that was not complained about earlier to the trial judge.

---

*While these time limits may appear overly restrictive and arbitrary, they are necessary for the orderly administration of justice. To allow for execution of the judgment, it is important that the issue of the finality of the decision be determined as soon as possible. It is also important that the appeal take place while the record is readily available. Since a transcript of proceedings is not ordinarily made until the appeal is filed, delay could result in loss of the reporter's notes or problems in translating them.

This requirement for a proper foundation places additional pressures on the trial attorney. A careless or incompetent attorney can destroy the client's chances for a successful appeal and at the same time destroy the client's chance to win at the trial level. Attorneys will make objections for the record even when they do not expect the trial judge to accept them. This is sometimes called protecting the record, or making a record for appeal.

It should be noted, though, that this foundation requirement is sometimes relaxed in criminal cases. There have been several cases, for example, in which the United States Supreme Court has ruled that the courts should not refuse to review violations of a defendant's constitutional rights simply because that defendant's attorney failed to make a timely objection.[4]

Legal as Opposed to Factual Issues

In reviewing a case appellate courts are supposed to consider only legal issues. (Legal issues involve interpretation and application of the law; factual issues involve the determination of whether a given event took place in a particular way.) In practice, however, the fact-law distinction tends to break down, and there are circumstances in which the resolution of a legal issue can require the court to review the facts.

Cases in which the appellate court must review a trial judge's interpretation of a statute or legal document such as a will or a lease offer examples of legal issues. Similarly, questions about the nature of the jury instructions or a decision on admissibility of evidence also present legal issues. Take, however, a party's appeal on the trial judge's decision to deny a motion for a directed verdict. In effect the appellant* is arguing that the evidence was so one-sided that it could only support one conclusion. Therefore, it is argued that the trial judge should have directed the jury to return a given verdict rather than giving them the choice of deliberating on several alternatives. Since it is a ruling on a motion, it is a legal question, but to reach a decision the appellate court must make a judgment about the strength of the evidence itself.

---

*The appellant is the party appealing the decision from the lower court. The party defending the lower court's decision is the appellee.

The appellate court can be drawn into similar evaluations of the facts in circumstances involving motions for judgment notwithstanding the verdict* and motions for a new trial. It should be noted, however, that when the appellate courts do review the facts they do so on a limited basis. Conflicts in the testimony and questions of credibility of the witnesses will be resolved in favor of the trial judge's position. Only where there is a lack of admissible evidence or where the trial judge's decision was clearly erroneous will the appellate courts reverse.

Reversible Error

If the appellate court does decide that the trial judge did make a legal error it must determine whether that error was prejudicial or merely harmless. Errors are defined as prejudicial when they likely affected the results. Harmless errors are classed as so minor and peripheral that they have no significant effect on the outcome. Only prejudicial errors are considered to be reversible errors.

Errors in the pleadings are usually considered to be harmless because the true facts can be emphasized at the trial. Errors in jury instructions are only considered reversible when there is reason to believe the jury may have been misled by them. It is also generally assumed that a judge presiding at a bench trial is less likely to be affected by incompetent evidence than a jury exposed to the same incompetent evidence.

In another aspect of the reversible error, the attorney who is appealing cannot be responsible for the error that is being appealed. In other words, the appellant cannot complain about the admission of inflammatory evidence if the appellant's attorney was the one who introduced it.†

---

*This motion asks the judge to reverse a jury's decision on the basis that the evidence was legally insufficient to support its verdict. This motion is also referred to as a Motion for a Judgment N.O.V. (*non obstante verdicto*), which means, literally, notwithstanding the verdict of the jury.

†An exception to this principle could occur in a criminal case where a different attorney is handling the appeal and is charging that the trial attorney's performance was incompetent.

FILING THE APPEAL

Once the decision to appeal has been made, the paralegal can promptly prepare a notice of appeal. Figure 10.1 presents an example. While the notice must be written and must contain specified information, there is usually no special format. The notice is filed in the trial court which rendered the decision being appealed and the most significant aspect is that it must be filed within some rather restrictive time limits.*

As soon as the notice of appeal has been filed, the paralegal should contact the court reporter and the court clerk to order appropriate portions of the official record. The court reporter is then instructed to prepare a written transcript of either selected portions or the entire trial† and the court clerk is asked to prepare copies of various official court records relating to the case. This request is often referred to as a praecipe‡ for record. Figure 10.2 shows a commonly used format for this request. The specific records ordered will depend on the nature of the case and the specific rules of the appellate court.

Either the paralegal or some other representative of the firm must, on behalf of the client, pay a filing fee with the appellate court and quite possibly file one or more bonds. In the federal courts, for example, the appellant must post a bond (usually $250) to secure payment of the costs on appeal. If the appellant wants to stay the judgment pending the outcome of the appeal, a supersedeas bond must be filed back in the trial court.§

---

*See discussion on page 358. Note that time limits and deadlines are very important not only at the filing stage but throughout the entire appellate process.

†Federal rules provide that "Unless the entire transcript is to be included, the appellant shall within the time above provided, file and serve upon the appellee a description of the parts of the transcript which he intends to include in the record and a statement of the issues he intends to present on the appeal." Federal Rules Appellate Procedure 10(b). The appellee can then order additional sections.

‡A praecipe is a formal request that the clerk take some action. Unlike a motion, it does not require a judge's approval.

§When the court stays a judgment, it permits the party who owed the judgment to withhold paying it until the appellate court has had an opportunity to review it. The bond provides a guarantee to the person to whom the judgment is owed that the money (plus interest) will be paid if either the appeal is dismissed or the judgment is affirmed.

FIGURE 10.1
Notice of Appeal

APPEAL TO THE APPELLATE COURT OF ILLINOIS
FOURTH DISTRICT
From the Circuit Court of the Eleventh Judicial Circuit,
McLean County

EMMA M. RENSLOW, as mother
and next friend of LEAH ANN
RENSLOW, a minor,
                    Plaintiff,

            vs   AT LAW NO. 75 L 8

MENNONITE HOSPITAL, a corporation, and HANS STROINK, M.D.,
                    Defendants.

NOTICE OF APPEAL

EMMA M. RENSLOW, as mother and next friend of LEAH ANN RENSLOW,
a minor, hereby appeals to the Appellate Court of Illinois, Fourth District,
from the Order of the Trial Court entered in this cause on June 4, 1975, sup-
plementing a previous Order of said Court dated May 5, 1975, dismissing
Counts VI through X of the original Complaint filed herein, and requests the
Appellate Court to reverse the decision of the Trial Court and direct the Trial
Court to sustain the Complaint as to Counts VI through X, and overrule or
deny the Motion of the Defendants to Dismiss the original Complaint, Counts
VI through X.

EMMA M. RENSLOW, as mother and
next friend of LEAH ANN RENSLOW,
a minor,
Plaintiffs

BY ___*Robert C. Strodel*___

One of Their Attorneys

ROBERT C. STRODEL
LAW OFFICES OF STRODEL & KINGERY, ASSOC.
900 First National Bank Building
Peoria, Illinois 61602
Phone: (309) 676-3612

FIGURE 10.2
Praecipe for Record (A Request to Clerk for the Official Record)

APPEAL TO THE APPELLATE COURT OF ILLINOIS
FOURTH DISTRICT
From the Circuit Court of the Eleventh Judicial Circuit,
McLean County

EMMA M. RENSLOW, as mother
and next friend of LEAH ANN
RENSLOW, a minor,

              Plaintiff,

vs   AT LAW NO. 75 L 8

MENNONITE HOSPITAL, a corporation, and HANS STROINK, M.D.,
              Defendants.

PRAECIPE FOR RECORD

TO: The Circuit Clerk of McLean County, Illinois
     McLean County Court House
     Bloomington, Illinois

You are hereby requested to prepare and make up a complete transcript of the record in your court in the above-entitled cause as to Counts VI through X inclusive to be used on Appeal to the Appellate Court of Illinois, Fourth District, including a placita for each term of court, all pleadings, all Orders, all papers of record, the Notice of Appeal and Proof of Service thereof, this Praecipe and Proof of Service thereof, and all Motions, Orders, and stipulations that may have been made relative to the preparation of said record, together with your certificate that the same is a complete transcript of all proceedings had in your court in said cause.

DATED this first day of July, 1975.

LAW OFFICES OF STRODEL &
KINGERY, ASSOC.

BY *Robert C. Strodel*

ROBERT C. STRODEL

ROBERT C. STRODEL
LAW OFFICES OF STRODEL & KINGERY, ASSOC.
900 First National Bank Building
Peoria, Illinois 61602
Phone: (309) 676-3612

PREPARING THE APPELLATE BRIEF

While there are minor variations from one court system to another, Figure 10.3 presents an overview of the various elements usually included in an appellate brief as well as the order in which they appear. Rather than examining the elements as they appear in the final product, this section shall instead discuss the elements in the order of preparation.

Digesting or Abstracting the Record

Since the appeal is based on the record of the case, it is essential that both the attorney and the paralegal be thoroughly familiar with all aspects of the pleadings and motions as well as the tran-

FIGURE 10.3
Composition of an Appellate Brief

COVER PAGE

TABLE OF CONTENTS
(Usually included only in longer, more complex briefs)

TABLE OF AUTHORITIES CITED
(Sometimes combined with a summary of the main points of the argument and labeled "Points and Authorities")

JURISDICTIONAL STATEMENT
(Designation of the type of action and the courts that are involved)

STATEMENT OF THE ISSUES PRESENTED

STATUTES INVOLVED
(Quotation of statutes or sections of statutes that are being interpreted)

STATEMENT OF THE FACTS

ARGUMENTS PRESENTED
(If the argument is complex, it should begin with a brief summary and then be divided into several parts)

CONCLUSIONS

APPENDICES
(Relevant excerpts from the record are placed in these appendices)

FIGURE 10.4
Sample Entries from a Digest of the Record

Testimony Related to Defendant Black's Alleged Failure to Hear Sgt. Leary's Dispersal Order

Sgt. Leary, in a "loud voice," gave an order for the demonstrators to leave the area.
Leary's Direct R-6

Sgt. Leary was not over 20 feet away from the demonstrators when he gave the order.
Leary's Direct R-10

Black did not hear Leary's dispersal order.
Black's Direct R-356

Lynn Allen, who was standing next to Black, did not hear Leary's, or anyone else's dispersal order.
Allen's Direct R-310

Suzanne Little, who was near Black, did not hear Sgt. Leary's dispersal order.
S. Little's Direct R-258

Testimony Related to Defendant Black's Arrest

---

script of the trial. This familiarity is best achieved by having the paralegal digest or abstract the record.*

The digesting process involves compilation of summaries of key parts of the record and indexing where in the record they appear. This digesting familiarizes the paralegal with contents of the documents and facilitates quick reference to original sources.

Several techniques can be used in preparing this type of digest. The most thorough one involves recording a summary for each distinct item on separate note cards. These cards can be arranged so that all allegations or testimony about a single fact can be

---

*An abstract of the record is a summary of its contents. The paralegal takes each section in order of appearance and summarizes the essential material. A digest involves not only summarizing the material but classifying and rearranging it.

Sgt. Little and several county officers tried to "move Black along." Black was holding onto a telephone pole.

Sgt. Little's Direct R-105

The county police were already restraining Black when Sgt. Little arrived.

Sgt. Little's Cross R-113 and 114

Sgt. Little did not give Black a dispersal order.

Sgt. Little's Cross R-122

Black was not given a chance to move on while Sgt. Little was there.

Sgt. Little's Cross R-114

Black was approached by a group of officers who ordered him to get off the street and move onto the sidewalk.

Black's Direct R-370
Allen's Direct R-314

Following the order to get off the street, an officer told Black to "move on." When Black asked where he was supposed to move to, he was grabbed by two officers.

Black's Direct R-370
Allen's Direct R-328 and 329

---

catalogued together regardless of where the pleadings or testimony appear.[5] Figure 10.4 provides an example of part of such a digest. The record being digested comes from a criminal trial in which Black and four other defendants had been charged with obstructing a peace officer by not obeying his order to disperse during a demonstration at a county jail.

Identifying the Issues

Prior to deciding to go ahead with the appeal, the attorney carefully considers the issues that form the basis of the appeal. A careful analysis of the digested record sharpens the focus of those issues and may lead to the discovery of additional issues.

The issues presented must relate to legitimately debatable

points. It is a waste to include frivolous issues that have no reasonable basis for support. The presentation of such groundless issues tends to weaken the brief's credibility.

On the other hand, it is a good policy to raise issues involved in fallback positions. In other words a brief can raise secondary issues for the court to consider if it rules against the primary issue. For example, one issue can assert that a supposed contract was not valid because there was a lack of adequate consideration. The next issue can then assert that the contract should be interpreted in such a way as to favor one's client's position. Also, one issue might assert a right of recovery based on a breach of contract theory while the next issue might be based on negligence.

Once the paralegal has a clear understanding of the issues the attorney intends to raise, one can proceed to draft the statement of the issues presented and then prepare the statement of the facts. Figure 10.5 presents examples of the issue statements from two different cases. *People v. Black* is the criminal case that was used in Figure 10.4. The appeal is designed to reverse the convictions of defendants Robert Reyes and Peter Black. *Astor v. Curry* is an appeal from a summary judgment in a civil case. Tim and Kassandra Astor had signed an agreement to purchase a mobile home through monthly installments. The home was located in a mobile home park operated by the seller. The trial judge had ruled that a key paragraph in the contract was properly interpreted as a month-to-month lease. Note that the issues are phrased in terms of the factual situations involved in each case.

FIGURE 10.5
Issues Presented for Review

People v. Black
1. Whether the evidence failed, as a matter of law, to establish that the Defendant, Robert Reyes, knowingly resisted or obstructed Sergeant Leary's order to disperse.
2. Whether the evidence failed, as a matter of law, to establish that the Defendant, Peter Black, knowingly resisted or obstructed Sergeant Leary's order to disperse.

Astor v. Curry
   Whether the Court erred in interpreting the Agreement as a matter of law and granting Summary Judgment upon that interpretation.

The paralegal should seek to present the issues so that they persuasively suggest the answer which favors the client's position.

Presenting the Facts

The facts of the case can be divided into two categories. One relates to the events which created the original dispute while the other reports the nature of the legal action taken and its outcome in the lower courts. Many brief formats start (after the cover page, table of contents, and so on) with a concise summary of the legal history of the case. This type of summary is sometimes called the jurisdictional statement because it establishes that the case falls within the jurisdiction of the appellate court where it was filed. Figure 10.6 shows examples of these sections from the same cases involved in Figure 10.5. Note how one has been summarized in three sentences, while the nature of the other case requires three paragraphs.

The summary of the legal history is usually quite straightforward and relatively easy to prepare. Much more skill is involved in preparing the statement of facts. This section seeks to summarize the various factual contentions involved in the legal action. Figure 10.7 shows an excerpt from the statement of facts in the *People v. Black* case. Obviously one wants to portray the facts in a manner most favorable to the client's position. While the writer should not ignore central facts unfavorable to the client, the amount of emphasis given to them and the nature of supporting materials can be persuasive.

Although the facts are usually presented in chronological sequence, there are times when the writer may wish to use a different pattern. Often a writer presents the most favorable materials first to capture the reader's initial sympathies.

Presentation of these facts should incorporate reference to the official record. The author should include a reference to the appropriate page number of the record showing when the fact in question was presented in court. To avoid breaking up the style, this documentation is provided by including the appropriate page numbers from the record in parentheses at the end of the sentence, as shown in Figure 10.7. When the facts are in dispute, the summary should reflect their disputed status.

While there are times when it is appropriate to include an exact

FIGURE 10.6
Sample Nature of the Case or Jurisdictional Statements

People v. Black

This is an appeal from a jury verdict finding the Defendants, Robert Reyes, Peter R. Black, and Harry Brent DeLand, guilty of a violation of chapter 38, section 31-1 of the *Illinois Revised Statutes*. In the same trial, Robert Sutherland and David Nelson were found not guilty by the jury. No question is raised on the pleadings.

Astor v. Curry

This is an appeal from trial court's order granting defendant-appellant's motion for summary judgment as to Count I of plaintiff-appellant's amended complaint. The trial court found as a matter of law that the only reasonable interpretation was that paragraph five of the written agreement was a lease from month to month and defeated plaintiff's claim. The court found no just reason to delay enforcement or appeal.

This cause involves an action brought by plaintiff-appellant TIM and KASSANDRA ASTOR, to recover from the defendant DAVID CURRY, money paid by the plaintiff to the defendant. The money represents the amortized amount of a contract for the purchase of a mobile home plus the amount expended for improvements to that mobile home. The case involves the interpretation and construction of a clause of the contract.

The defendant has not denied plaintiff's amended verified complaint nor submitted any affidavits to contradict any of the terms of plaintiff's complaint nor attacked the substance of plaintiff's complaint. The trial court granted summary judgment for defendant-appellee holding that clause five (5) of the contract constituted a month-to-month lease as a matter of law and could be terminated prior to the termination of the contract. The trial court entered judgment for the defendant-appellee and against the plaintiff-appellant as to Count One (I) of plaintiff's amended complaint.

---

quotation from someone's testimony or from some portion of a document, it should be done quite sparingly. It is generally better to paraphrase the item and let the judges read it directly from the record.

Developing the Argument

The argument section attempts to interpret both the meaning of the law and the extent to which that law is applicable to the facts of the case. A good argument skillfully combines analysis of the

FIGURE 10.7
Excerpt from the Statement of Facts

STATEMENT OF FACTS

On Sunday afternoon November 3, 1974, a group of people gathered in the vicinity of the McLean County Jail for a demonstration and protest against McLean County Sheriff John King. A large contingent of police from Bloomington, Normal, and the McLean County Sheriff's office were present to maintain order during the demonstration.

Sergeant Michael Leary of the Bloomington Police Department was in charge of a thirty-man police squad which was originally held in reserve at a secluded spot until approximately 2:45 P.M. (R-4) Responding to requests from his superiors, Sergeant Leary moved his squad to the county jail to prevent the demonstration from "getting out of hand." (R-4) When Sergeant Leary and his squad arrived at the McLean County Jail, he observed a group of about one hundred persons, some of whom were "more or less jeering and harassing" the police officers who were in position around the jail. (R-5) Police officer Bobby Friga, who had been stationed in the alley beside the jail for at least two hours prior to the arrival of Sergeant Leary, estimated the number of demonstrators as "approximately forty-five." (R-76) Officer Bob Little, who was also present at the scene, estimated the group at "eighty, maybe one hundred people" and agreed that there was a lot of shouting and jeering. (R-103)

At this point, Sergeant Leary testified that he ordered his police officers to form a line. (R-6) He then ordered the demonstrators to disperse and leave the area in a "loud voice." (R-6) Although other orders given to the demonstrators at a later time by Sergeant Leary were given over a bullhorn, Sergeant Leary admits that this first order was not given over the bullhorn. (R-10) Sergeant Leary testified that the demonstrators were not over twenty feet away from him when he gave the order. (R-6)

Without any further orders to the demonstrators, Sergeant Leary ordered his police line to move forward. (R-7) As the police line started to move forward, Sergeant Leary stated that some of the demonstrators fell down. (R-7) Members of Sergeant Leary's police squad tried to get the fallen demonstrators up and "move them along." (R-8) Right in the area where some of the demonstrators had fallen, "one subject turned and came back toward the line." (R-7) Sergeant Leary testified that the subject came back toward the police line to "counter the officer" but no further testimony was forthcoming from Sergeant Leary to describe any actions or conduct of the subject. (R-8) Sergeant Leary next testified that he grabbed the subject and told other officers to take him to the paddy wagon. (R-8) This subject was the Defendant Robert Reyes.

(Continued)

FIGURE 10.7 — Continued

The actual officer making the arrest of Robert Reyes was Bloomington Police Officer Bobby Friga. Officer Friga testified that Sergeant Leary "more or less pointed to a subject [Robert Reyes]" and told him to "arrest this guy." (R-79) While Officer Friga testified that Robert Reyes was arrested because he refused to leave the area, he admitted during cross-examination that he personally did not observe Robert Reyes do anything which would cause him to be selected by Sergeant Leary for arrest. (R-86)

---

facts in the record with an interpretation of relevant statutes, cases, and constitutional provisions. Digesting the record familiarizes the paralegal with the facts, while the legal research and analysis techniques discussed in Part Three provide the basis for interpreting the law.

The argument section of the brief should be divided into subsections that correspond to the issues defined in the "Issues Presented" section. Each of these subsections should begin with a single-sentence summary of the main point. It should be a restatement of the issue involved in the form of a statement rather than question. The statement should be phrased to favor the client's position and typed in capital letters. Moreover, it is usually wise to further subdivide these issue arguments with similar capitalized lead sentences. This subdivision scheme makes the argument easier to follow and increases its impact. Since these capitalized headings are so important, the writer should spend time revising and tightening them for maximum impact.

When the interpretation of the record is involved, the writer should highlight those sections which favor the client's position. This type of argument is directed at persuading the appellate court to accept the reasonableness of a particular interpretation. Figure 10.8 provides an example of how this approach was used in Black's brief.

At other times, the argument will focus on interpretation of a particular case, statute, or constitutional provision. In these cases the paralegal must utilize the techniques discussed in chapters 5 and 6. If a statute or constitutional provision is involved, one should utilize the plain meaning, legislative history, and contextual analysis approaches to build as strong an argument as possible. If case law is involved, one should emphasize

FIGURE 10.8
Example of an Argument Centering on Interpretation of the Facts

THE EVIDENCE FAILED, AS A MATTER OF LAW, TO ESTABLISH THAT THE
DEFENDANT PETER BLACK KNOWINGLY RESISTED OR OBSTRUCTED
SERGEANT LEARY'S ORDER TO DISPERSE

. . .

The entire evidence put forward by the State against Peter Black consists
of the testimony of Officer Bobbie Little. On direct examination, Officer Little
stated that as Sergeant Leary's police line moved northward on Roosevelt
Street, "we came in contact with a gentleman that refused to leave the area."
(R-105) The following dialogue between the Assistant State's Attorney and
Officer Little represents his description of the "contact" and the arrest:

[At this point the brief quotes verbatim from a section of Officer Little's testimony.]

Cross-examination of Officer Little probed the circumstances of the arrest
in more detail. Officer Little admitted that when he came up to Peter Black,
"Mr. Black was already being confronted by two or three county policemen at
this time." (R-113) Officer Little also admitted that the county policemen already had their hands on Peter Black, preventing him from any movement.
(R-114) Officer Little further testified that he had no conversation with the Defendant other than telling him that he was under arrest. (R-122)

The "county policemen" were not called as witnesses to testify against
Peter Black or identified by name. Yet, these county police officers are crucial
to the sufficiency of the State's burden of proving that Peter Black was guilty
of obstructing the orders of Sergeant Leary.

. . .

All three defense witnesses who testified regarding the arrest of Peter
Black explain the incident in similar terms. Peter Black testified that he did
not hear any order to disperse. (R-356) He also testified that he did not hear
any police officer giving orders over a bullhorn. (R-355) In this respect, Peter's testimony is entirely consistent with Sergeant Leary, who admitted that
he did not use a bullhorn to give the initial order to disperse. The Defendant
further testified that he was approached by a group of officers who told him
to move. (R-357) In response, the Defendant asked them where he was supposed to move. (R-357) One of the police officers also told Peter to get off the
street. (R-357) Peter stated that he moved off the street (Roosevelt Street)
onto the sidewalk on the grassy area between the curb and the sidewalk. (R-
369) He was then told by another police officer to move. (R-369) Peter Black
then testified that he again asked "move where?" (R-370) He further stated
that the verbal exchange between the group of police officers, presumably

(Continued)

FIGURE 10.8 — Continued

the "county policemen" referred to by Officer Little, lasted "ten or fifteen seconds at the most." (R-359)

The testimony of Lynn Allen, who was standing with Peter Black, is consistent. She testified that she did not hear any order to disperse. (R-310) She also testified that a group of police officers came up to them and told them to get on the sidewalk. (R-314) She and Peter Black asked the police officers what they were supposed to do. (R-328) Lynn also testified that the police officers pushed them with their clubs shortly before the police officers grabbed Peter Black. (R-328) Lynn further testified that after the police officers grabbed Peter Black he held onto the telephone pole. (R-316)

The testimony of Suzanne Little, who was standing with Peter Black and Lynn Allen, is consistent in all material aspects to the other defense testimony. Suzanne testified that the police officers who approached them told them to get off the street and move on. (R-292) She further testified that Peter Black was talking to the police officers and asking them why they had to move since they were on public property. (R-292)

It is important to note that the testimony presented by the defense witnesses indicates that Peter Black questioned the police officers and asked them why and where he should move. The Supreme Court has stated that mere argument with a policeman about the validity of an arrest or other police action does not constitute resisting or obstructing within the proscription of the statute. *People v. Roby*, 49 Ill. 2d 392, 240 N.E. 2d 595, Cert. denied 393 U.S. 1083 (1968). Officer Little testified that Peter Black was "unwilling to move" and "refused to leave the area." However, he admits that other police officers had already detained Peter when he arrived. He also admits that he had no conversation with the Defendant other than to tell him he was under arrest. None of the other police officers testified against Peter.

In summary, the evidence against Peter Black taken in its totality does not prove that the Defendant knowingly resisted or obstructed Sergeant Leary's order to disperse.

the extent to which factual situations involved in favorable cases are analogous to facts of the case being appealed. When cases are unfavorable one should emphasize the extent to which the situations are not analogous. One must remember also the difference between mandatory authority and persuasive authority.

Figure 10.9 provides examples of analogizing to a favorable case and distinguishing unfavorable ones. It is taken from the Defendant-Appellant's brief in the case of *Falco v. Bates*. The police had been holding a friend of Bates (named Wallraven) and

FIGURE 10.9
Examples of Arguments Centering on Interpretation of Precedent Cases

Interpreting a Favorable Precedent

> A VALID CONSIDERATION OR AN ESTOPPEL CANNOT BE FOUNDED UPON CIRCUMSTANCES THAT SHOW THE USE OF CRIMINAL PROCESSES TO COLLECT A PRIVATE INDEBTEDNESS.

Clearly, the plaintiff initiated the actions which resulted in the apprehension of Wallraven and his request for help. The record shows that the defendant, Bates, was the second party who gave a check to Wallraven while he was in the custody of a police officer. The law is quite clear on the use of the criminal process in obtaining payment of private indebtedness. The principle is examined in *Shenk v. Phelps,* 6 Ill. App. 612 (1880). *Shenk v. Phelps* presents a case with a fact situation similar to the case at bar. The appellant's son had obtained credit through false statements. A warrant for the arrest of Mr. Shenk's son was procured and the arrest was made by a deputized detective working for the creditor. The accused was not taken before the justice of the peace who issued the warrant, but held at the office of the detective agency. He was released upon Shenk's promise to pay the funds fraudulently obtained by his son. Shenk was sued on the note when he refused to pay. The court reversed a decision for the creditor, ruling that the consideration for the note constituted compounding a crime and was therefore void.

The Shenk court's ruling that the plaintiff's instructions to the jury were improper is instructive. The creditor offered the following instruction:

> If the jury find from the evidence that the defendant executed the note in question, knowing at the time of the execution of the same that he was executing a note, and for the amount, and payable as shown by the same, that he voluntarily assumed the debt or debts of his son, and understood the effect of what he was doing, and if the jury find from the evidence, that the consideration for said note, as between the plaintiffs and defendant, was the assignment to said defendant of the accounts against his son, and they were so assigned, and that at the time of the giving of said note, the defendant had notes due the said son in his possession or control, then the assigning of said accounts was a good and valid consideration, and the jury should find for the defendants.

The court continued:

> All that is said in this instruction may have been true and still the plaintiffs would not be entitled to recover if the jury further believed from the evidence that the defendant was induced to execute the note by an illegal use of the criminal process. *Shenk v. Phelps*, 6 Ill. App. 618 (1880).

(Continued)

FIGURE 10.9 — Continued

The court addressed directly the issue of equitable estoppel:

> The court (below) seems to have worked the principle of an equitable estoppel in order to give effect to a contract tainted with illegality. It was, in effect, saying the plaintiff has procured the execution of a contract by illegal means, and through an abuse of the criminal process of the State: but because the defendant has not returned so much of the consideration as he actually received, the plaintiff shall have a verdict. The cases are numerous to the effect that where a contract is void on the ground of public policy or against a statute, any attempt to enforce it will fail whenever the illegality appears — and the circumstances that one party has failed to perform his part of the agreement cannot operate as a waiver of such illegality. *Shenk v. Phelps*, 6 Ill. App. 619 (1880).

Distinguishing an Unfavorable Precedent

THE AFFIRMATIVE DEFENSE OF COMPOUNDING A CRIME DOES NOT HAVE TO BE PROVEN BEYOND A REASONABLE DOUBT IN ALL CASES.

The contention that when a defense of compounding a crime is tendered the crime of compounding must be proven beyond a reasonable doubt must be dealt with. *Zimmerman Ford, Inc. v. Cheney*, 132 Ill. App. 2d 871, 271 N.E. 2d 686 (1971); *Rudolph Stecher Brewing Co. v. Carr*, 194 Ill. App. 32 (1915); *Germania Fire Ins. Co. v. Klewer*, 129 Ill. 612 (1889); *Grimes v. Hilliary*, 150 Ill. 141 (1894).

In *Zimmerman Ford, Inc. v. Cheney*, a grandmother of a youthful purchaser of an automobile claimed lack of consideration for her co-signature because she thought her signing would prevent prosecution of the buyer. Her grandson had forged her original signature in order to purchase the automobile. She signed a replacement contract. Indicating that there was a sufficient consideration in the forbearance in repossessing the automobile to support the action on the grandmother's signature, the court stated:

> Plaintiff was solely interested in recovering its loss and bargained for that purpose. She only thought it would prevent prosecution which is distinguishable in legal effect from finding that a creditor has promised to forbear from prosecuting a crime.
>
> Moreover, proof has to be beyond a reasonable doubt: *Rudolph Stecher Brewing Co. v. Carr*, 194 Ill. App. 32, 37 (1915).

In the Stecher case the defendant, Carr, had endorsed a check that his client, Sarafin, presented to his creditor at the preliminary court proceeding against Sarafin, who had received $502 in goods from the creditor through a so-called confidence scheme. Sarafin was then admitted to personal recognizance bond and proceeded to stop payment on the check. Carr was sued as the endorser and tendered the defense of compounding of a crime. The suit was on the common counts alleging the delivery of goods. Noting the emphatic denial of the defendant's charge by the plaintiff and corroboration of the plaintiff's testimony the court stated this rule:

> We think that the law is well settled in this state that where the defense of compounding a crime is relied upon to defeat the plaintiff's action that then the burden is upon the defendant to prove the criminal offense alleged beyond a reasonable doubt, and that it is not sufficient that it be proven by a preponderance of the evidence. *Germania Fire Ins. Co. v. Klewer*, 129 Ill. 599; *Grimes v. Hilliary*, 150 Ill. 146. *Rudolph Stecher Brewing Co. v. Carr*, 194 Ill. 34.

. . .

It is important to note that the criminal act alleged in Germania, relied upon by the Stecher court, is quite different from the compounding of a crime. In Germania the act of burning down a building was alleged to defeat a claim on an insurance policy. That seems to be a more substantive crime, and, the allegation and proof of it of greater consequence, than an agreement between two parties to a suit to drop a criminal prosecution. Proof of the crime defeats the entire contractual obligation. In the present case, the defense of compounding a crime does not defeat the underlying obligation. Wallraven still owes Falco. Clearly, when one party emphatically denies the compounding agreement, very likely a secretive affair, the extraordinary burden of proof would be impossible to achieve, making the defense practically useless. Illinois law has, in fact, despite the above cases, not followed this rule; most such cases, as the one at bar, are distinguishable from the harsh rule of Zimmerman and Stecher. It will be found that the cases requiring proof beyond a reasonable doubt of the crime offered as defense to a contractual action have these things in common:

1. There is a clear contractual liability which but for the criminal act would be owing.
2. The wrong-doer himself is a party to the note or security in issue.
3. There is an alternative consideration upon which to base recovery.
4. There is no other public policy reason for denying recovery.

Applying these distinguishing characteristics to the Zimmerman case, for example, it can be seen:

1. That there was clearly an outstanding debt owing on the automobile sold by plaintiff to the defendant's grandson;

(Continued)

FIGURE 10.9 — Continued

---

2. That the grandmother became a co-signer for the grandson after she ratified her forged signature;
3. That consideration existed in the plaintiff's forbearing to repossess the automobile;
4. That no public policy issue was raised aside from the sole issue of compounding.

. . .

Thus it appears that there are more basic equitable and public policy reasons for the court to grant or deny recovery in the compounding cases and that the plaintiff cannot find much refuge in the few cases stating that proof beyond a reasonable doubt is required before a defense of compounding a crime can be sustained.

---

had threatened to arrest this friend if he failed to pay a motel bill he owed to the Falco corporation. Bates had written a check to the motel on the basis of the friend's promise to repay him the next morning and the police had then released the friend. When Wallraven did not pay him the money, Bates stopped payment. The corporation then sued Bates. The trial court found in Falco's favor and Bates appealed.

While the brief should provide adequate documentation of its assertion of legal principles, the writer should not overdo in this. When widely accepted general legal principles are stated, two or three case citations are quite adequate. If they are truly widely recognized, they are unlikely to be contested and need no further documentation. When the principle is more likely to be contested, the brief should emphasize more recent cases and those which are mandatory authority. Where persuasive authority is involved, it is better to cite cases from several different jurisdictions than to include only a long list of cases from the same jurisdiction.

When a citation follows the statement of a legal principle, it is assumed that the holding of that case supports the principle stated. If the principle being referred to or the quotation being used represents dictum* or comes from a concurring or dissenting opinion, it should be identified as such in parentheses following the citation. For example:

*It is a comment not essential to the decision of the case at hand.

National League of Cities v. Usery, 426 U.S. 833, 860 (1976) (Brennan, J., dissenting).

means that the quotation or principle appears on page 860 of Mr. Justice Brennan's dissenting opinion.

Moose Lodge No. 107 v. Irvis, 407 U.S. 163, 169 (1972) (dictum)

means that the principle enunciated on that page was a form of dictum. If the holding of a case is not clear, the word *semble* should be placed in parentheses after the cite. If the holding of the case being cited is contrary to the principle being presented, its citation should be introduced by the *contra* or *but see.* The term *cf.* means that while it is not a direct holding, the case is somewhat analogous and that it does offer some support for the principle being cited.

The brief may also emphasize probable impact as part of its argument. If a decision against the client will have an impact on a larger group of people, that should be emphasized in the brief. Where possible the brief should argue that justice and fairness require a decision supporting the client and that such a decision is consistent with the general public interest. This type of social consequences argument was made in the appellant's brief in the mobile home case. Part of that argument is included in Figure 10.10.

Summing It Up

After the argument has been drafted, revised, tightened, and still further revised, the paralegal should begin work on the conclusion section. This section consists of a concise summary of the nature of errors that were made by the lower court and a request that the appellate court take some specific action to change the lower court's decision. Sample conclusions are included in Figure 10.11.

Table of Authorities

Most appellate courts require some type of summary of the legal authorities cited in the brief. One common format lists all con-

FIGURE 10.10

Example of Argument Centering on a Sense of Equity and General Concerns of Public Policy

A further policy consideration must be made. The defendant was not only the seller of the mobile home but the lessor. If the lessor is permitted to represent to purchasers that they can live at the mobile home court until the agreement is paid in full, but later evicts them, the purchaser may be forced to not only remove himself, but be faced with the costly removal of a mobile home. Worse yet, the purchaser may be required to move his person without being allowed to remove the mobile home, resulting in a forfeiture of his rights under the purchase agreement. In the instant case, the seller violated a health statute requiring adequate supplies of water and constructively evicted prior to the actual eviction. Should the seller-lessor be allowed to profit from his wrongdoing? The seller could gain both the payments and the mobile home by simply evicting the purchaser, forcing the purchaser to find a new site for the mobile home and paying transportation costs, a burden which the purchaser may not be able to pay.

In the instant case, the purchaser paid all sums when due, and was not in default under the provisions of the agreement. The case might be different if the purchaser were in default under the lease or the principal payments. In this case, the seller-landlord received all payments, rents, and the mobile home. Seller-landlord has counterclaimed for the balance of the purchase price.

A decision in favor of defendant-appellee would work a serious hardship on purchasers of mobile homes. Since many of these homes are located in mobile home parks, and it is believed that seller-landlord relationships as in this case are not uncommon, purchasers will be left to the mercy of landlord-sellers who may control the environment in such a manner as to constructively evict contract purchasers, thus reselling the same chattel. If the vendees are unable to recover the amortization and improvements upon the chattel a seller-landlord may be able to unjustly enrich himself at the cost of the innocent purchasers.

The situation becomes acute, with the lack of legal remedies available in this relatively new area of single family dwelling. If the plaintiff had purchased a house without the land, choosing to rent the land, and the seller committed acts which interfered with vendee's rights as a tenant and in fact evicted the tenant and told him to remove (or not remove) the house, would the vendee have any remedy? This situation could easily arise in a commercial setting where complex tax laws favor leasing of non-depreciable assets (such as a building). There is no evidence that a "mobile" home is any more or less mobile than a small building, and, indeed, an older mobile home may be more difficult to move than a well-constructed building.

FIGURE 10.11
Examples of Conclusion Sections

People v. Black
   The evidence against both Defendants was insufficient as a matter of law to prove that the Defendants were guilty of a violation of Chapter 38, section 31-1 of the *Illinois Revised Statutes.* The convictions should therefore be reversed. At the least, judgment should be reversed and the Defendants granted a new trial.

Falco v. Bates
   The plaintiff claims that the defendant must pay the motel bill of a former customer because it accepted a check from the defendant in payment of that debt and in reliance thereon allowed the customer to leave its premises. All the testimony showed that the debtor was brought to plaintiff's premises by an officer of the local police department. In asserting that consideration for the check was the release of the debtor the plaintiff admits use of the criminal process in securing payment of a private indebtedness which violates the clear public policy of the State of Illinois. Having tendered no evidence of an alternative consideration or justification of the method of obtaining custody over its debtor, the plaintiff's action against the defendant must fail for voidness of the consideration and the decision of the lower court granting recovery to the plaintiff be reversed.

---

stitutional provisions, statutes, cases, and other types of authorities under generalized categories. In this system all the citations to federal constitutional provisions are grouped together. Federal statutes are cited in one group while state statutes are cited in another section. Municipal ordinances are grouped in still another category. Similarly, Supreme Court cases are separated from Circuit Court of Appeals decisions, and state cases are grouped by state. References to law review articles, encyclopedias, and other sources are grouped under a miscellaneous references section.

   Within each category the provisions of the constitutions and statutes are arranged according to the order in which they appear in the constitution itself or in the code. Court opinions, on the other hand, are usually arranged within each subcategory by alphabetical order. The citations should be accurate and complete. While United States Supreme Court cases are only cited to the official *United States Reports*, state decisions should include ref-

erence to the unofficial and official citations.* This table of authorities should then provide cross-references back to the pages of
the brief on which each citation appears. This allows the reader to
turn directly to all discussions of any particular case or statute.

As an alternative to the table just described, some appellate
courts require that the citations be arranged on the basis of sub-
points of the argument which they support. This approach was
used in the appellant's brief in *Falco v. Bates* in Figure 10.12.

When statutes or provisions of the constitution are involved,
some courts also require that the brief reproduce the text of the
specific provisions in question. When such Statutes Involved
sections are required, they are usually located at the front, near
the Authorities section.

Assembling Appendices, Table of Contents

The appellant's brief will usually include several appendices of
various supporting documents. Typically included are parts of the
pleadings, sections of the trial transcript, exhibits introduced as
evidence, and jury instructions. These materials should be arranged in a logical order and then given consecutive numbers
that tie in with the brief itself.

Depending on the court involved, the paralegal may also be
asked to prepare a table of contents. Such a table provides an
overview of the entire document and easy reference to specific
parts. It should include references to the pages on which the main
sections begin (i.e., issues presented, statement of facts) and the
subdivisions of the argument section. This will provide the judges
with a good overview of the structure of the argument itself
(much as a table of points and authorities does).

Preparation of the Cover Sheet

The one remaining section of an appellate brief is the cover page.
Here again, the brief must be carefully prepared to meet the

---

*This occurs because official state reporters are usually not readily
available to persons in other states. The judges and other attorneys are
most likely to be consulting West's regional reporters.

FIGURE 10.12
Excerpts from a Points and Authorities Section

THE AFFIRMATIVE DEFENSE OF COMPOUNDING A CRIME DOES NOT HAVE TO BE PROVEN BEYOND A REASONABLE DOUBT IN ALL CASES.

Zimmerman Ford, Inc. v. Cheney, 132 Ill. App. 2d 871, 271 N.E. 2d 682 (1971).

Rudolph Stecher Brewing Co. v. Carr, 194 Ill. App. 32 (1915).

Germania Fire Ins. Co. v. Klewer, 129 Ill. 612 (1889).

Grimes v. Hilliary, 150 Ill. 141 (1894).

Good Hope State Bank v. Kline, 303 Ill. App. 381, 25 N.E. 2d 425 (1940).

Shenk v. Phelps, 6 Ill. App. 612 (1880).

Williamsen v. Jernberg, 99 Ill. App. 3d 37, 240 N.E. 2d 758 (1968).

IN ASSERTING THE AFFIRMATIVE DEFENSE OF COMPOUNDING A CRIME IT IS NOT NECESSARY TO SHOW AN ACTUAL WRITTEN CHARGE IN THE PROSECUTION WHICH WAS DISMISSED.

Good Hope State Bank v. Kline, 303 Ill. App. 381, 25 N.E. 2d 425 (1940).

AN EQUITABLE ESTOPPEL CANNOT BE APPLIED WHERE THE FACTS SHOW THE PARTY ASSERTING THE ESTOPPEL OBTAINED HIS ADVANTAGE BY ILLEGAL MEANS.

Mills v. Susanka, 394 Ill. 439, 68 N.E. 2d 904 (1946).

Ptaszek v. Konczal, 7 Ill. 2d 145, 130 N.E. 2d 257 (1955).

POLICE CANNOT OBTAIN LAWFUL CUSTODY OF A PERSON EXCEPT AS PRESCRIBED BY STATUTE.

Ill. Rev. Stat., ch. 38, Sec. 107-2.

Ill. Rev. Stat., ch. 38, Sec. 107-6.

Ill. Rev. Stat., ch. 38, Sec. 107-14.

standards of each particular appellate court. In general, the cover page includes the name of the appellate court, the names of the parties, the docket number, the name of the court from which the appeal is coming, and the name and address of the lawyer submitting the brief. It should also contain a clear designation as to whether it is the appellant's or the appellee's brief and whether it is an initial brief or a reply brief. In designating the parties, it is also wise to indicate not only which one is bringing the appeal but which one was the plaintiff or defendant at the trial court level. In

FIGURE 10.13
Cover Sheet for an Illinois Appellate Court *(make up own #.)*

NO. 13444

IN THE
APPELLATE COURT
OF THE
STATE OF ILLINOIS

(this is correct for this assign.)

FOURTH DISTRICT

TIM and KASSANDRA ASTOR,
    Plaintiff-Appellants,

v.

DAVID CURRY,
    Defendant-Appellant.

Appeal from the Circuit Court
of the Eleventh Judicial Circuit
McLean County, Illinois
NO. 77-LM-403 *(# of case in cir. ckt. - make it up.)*
Honorable James A. Knecht
Judge Presiding

BRIEF AND ARGUMENTS OF PLAINTIFF-APPELLANTS *(Def-Appel Statement Brief + Argument)*

JOHN J. PAVLOU
STUDENTS' LEGAL SERVICES
Illinois State University
225 N. University, Suite 200
Normal, Illinois 61761

Attorney for Plaintiff-Appellants

JOHN J. TIELSCH
Of Counsel

* ORAL ARGUMENT REQUESTED

---

some jurisdictions a request for oral argument also appears on the cover sheet. Figure 10.13 shows a typical cover sheet for an Illinois appellate court.

COMPLETION OF THE APPELLATE PROCESS

When the appellant files the required number of copies of the brief with the appellate court, a copy is also sent to the attorney for the appellee who then has a set time limit to file the appellee's brief.

While this brief usually follows the same format as the appellant's brief it need not define the issues or characterize the facts in the same way that the appellate did. While the appellee's argument section should definitely respond to each of the points raised by the appellant, those points do not have to be treated in the same sequential order. The appellee should arrange the points and authorities in the order that will provide for their maximum persuasive impact. Each segment of the brief (cover page, points and authorities, argument, and conclusion) should be started on a separate page.

Up to this point various sections of three different appellant briefs have been used to illustrate various techniques. Figure 10.14 provides a sample appellee's brief. Note that the author of the brief did not include a statement of the facts because he did not disagree with the way they had been stated in the appellant's brief. Defendant Dennis Hale had been charged with the offense of aggravated battery in violation of section 12-4(b)(6) of the Illinois criminal code. The trial court judge had dismissed the charges on the basis that the information* failed to allege either the offense of aggravated battery or simple battery. The information in question had specifically charged that Hale had "willfully, unlawfully and knowingly without legal justification, made physical contact of an insulting and provoking nature with Elijah Rusk, by striking him with his fist, knowing said Elijah Rusk to be a peace officer engaged in the execution of his official duties." The state then appealed this trial judge's decision.†

After the appellee's brief has been filed, the appellant can then file a reply brief that attempts to respond to the appellee's line of argument and any new authorities that may have been introduced. Only the argument section is usually contained in this reply brief. One must be sure, however, to concentrate the argument on rebutting the points presented by the opponent and not simply restate what has already been said in the original brief.

Depending once again on the rules of the particular court and sometimes at the discretion of the appellate judges, the court may hear oral arguments on the appeal. When oral arguments are held, each side's attorney has an opportunity to make a verbal

---

*In Illinois a defendant can be formally charged with a felony through indictment returned by a grand jury or an information returned by the prosecuting attorney.

†While the double jeopardy clause prevents a state from appealing a not guilty verdict in a criminal trial, it does not prevent the state from appealing a judge's decision to invalidate an indictment or information.

FIGURE 10.14
Sample Brief for Appellee

NO. 14579

IN THE
APPELLATE COURT OF ILLINOIS
FOURTH JUDICIAL DISTRICT

PEOPLE OF THE STATE OF IL-
LINOIS,
 	
          Plaintiff-Appellant,
 	
    vs.
 	
DENNIS HALE,
 	
          Defendant-Appellee.
	Appeal from the Circuit Court
	of the Eleventh Judicial Circuit
	McLean County, Illinois
	
	No. 77-CF-147
	
	Honorable
	Wayne C. Townley, Jr.
	Judge Presiding

BRIEF AND ARGUMENT FOR DEFENDANT-APPELLEE

Fred B. Moore
LIVINGSTON, BARGER, BRANDT,
   SLATER & SCHROEDER
204 Unity Building
Bloomington, Illinois 61701
Telephone: (309) 828-5281

ORAL ARGUMENT REQUESTED

POINTS AND AUTHORITIES

A.

A DIFFERENT STANDARD IS APPLIED FOR REVIEWING THE SUFFI-
CIENCY OF AN INFORMATION OR INDICTMENT IN THE APPELLATE COURT
FROM THE STANDARDS FOR REVIEWING THE INFORMATION OR INDICT-
MENT WHEN THE ISSUE IS RAISED IN THE TRIAL COURT.

People vs. Pujoue, 61 Ill. App. 2d 335, 335 N.E. 2d 437 (1975)

People vs. Haltom, 37 Ill. App. 3d 1059, 347 N.E. 2d 502 (1st Dist. 1976)

People vs. Pfeiffer, 354 N.E. 2d 678 (3rd Dist. 1976)

DISCUSSION OF AN ISSUE NOT NECESSARY FOR THE DECISION OF AN
APPELLATE COURT IS NOT BINDING ON THAT APPELLATE COURT OR IN-
FERIOR COURTS.

People ex rel. Scott vs. Chicago Park District, 66 Ill. 2d 65 (1976)

B.

THE DOCTRINE OF STARE DECISIS DOES NOT PRECLUDE REEXAMINATION OF A QUESTION PREVIOUSLY DECIDED BY THE APPELLATE COURT.

Nudd vs. Matsoukas, 7 III. 2d 608, 131 N.E. 2d 525 (1956)

Bradley vs. Fox, 7 III. 2d 106, 129 N.E. 2d 699 (1955)

A STATUTE SHOULD NOT BE SO CONSTRUED TO RENDER ANY WORDS, CLAUSE OR SENTENCE SUPERFLUOUS OR MEANINGLESS AND IN ASCERTAINING THE LEGISLATIVE INTENT OF A STATUTE THE COURT MUST GIVE MEANING AND EFFECT TO ALL OF ITS PROVISIONS.

Peacock vs. Judge's Retirement System of Illinois, 10 III. 2d 498, 140 N.E. 2d 684, 686

Sternberg Dredging Company vs. Estate of Sternberg, 10 III. 2d 328, 140 N.E. 2d 125, 128–129

INSULTING AND PROVOKING CONDUCT OR CONTACT DIRECTED TOWARDS A POLICE OFFICER IS NOT A BASIS FOR THE CHARGE OF AGGRAVATED BATTERY, ABSENT SOME ALLEGATION OF HARM.

People vs. Nance, 26 III. App. 3d 182, 324 N.E. 2d 652 (5th Dist. 1975)

People vs. Crane, 3 III. App. 3d 716, 279 N.E. 2d 134 (5th Dist. 1971)

People vs. Benhoff, 51 III. App. 3d 651 (5th Dist. 1977)

People vs. Haltom, 37 III. App. 3d 1059, 347 N.E. 2d 502 (1st Dist. 1976)

THE VARIOUS PROVISIONS OF CHAPTER 38, SECTION 12-4 WERE INTENDED TO REMEDY VARIOUS SPECIFIC SITUATIONS.

People vs. Cole, 47 III. App. 3d 775, 362 N.E. 2d 432 (4th Dist. 1977)

Smith-Hurd Annotated Statute, Chapter 38, Section 12-4, Committee Comments 1961 and Historical Notes

ARGUMENT
A.

The State's argument seems to consist of two parts. The first is that the decision in *People vs. Meints*, 41 III. App. 3d 215, 355 N.E. 2d 125 (4th Dist. 1976), should have controlled the Trial Court's decision in this case and that the Trial Court is obligated to follow that decision, since it does come from the Fourth District.

This Court in the *Meints* decision did spend a substantial amount of time discussing whether or not an allegation that a party who was battered was harmed, would be necessary to state a charge of aggravated battery. This Court expressed a view in that decision that is contrary to opinions expressed by the First and Fifth District Appellate Courts in other cases. *People vs.*

(Continued)

FIGURE 10.14 — Continued

Nance, 26 Ill. App. 3d 182, 324 N.E. 2d 652 (5th Dist. 1975); *People vs. Crane,* 3 Ill. App. 3d 716, 279 N.E. 2d 134 (5th Dist. 1971); *People vs. Benhoff,* 51 Ill. App. 3d 651 (5th Dist. 1977); *People vs. Haltom,* 37 Ill. App. 3d 1059, 347 N.E. 2d 502 (1st Dist. 1976).

It is the Defendant's position that the question of whether or not an allegation of harm is necessary for a charge of aggravated battery, as opposed to an allegation of contact of an insulting or provoking nature, was not necessary for the decision in the *Meints* case. This Court correctly set forth the standard that was necessary to uphold the indictment in the *Meints* case. This Court concluded that "the indictment was sufficient to fully apprise Defendant of the offense charged, enabled him to prepare a defense, and will protect him from future prosecution for the same conduct." 355 N.E. 2d 125 at 129.

This Court was not required to decide whether or not the charge, as it was made against the Defendant in *Meints,* set forth the nature and elements of the offense charged. Where the issue of the correctness of the charge is first raised on appeal, the standard used in *Meints* is correct. Since the issue is raised in the Trial Court in this case, the *Meints* decision is inappropriate so far as being authority on the point. The discussion of whether or not the allegation of bodily harm was needed was not necessary to the decision in *Meints* and, therefore, amounted to dicta. This is what the trial judge in the present case referred to as an "aberration" in the *Meints* decision. He was not referring to the fact that this Court's opinion was inconsistent with other opinions. Instead he indicated that this Court's opinion was "an aberration which was a result of the fact that the Defendant. . . pleaded guilty." (R. Vol. II, 18) In other words, the Trial Court correctly recognized, as it must be assumed this Court recognized, that when a party raises the issue for the first time on appeal, the standard for reviewing the information or indictment differs from the standard used when the issue is raised in the Trial Court.

The Supreme Court of this State and other Appellate Courts have held that a more strict standard, requiring the information or indictment to set forth the nature and elements of the offense charged, is the standard to be applied where, as in the instant case, the information is challenged in the Trial Court. *People vs. Pujoue,* 61 Ill. App. 2d 335, 335 N.E. 2d 437 (1975); *People vs. Haltom,* 37 Ill. App. 3d 1059, 347 N.E. 2d 502 (1st Dist. 1976); *People vs. Pfeiffer,* 354 N.E. 2d 678 (3rd Dist. 1976).

Any portion of the *Meints* decision which discussed whether a statement of "harm" in the charge of aggravated battery was required should be treated as dicta, or at least inapplicable to the charge against Dennis Hale. In this case we are not determining whether or not the information was sufficient to fully apprise him of the offense charged, enabling him to prepare a defense to protect him from future prosecution for the same conduct. Here we are concerned with whether or not the nature and elements of the offense charged have been properly set forth. Discussion in *Meints* of matters that are not necessary for the decision is neither binding on this Appellate Court or upon the Trial Court. *People ex rel. Scott vs. Chicago Park District*, 66 Ill. 2d 65 (1976).

B.

The second part of the State's argument is that the charge in this case properly sets for the nature and elements of the offense of aggravated battery. Even if this Court feels the *Meints* decision has answered the question, they are not precluded by the doctrine of stare decisis from reexamining the question and reaching a conclusion contrary to the conclusions reached in the discussion in *Meints*. *Nudd vs. Matsoukas*, 7 Ill. 2d 608, 131 N.E. 2d 525 (1956); and *Bradley vs. Fox*, 7 Ill. 2d 106, 129 N.E. 2d 699 (1955).

In determining the meaning of the term "harm" as it is used in Chapter 38, Section 12-4 (b) (6), rules of statutory construction have been established by the Supreme Court of this State. Those rules include the rule of construction that "a statute should be so construed, if possible, that no word, clause or sentence is rendered superfluous or meaningless. . . ." *Peacock vs. Judge's Retirement System of Illinois*, 10 Ill. 2d 498, 140 N.E. 2d 684, 686, and that "in ascertaining the legislative intent of a statute, this Court is bound to give meaning and effect to all of its provisions, and they must be construed together." *Sternberg Dredging Company vs. Estate of Sternberg*, 10 Ill. 2d 328, 140 N.E. 2d 125, 128–129. If those standards are seriously applied with any thought, it seems almost impossible to say that "harm" is synonymous with "battered." Those two terms are used in Sections 12-4 (b) (6) and 12-4 (b) (8) and in applying the rules of construction some separate meaning must be given to each. The guidance of the Supreme Court is being ignored if those are treated as being synonymous.

The State argues that in order to carry out the intent of the legislature, their interpretation of the statute must be followed. However, that assumes that the legislature intended to mean the same thing in each subsection of the statute in question but did not use the same language. This Court has recognized in other cases that the various provisions of Chapter 38, Section 12-4 have been intended to remedy various specific situations. *People vs. Cole*, 47 Ill. App. 3d 775, 362 N.E. 2d 432 (4th Dist. 1977). The various subsections were not adopted at the same time and they were not intended to correct the same condition. Obviously, there is no unanimous underlying legislative purpose for the entire statute. Smith-Hurd Annotated, SHA Chapter 38, Section 12-4, Committee Comments-1961 and Historical Notes. There is no basis for saying that the legislature intended the same meaning should be applied to terms that are on their face different. It is quite plausible and believable that the legislature felt that contact causing harm of a physical type to a police officer or peace officer is a much more serious matter than contact that does not cause harm but is merely provocative or insulting. Nor is it

(Continued)

FIGURE 10.14 — Continued

---

proper for this Court to say that contact that is insulting or provoking to a peace officer engaged in his official duties is more serious or less serious than the same contact or conduct directed toward a private citizen but made in a public place or on a public way.

If the legislature had intended that insulting or provocative physical contact with a peace officer should amount to a felony of aggravated battery rather than a misdemeanor of simple battery, they could have so stated. However, the terms actually employed by the legislature may not be glossed over only because it is felt by this Court or this State that acts of harassment or interference directed against persons in positions of authority constitute a greater social evil than similar acts directed in public places against private citizens. *People vs. Benhoff*, 51 Ill. App. 3d 651 (5th Dist. 1977). The decision of what is to become a felony and what is to be a misdemeanor is one that is left for the legislature and not for the Appellate Courts.

The Supreme Court of this State has not ruled on the question raised in this appeal. It is apparent that decisions from the First and Fifth Districts in the *Nance, Crane, Benhoff*, and *Haltom* cases held that a charge such as that placed against Dennis Hale is not sufficient when objection is raised in the Trial Court. As has been mentioned before, the *Meints* case involved objection that was raised in the Appellate Court for the first time. The same is true of other cases cited by the State in its brief. The two other Fourth District decisions cited by the State, *People vs. Lutz*, 10 Ill. Dec. 587, 367 N.E. 2d 1353 (4th Dist. 1977); and *People vs. Hurlbert*, 41 Ill. App. 3d 300, 354 N.E. 2d 652 (4th Dist. 1976), this Court decided the cases without the necessity of determining whether or not the nature and elements of the offense were properly set forth. Again in those cases there was discussion that is in agreement with the decision in *Meints*, but the cases were decided on other grounds.

---

presentation of his side's position. During these presentations, the judges will usually interrupt with their own questions. These questions probe weak points in the argument and explore the implications of particular lines of reasoning.

With or without the benefit of oral argument, the judges study the matter for an indefinite period of time until they have reached a decision (by majority vote) and have written opinions explaining their positions. While these decisions are ordinarily based primarily on materials contained in the briefs, they usually have law clerks check all the authorities and sometimes even find additional cases that apply to the arguments.

The decision then usually involves either affirming the lower court's action or sending the case back down (remanding) to the

The Defendant urges this Court to follow the lead of the First and Fifth Appellate Court Districts in following the rules of construction set forth above. This Court should either treat the present case as one of first impression in the Fourth District and affirm the ruling of the Trial Court dismissing the charge of aggravated battery or reconsider its discussion in *Meints* and the subsequent cases in light of the directions set forth by the Supreme Court and the decisions of other Appellate Courts of this State.

CONCLUSION

Wherefore the Defendant, Dennis Hale, respectfully requests that this Court affirm the ruling of the Trial Court dismissing the information.

Respectfully submitted,
Dennis Hale, Defendant-Appellee

By Fred B. Moore
LIVINGSTON, BARGER,
BRANDT, SLATER &
SCHROEDER
204 Unity Building
Bloomington, Illinois 61701
Telephone: (309) 828-5281

COUNSEL FOR DEFENDANT-APPELLEE

lower court for reconsideration. If the nature of the case is such that a new trial is not required to supplement the factual record, the judges may simply enter a final judgment. Depending on court structure and nature of the case, however, the losing party might still appeal the case to yet a higher level appellate court. If that occurs the record is forwarded to the higher court and new briefs are again filed.

SUMMARY

Appellate work is a particularly challenging aspect of law. It is an area that involves much time in research and writing. Qualified paralegals can make major contributions in the appellate process.

As with other stages in litigation, timing is important. Generally, a case cannot be appealed until the final judgment has been entered. Once that judgment is final, the appeal must be registered within a given time limit. While there are exceptions to both of these principles they are relatively limited. Furthermore, the attorney must have laid a proper foundation at the trial level. The appellate courts insist that the attorneys must have raised a proper objection at the trial itself before they can use the incident as the basis for an appeal.

While the appellate process limits its focus to legal issues as opposed to factual ones, there are circumstances in which factual considerations blend into the legal issues. The review of a denial of a motion for a directed verdict, a motion for judgment notwithstanding the verdict, and a motion for a new trial are all examples of this blending.

Finally, it is not sufficient to merely allege that a legal error took place. It must be shown that the error was prejudicial rather than harmless.

The appellate process formally begins with filing a notice of appeal. The clerk of that court and the court reporter are then instructed to prepare copies of the official court records and the transcript of the trial itself.

Once these materials have been compiled, the paralegal should prepare a digest or abstract of the record. Such a document then becomes the basis for identifying the appealable issues and writing the fact section of the brief. Legal research must be undertaken to test the strength of potential issues and to ultimately provide the authorities to be cited in the brief.

The brief should be a persuasive document. While it cannot alter or ignore important facts, the brief can present an interpretation of those facts most supportive of the client's position. The issues should be phrased to suggest the answer that favors the client's position. The argument section should weave an analysis of the facts together with an interpretation of the law. The argument should emphasize precedent cases that support the client's position and attempt to distinguish those which do not. The writer should use whichever method of statutory or constitutional analysis (plain meaning, legislative history, or contextual analysis) which best supports the position being advocated.

When completed, the appellant's brief should consist of a cover page, table of contents, table of authorities cited, jurisdictional statement, statement of the issues presented, list of statutes involved, statement of the facts, the arguments, conclusion, and appendices (relevant excerpts from the record). The appellee's brief follows the same general format, though it need not define the issues in the same way. While the arguments section attempts to refute the arguments of the appellant, it need not address those arguments in the same sequential order. The reply brief consists solely of a cover sheet and the arguments section.

The paralegal's role in preparation of the brief will depend on that paralegal's understanding of the issues involved and his or her writing ability. The paralegal will almost certainly be involved in digesting the record and some of the legal research. The extent of direct participation in drafting the brief itself will depend on the paralegal's legal sophistication and writing skills. One must recognize, however, that writing styles are personal and the attorney may choose to revise part of it for stylistic reasons.

KEY TERMS

abstract of the record
affirm
appealable issue
appellant
appellee
but see
cf.
contra
cover page
dictum
digest of the record
factual issue
final judgment
harmless error

judgment notwithstanding the verdict
jurisdictional statement
legal issue
motion for a directed verdict
motion for a new trial
notice of appeal
praecipe
prejudicial error
remand
reversible error
semble
statement of the issues presented
supersedeas bond
table of authorities cited

REVIEW QUESTIONS

1. Why doesn't everyone who loses a court case appeal it to a higher level appellate court?

2. What conditions must be satisfied before an appellate court will agree to hear an appeal?

3. What constitutes laying a proper foundation for an appeal?

4. Why are errors in the pleadings usually considered to be harmless errors?

5. What is the difference between the statement of the facts and the jurisdictional statement?

6. What is the best way to organize the argument section of the brief?

7. What form of notation should be used to indicate that one is quoting from a concurring opinion rather than the opinion of the court?

8. What are the primary differences between the appellant's brief and the appellee's brief? How does a reply brief differ from either of the above?

DISCUSSION QUESTIONS

1. Why do appellate courts generally insist that a final judgment be entered before they will review the matter? When, if ever, should the courts deviate from this rule?

2. Why do the appellate courts generally limit their review to situations in which the attorney raised the appropriate objection at the trial? Is it fair to punish the client for the attorney's mistake?

3. To what extent should the appellate courts review the factual determinations of a judge or jury? Should greater deference be shown to judges than to juries?

4. What are the advantages of digesting a record as opposed to simply abstracting it?

PROJECTS

1. Locate the rules for appellate practice in your state. Now an-
    swer the following questions on the basis of those rules: (a) Is
    a praecipe for the record required, and if so, when should it
    be filed? (b) What should be done if there is no verbatim tran-
    script of the trial available? (c) Who must pay the cost of hav-
    ing the record produced? (d) Are there limitations on the
    number of pages included in a brief? (e) What are the time
    limits for filing of briefs? and (f) Under what circumstances
    is oral argument available?

2. Take the legal memorandum you wrote for project 6 in chap-
    ter 7 and use it as the basis for an appellant's brief. As-
    sume that the trial court had ruled against your client's de-
    fenses and had ordered her to surrender possession of the
    apartment.

3. Now write a brief for the appellee in the same case as no. 2
    above.

REFERENCES

1. Federal Rules of Appellate Practice 4 (a).

2. *Pittsburgh Towing Co. v. Mississippi Valley Barge Line Co.*, 385 U.S. 32,
87 S. Ct. 195, 17 L. Ed. 2d 31 (1966); *Dyotherm Corp. v. Turbo Mach. Co.*, 434 F.
2d 65 (3rd Cir. 1970).

3. *See Wainwright v. Sykes*, 433 v s. 72, 97 S. Ct. 2497, 53 L. Ed. 2d 594
(1977).

4. Federal Rules Criminal Procedure 52(b) and see *Henry v. Mississippi*, 379
U.S. 443 (1965); *Fay v. Noia*, 372 U.S. 391 (1963); and *Wainwright v. Sykes,* 433
v s. 72, 97 S. Ct. 2497, 53 L. Ed. 2d 594 (1977).

5. *See* chapter 5 in Mario Pittoni, *Brief Writing and Argumentation* (Brooklyn, N.Y.: The Foundation Press, 1967).

PART V

CAREER PERSPECTIVES

Part I introduced the American legal system and the paralegal's role. Parts II, III, and IV discussed and developed several fundamental paralegal skills. This final section discusses personal considerations to remember when evaluating a career in the paralegal field.

CHAPTER 11

Perspectives on a Paralegal Career

People select occupations for many reasons. Salary levels, working hours, and the availability of positions are usually prime considerations. Paralegal salaries have and probably will continue to vary according to city and firm. A few experienced paralegals will be paid more but most salaries will fall between a secretary's wages and an attorney's earnings. A paralegal may occasionally work overtime or at odd hours but it is generally a nine-to-five, five days a week job. As discussed in chapter 2, the use of paralegals is likely to continue expanding.

A career choice, however, should be based on less tangible factors as well. Every job carries with it certain psychological satisfactions and frustrations. This chapter reviews some of these psychological considerations to help the reader make a more knowledgeable decision about a paralegal career.

Any discussion such as this involves generalities. A source of satisfaction for one individual may be a source of frustration for another. Readers therefore must examine the various points based on their own personalities. Job enjoyment, of course, also greatly depends on the personalities of co-workers. A dull and tedious job can sometimes be tolerated when there are understanding and accommodating supervisors and colleagues, and the best of jobs can be ruined by incompatible personalities.

ADVANTAGES

One of the advantages of the paralegal field is the wide variety of available positions. Chapter 2 provided a brief overview of the primary tasks involved in the various specialties. The paralegal should try to find a position with the tasks he or she performs best and finds the greatest satisfaction in. An individual who is very shy and who might not possess highly developed oral communications skills would probably not excel at interviewing clients or taking statements from witnesses. On the other hand, the same individual might perform very well working in a probate area where the primary duties involve assembling information about the financial assets and liabilities of the deceased. A person who thrives on personal contact would probably not be very happy drafting corporate bylaws or calculating inheritance taxes, yet might enjoy being an intake worker in a legal aid office or an investigator.

Even when the paralegal does not have much personal contact with the client, there is the satisfaction of being on a team providing a very important service to people. (Although corporations are often clients, the outcome affects real people.) The paralegal's actions can contribute significantly to the resolution of the client's legal problem.

There is also a certain glamour in the legal field. Lawyers and trials have often been the subjects of television and movie dramas. If the paralegal works in the litigation field, it is always possible that the case will eventually be reported in the press.

One final advantage of working with legal problems is intellectual stimulation. While the completion of standardized forms in a routine residential real estate transaction may not offer much challenge, there are occasions when a paralegal is confronted with problems that demand intellectual rigor and innovative solutions. Breaking through a client's defenses in an interview, locating a missing witness, and finding a precedent are activities that can be a challenge to anyone. Paralegals, like lawyers, often revel in the pure intellectual fascination of law.

DISADVANTAGES

Anyone working as a paralegal must be prepared to face a variety of frustrations. Some vary with the specialty and the size of the office. For example, the paralegal in a very large firm may feel too specialized and isolated. Few individuals appreciate the prospect of spending months digesting depositions from a single large antitrust case. On the other hand, paralegals in small firms occasionally complain they are expected to perform too many nonparalegal functions, from typing to running errands.

Other frustrations are often the product of poor supervision. Some firms tend to give major projects to paralegals without giving them either adequate background or instructions. The problem is sometimes further complicated by the lack of adequate time to do the work correctly.

Fundamental problems can arise from the lack of a clear, mutually understood definition of the paralegal's role in the organization. This confusion involves not only the definition of the type of work assigned to the paralegal, but also such matters as personnel policies.

Many organizations treat paralegals like clerical personnel some of the time and at other times like lawyers. Paralegals usually feel they get the worst of both worlds. Lawyers typically fail to give paralegals the credit and status they deserve. Secretaries (who may be jealous of the paralegal's position or simply not understand it) often fail to show the respect and cooperation the paralegal believes is deserved. The situation is further aggravated when clients are also confused about the paralegal's functions and responsibilities.

Paralegals also experience frustrations when they are not allowed the freedom to perform the complete range of duties this text has suggested. They believe they are capable of assuming more responsibility than is being delegated to them.

Finally, paralegals complain that their positions are "dead end jobs" with no room for advancement. In some law offices they might legitimately look forward to a type of managerial position supervising other nonlegal personnel, but these positions are relatively scarce.

EXPANDING OPPORTUNITIES

The disadvantages and common frustrations mentioned in the previous section have been included to give a realistic appraisal of paralegal careers. However, many of these supposed disadvantages can be overcome by an alert and resourceful paralegal.

Before accepting a paralegal position, the employer's view of the paralegal's role in the mission of the organization should be determined. Too often paralegals accept positions without analyzing their potential for professional growth.

After the paralegal has been on the job for a while, opportunities may arise to expand the employer's utilization of the paralegal's skills. Many lawyers have never considered assigning certain responsibilities to a paralegal because they have not believed a nonlawyer would be capable of handling them. Paralegals who understand the dynamics of delegation and supervision may be able to open the employer's eyes to their true potential.

When delegating authority, a good supervisor clearly explains not only what needs to be done, but how it fits into the larger plan. This gives the employee a basis for making judgments and gives the worker a greater sense of accomplishment. A good supervisor also sets specific time limits and seeks interim feedback. The time limits serve as a guide in assigning priorities in the distribution of time. The interim feedback can serve several useful functions. It tends to prevent the paralegal from becoming sidetracked or spending too much effort on what the supervisor believes to be a minor point. It allows questions to be raised about items that could not have been anticipated in advance. It also lets the supervisor redefine or redirect the task on the basis of information the supervisor did not anticipate.

If a supervisor does not follow these principles of delegation, the paralegal should attempt to lead the supervisor into the specifics of good delegation by asking enough questions to clarify the assignment and the applicable time limits, and should provide the supervisor with an interim report even when it has not been specifically requested. When tasks are assigned following this model of delegation, the outcome will be more satisfactory for both the supervisor and the paralegal. The supervisor is more likely to achieve his goals and the paralegal will work more efficiently and with less frustration.

The paralegal should always remember that the attorney is ultimately accountable for the result of the work, and, therefore, the paralegal cannot expect to be granted additional responsibility until the attorney is confident that it can be handled. Since not all paralegals are equally capable, each must establish personal credibility by successfully performing increasingly more difficult tasks. The paralegal should not be hesitant about seeking additional responsibility, but should expect to earn it.

In those cases where the paralegal cannot expand the duties of the position to a level that matches his or her ability, an alternative position should be sought. Usually this would be another paralegal position with a different employer, but sometimes paralegals move into related managerial positions. In government agencies, insurance companies, banks, and other private business corporations paralegals can sometimes move into a general management within the same organization. Some paralegals have successfully developed their own business doing freelance and consulting work. Others have branched off into the sales of law office systems. Increasing numbers are going on to law schools to become lawyers themselves.

ACCEPTING RESPONSIBILITY

The acceptance of the paralegal profession carries with it the assumption of the ethical responsibilities detailed in chapter 3. Paralegals have the responsibility of avoiding the unauthorized practice of law. They cannot let their vast knowledge of the law seduce them into giving legal advice to either the employer's clients or personal friends.

Confidentiality is very important. While the paralegal could easily be the center of attraction at a party by offering interesting anecdotes about cases, such comments violate a fundamental ethical responsibility. What is learned in the office should stay in the office.

Paralegals also have a responsibility to both the client and the attorney to perform to their capacity. The client's personal and financial interests are at stake, as is the attorney's reputation. Paralegals should research and draft the work for the case as if it were their own.

SUMMARY

Like any occupation, a paralegal career has both advantages and disadvantages. The student paralegal should be aware of both. Many of the potential disadvantages can be eliminated or reduced if the choice of the specialty and the size of the organization are based on well-assessed interests and abilities. The profession can provide an exciting and intellectually challenging way to have a tangible impact on fellow human beings.

Selected
Bibliography

General Overview of the Legal System

Abraham, Henry J. *The Judicial Process*. New York: Oxford University Press, 1975.

Brody, David Eliot. *The American Legal System: Concepts and Principles*. Lexington, Mass.: D.C. Heath, 1978.

Cole, George F. *The American System of Criminal Justice*, 2d ed., North Scituate, Mass.: Duxbury, 1979.

Glick, Henry R., and Vines, Kenneth N. *State Court Systems*. Englewood Cliffs, N.J.: Prentice-Hall, 1973.

Goldman, Sheldon, and Sarat, Austin. *American Court Systems*. San Francisco: W. H. Freeman, 1978.

Holten, N. Gary, and Jones, Melvin E. *The System of Criminal Justice*. Boston: Little, Brown, 1978.

Jacob, Herbert. *Justice in America*, 3d ed., Boston: Little, Brown, 1978.

Kolasa, Blair J., and Meyer, Bernadine. *Legal Systems*. Englewood Cliffs, N.J.: Prentice-Hall, 1978.

Lewis, Anthony. *Gideon's Trumpet*. New York: Random House, 1964.

Mayers, Lewis. *The Machinery of Justice: An Introduction to Legal Structure and Process*. Totowa, N.J.: Littlefield, Adams, 1973.

McLauchlan, William P. *American Legal Processes*. New York: John Wiley, 1977.

Mermin, Samuel. *Law and the Legal System.* Boston: Little, Brown, 1973.

Neubauer, David W. *America's Courts and the Criminal Justice System.* North Scituate, Mass.: Duxbury, 1979.

The Development, Education, and Functions of Paralegals

Ader, Mary (ed.). *A Compilation of Materials for Legal Assistants and Lay Advocates.* Evanston, Ill.: National Clearinghouse for Legal Services, 1972.

American Bar Association Special Committee on Legal Assistants. *Certification of Legal Assistants.* Chicago: American Bar Association, 1975.

——. Liberating the Lawyer: *The Utilization of Legal Assistants by Law Firms in the United States.* Chicago: American Bar Association, 1971.

——. *The Paraprofessional in Medicine, Dentistry, and Architecture.* Chicago: American Bar Association, 1971.

American Bar Association Standing Committee on Legal Assistants. *Approval of Legal Assistant Education Programs.* Chicago: American Bar Association, 1977.

——. *Legal Assistant Education: A Compilation of Program Descriptions.* Chicago: American Bar Association, 1977.

Brickman, Lester. "Expansion of the Lawyering Process Through a New Delivery System: The Emergence and State of Legal Paraprofessionalism," 71 *Columbia Law Review* 1153 (1971).

Bruno, Carole A. *Paralegal's Litigation Handbook.* Englewood Cliffs, N.J.: Institute for Business Planning, 1979.

Day-Jermany, Catherine. *Status Report on Paralegal Training and Career Development.* Washington, D.C.: Legal Services Corporation, 1977.

Fairbanks, Sally S. "Assistants in the Personal Injury Case," 10 *Trial* 74 (Sept./Oct., 1974).

Frey, William. "A Short Review of the Paralegal Movement," 7 *Clearinghouse Review* 464 (Dec. 1973).

Gilhood, Gilliam R. "Working Together: Professional and Paralegal," 14 *Trial* 54 (Feb. 1978).

Grove, Chester S. "Estate Work: A Happy Hunting Ground for the Paralegal," 19 *Practical Lawyer* 73 (Mar. 1973).

Haemmel, William G. "Paralegals/Legal Assistants — A Report of the Advances of the New Professional," *American Business Law Journal* 112 (1973).

Larbalestrier, Deborah. *Paralegal Practice and Procedure: A Practical Guide for the Legal Assistant.* Englewood Cliffs, N.J.: Prentice-Hall, 1977.

Larson, Roger. "Legal Paraprofessionals: Cultivation of a New Field," 59 *American Bar Association Journal* 631 (June, 1973).

Park, William R. (ed.). *Manual for Legal Assistants.* St. Paul, Minn.: West, 1979.

Statsky, William P. *Introduction to Paralegalism.* St. Paul, Minn.: West, 1974.

Strong, Kline D. "In-Office Training of Legal Assistants: Why and How," *Case and Comment* 38 (Mar./Apr. 1974).

Strong, Kline D., and Clark, Arben O. *Law Office Management.* St. Paul, Minn.: West, 1974.

Unauthorized Practice of Law and Legal Ethics

Bloom, Murray Teigh. *The Trouble with Lawyers*. New York: Simon and Schuster, 1969.

"Control of the Unauthorized Practice of Law: Scope of Inherent Judicial Power," 28 *University of Chicago Law Review* 162 (1960).

Derby, Lloyd. "The Unauthorized Practice of Law by Laymen and Lay Associates," 54 *California Law Review* 1331 (1966).

Freedman, Monroe. *Lawyer's Ethics in an Adversary System*. Indianapolis, Ind.: Bobbs-Merrill, 1975.

Hazard, Geoffrey. *Ethics in the Practice of Law*. New Haven, Conn.: Yale University Press, 1978.

Kaufman, Andrew. *Problems in Professional Responsibility*. Boston: Little, Brown, 1976.

"Law Clerks and the Unauthorized Practice of Law," 46 *Chicago-Kent Law Review* 214 (1969).

"Legal Paraprofessionals and Unauthorized Practice," 8 *Harvard Civil Rights and Civil Liberties Law Review* 104 (1973).

"On the Question of Negligence: The Paraprofessional," 4 *University of Toledo Law Review* 553 (1973).

Park, William R. (ed.). *Manual for Legal Assistants*. St. Paul, Minn.: West, 1979.

"Remedies Available to Combat the Unauthorized Practice of Law," 62 *Columbia Law Review* 501 (1962).

Statsky, William P. *Introduction to Paralegalism*. St. Paul, Minn.: West, 1974.

———. "Paralegal Advocacy Before Administrative Agencies," 4 *University of Toledo Law Review* 439 (1973).

"Symposium: The Role of the Nonlawyer in Estate Planning," 36 *Unauthorized Practice News* (Nov. 1971).

"Symposium: The Unauthorized Practice of Law Controversy," 5 *Law and Contemporary Problems* 1 (1972).

"The Unauthorized Practice of Law by Laymen and Lay Associates," 66 *Columbia Law Review* 1131 (1966).

"The Unauthorized Practice of Law by Lay Organizations Providing the Services of Attorneys," 72 *Harvard Law Review* 1334 (1958).

Wise, Raymond. *Legal Ethics*. New York: Matthew Bender, 1970.

Interviewing and Investigation

Akin, Richard. *The Private Investigators Basic Manual*. Springfield, Ill.: Charles C. Thomas, 1976.

Baer, Harold, and Broder, Aaron J. *How to Prepare and Negotiate Cases for Settlement*. Englewood Cliffs, N.J.: Prentice-Hall, 1976.

Bailey, F. Lee, and Rothblatt, Henry B. *Fundamentals of Criminal Advocacy*. Rochester, N.Y.: Lawyers Co-operative, 1974.

Benjamin, Alfred. *The Helping Interview*, 2d ed., Boston: Houghton Mifflin, 1974.

Binder, David, and Price, Susan. *Legal Interviewing and Counseling: A Client-Centered Approach.* St. Paul, Minn.: West, 1977.

Bruno, Carole A. *Paralegal's Litigation Handbook.* Englewood Cliffs, N.J.: Institute for Business Planning, 1979.

Freeman, Harrop A., and Weihofen, Henry. *Clinical Law Training — Interviewing and Counseling.* St. Paul, Minn.: West, 1972.

Golec, Anthony. *Techniques of Legal Investigation.* Springfield, Ill.: Charles C. Thomas, 1976.

Gordon, Raymond, *Interviewing: Strategy, Techniques, and Tactics.* Homewood, Ill.: Dorsey, 1975.

Hogan, John J. *Criminal Investigation.* New York: McGraw-Hill, 1974.

Ivey, Allen E. *Microcounseling: Innovations in Interviewing Training.* Springfield, Ill.: Charles C. Thomas, 1971.

Larbalestrier, Deborah. *Paralegal Practice and Procedure: A Practical Guide for the Legal Assistant.* Englewood Cliffs, N.J.: Prentice-Hall, 1977.

Makay, John J., and Gaw, Beverly A. *Personal and Interpersonal Communication: Dialogue with the Self and with Others.* Columbus, Ohio: Charles Merrill, 1975.

Park, William R. (ed.). *Manual for Legal Assistants.* St. Paul, Minn.: West, 1979.

Philo, Harry M.; Robb, Dean A.; and Goodman, Richard M. *Lawyers Desk Reference: Technical Sources for Conducting a Personal Injury Action,* 5th ed., Rochester, N.Y.: Lawyers Co-operative, 1975.

Rothstein, Paul F. *Evidence in a Nutshell.* St. Paul, Minn.: West, 1970.

Royal, Robert F., and Schutt, Steven R. *The Gentle Art of Interrogation: A Professional Manual and Guide.* Englewood Cliffs, N.J.: Prentice-Hall, 1976.

Scott, James D. *Investigative Methods.* Reston, Va.: Reston, 1978.

Shaffer, Thomas. *Legal Interviewing and Counseling in a Nutshell.* St. Paul, Minn.: West, 1976.

Statsky, William P. *Introduction to Paralegalism.* St. Paul, Minn.: West, 1974.

Stuckey, Gilbert. *Evidence for the Law Enforcement Officer,* 2d ed., New York: McGraw-Hill, 1974.

Uviller, H. Richard. *The Processes of Criminal Justice — Investigation,* 2d ed., St. Paul, Minn.: West, 1979.

Legal Research, Analysis, and Writing

Board of Student Advisers, Harvard Law School. *Introduction to Advocacy: Brief Writing and Oral Argument in Moot Court Competition.* Mineola, N.Y.: Foundation, 1970.

Bruno, Carole A. *Paralegal's Litigation Handbook.* Englewood Cliffs, N.J.: Institute for Business Planning, 1979.

Cohen, Morris. *How to Find the Law,* 7th ed., St. Paul, Minn.: West, 1976.

———. *Legal Research in a Nutshell,* 3d ed., St. Paul, Minn.: West, 1977.

Dickerson, Reed. *The Fundamentals of Legal Drafting.* Boston: Little, Brown, 1965.

Jacobstein, J. Myron, and Mersky, Roy M. *Fundamentals of Legal Research.* Mineola, N.Y.: Foundation, 1977.

Levi, Edward H. *An Introduction to Legal Reasoning.* Chicago: University of Chicago Press, 1948.

Mermin, Samuel. *Law and the Legal System: An Introduction.* Boston: Little, Brown, 1973.

National Association of Attorney's General. *Computerized Research in the Law.* Raleigh, N.C.: The Committee on the Office of Attorney General, 1976.

Park, William R. (ed.). *Manual for Legal Assistants.* St. Paul, Minn.: West, 1979.

Pittoni, Mario. *Brief Writing and Argumentation.* Brooklyn, N.Y.: Foundation, 1967.

Price, Miles O., and Bitner, Harry. *Effective Legal Research,* 3d ed., Boston: Little, Brown, 1969.

Reed, Horace E.; MacDonald, John W.; Fordham, Jefferson B.; and Pierce, William J. *Materials on Legislation,* 3d ed., Mineola, N.Y.: Foundation, 1973.

Rombauer, Marjorie Dick. *Legal Problem Solving: Analysis, Research and Writing,* 3d ed., St. Paul, Minn.: West, 1978.

Sprowl, James A. "Computer-Assisted Legal Research: West Law and Lexis," 62 *American Bar Association Journal* 320 (1976).

_____. *A Manual for Computer-Assisted Legal Research.* Chicago: American Bar Foundation, 1976.

Statsky, William P. *Introduction to Paralegalism.* St. Paul, Minn.: West, 1974.

_____. *Legal Research, Writing and Analysis.* St. Paul, Minn.: West, 1974.

Statsky, William P., and Wernet, R. John, Jr. *Case Analysis and Fundamentals of Legal Writing.* St. Paul, Minn.: West, 1977.

A Uniform System of Citation, 12th ed., Cambridge, Mass.: Harvard Law Review Association, 1976.

Zelermyer, William. *The Process of Legal Reasoning.* Englewood Cliffs, N.J.: Prentice-Hall, 1963.

Civil and Criminal Procedure

Amsterdam, Anthony G.; Segal, Bernard L.; and Miller, Martin K. (eds.). *Trial Manual for the Defense of Criminal Cases.* Philadelphia: American Law Institute, 1974.

Baer, Harold, and Broder, Aaron J. *How to Prepare and Negotiate Cases for Settlement.* Englewood Cliffs, N.J.: Prentice-Hall, 1967.

Bailey, F. Lee, and Rothblatt, Henry B. *Fundamentals of Criminal Advocacy.* Rochester, N.Y.: Lawyers Co-operative, 1974.

Blanchard, Roderick. *Litigation and Trial Practice for the Legal Paraprofessional.* St. Paul, Minn.: West, 1976.

Bruno, Carole A. *Paralegal's Litigation Handbook.* Englewood Cliffs, N.J.: Institute for Business Planning, 1979.

Fleming, James. *Civil Procedure.* Boston: Little, Brown, 1977.

Franklin, Marc A. *The Biography of a Legal Dispute.* Mineola, N.Y.: Foundation, 1968.

Green, Milton D. *Basic Civil Procedure.* Mineola, N.Y.: Foundation, 1972.

Halverson, James T. "Coping with the Fruits of Discovery in the Complex Case — Systems Appeal to Litigation Support" 44 *Anti-Trust Law Journal* 39 (1975).

Israel, Jerold H. and LaFave, Wayne R. *Criminal Procedure in a Nutshell.* St. Paul, Minn.: West, 1971.

Kamisar, Yale; LaFave, Wayne R.; and Israel, Jerold H. *Cases, Comments and Questions on Basic Criminal Procedure*, 4th ed. St. Paul, Minn.: West, 1974.

Stern, Steven T. (ed.). *Introduction to Civil Litigation.* St. Paul, Minn.: West, 1977.

Uviller, H. Richard. *The Process of Criminal Justice — Adjudication*, 2d ed., St. Paul, Minn.: West, 1979

Administrative Law

Davis, Kenneth Culp. *Administrative Law in the Seventies.* Rochester, N.Y.: Lawyers Co-operative, 1976.

———. *Administrative Law Text*, 3d ed., St. Paul, Minn.: West, 1972.

Gellhorn, Ernest. *Administrative Law in a Nutshell.* St. Paul, Minn.: West, 1972.

Jaffe, Louis L. *Judicial Control of Administrative Action.* Boston: Little, Brown, 1965.

Krislov, Samuel, and Musolf, Lloyd D. (eds.). *The Politics of Regulation.* Boston: Houghton Mifflin, 1964.

Larbalestrier, Deborah E. *Paralegal Practice and Procedure: A Practical Guide for the Legal Assistant.* Englewood Cliffs, N.J.: Prentice-Hall, 1977.

Marshaw, Jerry L., and Merrill, Richard A. *Introduction to the American Public Law System.* St. Paul, Minn.: West, 1975.

Mezines, Basil J.; Stein, Jacob A.; and Gruff, Jules. *Administrative Law.* New York: Mathew Bender, 1977.

Robinson, Glen O., and Gellhorn, Ernest. *The Administrative Process.* St. Paul, Minn.: West, 1974.

Shapiro, Martin. *The Supreme Court and Administrative Agencies.* New York: Free Press, 1968.

Statsky, William P. *Introduction to Paralegalism.* St. Paul, Minn.: West, 1974.

———. "Paralegal Advocacy Before Administrative Agencies." 4 *University of Toledo Law Review* 439 (1973).

Index

C

Caption. *See* Appellate brief
Case analysis
  brief format, 162–164
  concurring opinion, 378
  decision, 152, 154–155, 158–161
  disposition, 150, 155, 162–165
  dissenting opinion, 378
  facts, 150–151, 155–157, 161–162
  holding, 159–161, 163
  issues, factual v. legal, 158, 161
  issues, general, 150, 154–155, 158, 163
  judicial history, 150–151, 155, 157–158, 163
  precedent, 142, 150, 158, 165–176
  reasoning, 152–155, 161, 164
    (*see also* Contextual analysis; Legislative history; and Literal approach)
  stare decisis, 165–168, 176–177, 185
Case brief, 162–165 (*see also* Case analysis)
Cause of action, 27, 286, 301
Certification, 45–49
Certiorari. See Writs
c.f., 379
Challenge for cause, 24
Citations
  administrative, 208
  court cases, 143–149
  Harvard Citator, 143
  ordinances, 182
  parallel, 148, 259
  secondary sources, 262–263
  Shepard's, 245–246, 256, 259–260
  statutes, 182–183
  use in appellate brief, 378–379, 381–383
Civil law, 7–9, 11–14, 25–28
Civil Service Commission, 40–41, 337

Class action, 282
Clearly erroneous test, 351, 361
Closed questions, 97–98
Codes
  Code of Federal Regulations, 203, 248, 250, 342–343
  Code of Professional Ethics (*see* Ethics)
  Code of Professional Responsibility (*see* Ethics)
  Federal Code Annotated, 181, 183
  U.S. Code, 181, 183, 242, 342
  U.S. Code Annotated, 181, 183, 242, 243, 245
  U.S. Code Congressional and Administrative News, 181, 183, 245, 248
  U.S. Code Service, 181, 183, 242
Commercial law, 11–12
Common law, 6, 165, 202
Compensatory damages, 293
Complaint
  allegations, 287–292
  amending, 295
  caption, 286–287
  criminal, 302
  damages, 293
  jury demand, 290–292
  prayer for relief, 290–293
Compulsory joinder, 282
Computer assisted research, 261
Concurring opinion. *See* Case analysis
Congressional Index, 248
Congressional Record, 248
Constitutional law
  ambiguity in, 209–210
  legislative history, 210
  literal interpretation, 209–210
  role of precedent, 165
  source of, 7
Contextual analysis, 185, 193–197, 202, 372
Contra, 379